Uneven Futures

Uneven Futures

Strategies for Community Survival from Speculative Fiction

Edited by Ida Yoshinaga, Sean Guynes, and Gerry Canavan

The MIT Press
Cambridge, Massachusetts
London, England

The MIT Press would like to thank the anonymous peer reviewers who provided comments on drafts of this book. The generous work of academic experts is essential for establishing the authority and quality of our publications. We acknowledge with gratitude the contributions of these otherwise uncredited readers.

This book was set in ITC Stone Serif Std and ITC Stone Sans Std by New Best-set Typesetters Ltd. Printed and bound in the United States of America.

Library of Congress Cataloging-in-Publication Data

Names: Yoshinaga, Ida M., editor. | Guynes, Sean, editor. | Canavan, Gerry, editor.
Title: Uneven futures : strategies for community survival from speculative fiction / edited by Ida Yoshinaga, Sean Guynes, and Gerry Canavan.
Description: Cambridge, Massachusetts : The MIT Press, 2022. | Includes bibliographical references and index.
Identifiers: LCCN 2021060554 (print) | LCCN 2021060555 (ebook) | ISBN 9780262543941 (paperback) | ISBN 9780262370165 (epub) | ISBN 9780262370172 (pdf)
Subjects: LCSH: Speculative fiction—History and criticism. | Science fiction—History and criticism. | Communities in literature. | LCGFT: Literary criticism.
Classification: LCC PN3448.S64 U54 2022 (print) | LCC PN3448.S64 (ebook) | DDC 809.3/876—dc23/eng/20220214
LC record available at https://lccn.loc.gov/2021060554
LC ebook record available at https://lccn.loc.gov/2021060555

10 9 8 7 6 5 4 3 2 1

Contents

Introduction: It's the End of the World as We Know It—or So We Hope

Ida Yoshinaga, Sean Guynes, and Gerry Canavan

The future is already here, as William Gibson once said; it just isn't very evenly distributed. This sense of a dread futurity shooting irregularly and unfairly across a troubled present is key to twenty-first-century politics: digital futures that alternately liberate and control, a global capitalist consensus now so riven by crisis that it seems ready to explode into neofascism or other toxic forms of collectivism, an Earth poised for destruction by climate change at the very moment that technological transcendence of the material plane seems finally possible, to name a few.

Some have names for this supposedly unprecedented era: neoliberalism, neofeudalism, the Anthropocene, the Great Acceleration, the Capitalocene, the Plantationocene, the Cthulhucene, postnormality—all useful catch phrases for identifying the origins of a particular set of (interrelated) problems plaguing these awful times. Yet many others—say, humans and animals and others in the Global South or in the internal colonies of hyperpowers like the United States—might recognize this historical conjuncture as yet another manifestation of the always ongoing apocalypse of the colonial episteme that forever changed the world in the wake of that *annus horribilis* 1492. We face violence slow and fast; we declaim the daily yoke of capital, patriarchy, heteronormativity, ableism, race, empire, and more; we do so across unequal battle lines, pitted against one another, fighting over scraps.

Twenty-first-century life—with its intensified mining of human data by corporations that aim to explode the limits of both biotechnological commodification and labor exploitation, and with its stratifying economic transformations in wake of the global financial crisis and the Great Recession threatening to wreak havoc upon both the environment and human embodiment—exemplifies such contradictory futures in the historic consumption of science fiction and fantasy texts.

The explosion in SF stories across different media, from the late twentieth century through the present, has made those of us in the field of science fiction studies rethink our community's taken-for-granted identity, orientation, stakes. An earlier generation of scholars had organized itself around Darko Suvin's structuralist definition of science fiction as the "literature of cognitive estrangement." Language like Suvin's (with his emphasis on SF as a *literary* form with a linguistic effect upon readers) revealed a need to prove that SF *deserved* the same level of academic attention as, say, Shakespeare or Joyce or Austen. Today, most of us who talk about SF don't worry so much about whether we're allowed to talk about what most of us now call, purposefully vaguely, *SF* in academic papers or at conferences; moreover, many of us have moved beyond worrying too much about what is and isn't SF (as opposed to fantasy or horror or any other permutation of the broad range of still unsatisfactorily undefined *fantastic* or *nonmimetic* genres). In part, this is because the Suvinites won their argument with their imagined traditionalist counterparts, and the literary appropriateness of SF and related speculative genres is now taken more or less as a given; it's also in part because the genre(s) of SF permeate our everyday now, whether in the bookstore, at the movie theater (or bookmarked streaming service), or on the news. What could be more estranging than the times we're already living through, which blur uncomfortably into SF territory day by day?

In an era in which ecological disasters, global pandemics, and neoimperial invasions now regularly serve to expose and intensify these deep political-economic inequalities, where has SF anticipated emergent futures and given us strategies to survive the present? *Uneven Futures: Strategies for Community Survival from Speculative Fiction* brings together forty-odd critics, artists, and activists who each take up some core text of the genre with an eye toward the collective articulation of a new paradigm for thinking of SF as suitable to a milieu in which corporations dominate both the means of production and the means of distribution, and in which governments utilize powerful surveillance and carceral technologies, feeding our most cherished fantasies and our most terrifying nightmares. With an eye toward broad community adoption and practical use, and an activist sensibility, *Uneven Futures* is about the estrangements of SF that lead us to other cognitive models of futurity, belonging, and hope. Each chapter of the book takes up its own key genre text drawn from a broad understanding of *speculative fiction* as including, among other generic dispositions, science fiction, fantasy, horror, and the weird. The editorial principle of a given text's inclusion rests on the case that an essayist makes for the text as a document of an uneven future but one that also gives humankind strategies for survival.

We hope this book centers community, not only as a strategy for survival in dark times as illuminated through the lessons of the forty-odd disparate SF texts our authors engage with, but also as a method of textual curation and intellectual curiosity. We further hope the wealth of media and contributors—from well-known SF novelists to social justice activists to video game designers to scholars—prevents the collection from becoming, as too much criticism in SF studies still too easily does, an overlong testament to the nostalgia of middle-aged white men who, as boys, imagined colonizing the universe through space travel. Instead, we have sought to reflect the culturally and regionally rich array of populations to which our uneven futures belong. Huge gaps still haunt our selection: we were unable to procure pieces by working scientists such as AI designers, specialists in Islamic SF, writers or artists from Africa, Russian or central Asian film scholars, or indie science fiction/fantasy film auteurs, among many other missing possibilities—opportunities for future continuations of the project begun here. Nevertheless, this book brings together those who write SF and who write reviews and criticism of SF as fans with those whose scholarly careers revolve around studying SF. In bringing members of these communities together, we sought to forge new paths toward collective inquiry into the genre we all love—in different ways, capacities, and languages of redress, to be sure, but all enjoy nonetheless.

As editors, we gave our writers one remit: choose an SF text you love and explore how it helps us think of ways to live in, survive, and grow beyond the inequalities and injustices of our times, with *SF*, *love*, *survive*, and *our* all open-ended categories that assume no clear or final definitions. The political concerns our authors brought to the book were as urgent as they were varied, surprising and inspiring us with their often unexpected dimensions. The texts they chose spanned continents, centuries, ideologies, languages, media, genres, and more. Some are deliberately utopian in character; others are deeply disturbing. But they possess a unity of perspective and purpose: *Uneven Futures* is neither a cabinet of randomly selected, obscure curiosities nor a handbook for the major media franchises but a guidebook to the new

SF megatext as a vibrantly dialogical and enduringly ethical methodology for our collective future.

We have organized essays around four major approaches to the uneven futures and presents we face, based on the ways in which contributors address the problems their texts raise and the tools communities take up to respond. We have subdivided chapters into four sections: Emergence, Rupture, Transformation, and Revolution. Each of these represents a collective strategy for survival, but we recognize—as do our contributors—that these strategies are neither static nor completely separate from one another: in rupture there is emergence and transformation, in revolution there is rupture and transformation through emergence, and so on. We have thus divided chapters into sections based on the focus of the contributors' interpretations and encourage you to read creatively across the book as you see fit. We have adopted a common structure for chapter titles, allowing readers to easily comb over the table of contents, grasp the text selection, and discover the strategy for survival provided in the text (per the contributor's interpretation). The first half of each chapter title furnishes basic text info (author/creator name, text title, year of publication), the second half a brief gloss of the strategy that text provides. We hope the indexical chapter titles, while lengthy and a little idiosyncratic, might provide an alternate point of entry to the book, allowing readers to plot their own courses into the future.

Pieces in the Emergence section focus on how the affective dimensions of empathy, affinity, and solidarity serve as powerful agents for driving community responses in times of social strife and change. The texts surveyed in this section provide a framework for organizing emergent groups and networks in uncertain times. The second section, Rupture, builds on these emergent community paradigms by turning to speculative works that symbolically (or actually) interrogate and challenge normative orders. Authors emphasize the rupturing capacity of speculative fiction to break through the uneven futures of the present by making their inequality radically apparent. Transformation thinkpieces focus on speculative texts that offer and/or model community solutions within crisis-ridden systems, highlighting strategies of harm reduction, reconnection, reformation, and the building of alliances/coalitions across systemic differences to move toward deep structural change. Finally, Revolution highlights the ideological and material revolutions of speculative fiction, whether the subaltern rising against the elite or a new way of imagining solidarity and boldly reorganizing the very nature of communities, reconsidering relationships and practices in the face of harsh political and economic divisiveness.

An interlude between Rupture and Transformation, by editor Ida Yoshinaga, contextualizes a new approach to SF studies in terms of both the academic contributions of global science fiction and Indigenous Futurisms, and the "productive turn" of diverse science fiction created across media, which are together transforming core definitions of the genre. Yoshinaga calls this paradigm Science Fiction Studies 3.0—a justice-centered thought experiment to survive an era of futurity in crisis. This interlude frames the project of *Uneven Futures* both within SF studies as an academic discipline, staking a claim about how we can do our work differently but also, by virtue of its open-ended call for engagement, as seeking a broader community of critics and creators already engaged in thinking science fictionally, learning what SF moments, modes, and movements mean to their own knowledge networks. Toward such expanded genre exploration, we have also attended to linguistic issues, by respecting writers' choices to not italicize words from Indigenous and First Nation languages or words reclaiming community languages toward their cultural or decolonial revival.

When we approached our contributors, we sought an archive of hope and found treasures in the words and ideas they brought back to us. In the spirit of our vision for this volume, we share them with you now and encourage your response, engagement, and enjoyment alongside ours. We call on you to make this more than a book, now published and done: to make it a living text—an evolving lesson plan, an unending dialogue, an invitation to community. Fight it, love it, talk back to it, use it, challenge it, live with it—but above all, help us find new, better, other, tried and forgotten, or untried ways to be.

I Emergence

1 Samuel R. Delany, "The Star Pit" (1965) / Moving On, as Far as You Want

Kirin Wachter-Grene

Out here it is never cold and never hot. Dangling their feet over the Edge through the broken place in the fence, mechanics Vyme (an emotionally stunted Black forty-two-year-old) and Ratlit (a wizened white thirteen-year-old) commiserate over their impoverished childhoods and relative immobility, watching star-flecked infinity fall away beneath their boot soles. They repair the ships others use to travel intergalactically. Unable to get out, they emerge at night to bathe in the stasis field's world-wind, feeling it whip teasingly at their garments. In Samuel R. Delany's "The Star Pit," we sit with these former Earthlings at their outer limits. But even here, a representationally unfamiliar place at the galaxy's periphery, it feels the same as the world we know: structural dynamics demarcate people's access and progress. "The Star Pit" is a novella about the alienated labor that maintains inequitable complex systems and the necessity of empathetic reciprocity across class, race, gender, and age. SF readers are likely familiar with Delany's claim that science fiction helps to think about the present, but his speculative worldbuilding is not solely allegorical. Delany brings a realist sensibility to bear on systems analysis and materialist critique.

As I write this, early in summer 2020, the so-called once-in-a-century SARS-CoV-2, or COVID-19, pandemic is wreaking global havoc. Almost ten million people have been infected worldwide and over four hundred thousand have died, with Americans comprising more than a quarter of fatalities. These statistics will likely be dwarfed by the time this piece is published. Black Americans are disproportionately suffering, dying from the virus at three times the rate of white people, excessively affected by the nation's economic downturn, produced by the virus. And all this when the collective rage and grief over American anti-Black racism has reached a boiling point, spilling out into the nation's streets as hundreds of thousands of citizens demand structural change in the face of racist police violence and a criminal justice system that incarcerates Black people at more than five times the rate of whites.

The COVID-19 crisis and current civil unrest, the injustice and inequality they starkly reveal, are connected. They are symptomatic of a continual state of emergency rather than discrete moments or events. Taking the disproportionate amount of Black people in prisons, jails, and detention centers as an example, one can see how Black Americans are at greater risk for exposure to the virus due to congregate, carceral living. It is not a cliché to acknowledge racism is a public health crisis, too; anti-Blackness is a precondition for COVID-19. As is the case in "The Star Pit," structural containment renders some groups of people disproportionately vulnerable to class-based inequities.

Consider also that many Black people, who have maintained jobs during this worst economic downturn since the Great Depression, are the so-called essential workers depended upon to sustain the economy. They are our grocery store clerks, our delivery drivers and mail carriers, our meatpackers, our Amazon warehouse employees, our public transportation operators. They are praised as heroes; without them, supply chains would break down. Yet our dependence on these essential workers, and their dependence on an often scanty paycheck to get by in an advanced capitalist system unfairly skewed along lines of race and class, greatly increase their exposure to the virus, accelerating their risk of severe illness and death. They are treated as expendable, without government concern or provisions for their safety.

If these latest developments in our continuous state of emergency reiterate anything instructive, it is that human civilization is globally interdependent, its division of labor inextricably intertwined with the economic conditions of local social environments. A complex system such as advanced capitalism, and the white supremacy that drives and profits from it, maintains (temporary) survival for some at the disregard and devastation of others. Such a system, known as *racial capitalism*, is precarious at best and unsustainable at worst in the face of present and future events such as the COVID-19 eviction crisis, the rise of wildfires in economically vulnerable neighborhoods, looming climate change, and other catastrophes that will continue to impact global BIPOC communities disproportionately. In "The Star Pit," we see a representation of environmental racism in the drought initiated by biological warfare that kills many in Vyme's procreation group, including Vyme's oldest son Antoni and Antoni's mother. We must divest from whiteness and its trappings. Civilization depends on it. But knowing many of us are reluctant or downright unwilling to relinquish power and privilege, how does humanity coexist, moving within the disproportionate, artificial boundaries we have constructed while equitably restructuring what that coexistence might look like? Accountability to one another means recognizing our relationality, dismantling unjust horizons so as to restructure reciprocal horizontality.

* * *

"The Star Pit" is a story of complex systems—systems comprised of multiple interlocking components such as an ecosystem, the global climate, or the universe—and how organisms relate therein. Delany wrote "The Star Pit" as a twenty-two-year-old queer Black man living in Manhattan during the postwar wave of suburban white flight. This historical context matters because "The Star Pit" is a story about mobility—those who have it and flaunt it with abandon and those whose access is nightmarishly circumscribed—a reality Black and queer Americans living in the early 1960s experienced to differing degrees (as they do today). "The Star Pit" emphasizes the experiences of one such essential worker. Vyme is a former Earthling living in the Star Pit—a truck stop on the Milky Way's galactic rim. The Star Pit, poised on the edges of the promise of spacial infinity, is the furthest Vyme can go—a fact that makes him profoundly distraught. His worldview is informed by analyzing complex systems—including his childhood ant farm, ecologariums (outsized or minuscule self-sustaining terrariums), procreation groups, and intergalactic trade—and feeling trapped by their interconnections. Delany uses these examples to meditate on the claustrophobic affordances required by our circular life stages and systems of reproduction, both biological and capitalistic. Nevertheless, as Vyme tells Antoni, life insists we grow continuously within such bounds. The tension arises when some peoples' horizons stretch farther than others, and some lives and livelihoods seem endlessly expansive at others' expense.

As a mechanic, Vyme repairs the ships of the dubiously privileged "golden." Their mobility-based privilege stems from weird physics past the galactic barrier at the edge of the Milky Way, which kills most human beings who attempt to traverse it, condemning them to insanity and death.

But the golden (who are various races, not just white) are exceptional, able to make this journey and bring back exotic material from outside the galaxy for trade. Though the golden unpleasantly flaunt their uniqueness and are widely resented for being extraordinary, they are also exploited, prized because the government manipulates their abilities for nefarious purposes, using them to procure raw resources for biological warfare that the non-golden wage.

Due to their seemingly unlimited access to travel and pay from this government, the golden "live by their own laws and walk their own ways." It is thus tempting to merely read goldens as representative of white supremacy and beneficiaries of white privilege, an interpretation perhaps complicated by the fact that some golden are Black and Asian.[1] While their advantages are undeniable, it is essential to acknowledge goldens' many vulnerabilities; they are considered "psychological freaks with some incredible hormone imbalance" who need to have experienced deep trauma "that makes life in interstellar society painful or impossible" to survive intergalactic journeys.[2] And if they lack what is necessary, the government implants psychosis. In a way, they are also essential workers, both necessary to this government's political economy due to the sudden boom in intergalactic trade and, as such, prized and exploited despite or because of stigmatized, "environmentally conditioned" aspects of their identities. Often when golden return from these trips, as much as they swagger, they also suffer acute, yet treatable, psychic shock; some also feel confined in this biocapitalist arrangement of coercion/consent. Even the most privileged within the novella suffer under the same oppressive system they help perpetuate and benefit from. Nevertheless, golden mobility "messes up [Vyme's] picture of the universe" because it throws into stark relief the inequity of oppression, always contextual, experienced and felt by degrees along the fault lines of social class.[3]

At its core this is a story about the alienated labor, Vyme's and goldens' included, that maintains an inequitable, unsustainable complex system of interconnected crises large and small that reveal dependence on marginalized people—an (im)balance that causes many to die. Even among golden, "there are no familial inheritance laws . . . only rights of plunder."[4] The government needs golden; golden and the government need Allegra, a projective telepath employed at age eight in a sadistic pattern of withholding drugs and increasing dosage to force her to work harder to help golden process their psychic shock; Allegra needs Ratlit, a thirteen-year-old boy who procures for her the drugs she requires; Ratlit needs Allegra—desperate to travel intergalactically, he uses Allegra's hallucinatory projections to view inaccessible worlds; Ratlit, Sandy, and Vyme need intergalactic trade (warfare) to sustain their jobs as mechanics for the goldens' ships; and the golden need ships or they are out of work. Knowing that "you can't fight reality," as Vyme tells Ratlit, many of these alienated laborers die or try unsuccessfully to kill themselves as a result of these unequal, dependent social relations.[5] So what does Vyme *really* need in the midst of such claustrophobia? The possibility of freedom from suffering as a result of *causing* suffering. As he cries during his aborted suicide attempt near the novella's end, "I *don't* want to hurt anybody any *more*."[6]

But there is no getting out of this dynamic, no outside of society, a principle Delany has always maintained in his critical and fictional work, including his most speculative. "I never let myself pretend," he tells us, "that I have somehow transgressed the social—so that I will not think I have freed myself of the responsibility of telling the entailed social truths I see."[7] Racial capitalism's deep embeddedness is one of those truths. The classic opening lines of Delany's "Racism and Science Fiction" read, "Racism for me has always appeared to be first and foremost a system," one "largely supported by material and economic conditions at work in a field of social traditions . . . [that] isolate and segregate the people of one race, or group, or ethnos from another."[8] White people perpetuate a complex system of racial capitalism that depends on and maintains humanity's collective alienation so as to delude ourselves that we are free and safe. But what is freedom, the novella provokes, other than cruelty and selfishness, a way to temporarily benefit yourself regardless of its impact on others? Such freedom will lead to our collective demise, and none of us are safe.

* * *

How, then, to think of survival? "There are certain directions in which you cannot go," Vyme considers at the novella's end, recalling his employee Sandy's earlier insights. So you "choose one in which you can move as far as you want." "You can grow," Vyme thinks, "or you can die."[9] Delany seems to suggest that one cannot delimit their growth on the basis of containment, fitting for a story about both accepting and pushing against boundaries. Yes, as Delany claims, racism is our "total surround," but the choice of how and in what direction one moves remains an autonomous determination.[10] Furthermore, as Vyme stresses to Antoni, one must always mentally expand. The latter, he underscores, is what is most important because it never stops. An overemphasis on oppression often obscures the countless ways Black people have always defined their own subjectivity, power, and pleasure. Much of the history of Black people in America emphasizes thriving despite constraint. But this economic system, created by whites, is disgraceful and untenable. Knowing that there is no outside to the social, no galaxy we can escape to while we burn our world down, how do we move within oppressive structures as we simultaneously work to abolish them?

Fortunately, there is more to Delany's famous assertion that "science fiction is a tool to help you think . . . about the present—a present that is always changing."[11] In "The Star Pit," there are always further places to go even within containment, and the future, as they say, is unwritten. Some claim in this moment of seemingly imminent collapse that the American experiment is dead. Others rejoice in that supposition as we are called to reimagine, remake, reworld. For white people to grow, there must be a recognition that the racial capitalist system threatens and constrains all people. Alienation keeps us from questioning this logic and from recognizing that we all already possess the resources and tools we need to flourish anew. As Alegra's dying insight illuminates, none of us can "get out" if one group's "freedom" depends on the entrapment of others. Armed with this knowledge, we might reach toward one another with, in Vyme's words, a "raging tenderness," as Vyme himself moves toward An, a fourteen-year-old golden in need of work in the Star Pit at the novella's conclusion. An, who refers to Vyme as "brother," reminds Vyme of his deceased son, Antoni. In turn, An becomes to Vyme, in that moment of recognition, "little brother"—and it is An who teaches Vyme that golden, too, are trapped, a lesson Vyme is eventually receptive to because it emerges from an empathetic connection. Later, Vyme learns, much to his shock, that Sandy was married to a golden, and An is Sandy's brother-in-law.

There is no outside the social; we move in concert with others—including with those so seemingly different outside of and within our kinship groups—in our continual states of emergency and our suffering biosphere. By simultaneously acknowledging our limitations and restructuring society from within, we might identify alternative directions in which to proceed.

We have always had our abolitionist visionaries (Angela Davis, Ruth Wilson Gilmore, and Mariame Kaba, to name a few) who both acknowledge our historical and present material conditions and urge us to take audacious steps along attainable routes far too few dare to travel. Kaba, in fact, refers to abolition as a *horizon*.[12] What is possible? As we imagine and build, we cannot depend on nor expect Black people and allies long aware of what others refer to as *events unforeseen* or *unprecedented* to do all the speculative, generative, and concrete labor.

The question (one James Baldwin posed many times) remains: Will white people awaken to the fact that white supremacy—maintained consciously and unconsciously to the extent that it constitutes our total surrounds—is an impoverished and unsustainable system for *all*? When compounded crises such as the COVID-19 pandemic, police violence, and climate catastrophes that disproportionately impact BIPOC communities increasingly arise, we can no longer be dependent on people who are marginalized to sustain the status quo of seemingly endless white horizons. To adapt—to grow or die—we must recognize and refuse the multiple tethers of those horizons that bind. As our collective precarity magnifies and intensifies, we need to recognize that our lives and so-called freedoms depend on the thriving of all. The conditions of our coexistence (labor, economics, caretaking, vulnerability, and power) must be radically reassessed and redistributed. But beyond reallocation, transforming the structures of logic that confuse violence and necropolitics for freedom and safety remains our calling.

Notes

1. Delany, "Star Pit," 23.
2. Delany, "Star Pit," 22–23.
3. Delany, "Star Pit," 58.
4. Delany, "Star Pit," 36.
5. Delany, "Star Pit," 26.
6. Delany, "Star Pit," 66; emphasis in original.
7. Rowell, "Interview with Samuel Delany," 41.
8. Delany, "Racism and Science Fiction," 73.

9. Delany, "Star Pit," 18.

10. Delany, "Racism and Science Fiction," 84.

11. Delany, "Necessity of Tomorrow(s)," 13.

12. Duda and Kaba, "Horizon of Abolition."

Bibliography

Delany, Samuel R. "The Necessity of Tomorrow(s)." In *Starboard Wine: Notes on the Language of Science Fiction*, 1–14. Middletown, CT: Wesleyan, 2012.

Delany, Samuel R. "Racism and Science Fiction." In *The Atheist in the Attic*, by Samuel R. Delany, 72–94. Oakland, CA: PM Press, 2018. First published 1998.

Delany, Samuel R. "The Star Pit." In *Driftglass*, 13–71. New York: Signet, 1971. First published 1965.

Duda, John, and Mariame Kaba. "Towards the Horizon of Abolition: A Conversation with Mariame Kaba." The Next System Project. November 9, 2017. https://thenextsystem.org/learn/stories/towards-horizon-abolition-conversation-mariame-kaba.

Rowell, Charles H. "An Interview with Samuel Delany." In *Conversations with Samuel R. Delany*, ed. Carl Freedman, 26–53. Jackson: University Press of Mississippi, 2009.

2 Lionel Davidson, *Under Plum Lake* (1980) / YA Time Out of Joint

Rebekah Sheldon

During summer vacation, Barry, the twelve-year-old narrator of Lionel Davidson's *Under Plum Lake*, discovers a hidden civilization under the tidal pool formed by the cliffs of Cornwall while his family visits a seaside resort. Exploring the cliff caves one day, he meets a captivating boy who leads him down a tunnel and out into the land of Egon. The strange boy, Dido, shows Barry the wonders, pleasures, and possibilities of Egon beyond the scope of his imagining. With Dido, he rides on thermal jets, eats the fruits of the pleasure tree, and learns an alternate history of the world.

Following the language of SF's utopia subgenre, Egon is a space apart. Barry's growing understanding of Dido's world causes him, and the reader along with him, to reassess his own assumptions and expectations of life while in Egon's light. Yet as Dido repeatedly reminds him, the world that he shows Barry is one that Barry can never possess. He can neither remain in Egon nor take any of the things he learns there back *up above*. His biological development will not allow him the range or power of understanding that the people of Egon possess. For as much as his new friend appears also to be a kid on the cusp of adolescence, Dido is in fact ninety-nine years old: "He said the difference between us was the difference between people and dogs in the world above. He said people above lived seven times longer than dogs. But people in Egon lived over seven times longer than *people* above. He said they lived to seven or eight hundred years. They developed more slowly. There was more of them to develop."[1] Like Barry, Dido is still a minor and thus a ward of his parents, but Barry can see that he is in fact a "very old man. He was older than my grandparents, older than anyone I knew or had even heard of."[2] So Barry is, in effect, too young to do what Dido does. And he always will be. Every experience overwhelms him. As

Barry tells us in the secret journal of his memories that is the text of the book, he has trouble taking in Dido's explanation of the differences in their aging processes, because they were in the shower while Dido was explaining it and "the shower was so fantastic, I hardly heard him."[3] Barry's experiences in Egon are all like this; they are of pleasures so exquisite as to be a kind of self-immolation. "I forgot who I was," he tells us more than once.[4] On one notable occasion, he dies. The recklessness that Dido encourages in Barry causes his death, but Dido and his father use their advanced technology to reconstruct his personality and bring him back to life.

It is these too-early encounters with utopia that leave Barry so violently unmoored, so out of joint with the developmental sequence expected of children. When Barry is eventually forced to leave Egon, Dido and his father erase Barry's memory. But something goes wrong with the process, perhaps precipitated by his death and reconstruction, perhaps from the many times Dido has experimented with memory erasure on Barry, perhaps simply from the intensity of his exposure. Whatever the case, the result is that Barry does not forget. In fact, the longer he spends back in Cornwall, the more of his memories return to obsess him with their haunting, impossible promise of dangerous sweetness. By Barry's thirteenth birthday, he feels himself to be "an old man, far older than my parents."

One way to understand this is as a novel of moral hazard about pleasures that come too early and stories that promise too much. In this way, *Under Plum Lake* gives voice to the persistent fear that readers of science fiction and other popular genres are arrested in early adolescence by their attachment to escapist literature. The quip that the golden age of science fiction is twelve—both an insult and a truism capturing the catalog of many an SF reader's adolescence—turns this difficult bond into an epigram. And while it is certainly a witty one, its sly displacement of chronology for chronicle also highlights something important about the taken-for-granted relationship between adolescence and science fiction: the prominence of time, timing, and development in both the genre and its typical readers' stage of life.

It is hard to separate modern conceptions of childhood from the idea of timing. Since the child-saving movements of the Progressive Era, norms of discrete childhood-developmental stages have seemed key to achieving adulthood.[5] Queer theorists of childhood and adolescence have noted how closely that achievement is tied to the reproduction of the family.[6] It is no mistake that stunted development is often the slur used against gays and lesbians, whose sexuality is seen as a failure to leave an earlier and less adult sexual stage. What Elizabeth Freeman has termed *chrononormativity* names the idea that a meaningful life is a life in which childhood fantasy, including Freud's famous polymorphous perversity, gives way to adult heterosexuality.[7] Timing matters to childhood insofar as a proper adult is a straight adult. Barry is unable to *grow up* and take his proper place in the world because he is now *too old*, having been exposed to pleasures against which nothing in his world can compare. Like the children who cavort with ghosts in Henry James's *The Turn of the Screw*, Barry's secret knowledge has left him prematurely aged. In its analogy of Egon with utopian science fiction, the novel suggests that such a fate may meet any child who wanders too early into such esoteric realms. Stunted development, in other words, is here a wound of the genre. Science fiction, like the world of Egon, offers pleasures so rich no realism will ever again suffice.

But stunted development isn't really a matter of age but of interests. Barry's problem is not so much that he won't mature (he is in some sense already too old), but rather that he won't abandon the attachments that seem to the adults in his life like irresponsible fantasies of escape. That is, he won't denigrate his knowledge as delusion; he won't dismiss as impossibility what he knows to have been true. He holds on, in other words, to the idea that another world, another form of social organization, another order of desire and pleasure, is not only possible but in fact continuously operating alongside this one. If, as Kathryn Bond Stockton argues, a child's ostensibly endearing difference from adults is also the thing that must be lost in order to gain adulthood, then Barry's excessive attachment to childish stories doubles what Stockton understands as the originating queerness of the child, as the site of a difference both celebrated and doomed to be eradicated. Barry's refusal to accept our consensus reality as singularly true stunts his trajectory toward heteronormative social reproduction and puts his time out of joint, making him grow laterally rather than linearly, fattening around his adult-like fixation on an irrational, unrealistic, impossible dream of self-shattering enjoyment.

Genres like science fiction, fantasy, and utopia take their associations with childhood from the idea of *wonder*, treated nostalgically by adults as once beloved but now overcome genres of unreal escape. In her book *Re-Enchanted*, Maria Sachiko Cecire charts the way C. S. Lewis and J. R. R. Tolkien together forged an association among children, England's medieval past, and metaphysical wonder. Through their Oxford curriculum, as well as in their novels and essays, Lewis and Tolkien sought to instill an alternative pedagogy of wonder against the modern principle of linear, secular time. Cecire demonstrates that Lewis and Tolkien found in children's literature an ideal place for magic and other metaphysics routinely denigrated as outmoded, "regressive," or "infantile" and so no longer understood as viable in the sober adulthood of rational modernity.[8] By the twentieth century, childhood as *that which must be left behind* had already come to seem synonymous with the lost premodern past, somewhere that must be left behind in order for proper adulthood to take hold. Tolkien and Lewis sought to use wonder to forge an aesthetic and affective comportment that might persist into adulthood as nostalgia—and so even they continue to employ a developmental telos. Children's fantastic literature figures as a ghost of itself (as always already in the past), the child whose queer attachment to other forms of knowing and being it both desires and dismisses.

In this sense, the genres of children's fantastic literature operate as containment, first by registering the social and epistemological differences of childhood modes of knowing compared to those of adulthood, and then assimilating childhood modes of knowing to a superseded personal and national past. And yet, I want to argue, the child's epistemological queerness cannot be simply excised. Children's fantastic literature encourages childhood's energetic attachment to the possibility of another world in order to contain it as the lost past. That it must be contained indicates that those qualities are also necessary. I want to take seriously childhood's affinity with other worlds and ways of knowing not as a metaphor or even as a discursive construction but rather as a threatening potentiality, superseded by adult rationality but nonetheless continuously operating in rationality as epiphany, a combination often corporatized as innovation or managed as creativity.

Children's fantasy is the genre that most explicitly associates childhood with the past. However, wonder at the possibility of historical difference figured through the child's queered form of knowing and contained as nostalgia happens across all fantastic fictions for children. Fantasy fiction does so through the past; young adult dystopias do so by comparing the dystopian future to the present and against the possibility of another world. Young adult dystopias contain the potential differences of childhood by restoring the present. A teen on the cusp of adult knowledge is tasked to sacrifice for the good of the whole. The conditions of this sacrifice expose the teen to a new understanding of the world. In its light he chooses instead to rebel, to reject his societies, figured as infantilized, and to force everyone to grow up for their own good. His rebellion saves the society from its stunted development and returns the real utopia of a restored present—the present of the reader. Scott Westerfeld's *Uglies*, James Dashner's *Maze Runner*, Veronica Roth's *Divergent*, China Miéville's *Railsea*: these young adult dystopias may attribute different causes for the dystopian social organization of the setting (state-mandated beautification surgery, educational testing, division into specialized worker classes, end-of-history ideology), but they all engage the device of the young adult hero's sacrifice to restore the reader's idealized present.

The teens of contemporary YA dystopias find it harder to live in unjust societies once their eyes have been opened to systemic inequities, rather than to sacrifice themselves in the pursuit of the restoration of a lost order. Each novel narrates knowledge shifts the teen protagonist experiences—from true believer through the moment of recognition to the choice to rebel. The plotting intimates that the teen's identity is only artificially shaped by the influence of his or her society. Underneath those superficial values is a longing for what the novels pose as true and enduringly human values: family, choice, love, and individual autonomy. Hidden but still vital under the carapace of dystopian control, these "true" values are the essence of the human. Redeemed before the onset of adult fixity, turned inward and away from external influence, the teen expresses the truth of humanity and so redeems the adult world from the distortions of culture.

YA dystopian fictions, in other words, *manage as plot* the crisis brought on by the queer innocence of childhood and its stubborn affinities with ways of knowing that must be shed and replaced by proper adulthood. They proffer escape from social norms but only as a moment of crisis in which the protagonists freely and sometimes fiercely choose to grow up and reproduce our consensus reality as the best of all possible worlds.

In this context, *Under Plum Lake* becomes visible less as a work of utopian fiction than as a rejection of dystopia, a rebellion against dystopia's generic pattern, a dystopia whose protagonist refuses to see the world it describes as bad. Barry experiences profound ambivalence after being exposed to Egon. His forced return leaves him physically depleted and mentally anguished. Even though they erase his memory, he is left with the feeling of something missing in the world. "I couldn't concentrate on anything," he writes. "I kept looking out of the window. I had a feeling I'd lost something. I couldn't think what it was. But I couldn't think of anything else either."[9] As he recovers, this feeling of something missing starts filling in with fragmentary details and he experiences longing mixed with despair, attachment, rage, vulnerability, and a compulsive refusal to move on. These feelings make *Under Plum Lake* a kind of seduction narrative. In Davidson's version, though, it is the genre of utopian imagining that seduces and wounds, given the dictates of adult realism. He is stunted in his development because he refuses to put away fantasies that could be realities. Once Barry encounters utopia, he cannot grow up in the way Dido's people can, but neither can he grow up in the more conventional sense. Having been exposed too early to the possibility of *otherwise*, he can no longer accept his place in his world.

In this way, *Under Plum Lake* suggests that young adult dystopias channel rather than eradicate the epiphany-driven energies of childhood toward normative ends. In doing so, they tell us that another order is not only possible but also, like Dido's Egon, the subterranean support for the reproduction of the present. In this time of catastrophe, when dystopia seems closer than ever, it is easy to feel as dystopias suggest we do: that our normal is truly the best of all possible social organizations. Through Barry's anguished attempt to retain his memories of Egon, *Under Plum Lake* calls on us too to remember what we lose when we accept that the only alternative is the realism of the present.

Notes

1. Davidson, *Under Plum Lake*, 53.
2. Davidson, *Under Plum Lake*, 94.
3. Davidson, *Under Plum Lake*, 54.
4. Davidson, *Under Plum Lake*, 5.
5. Platt, *Child Savers*; Ward, *Black Child Savers*.
6. Stockton, *The Queer Child*; Owen, *A Queer History of Adolescence*.
7. Freeman, *Time Binds*.
8. Cecire, *Re-Enchanted*, 16.
9. Davidson, *Under Plum Lake*, 132.

Bibliography

Cecire, Maria Sachiko. *Re-Enchanted: The Rise of Children's Fantasy Literature in the Twentieth Century*. Minneapolis: University of Minnesota Press, 2019.

Davidson, Lionel. *Under Plum Lake*. New York: Knopf, 1980.

Freeman, Elizabeth. *Time Binds: Queer Temporalities, Queer Histories*. Durham, NC: Duke University Press, 2010.

Owen, Gabrielle. *A Queer History of Adolescence: Developmental Pasts, Relational Futures*. Athens: University of Georgia, 2020.

Platt, Anthony M. *The Child Savers: The Invention of Delinquency*. New Brunswick, NJ: Rutgers University Press, 2009.

Stockton, Kathryn Bond. *The Queer Child, or Growing Sideways in the Twentieth-Century*. Durham, NC: Duke University Press, 2009.

Ward, Geoff K. *The Black Child Savers: Racial Democracy and Juvenile Justice*. Chicago: University of Chicago Press, 2012.

3 Brian Henson and Rockne O'Bannon, *Farscape* (1999–2003) / Radical Compassion

Emmet Asher-Perrin

In the very first episode of Rockne S. O'Bannon's space opera series *Farscape*, displaced human astronaut John Crichton (Ben Browder) asks an alien named Aeryn Sun (Claudia Black) if she could find it within herself to show their purported enemies some compassion. Both of them have been injected with "translator microbes" that help them understand each other's languages, but Aeryn appears perplexed by the request: "Compassion? What is compassion?"

It's a by-the-numbers culture clash heightened by a science-fictional premise: John has just learned that Aeryn's language has no word equivalent to *compassion*. She is a soldier, bred for service as part of a fascist military force known in their part of the galaxy only as the Peacekeepers. Among the ranks of her people, any form of emotional, mental, or physical fragility is something to be buried or excised. She has no word for compassion because it is not an attribute her people value, but rather an inconvenient glimmer of weakness that she must repress.

This is where *Farscape* begins—a television show about an American astronaut who, upon being unceremoniously slung down a wormhole, finds himself stuck on the other side of the universe aboard a living ship, *Moya*, crewed by escaped prisoners and an exiled Peacekeeper. There are plenty of SF television shows and films that focus on the trials of a specific crew and vessel, but *Farscape* distinguished itself from the start with this exchange, an acknowledgment that empathy is an active decision in need of cultivation rather than passive state. By illustrating that one of their main characters has no working grasp of those tools, the show positions itself as a map toward cultivating radical compassion as Aeryn, John, and the rest work together to create empathic bonds. In creating that map, the characters of *Farscape* developed a community that caters to their multifaceted needs, supports its members in times of turmoil, and puts an end to a galactic war between the Peacekeepers and their enemies, the Scarrans.

Aeryn's reeducation is central to what *Farscape* accomplished during its four seasons: she is essentially a fascist military combatant, brainwashed from birth, who finds the strength to deprogram herself once she realizes that she is loved and valued beyond her conditioning and Peacekeeper identity. Some of that love is romantic in her burgeoning and tumultuous relationship with John Crichton, but it is also familial and platonic in the love she receives from, and eventually learns to openly return to, her friends about *Moya*. Aeryn bonds with their ship's custodian, Pilot, after being injected with his DNA; she forms a fighter's camaraderie with the Luxan warrior D'Argo; she finds spiritual guidance in Delvian priest Pa'u Zotoh Zhaan; and she discovers the little sister she never had (or likely wanted) in the antics of the young Nebari named Chiana. Over her years away from the Peacekeepers, Aeryn learns to separate out the parts of her old life that are still useful, keeping discipline and strength as core tenets of her person while making room for humor and messier emotions. She searches for compassion within herself and finds an unending resource that carries her beyond her fealty to a gargantuan military force, coming out the other side fulfilled and more vibrant than ever.

This pattern is replicated among her shipmates, often in the most unexpected places, and realized in surprising ways. Two of the show's main cast—Rygel and Pilot—are physically embodied as puppets created by the Jim Henson Company, imbuing their manufactured forms with the same tangible pathos that the Muppets have received since their inception. Rygel XVI, deposed dominar of the Hynerian Empire, begins his tenure on the show determined to sell out his cohorts at the first and best opportunity. But although Rygel's schemes frequently cause trouble for his companions, he is always given the opportunity to redeem himself, and always finds himself taking it. Former Peacekeeper captain Bialar Crais has even more to make up for, being responsible for Aeryn's exile and for chasing Crichton across the galaxy out of a misplaced desire for vengeance. But Crais works hard to unlearn what the Peacekeepers taught him, departing from their service in search of honor and peace on his own terms. D'Argo's species is subject to fits of "hyper-rage" in addition to aggressive tendencies, and he often has difficulty controlling his temper, even among comrades.

But the Luxan reckons with that rage over time, confronts its toxicity, and embraces the more gentle aspects of his person, always finding forgiveness and respect among his friends regardless of his mistakes.

The greatest cultivator of empathy on *Farscape*, however, is the ship itself—or rather, *her*self. The navigator and single point of communicative contact with *Moya* is Pilot, a being physically bonded to the ship as a symbiotic unit. Pilot and *Moya* can feel each other's pain, and because *Moya* is alive, the crew is obligated to consider her needs, fears, and autonomy. When *Moya* is pregnant, the crew has to forego "starburst," a Leviathan's single defense maneuver that puts distance between them and threats. When *Moya* is injured during the extermination of vermin that the crew are responsible for bringing on board, they have to help her heal and give her time to recover. When *Moya* is scared or worried, she occasionally behaves erratically, and the crew has to weather that in the same way that they would weather an emotional outburst from any of their number. *Farscape* drastically reshapes the dynamic of crew and spaceship familiar from TV shows like the Star Trek franchise, where no matter how much damage a ship takes, it can be seemingly and miraculously repaired with no concern for the vessel itself; in effect, *Farscape*'s ship becomes a metaphor for our own ecological concerns and stressors. Because *Moya*'s crew is a community housed in a living being, their community *becomes* a living thing itself, and in turn serves as a reminder to offer that community—each constituent part being integral to the whole—the consideration and care it deserves.

Empathy isn't the only method by which *Farscape* excels in community-building. While most of the actors on the show are white—a mark of having been produced in Australia in the late 1990s and early 2000s—within the fictional premise of the series, *Moya*'s crew is an assemblage of different species, cultures, religions, and life experiences. Different lifeways abound, often clashing, but still finding ways to coexist. Romantic and sexual encounters are frequent, common, and often interspecies, and the kink factor in these encounters is widely broadcasted and frequently bound up in BDSM tropes, making nearly every character on the show functionally queer to some degree, a fact that is never so much as commented upon by any of them. And it would be remiss to neglect the truly remarkable manner in which *Farscape* handles disabilities, both mental and physical, within the context of its narrative. Nearly every character on the show displays some form of neurodivergence or physical disability, or both at once—a commonality relatively rare in fiction across the board, particularly at the level of detail the series employs.

The show demonstrates a pointed awareness that disability is also conditional to the environment one operates within; for example, Rygel spends most of the show sitting in a hovering chair called a ThroneSled because his limbs are too small to carry him effectively about the ship when compared to his larger, long-legged shipmates. But Rygel is not immobile by Hynerian standards; his species appears to be amphibious, his body designed to move in water. What's more, Rygel's seeming lack of mobility leads to a reservoir of knowledge, skill, and expertise where *Moya*'s ducts and ventilation are concerned. Rygel's size and penchant for secrecy give him an impressive working knowledge of the smaller spaces on the ship that the majority of the crew cannot match.

Physical disability isn't the only point of misunderstanding regarding Rygel; while the former dominar is often berated by the rest of the crew for being greedy and selfish, some of this appears to be related to post-traumatic stress disorder, which many of his compatriots experience to varying degrees. Rygel's perceived gluttony is a bound-up response to trauma, connected to the years of uncertainty and torture he suffered at the hands of the Peacekeepers, making his motives always more complex than they seem.

John Crichton also suffers from PTSD, which visibly worsens throughout the show as he's subjected to increasing levels of stress and violence. *Farscape* is one of the few narratives that properly acknowledges the mental toll exacted by being exposed to a universe's worth of new experiences while your own touchstones disappear. Crichton's sense of impending doom expands while his points of reference contract and grow distant the longer he is away from home. One of the astronaut's most entertaining traits—his tendency to frame everything through Earth pop culture references—is a testament to that difficulty, a deliberate ploy to recontextualize all the things he sees that he cannot codify or assimilate quickly enough. And to make his road rockier, he ends up burdened by hallucinations in the form of a "neural clone" planted in his mind by another Peacekeeper enemy, a Scarran-Sebacean hybrid known as Scorpius.

Because this is *Farscape*, Scorpius is far more than a cardboard cutout villain, eventually becoming a member of *Moya*'s crew who aids in their journey. Much like Crais, he performs a contextual turn from foe to unnerving ally, whose motivations and goals are thoroughly understood even when they're far from laudable. The show spends a great deal of time unpacking Scorpius's physical disabilities as well, treating them as a means to better appreciate his perspective rather than a shorthand for inequity and evil. Descended from one species that goes comatose in the presence of heightened temperatures and another that produces intense heat physiologically, Scorpius's own body is constantly battling itself. To regulate his temperature properly, the Peacekeeper commander wears a custom-made coolant suit—one that necessitates the frequent insertion of cooling rods *directly into his brain*. It is simultaneously a source of unimaginable vulnerability, requiring an assistant or helper to change out the rods on his behalf, and a testament to all that Scorpius is capable of overcoming.

At the same time, Scorpius's manner of dealing with his disability is something of an aesthetic, built in accordance with his style to suit his personality, an aspect that is often left disregarded when imagining how disability might be integrated into personal and daily life. To say that Scorpius spends every waking hour as a fully equipped dom is putting it far too mildly: his coolant suit is constructed of head-to-toe armored shining black leather, complete with codpiece, head mask, and a tailcoat. He is shown to be attractive to a variety of peoples and species throughout the series' run, demanding loyalty and adherence to his commands, and bestowing bondage, sexual satisfaction, career advancement, and protection on those who please him. The suit's functionality is part of that arrangement; Scorpius prefers to have those in his inner circle exchange his cooling rods, a carefully selected handful of people. In effect, he builds the mechanisms that support his disability around the persona he wishes to project, and manages the task with devastating panache.

The crew of *Moya* are accustomed to these differences of mind, of body, of behavior, and they develop their own systems for handling them over their years spent cooped up together. They know that there are times when D'Argo needs to be left to cool off because he's too angry; that Rygel will clean out the kitchen if he's upset or nervous; that Crichton needs to be held back sometimes so he doesn't injure himself as he hallucinates a version of Scorpius that's wearing a hideous Hawaiian shirt; that Stark will fidget and stare at people long past their point of comfort and repeat phrases when he's stressed; that Chiana's first instinct is to do the opposite of what someone tells her as a response to growing up in a homogenous culture that punished any form of variance. That doesn't mean the show eschews conflict as it basks in a cooperative glow of fellowship; if anything, it's just the opposite. More often than not, *Moya*'s little found family members are at each other's throats, chaos ensues, and everyone comes out the other end bruised and exhausted. And this is important: communities aren't built on agreement, but on understanding.

It's that constant momentum toward greater interpersonal understanding that *Farscape* chisels away at, piece by pebbly piece. For a show that focuses so much on imagery and action and spectacle, it's incredible how much of the story can be found in scenes that are merely two people talking about how they feel. Or even *not* talking—just two people taking up space in a companionable silence. Communication is the vehicle of understanding, the facilitator of community-building, and this continues to evolve throughout the show. The more *Moya*'s crew communicates, the better they understand one another, the more they are capable of withstanding and surmounting odds together. It's astounding that the show managed to impart this when it was famously mired in production roadblocks that made it difficult to adhere to its planned arc: from the departure of beloved actors to studio interference born of having producers on three different continents to its premature cancellation after season four—which led to widespread outcry and a fan-led campaign that got the show its miniseries ending.

Crichton often bemoans the fact that his plans are terrible, but every time he wants to rob a Shadow Depository or infiltrate a Gammak Base or sabotage Peacekeeper military research, he's always got a few friends reckless enough to go along with what he's got in mind, if it means keeping more people safe. They learn time and again that they're stronger when they act as a unit, when they trust each other and work toward common goals. But the reason they do it is far more sentimental than any of Crichton's friends would be comfortable reckoning with: it is because understanding begets love.

In the very first episode of *Farscape*, Aeryn Sun tells John Crichton that being a Peacekeeper is her duty, what she was born for, but Crichton's not buying it. Yet rather than denigrate that perspective, he comes at the problem from a different angle, offering up a simple statement: "You can be more."

This is what *Farscape* believes. That every single one of us can be more than what we're told or raised or intended to be. That the bridges we build and the love we offer can help us discover community and greater purpose. And that if we support one another with that knowledge, that steadfast belief, there is truly no limit to what we might accomplish. *We* can be more, collectively, then we ever were apart. Like the bond between *Moya* and her Pilot, our shared camaraderie and experience and trust have the ability to carry us far—to the stars, and between them, and to whatever lies beyond.

4 Shovon Chowdhury, *The Competent Authority* (2013) / CTRL+ALT+DELETE Humanity

Sami Ahmad Khan

This chapter is dedicated to the loving memory of Barkat Zaman Khan, my father: a utopia within him, he left in dystopia without. It is also dedicated to Shovon Chowdhury—who left us laughing at the folly of our ways.

The wall has finally been built.

Whether it first appeared in speculative fiction to later get projected on our collective psyches or whether it is but a manifestation of the wall(s) permanently etched in our own minds is a petrifying question. Philosophers have debated the nature of reality, its constituent elements and conditions, and whether/how it shapes the art of an age since time immemorial. Literature often negotiates with such empirical "reality," and SF, the literature of "what if," almost always becomes the literature of "what now." The constructed realities in *The Matrix* and *Dark City*, the "force" in *Star Wars* and the "chaos" in *The Witcher*, and SF's own movement from *Flash Gordon* to Joanna Russ's *The Female Man*—all exhibit in different ways how art, reality, markets, and politics shape literary narratives.

Which is why I assert that huge, magnificent walls have already been built in SF. In science fiction, they keep the kaiju out; in fantasy, they save us from the White Walkers; and in (Islamic) mythology, they keep Yajuj and Majuj (Gog and Magog) at bay. The dystopian aspects of SF—science fiction, fantasy, and myth—have always laid the groundwork for the metaphorical walls to *be*. Our times are dark and full of programmed (t)errors: around the time my home city, New Delhi, witnessed a polarizing (state) election campaign in early 2020, a horrifying communal riot tore through the streets. India inched toward implementing Nuremberg-inspired laws directed toward its minorities, a pandemic gripped the world, a series of localized earthquakes jolted us, the air turned toxic, and India and China (and not just Pakistan)—a mushroom on top of *this* cake—almost went to war. In a world order where truth is stranger than fiction, where global warming doesn't exist, where hatred/violence has become acceptable currency, where Australian bushfires have killed more than a billion beings, where the United States is inches away from invading another country, and where my own country—India—is in the grip of bloodied mass agitations, genocide of the other seems to be the only/final solution. SF, a la Kubrick, tosses bones of contention upward in the skies and forward in time toward our futures. While aware of the fractal linkages among language/literature, thought, and reality, this essay is not about those intersections per se; it is, rather, about how empirical reality finds itself reflected and refracted (albeit in a distorted, temporally delayed way) via and in Indian SF, and how/whether it can help us survive the twenty-first century. Will 2020 translate into a metaphor for this entire century?

Sometimes the answer to this question of survival and Indian SF can be a yes—depending on how you phrase the question. Let's turn to India's Anglophonic science fiction about surviving our current predicament. India is mutating rapidly; its science fiction reifies the concerns of a society where technology is beginning to permeate all spheres of existence. Darko Suvin reads science fiction as a "specifically roundabout way of commenting on the author's collective context"; Ursula K. Le Guin finds the genre "descriptive" and not "predictive"; and Samuel R. Delany views it as a narrative convention that employs the "future" to present distortions of the "present."[1] Using English-language SF from India is a conscious choice/location/network from which to write back. English is a global lingua franca, which Indians have appropriated from their erstwhile colonizers with zeal. Contemporary India itself, in the throes of unparalleled technological and social change, has the three-body problem of an ancient civilization caught between global market forces; localized, irredentist right-wing powers' reassertion; and a left-liberal resistance to the previous two, three factors shaping Indian SF's trajectory.[2] Such notional flux activates identities of caste, religion, gender, class, nationality, and so on, and Indian SF merges reality and fiction, literature and politics, and past, present, and future.

This is evident in contemporary works. Rimi Chatterjee's *Signal Red* (2005) paints a neofascist India of the near future, testing WMDs on its own citizens; Mainak Dhar's *Zombiestan* (2012) treats Islamist terror as a zombie infection that sweeps across the world; Ruchir Joshi's *The Last Jet-Engine Laugh* (2001) showcases an existential threat to India from a Pakistan-Saudi

Arabia-USA alliance; and Suraj Clark Prasad's *Baramulla Bomber* (2013) fears a Communist Caliphate (after a de facto Pakistan and China entente). Anil Menon's *The Beast with Nine Billion Feet* (2009) uses genetic engineering to question the ethics of late capitalism; and Jugal Mody's *Toke* (2012) uses Hindu gods (Vishnu and Shiva) to indict commodity fetishism, conformism, and bourgeois values. Environmental concerns are encoded (among other things) in Kenneth Doyle's "Rain," Sukanya Datta's "Taking a Shortcut," and Prayaag Akbar's *Leila* (2017). Shiv Ramdas' *Domechild* (2013), Vatsala Kaul's "Catatonic" (2007), and Payal Dhar's "The Coward" (2007) foreground AI and digital threats. Identities become problematic too: Priya Sarukkai Chabria's *Generation 14* (2008), Vandana Singh's "Almaru" (2007), and Rahul Srivastava's "The Unknown Firewalls" (2007) engage with the intermeshing of caste and class within a hierarchical, oppressive society. Manjula Padmanabhan's *Escape* (2008), Indrapramit Das's "Sita's Descent" (2012), and Vandana Singh's "The Woman Who Thought She Was a Planet" (2008), to cite just three examples, attack sexism, male chauvinism, and the systematic neutralization of women in a country. *Si vis pacem, para bellum.* If you want a utopia, prepare for a dystopia.

Moreover, the metaphorical reimagining of dystopias becomes the strength of (Anglophone) Indian SF, a movement not toward nihilism, anarchy, didactic prescriptions, or enforced top-down codes of ethics but toward a framework of morals, harmony, and balance. While the thematic relevance—and the epistemes which link such narratives to the times in which they are rooted—is hard to miss, contemporary Indian SF composed in English goes beyond a simple representation of the times in which it is forged and consumed. Through its (primarily) dystopian visions, Indian SF reflects a need for tolerance and acceptance in our present times—a warning shot fired across the bow of time. Interestingly, though most of the texts mentioned previously may promise (at least) the possibility of redemption based on the "feedback" we receive from, say, dark futures,[3] I feel some SF differs due to its satirical roots of black comedy—like Shovon Chowdhury's *The Competent Authority* (TCA). Rather than the wishing-away of the walls in our minds, TCA yearns for a wishing away of the minds themselves. Nagarjuna writes that there is "pleasure when a sore is scratched," but "to be without sores is more pleasurable still."[4] The tranquility of this message is interpreted by select Indian dystopias thus: though there are pleasures in the genocide of others, to be without others is perhaps more pleasurable still.

TCA doesn't shy away from others. In the novel, Mumbai has been nuked, Delhi is in the middle of a postnuclear reconstruction, the Indian state of West Bengal has seceded and now operates as a protectorate of China, and Maoists run amok across India. The novel paints a near future in which the People's Republic of China nukes India after the Indian prime minister feeds a snack to a child regarded to be the next Dalai Lama. Social order collapses, political boundaries change, and large parts of the country are rendered uninhabitable. Those who survive face environmental disasters, water riots, gender clashes, economic inequalities, political strife (class warfare), social upheavals (caste clashes), and the consequences of historical blunders (the partition of India, for example). The radiation also creates telepaths and mutants—except this time Professor Xavier is not there to shepherd them.

Within this scenario, an Orwellian "deranged bureaucrat" emerges: the *competent authority*, implying any person/organization invested with the power to perform specific functions. As head of the Bureau of Reconstruction within a de jure democratic republic, the competent authority uses his powers to subvert constitutional (and human) values. For example, he exhorts the Indian military to attack China because "it is big, close, and hard to miss."[5] Through the sluggish, eponymous competent authority, TCA riles against state inefficiency, political hypocrisy, red tape, and bureaucratic complacency: the elite Indian Administrative Service—India's bureaucratic steel frame—is regarded as the "biggest mafia racket in human history."[6]

The novel also indicts commodity fetishism, neoimperialism, and neoliberal capitalism: the Bank of Bodies, voted "India's most valuable company" for the third year in a row, extracts organs out of the living poor for the benefit of the rich. Slavery, too, is back in business: industrialist Verma purchases a doctor from Slaves R Us, and his factory runs on slave labor. Nepotism and the military-industry-state nexus are evident in the prime minister (who comes from a long line of PMs) and in the relationship between a bureaucrat (Mehta) and the wealthy Verma. TCA is replete with gender crimes, violence, and sexism: "the precipitous drop in the number of available women had led to a lot of men turning on their own kind."[7] The Haryanvi horror, who is "a perverted pimpernel, buggering the rich, and cheering up the poor," sharpens the satire, especially since he is from the Indian state of Haryana (with a skewed sex ratio).[8] TCA also lampoons how "gurus," under the garb of religion, fill their coffers at the expense of those they are supposed to enlighten: for example, Dharti Pakar, who "had started his career as a management consultant, before realizing that his talent could be put to better use," and Sri Sri Yo Yo, a rapper who turns to spirituality and its monetization.[9] Global climate change also appears via the imagery of a postnuclear society in which air and water are now (even more) precious commodities and antiradiation swimsuits are all the rage. Also, some (such as Verma) treat South African private security contractors (who safeguard Verma's factories against Maoist thrusts) with disdain; they also ride a xenophobic wave, as evidenced by how China (which has ostensibly deployed telepaths against India) is seen as the fountainhead of evil.

The protagonist of TCA is a twelve-year-old mutant (Pintoo) who lives in a ghetto (Shanti Nagar). Pintoo is assaulted by Medical Military Commandos and divested of a hand because Pappu, the son of industrialist Verma, requires the limb, and the Bank of Bodies readily procures it. However, unwilling donor Pintoo soon develops superpowers and then comes in contact with people from the left, center, and right of the political spectrum. After due deliberation, Pintoo realizes that the best way to heal his world is by preventing it from coming about in the first place. He identifies first problems and then the (temporal) solutions that might correct history. For example, he regards the main reasons behind India's dystopia to be weaponization/militarization (which Pintoo feels could be checked by stopping India's nuclear weapons tests), communalism (which could be toned down by preventing the Muslim League's Direct Action Day of 1946), and India's rightward shift (which he intends to stop by ensuring that Mahatma Gandhi is not assassinated by a religious zealot in 1948). Using his psychokinetic powers, he sends three people back in time to stop these colossal events from taking place: a pessimistic officer (Chatterjee), a dirty cop (Pande), and the last surviving member of Al Qaeda (Ali).

The novel can be explicated via what I call the "transMIT thesis," which advances how Indian SF "exists across the intersecting domains of technology, materiality/politics/ideology and mythology" and "transmits to its readers (emergent) technology, (sedimented) mythology and (mutating) ideology."[10] TCA also foregrounds newer technologies that disrupt and (literally) deform (e.g., efficacious organ transplant technologies), mythologies that contour normativity (e.g., Guru Dharti Pakar and his disciples), and ideologies that are locked in perpetual combat (e.g., Islamism, Maoism,

Hindutva). TCA thus constructs three kinds of others for India: the first paradigm is religion (Islam), the second is the nation-state (China, Pakistan), and the third is political ideology (Maoism, Islamism).[11]

The placement of these semantic markers gains immense sociopolitical relevance. At a time when religious fault lines are openly visible, TCA interrogates communalism throughout its body (and that of India): the ugly spat between Tarun-da and the ancient headmaster over Islam in India, Jinnah, and the 1947 partition provide one such example. The Shakahari Sena (SS; Vegetarian Army)—which raids and vandalizes public establishments and forces people to take an oath of vegetarianism—represents mobs who are hand in glove with a neofascist state: not only is the SS "a religio-political organization" to which "the normal principles of law and order [do] not apply," its members are also "shock troops against Islamic Terror."[12] The poison of communalism runs so deep that when Ghanashyam Das, an actor, pretends to be national hero Netaji (S. C. Bose) and tries to pacify a bloodthirsty mob during the Direct Action Day of 1946 through an emotional appeal to patriotism and goodness, "a shot rang out" and the would-be Netaji "fell, clutching his chest, a bloodstain swelling across his khakis."[13] My reading of the TCA's presentation of communalism is so poisoned by this bitter event, by the murder of the actor representing the beloved leader, that I comprehend that such fanaticism could never have a hopeful outcome.

The novel also fuses the paradigms of caste and class (which often go together in the Indian context) with the low-intensity conflict between Shanti Nagar (a ghetto run by a eunuch called Shanti Bai) and the posh, upper-class/caste localities of Delhi as one example. These battles between the haves and the have-nots highlight the vast disparities between the rich and the poor, and the urban and rural populaces, in India's future. TCA thus establishes a link among India's yesterday (with references to India's freedom struggles and the principles under which it was forged), today (by foregrounding contemporary sociopolitical problems), and tomorrow (with warnings of the shape of things to come).

Dystopias in Indian SF become not just about warning, horror, and fear: they also morph into narrative modes of morality in which resistance to power structures transforms into a resounding act of agency. But do we really deserve to survive?

Sometimes the answer can be no.

TCA is not just about saving us from current crises (by depicting them); it is more about taking us out of the rat race in order to survive by reaffirming that the only *real* crisis that afflicts us is *us*. We live in glass houses, on a planet almost completely glassed. God ended with Friedrich Nietzsche, philosophy with Martin Heidegger, the centrality of an author-God with Roland Barthes, and history itself with Francis Fukuyama (and perhaps even *Doctor Who*): now mankind must end too—or all realities will end. For the betterment of the planet, it is imperative that we *don't* survive. John Snow must die once to defend the realm; Harry Potter must die once to destroy the horcrux of Voldemort within; Gandalf the Grey must die once to become Gandalf the White; Alex Murphy must die once to become RoboCop: similarly, humans—as we exist today—must die once to save the planet. A metaphorical self-extermination, a killing of the devil within, a mental seppuku seems to be the only way out for the human race. The way forward entails a fundamental reorientation of what it is to be human—and a radical change in the mentality that projects an anthropocentric dictatorship on our reality. Earth needs humanity, not humans; human beings come and go; our innate insaniyat (humanity) must never be lost in the mists of time. It is time to reboot humanity.

If that does not (or cannot) happen, then we must remember that the dinosaurs went extinct almost sixty-five million years ago; now it's time we should do the same. Maybe after a million years, flora and fauna might evolve their own cultures, create their own civilizations, excavate human bodies to use as fuel/food, come up with newer ways to fight wars, leech off the planet's resources, divide themselves into us versus them, witness their own doomsday prophecies coming true, and ultimately compose their own science fiction(s) after their respective industrial revolutions.

It is time anthropocentric perspectives within humanity make an exeunt from Earth, pursued by a radioactive bear. Let a forest grow where we used to live and die.

At least our planet would survive.

Barely.

Notes

Acknowledgments go to Anup Beniwal, Ashutosh Mohan, and Vivek Sachdeva of GGSIP University; Bodhisattva Chattopadhyay of the University of Oslo; and the editors of this volume for thought-provoking conversations. This article emerged out of discussions about a project that has received funding from the European Union's Horizon 2020 research and innovation program, under Marie Skłodowska-Curie grant agreement no. 101023313.

1. Suvin, *Metamorphoses*, 84; Le Guin, "Introduction," xii; Delany, qtd. in Csicsery-Ronay, *Seven Beauties*, 78.

2. Khan, *Star Warriors*, 31.

3. Csicsiery-Ronay, *Seven Beauties*, 198.

4. Nagarjuna, "Think Now."

5. Chowdhury, *Competent Authority*, 204.

6. Chowdhury, *Competent Authority*, 90.

7. Chowdhury, *Competent Authority*, 4.

8. Chowdhury, *Competent Authority*, 92.

9. Chowdhury, *Competent Authority*, 62.

10. Khan, *Star Warriors*, 22.

11. I describe "others" of Indian SF further in Khan, "Others in India's Other Futures."

12. Chowdhury, *Competent Authority*, 151–152.

13. Chowdhury, *Competent Authority*, 426.

Bibliography

Akbar, Prayaag. *Leila*. New York: Simon and Schuster, 2017.

Chabria, Priya Sarukkai. *Generation 14*. Delhi: Penguin, 2008.

Chatterjee, Rimi. *Signal Red*. Delhi: Penguin, 2011.

Chowdhury, Shovon. *The Competent Authority*. Delhi: Aleph, 2013.

Csicsery-Ronay Jr., Istvan. *The Seven Beauties of Science Fiction*. Middletown, CT: Wesleyan University Press, 2008.

Das, Indrapramit. "Sita's Descent." In *Breaking the Bow: Speculative Fiction inspired by the Ramayana*, edited by Anil Menon and Vandana Singh, 105–114. Delhi: Zubaan, 2012.

Datta, Sukanya. "Taking a Shortcut." In *Worlds Apart*, 240–262. Delhi: National Book Trust, India, 2012.

Dhar, Mainak. *Zombiestan*. Delhi: Duckbill, 2012.

Dhar, Payal. "The Coward." In *Shockwave and Other Cyber Stories*, 31–43. Delhi: Puffin, 2007.

Doyle, Kenneth. "Rain." In *It Happened Tomorrow*, 242–250. Delhi: National Book Trust, India, 1993.

Joshi, Ruchir. *The Last Jet-Engine Laugh*. Delhi: HarperCollins, 2001.

Kaul, Vatsala. "Catatonic." In *Shockwave and Other Cyber Stories*, 91–105. Delhi: Puffin, 2007.

Khan, Sami Ahmad. "The Others in India's Other Futures." *Science Fiction Studies* 43, no. 3 (November 2016): 479–495.

Khan, Sami Ahmad. *Star Warriors of the Modern Raj: Materiality, Mythology and Technology of Indian Science Fiction*. Cardiff: University of Wales Press, 2021.

Le Guin, Ursula K. "Introduction." In *The Left Hand of Darkness*, xi–xvi. New York: Ace, 2000.

Menon, Anil. *The Beast with Nine Billion Feet*. Delhi: Young Zubaan, 2009.

Mody, Jugal. *Toke*. Delhi: HarperCollins, 2012.

Nagarjuna. "Think Now." *The Pioneer*, June 12, 2013, https://www.dailypioneer.com/2013/columnists/think-now--nagarjuna--indian-buddhist-philosopher.html.

Padmanabhan, Manjula. *Escape*. Delhi: Picador, 2008.

Prasad, Suraj C. *Baramulla Bomber*. Delhi: Niyogi, 2013.

Ramdas, Shiv. *Domechild*. Delhi: Penguin, 2013.

Russ, Joanna. *The Female Man*. New York: Bantam, 1975.

Singh, Vandana. "Almaru." In *Shockwave and Other Cyber Stories*, 1–18. Delhi: Puffin, 2007.

Singh, Vandana. "The Woman Who Thought She Was a Planet." In *The Woman Who Thought She was a Planet and Other Stories*, 39–54. Delhi: Zubaan, 2008.

Srivastava, Rahul. "The Unknown Firewalls." In *Shockwave and Other Cyber Stories*, 124–139. Delhi: Puffin, 2007.

Suvin, Darko. *Metamorphoses of Science Fiction: On the Poetics and History of a Literary Genre*. New Haven, CT: Yale University Press, 1979.

5 Sofia Samatar, "How to Get Back to the Forest" (2014) / Shaping and Sharing Feelings

Steven Shaviro

"'You have to puke it up,' said Cee. 'You have to get down there and puke it up. I mean down past where you can feel it, you know?'" Sofia Samatar's short story "How to Get Back to the Forest" begins with this visceral appeal.[1] A bunch of teenage girls are huddled together, in an institutional bathroom, in the middle of the night. The girls are on edge; they have been forcibly separated from their families and brought to this new place. The atmosphere is menacingly sterile: "everything was so white and bright in that moment, mirrors and fluorescent lights." Tisha, the story's narrator, remembers it vividly. Her best friend Cee (short for Celia) sticks her toothbrush down her throat, in order to make herself vomit. "She looked completely bizarre, her wide cheekbones, her big crown of natural hair, sort of a retro supermodel with a glistening mouth, her eyes full of excitement." Once Cee succeeds in making herself puke, all the other girls compulsively join in. One after another, they feel "sort of dizzy and sick"; then they are suddenly overcome, and they let loose. "*Blam* . . . *Splat* . . . *sploosh.*" Everything is a mess of "puke and blood." The girls are all "absolutely crying with laughter . . . We just sort of looked at each other and screamed. It was mayhem."

This is an incident of what psychologists call *mass sociogenic illness*, or *hysterical contagion*: dysfunctional behavior, with no organic basis, that spreads like an infection through an entire group, driven by involuntary imitation.[2] Usually such episodes involve "a preponderance of female participants," although in point of fact "no one or group is immune."[3] Patriarchal medicine tends to classify such a contagious outburst as feminine, and especially as a girls' affliction, because it involves sympathetic identification and emotional abandon—as opposed to calm, dispassionate rationality.

"How to Get Back to the Forest" begins by describing this outburst because it is a story about the shaping and sharing of feelings—or what might be called, in more technical language, the *modulation of affect*.[4] Societies are held together much more through common structures of feeling than through processes of rational deliberation.[5] But structures of feeling are inherently unstable; they tend to change over the course of time. The modulation of affect is a never-ending process. It can be socially disruptive, especially when it erupts spontaneously, from the bottom up, through a process of imitative contagion—as is the case that night in the girls' bathroom. But similar mechanisms are at work when affect is deliberately and designedly modulated, from the top down, in the interest of social control. This is the overall situation in the world of the story. Structures of feeling are inculcated, reinforced, and maintained through such continually reiterated procedures as institutional training, bodily rehearsal, and the social management of expectations.

In the world of "How to Get Back to the Forest," children are taken away from their parents at an early age and sent to age- and gender-segregated sleepaway camps. They never see their parents again. Instead, they keep "Parent Figures": personal objects (lamps, notebooks, stuffed animals, "calendars and catcher's mitts and scarves") upon which they are supposed to refocus their emotional attachments—but upon which they are also warned "not to *fixate*." These Parent Figures are what psychologists call *transitional objects*, enabling the movement from infantile dependency to a supposedly greater degree of self-sufficiency—but only within socially approved parameters.[6] The campers "have Parent Figures, so that they can always be reminded of what they've lost, so that they can remember they need what they have now." This is an oddly ambiguous statement, which seems to mean that the Parent Figures help to make sure that these young people will never revert to their actual parents, but rather just memorialize them—which facilitates the process of transferring their attachments to their new situation and surroundings. "It's okay to be sad" over your losses, but you must also learn how to move on.

In camp, the teenagers are taught "Life Skills," which are supposed to guide them in how to take care of themselves forever after. They learn how to be "connected with people and with nature." They are also "told to find a hobby": this involves experimentation, since "a million choices" are open to them. It doesn't really matter just what your hobby is—as long as you have one. You are free to choose nearly anything at all; the only thing forbidden is not to choose. Above all, "camp [is] on its own calendar—*a special time of life.*" Camp is "the time of friends and of the earth." The connections you make at camp are all-important: "you have each other now. It's the most special bond in the world." In fact, the "other campers" you meet here will be "the people you'll know for the rest of your life! Now, I want you to turn to the person next to you and say, *Hi, Neighbor!*"

There are lots of planned activities at camp. You are urged to "participate in classes and hikes and shopping sprees and mixers." It's noteworthy that "shopping sprees" are included here alongside all the other activities; camp is not about self-sacrifice but about channeling socially sanctioned and economically prosperous modes of enjoyment. In any case, everyone is exhorted to get involved, which means to do what everyone else is doing: "the important thing was always to *participate* . . . It didn't matter where you came from or who you loved, *just join in!*" Conformity is largely enforced through persuasion and example. The authorities only resort to violent coercion when everything else has failed.

The mixers are special occasions because they are the only activities that bring girls and boys together. In this way, they offer opportunities for rehearsing what the society sees as gender-appropriate behavior. Tisha remembers the "fun" of "shaving [her] legs for the mixer. Wearing red shoes." (The shoes had "flowers on the toes," which made them distinctively femme-ish.) The point of the mixers is to meet your eventual life partner. Heterosexual coupling remains the norm; but same-sex attachments are tolerated, so long as they are (like the heterosexual ones) monogamous and long-term. Even the "queer girls had to go to the mixers; you could take your girlfriend, but you had to go"—and you are expected to have "fun" there, just like everybody else.

By the end of their time at camp, everyone is supposed to have found their spouse and their circle of friends; they are also assigned their life work. Tisha and her cohort are enrolled into Food Services, though she notes that "three out of five graduating classes join the army." Once you have left camp and become an adult, the rest of your life is permanently set. You work at your preassigned job, you live with your life partner, you occasionally see the friends you made in camp ("once a week we have dinner with some of the gang"), and you "do the usual stuff, hobbies and vacations." You are forcibly kept as healthy as possible with "all those check-ups, so regular, everyone gets them . . . *good health is everybody's business!*"

Once camp is done, time congeals, as if it had stopped passing. You have no future beyond this endless repetition of the same. And you have no past either—except for your memories of camp itself. People tend to keep their Parent Figures for the rest of their lives; but nobody is able to actually remember "what [their] parents looked like," or anything else about them. Indeed, one of the things the teens are taught at camp is that "forgetting isn't so wrong. It's a Life Skill . . . forgetting was natural. Forgetting helped us survive."

The story's power comes precisely from the fact that Tisha never questions the society in which she lives. She takes its customs and institutions entirely for granted; they are woven so seamlessly into the fabric of her everyday life that she cannot imagine that they could ever be different. Readers are initiated into the world of the story by the way it slides smoothly, and almost imperceptibly, from details that are entirely familiar (such as exhortations to "always be yourself") to ones that can only seem altogether bizarre (like the forcible removal of children from their parents at the age of eight). Tisha illustrates this cognitive estrangement with a symptomatic verbal tic: every time she tells us something horrific that happened at camp, she follows it up immediately, in the same paragraph, with a non sequitur insisting that "camp was so fun" (repeated three times in a story of less than six thousand words).

Nonetheless, despite her insistence to the contrary, Tisha is disaffected and depressed. She cannot really express her discontent, but it comes out in her physical feelings, in her bodily sensations, and in her habits. In the present time of the story, Tisha says of her life with her husband Pete: "We're okay . . . we make it work, you know?" Yet we learn in passing that Tisha no longer sleeps in the same bed with Pete; she doesn't even touch him anymore if she can avoid it. She suffers from insomnia: "At night I feel so sick, I walk around in circles." At best, if she can calm herself down sufficiently, she spends the long nights sitting alone in the living room, in the dark, curtains open so that she can "watch the lights of the city."

Tisha dismisses her distress by saying, as if with a shrug, that "it's just how I turned out." There's nothing to do about it. But she still dwells on the memories of her friendship with Cee, which was something special, something she doesn't have any more. Forgetting may be a Life Skill, but she is unable to forget the trauma of losing Cee. Tisha knows that Cee is gone forever, and yet she continually looks for her, "on the buses and in the streets," and every time "the bus passes shattered buildings, stick people rooting around in the garbage." Tisha also dreams about Cee, on the rare occasions that she is able to sleep at all. And when she wakes up again, she finds herself writing compulsively about her lost friend, and the time they spent together in camp. She writes the words of the very story that we are reading. It's yet another instance of mimetic contagion.

The reason that Cee makes herself puke in the bathroom, Tisha tells us, is that she imagines that she, and everybody else, has a "bug" implanted inside them, "where you've got less nerves in your esophagus. It's like wired into the side, into the muscle." The bug is a tool of affective modulation and control; it works "to track you or feed you drugs." In other words, the bug monitors your actions and modifies your feelings. Cee complains that "she could feel bug juice seeping into her body. Every time she was going to be angry or afraid, there'd be this warmth in her chest, a feeling of calm spreading deep inside." Tisha admits to a similar sort of experience: whenever she is feeling sick, she says, she also starts to feel "waves of something else, something that calms me, something that's trying to make the sickness go away." This is affective modulation in action: you are forcibly prevented from feeling bad.

Tisha tries to convince us, and also herself, that the bug Cee is obsessed with doesn't really exist. "You cannot feel your bug," she writes; "I've pressed so hard on my chest. I know." She suggests that Cee's claim is just "another dumb story," one of the many "stupid" rumors that pass among the girls at camp. But Tisha also tells us that she actually saw Cee's bug, that night in the bathroom. Cee kept on puking, over and over; until finally "something flew into the toilet with a splash . . . there in the bowl . . . lay an object made of metal." This object even "actually looked like a bug. Sharp blood-smeared legs." That should have resolved things, except that Tisha was so terrified by the sight that she immediately "flushed the toilet" to get rid of it. This allows her to remain forever uncertain about what she actually did or did not see in the toilet bowl. "What if there wasn't anything in it?" she wonders. "What if somebody'd dropped a piece of jewelry in there, some necklace or brooch and I thought it was a bug?" Tisha eventually convinces herself that "the whole bug thing was a mistake, a hallucination."

Whether or not it actually exists, however, the bug is powerfully emblematic of how the regime of affective modulation works. If Cee is the only one who complains about the bug, or even believes that it exists, this is because she is the only girl in the group who actively resists the camp's affective pedagogy. Tisha tells us that Cee was rebellious "right from the day we arrived; she was brash, messy Cee *before* the night in the bathroom, before she supposedly puked out her bug." And even after that night, Tisha says, "I couldn't see any difference" in Cee's behavior; and she reiterates, with emphasis: *"I could not see any difference."*

Cee is the quintessential bad girl: the one who rejects any sort of discipline, who tries to run away at every opportunity, and who always asks smart-ass questions that her teachers cannot answer. She refuses to be pacified. Her own contagious, hysterical affect is a sort of counterprogramming, her effort to undo her own conditioning. Cee is constitutionally incorrigible: she simply will not and cannot be assimilated into this society. That is why she is finally taken away by force—the final resort when affective modulation does not work. A counselor tries to assure Tisha that "it's okay, Cee's just sick, she's going to the hospital." But Tisha knows that she will never see Cee again.

"How to Get Back to the Forest" recalls the currently dominant paradigm for dystopian narratives, especially in young adult (YA) fiction. The story portrays an oppressive future society, extrapolated from recognizable present-day conditions. And it focuses on the plight of adolescent girls in this society. Nevertheless, Samatar does not give us an exhilarating tale of liberation in which—as my own teenage daughter once disparagingly summarized the entire YA dystopian genre to me—a perky young woman finds the right boy, and together they save the world. Rather, the story reminds us how difficult it is to fight a sort of oppression that largely works by forming us internally: getting inside our heads, and modulating and shaping our very desires. Spectacular displays of power like the Hunger Games are ultimately less efficacious than those unspectacular practices by means of which oppression is internalized and naturalized. Power insinuates itself into the nooks and crannies of everyday life, and operates through the passive consent and complicity of its victims.

"How to Get Back to the Forest" responds to this latter sort of power by evoking a deep and morbid distress: a grief that cannot be sublimated into the sort of gentle sadness that the girls at camp are encouraged to accept and even cherish. Tisha cannot use her sadness in order to transition and move on. She cannot forget her bad attachment to Cee because she cannot purge herself of her self-reproach for not living up to the full measure of Cee's rebellious anger. After Cee pukes up the bug, she tells Tisha that now it is her turn. But Tisha is unable to do it: "Cee, I couldn't, I really couldn't . . . I couldn't do it that hard, I remember the look in your eyes; you were so disappointed." Even worse, Tisha remembers how, when Cee proposed running away, she responded that "it was the stupidest thing I'd ever heard." Running away is impossible, whether in camp or more generally in the world of the story. Everything is heavily "monitored"; "there [is] no way to get outside." Indeed, there may well not even be any such thing as an *outside* to get to.

If Tisha were ever able to get over her loss of Cee, this would mean giving up her very capacity to feel anger or anxiety or (especially) loss. Instead, Tisha clings to her memory of how, that night in the bathroom, "some kind of loss swept through all of us, electric, and you'd started it, you'd started it by yourself, and we were with you in that hilarious and total rage of loss." This superordinate sense of loss is the story's gift to us; it works as an affective trigger to destabilize the present.

In addition to that night in the bathroom, Tisha also remembers the evening when she left a mixer with Cee and followed her off into the forest. Tisha didn't enjoy it at the time; she complains that "it was weird and sticky in there, and sort of dark, and the weeds kept tickling my legs." Even worse, she remembers the embarrassment of suddenly having to "take a dump" right there in the woods. Afterward, she "wiped [herself] on the leaves." She marvels that Cee "took my hand again right after I was done. She took my disgusting hand." Taking a dump, like puking, is a visceral experience; the body violently expels some loathsome soft or fluid substance. (There are moments of crying in the story as well). Such expulsion is the loss that forever binds Tisha to Cee. "I felt like I wanted to die," Tisha says, "and at the same time, I was floating."

The girls eventually find "a clearing in the woods. Stars above us in a perfect circle." Tisha remembers staring up at those bright objects, so far away, admiring them but also giving them the finger: "It was like there was a beautiful starry place we'd never get into—didn't *deserve* to get into—but at the same time we were better than any brightness. Two sick girls underneath the stars."

Transcendence and abjection go hand in hand. The moment doesn't last; soon enough, the counselors find the girls and bring them back to camp. Later on, Tisha conflates her memories of the two evenings: "I dream you're beside me, we're leaning over the toilet, and down at the very bottom there's something like a clump of trees and two tiny girls are standing there giving us the finger."

What is the weight of these dreams and memories? What can they actually *do*? Of course, Tisha cannot reverse the flow of time, return to when she was in camp with Cee, and do things over differently. But in those visceral movements of the flesh, those violent expulsions of puke and shit and blood and tears, the machinery of affective modulation goes into overdrive and spirals out of control. That hysterical contagion, that electric sense of loss, those shared moments of sickness: all these bodily convulsions bring the girls together, create something that "swept through all of us," that belongs to everyone and no one, that makes them more together than just the sum of their individual selves. Perhaps all these moments, in their effervescence, provide us with a map of *how to get back to the forest.* "Let's lose it," Tisha finally writes; "let's lose everything . . . we should both be sick, everybody should lose it together." Or as Cee already put it, near the beginning of the story: "It's something we can't imagine. We don't have the tools. Our bodies don't know how to calculate what we're missing. You can't know till you get there."

Notes

1. Samatar, "How to Get Back to the Forest." All subsequent quotes are from this source unless otherwise noted.

2. Weir, "Mass Sociological Illness"; Gehlen, "Toward a Revised Theory."

3. Weir, "Mass Sociological Illness," 36.

4. Clough, "New Empiricism."

5. Williams, *Long Revolution.*

6. Litt, "Theories of Transitional Object Attachment."

Bibliography

Clough, Patricia. "The New Empiricism: Affect and Sociological Method." *European Journal of Social Theory* 12, no. 1 (2009): 43–61.

Gehlen, Frieda L. "Toward a Revised Theory of Hysterical Contagion." *Journal of Health and Social Behavior* 18, no. 1 (March 1977): 27–35.

Litt, Carole J. "Theories of Transitional Object Attachment: An Overview." *International Journal of Behavioral Development* 9 (1986): 383–399. https://doi.org/10.1177/016502548600900308.

Samatar, Sofia. "How to Get Back to the Forest." *Lightspeed*, March 2014. https://www.lightspeedmagazine.com/fiction/how-to-get-back-to-the-forest/.

Weir, Erica. "Mass Sociogenic Illness." *CMAJ* 172, no. 1 (January 4, 2005): 36. https://doi.org/10.1503/cmaj.045027.

Williams, Raymond. *The Long Revolution.* London: Chatto & Windus, 1961.

6 Tade Thompson, Wormwood Trilogy (2016–2019) / Africanfuturism's Salvage Utopianism

Hugh Charles O'Connell

Tade Thompson's Wormwood trilogy,[1] *Rosewater, The Rosewater Insurrection,* and *The Rosewater Redemption,* is one of the most intriguing and challenging series to come out of the post-2000 boom in Africanfuturist SF. The series is set in Nigeria in the fictional town of Rosewater, which grows up around a mysterious alien artifact dubbed Wormwood, and it turns on the various world-altering potentials and world-ending threats it heralds. The series unites these divergent ends by turning to salvage, a living within and through the end-time. Salvage as culmination is a narratively dicey act: it can neither fully erase the ill conditions nor provide something from outside of them. It must work from within the ruins, admitting the ruin while also seeing past it. In doing so, salvage drives a wedge between the supposed synonyms of eschatology and apocalypse, thus providing a critical strategy for an Africanfuturism encumbered by a necrotic late capitalism and uneven development.

To invoke William Gibson's memorable phrase, the uneven distribution of the future is not only a constituent aspect of global capitalism, but something hard-baked into the very world-building of Africanfuturist SF. Such unevenness as both engine *and* product of the global political economy results in a growing series of overlapping and recursive crises that have become normalized as the operative conditions of existence. In this sense, "Africa," as a neoimperial geopolitical sign, is defined by crisis, and any sense of its future is therefore necessarily circumscribed and foredoomed by the crises that inexorably drive it toward its fated apocalypse. This neoimperial view positions crisis as apocalyptic eschatology: end-of-history prediction and fulfilment. The Wormwood trilogy confronts this head-on by pitting itself within and against this very concept.

What is at stake, then, is how to salvage a future from the conditions of eschatological crisis. How do we think within such dystopianism? To this end, the series turns away from the mystical-cum-capitalist eschatology of world-ending crisis and toward a radical, materialist apocalyptic possibility. Such a materialist apocalypse reveals rather than revels in the end-time conditions that blocked futurity in the first place, freeing us from fait accompli by returning to politics, strategy, and decision. One way this alternative sense of apocalypse—what I'm calling *salvage utopianism*—is expressed is by sifting through the detritus of capitalist modernity to reappropriate its means toward new ends. As one of the principal characters, Oyin Da, surmises—connecting Nigeria's circumscribed future to its colonial past—it's a question of "how to save the world from aliens, yet keep their infrastructure."[2]

Given the series' dense narrative layering, even a cursory description of its basic plot quickly becomes unwieldy. Reduced to an elevator pitch, I'd describe it as a slow-motion apocalypse meets biopunk meets first-contact invasion narrative. The key plot points revolve around an alien fungus that transforms humans and much of the planet's biome at the cellular level—a process that has been taking place over many millennia. The alien species—referred to as Homians—have been suffusing Earth's biosphere with "xenoforms," a sort of alien fungal spore that reacts with the fungus on human skin. This interaction creates the "xenosphere," a realm of pure information extracted from every living human being. Unknown to most, the minds of all living humans are constantly connected to the xenosphere, and they can be read and affected by those who can access it, such as the aliens and a few humans known as "sensitives." These same spores also begin to replace the cells of humans, resulting in a slow process whereby humans become more and more Homian (and some Homians more human). The oscillating tension between symbiotic hybridity and predatory colonization animates much of the series.

Although this process has been going on literally since the inception of humanity, the presence of aliens is only made widely known to humans once the Homians send various advance colonial "footholders" to Earth after the xenosphere has been established and supplied the Homian civilization with enough information about the planet to know it is inhabitable. The arrival of one such footholder—dubbed Wormwood—sets the series in motion. A large "amoeboid blob of alien organic matter," Wormwood crashes down in Hyde Park in 2012.[3] After some half-hearted efforts to make contact with it, the British government attempts to annihilate Wormwood by detonating a nuclear bomb. The attack fails, and Wormwood subsequently burrows into and through the earth before surfacing in Nigeria, not far from Lagos, in 2055.

Upon surfacing, Wormwood forms a domed alien city named Utopicity by the locals, which serves as an alien compound, housing Wormwood, Anthony (Wormwood's human avatar), a number of other alien creatures, and some humans. Moreover, Utopicity also interacts with the local community, supplying power to Rosewater, the titular Nigerian town that grows up around it. The city of Rosewater, in turn, functions as a sort of mystery cult, a haven for the sick and injured who seek to be miraculously healed by the alien entity, as well as for numerous opportunists, criminals, and other xenocurious folks. Focusing on the contact zone of Rosewater-Utopicity and the new relationships that arise between humans and Homians, the narrative juxtaposes utopian posthuman hybrid possibilities with dystopian imperial genocide—the possibility of radical new worlds and the worst of our old (and contemporary) worlds.

Named, as one alien has it, for "a doomsday asteroid out of one of their most tedious books," the Wormwood invasion is indelibly linked to the poisoning of the Earth and the end-times prophecies of Revelations.[4] Under the guise of universal history, the apocalyptic eschatology of Revelations in effect neutralizes materialist history and arrests utopian possibility as it encompasses everything within the totalizing death-drive of its predetermined, singular narrative endpoint. Given the Homian plan's long, unfolding, pervasive history, its developmental schema, and the narrative revelation of this information, the trilogy's biopunkish, first contact trappings ultimately enclose such an eschatological apocalypse narrative.

Reworked through alien invasion, however, this Christian eschatological narrative is transposed onto the necropolitical drive of imperial capitalism. The various intertwined aspects of this alien invasion mediate three of the principal drivers of our precarious global present: (neo)imperialism; technoenabled surveillance capitalism and its reduction of human life to data sets to be extracted and financialized; and the catastrophic climate crisis often theorized under the rubric of the Anthropocene. While all three can serve as separate critical lodestars through which the present can be analyzed, the narrative suggests that they are necessarily entangled in a hypercrisis event that is ubiquitous, inescapable, and world-ending. This hypercrisis event acts as a predation on Nigeria's future and thus forms the limits against which both apocalypse and Africanfuturism are measured in the series.

We can regard this concept of the hypercrisis event in relation to Evan Calder Williams's *Combined and Uneven Apocalypse*. Williams calls for a new non-Christian, nonteleological, noneschatological notion of apocalypse for the age of capitalist crisis and environmental catastrophe. Contrasted with the cyclical repetitions of crisis and the empty void of catastrophe, Williams argues that apocalypse is an end with revelation; etymologically, it's a "lifting of the veil" that intervenes in and negates the conditions of both crisis and catastrophe. Directly countervailing Christian notions, this renewed apocalypse "is the end of a *totality*, here meaning not the sum of all things but the ordering of those things in a particular historical shape. . . . This doesn't mean *total destruction* but rather a destruction of *totalizing* structures, of those universal notions that do not just describe 'how things are' but serve to prescribe and insist that 'this is how things must be.'"[5] Such an apocalypse would be the revelation and negation of the imperial-capitalist-Anthropocene problematic undergirding our present and the trilogy's world-building. Apocalypse thus becomes a way to salvage the future from the jaws of eschatology and the ravages of global modernity.

In the series, this is most clearly associated with Oyin Da and her interdimensional, peripatetic time-machine-cum-sanctuary, the Lijad. In order to create the Lijad, Oyin Da salvages the tech left behind by British imperialists and keeps it working by "cannibalizing" parts from the Nigerian government. Such reappropriation similarly leads away from teleology and certainty as the Lijad and Oyin Da herself are associated with nonlinearity and quantum possibility. The Lijad acts as a refuge for political dissidents, leftist utopians that desire an existence outside of the repressive confines of the present. It exists in "a potential of locations, the different spaces between various heres . . . in a dimension of several unknowable possibilities."[6] Upon encountering Oyin Da and the Lijad for the first time, Kaaro, a sensitive and the protagonist of the first novel, notes the experience as a "convergence of possibilities."[7] This is later reflected in the structure of Oyin Da's mind, which, via his access to the xenosphere, Kaaro can read: "There is . . . an untamed playful expansion of possibilities and alternatives. She has four trains of thought going at once."[8]

We later learn that the Lijad's quantum positionality, time travel, and interdimensional capabilities are in reality aspects of the xenosphere and that Oyin Da has been manipulating this realm all along for reasons that are far outside of its data-extractive and colonizing purposes. She thus hacks the xenosphere as a means for informational time travel in order to salvage and reactivate lost potentialities. Indeed, it is the xenosphere itself—and the creation of sensitives like Kaaro or residual information-personality constructs of the now dead like Oyin Da—that will be used to repel the Homian invasion through various acts of salvage and recombination.

And yet, in the constant conceptual shifts that the series ceaselessly challenges its readers with, this same utopian repurposing of the xenosphere is intimately entangled with its most troubling, dystopian turn: genocide. In the series' third act, the utopian possibility of human-alien hybridity has been annulled, and we are left with the naked aggression of settler colonial politics and what postcolonial critic Achille Mbembe refers to as *necropolitics*—the sole right over the distribution of death that sustains this relationship.[9] "'It was always going to come down to humans versus aliens,' says Femi. 'That's all it ever was.'"[10] Within this narrative framing, all other possibilities collapse, and we are left in the Manichean bind of colonizer and colonized, the living sovereign and the disposable dead. Following at least one thread of Frantz Fanon's anticolonial thoughts on the inescapable foundational role of violence that underwrites the colonizer-colonized relationship, the colonized have no choice but to kill the colonizers if they want to be free.[11] Notably, it is through the xenosphere that genocide takes place: either the humans will be fully replaced by the Homians, or the humans will annihilate the Homians.

Genocide, then, becomes the limit thought of the series' salvage utopianism, threatening to turn it into its opposite by rearing the ugly head of colonial eschatology as the inevitable outcome. That is, despite the trilogy's exploration of radical quantum possibility and the mutability of time and its own overt narrative dismissals of apocalyptic eschatology, it drifts into a straight alien-versus-human narrative. The Manicheanism of alien or human genocide smuggles such apocalyptic eschatology back in under the weight of narrative exigency: kill or be killed. Reversing the alien colonizer's monopoly on the distribution of death through the xenosphere, Kaaro becomes "the most successful mass murderer in history" and destroys the entire race of uploaded Homians.[12] As narrative recompense for this act, the potential site of posthuman utopia—Utopicity-Rosewater—is rendered a degraded monument to this inimical impasse: a contaminated "no-man's-land" populated by "Hellish carnivores, hybrid creatures that defy description, sentient green slime, and chemical contaminations at every turn."[13]

There's a sense, then, that the genocide that ends the series and the festering wound of Rosewater that it results in are due to this founding moment of colonial logic. It's a limit point that returns to haunt the narrative, constraining its other more utopian gestures and possibilities before smothering them under the weight of historical exigency; the expected and the teleological come back to extinguish the realm of possibility. Tellingly, the last chance for humanity here is explicitly related to the colonial past. Oyin Da tells Kaaro: "They did not hesitate. If they were in our shoes, they would not. I am sorry, my friend. I know what this will do to us, to all of us. I am putting rot in our souls for all time, but this moment is our best shot at stopping the [invasion], our time-machine moment, our travel-back-and-kill-Leopold II moment."[14]

There is, of course, a great deal of risk in turning to genocide as metaphor, at once allegorical (in the sense that the Homian invasion needs to be read through European imperialism) and extrapolative (in the sense that the future is still not only in relation but also in thrall to the imperial past, making salvage utopian possibilities impossible). In the trilogy, the aliens stand in for settler colonialism and genocide for the eradication of this systemic violence. Genocide therefore figures as a totalizing response to the totalizing conditions that produce our uneven futures. It's a call to decenter, to remove the systemic barriers. With metaphors, it's easy to confuse the vehicle for the tenor. However, in risking the conflation—the figuration of genocide for literal genocide—Thompson's apocalyptic narrative reveals the very grounds of our own unevenness, the genocides that conditioned, gave birth to, and continue to structure global modernity.

Going one step further down the metaphoric chain, given the series' focus on the aliens' literal transformation and colonization of Nigerian bodies, it ultimately seems that genocide stands in for what Kenyan novelist and postcolonial theorist Ngũgĩ wa Thiong'o calls a *decolonization of the mind*: the need to divest oneself from the colonizer's worldview enforced through the prescription of their language.[15] If we accept utopian studies scholar Ruth Levitas's claim that utopianism is first a habit of mind, a retraining of our desires that must take place in order to sharpen our political practice, then utopianism must be rid of this inimical limit of modernity for salvage to take place.[16]

Fittingly, at the end of the narrative, the former site of Rosewater-Utopicity returns as a site of both xenobiological threat and resource: "There's danger, but there are organic abominations that might have biomedical applications, and there might be energy resources."[17] In a sense, this returns us to the very beginning of the series and its founding questions of how to understand the symbiotic/predatory relationship of humans and aliens in this new space, of whether Utopicity is resource or destruction, life or death, possibility or catastrophe. To really begin to answer these questions, the series suggests, the undergirding problematic of capitalist imperialism needs to be revealed and extirpated from dystopian determinations in order to begin approaching such potential utopian horizons of living on in our transformed world. While the narrative pushes toward the monstrous teleological, eschatological ends of genocide, at its heart it seems to desire something different. Thus, it ends on the note of salvage utopian possibility that it initially foregrounds as Oyin Da heals and recreates the space of the xenosphere so that it is no longer a site of control and determination, but one of possibility and potentiality.

As Kim Stanley Robinson has recently argued, the contemporary dominance of dystopian SF is often narratively invested in and thereby heightens the sense of the universally encapsulating foregone conclusions of contemporary crises, resulting in a resigned pessimism.[18] There is no spatial outside or temporal beyond, and thus nothing is to be done. Hence the need for salvage. In thinking with Thompson's Wormwood trilogy, we can experience Africanfuturism—a mode of resistance heightened by the eschatological experiences of bureaucratic colonialism, economic neoimperialism, and a world ravaged by climate change—as inveighing against the dystopian allure of eschatology and exhorting us to instead contend with the historicity of crisis. Invoking the notion of crisis as historically constituted, rather than predetermined or purely contingent, the Wormwood trilogy teaches us to think dialectically about apocalypse as the progenitor of the limits and horizon of utopian futurity. Ultimately, then, rather than giving over to eschatology, the Wormwood trilogy offers a form of salvage utopianism, a living and thriving from within the ruins wrought by the conjoined, destructive ends of imperialism, neoliberalism, and the Anthropocene that is instructive for our contemporary moment.

Notes

1. Thompson, *Rosewater*; Thompson, *Insurrection*; Thompson, *Redemption*.
2. Thompson, *Redemption*, 90.
3. Thompson, *Rosewater*, 233.
4. Thompson, *Redemption*, 331.
5. Williams, *Combined and Uneven Apocalypse*, 5.
6. Thompson, *Rosewater*, 216.
7. Thompson, *Rosewater*, 196.
8. Thompson, *Rosewater*, 213.
9. Mbembe, "Necropolitics."
10. Thompson, *Redemption*, 285.
11. Fanon, "On Violence."
12. Thompson, *Redemption*, 363.
13. Thompson, *Redemption*, 365.
14. Thompson, *Redemption*, 327.
15. Thiong'o, *Decolonising the Mind*.
16. Levitas, *The Concept of Utopia*.
17. Thompson, *Redemption*, 371.
18. Robinson, "Dystopias Now."

Bibliography

Fanon, Frantz. "On Violence." In *The Wretched of the Earth*, translated by Richard Philcox, 1–51. New York: Grove Press, 2004.

Levitas, Ruth. *The Concept of Utopia*. Syracuse, NY: Syracuse University Press, 1990.

Mbembe, Achille. "Necropolitics," translated by Libby Meintjes. *Public Culture* 15, no. 1 (2003): 11–40.

Robinson, Kim Stanley. "Dystopias Now." *Commune*, November 2, 2018, https://communemag.com/dystopias-now/.

Thiong'o, Ngũgĩ wa. *Decolonising the Mind: The Politics of Language in African Literature*. Nairobi: East African Educational Publishers, 1986.

Thompson, Tade. *Rosewater*. Lexington, KY: Apex, 2016.

Thompson, Tade. *The Rosewater Insurrection*. New York: Orbit, 2019.

Thompson, Tade. *The Rosewater Resurrection*. New York: Orbit, 2019.

Williams, Evan Calder. *Combined and Uneven Apocalypse: Luciferian Marxism*. Winchester, UK: Zero Books, 2011.

7 Brit Marling and Zal Batmanglij, *The OA* (2016–2019) / Science Fiction's Affective Praxis

Sherryl Vint

Brit Marling's and Zal Batmangli's *The OA* is difficult to summarize and perhaps is not immediately recognizable as speculative fiction. In part it is the story of Prairie Johnson, played by Marling and also known as the OA, who is kidnapped and experimented upon by Hunter Aloysius Percy, also known as Hap, a medical doctor obsessed with near-death experiences (NDEs). It is also the narrative that an escaped Prairie tells to an eclectic group of mostly teenagers whom she meets after she is returned to her parents: Prairie's tale is about the captivity, but more importantly it is about the other realms she and her fellow captives were able to visit during their NDEs and the powers they slowly gain through their suffering to open doors to those realms. These powers manifest as five movements (a pattern of choreography) and enable access to a multiverse of worlds and possibilities. Their first successful execution of these movements restores someone to life.

The OA is ultimately a story about stories, a complex meditation on the power of narrative to lift us out of the quotidian, thereby to see possibilities for accessing another experience of the world. It carefully negotiates between two possible readings that are both kept plausible throughout Part 1: that everything the OA says about spiritual powers and transit between worlds is literally true, or that her story is a metaphor to describe traumatic experiences of imprisonment and torture whose materiality she cannot express but whose affect she must process and communicate. The metafictional turn at the end of Part 2 pushes this structure one step further, suggesting that just as the OA's diegetic audience can still benefit from her story and intervention, even if it turns out that she is speaking metaphorically rather than recounting real experiences, so too might the audience of the series *The OA* be moved to material, transformative change through the medium of its fictional story. The OA's evocation of the resilience, community, and nurturing that she and other captives find together as they learn the movements becomes a medium through which the listening teenagers are able to imagine themselves and their lives in new ways, to survive their own experiences of damaging isolation, which include struggles with gender identity, alienation from the values promoted by their parents, and economic hardship. She shows them how the captives became a group whose collectivity helped them overcome the limitations of their context and, through them, the narrative suggests ways viewers might extend her lessons into their own lives.

One of the series' central metaphors is about the power to see things differently: Prairie began her life as a child in Russia and lost her sight due to a bus accident and an NDE. She is later orphaned and adopted by the Johnsons (and renamed Prairie) and remains blind as an adult until a significant NDE during HAP's experiments, after which she regains her sight. In both instances she sees herself talking to a shaman, Khatun, in a Bardo space and deliberately decides to return to the realm of the living: to stay dead means to avoid pain, she is cautioned, but the OA prefers to accept the struggle of life, which also includes the possibility for change. The Bardo is easier, but static. Crucially, during the OA's second NDE, to stay means to leave the others behind in captivity, a choice she refuses. The OA is given the first of the five movements as a reward for this validation of solidarity, and Khatun also suggests that this is the beginning of a deeper self-knowledge that will eventually prove the pathway to a more meaningful kind of freedom: freedom to make a better world rather than freedom from the limitations of the existing one. Khatun tells her that "to exist is to survive unfair choices." The series thus refuses a stereotypical narrative that might explore survival as vindication: there is never any question that the world is unfair, and no transcendental system of justice will right these wrongs. Still, from within our given circumstances, we can find grace and solidarity, can continue to exist without falling into the negativity of bitterness that allows these unfair choices to continue to damage us ever after, to mark us as products of trauma and that alone.

The OA and her four fellow captives work to obtain, master, and use the given movements in the interests of a world of greater compassion and inclusivity, in contrast to Hap, who seeks to harvest their accomplishments for his own benefit. The difference between their methods is telling: the captives are imprisoned for years, providing solace to one another and creating community even though physical barriers prevent them from ever touching; Hap wants the easy and instant achievement he believes can come from the special powers granted to NDE survivors—yet is never willing to risk his own life. The OA and her main confidant, Homer, model what it takes to build a better world through long-term commitment and training, trial and error, the capacity to sustain hope even through dark experiences. Hap wants to manipulate their power and is jealous of their bond but can only imagine access to a better future through appropriation rather than contribution.

Collectivity is central to the series' themes. The OA is separated from the others and returned to the Johnsons in an emotionally distraught state, the sequences that open the series and set the stage for a complex narrative that weaves together this present with depictions of her past as she tells her story to her new group of comrades. Along with four teenagers, she recruits a disillusioned high school teacher, BBA (Betty Broderick-Allen), and trains them to do the movements—in order, she tells them, to open a door and save the other captives. At their first meeting, the OA promises this new group that she will show them "what you might do together, how you could help people that you'll never meet." She insists that it is important that her listeners imagine that they are part of the experience, to embrace it "as if you are me," for the stakes to be evident. *The OA* thus fosters empathy and intense bonds among people across seemingly impenetrable difference: although they all attend the same school, the recruits are an improbable collective including a transgender boy, a high school bully, a closeted honors student, an orphan, and a teacher. Through the power of story, the OA brings people together who otherwise would not interact—and, more importantly, she forces them out of their habituated performances of self. They must interact as people rather than as social roles—what she calls a focus on the "invisible self" rather than the outer self.

As the bully Steve's trajectory powerfully demonstrates, when people are jarred out of their habituated roles and responses, new possibilities emerge: options so new they are imaginable only as alternative realities or parallel worlds. The OA's refusal to be afraid of him compels Steve to interact with her on a level other than intimidation, leading to banal conclusions about bullies—they are driven by their own insecurities and fear—but here elevated to something more profound: the vision of the better person that becomes available to Steve as part of a collective oriented toward doing good in the world, concerned with others rather than just with self. Discussing Steve with BBA in an early episode, the OA posits Steve's bad behavior as sensitivity to the disturbances and injustices of "this realm," challenging BBA's narrative of Steve as a lost cause whose delinquency disrupts the learning of other students. The OA suggests that BBA examine her own perception of being a teacher and what it might mean to dedicate herself to those students who need her most, instead of to those who are already on promising trajectories. Through this conceit of personality as "attunement" to and expression of the surrounding culture, *The OA* links the idea of parallel worlds to the kinds of selves that we each might become across a range of worlds. The utopian project of changing the world, then, can begin with changing oneself and one's habituated responses, thereby attuning to another modality of the real and bringing it closer to materialization.

The phrase "with perfect feeling" is frequently used to describe the proper performance of the movements. It is not simply a matter of going through rote gestures but of committing to the belief in the possibility of the better world that they symbolize. As mentioned earlier, the first time they are able to effect material change with the movements, they bring Scott, a captive killed by Hap's experiments, back to life. Yet they begin this performance in conditions of grief and despair: Scott is dead, the OA and Homer are estranged, and all hope seems lost. At first Homer and the OA perform alone, giving voice to their grief and anger with one another and with the situation through their performance; as they continue, the very act of committing to the movements shifts the affect from despair to possibility. The "unfair choices" of the world remain, their pain remains, and yet the movements also open the door to create something new from this trauma rather than merely to dwell in it. This is the "perfect feeling" that must continually and collectivity be renewed with our choices, the series suggests. Scott revives and announces that the movements do things "we cannot imagine"; they "open a tunnel to a dimension of freedom." Cultivating this dimension through their movement art becomes the captive group's mission. And in the finale of Part 1, when a school shooter terrorizes campus, the OA's new recruits use the movements to intervene, to change the context. The movements do not stop the shooting, but they do distract the shooter long enough that the police are able to disarm the shooter. More importantly, they affirm the group in their chosen identities as better people who seek to make a positive change in the world—and this is the case whether the movements really are doorways to other realms and the OA's story is literally true *or* if the OA is speaking metaphorically as a way to process a more mundane act of violence, a young girl being kidnapped and held captive.

The OA is thus an exemplar of why and how SF can be important as a tool for social change. Ernst Bloch's work in *The Principle of Hope* has been foundational for the ways academics and activists understand and use the genre. Bloch names Not-Yet-Consciousness the immanent field of desire for an unalienated world that finds a ghostly hint of expression in aspects of quotidian life—daydreams, the fantasies of popular culture, love and erotic desire. He is careful to distinguish this utopian and anticipatory Not-Yet-Consciousness from reactionary, backward-looking responses to the inadequacies of the present: utopian hope stands against fear, it expands people and their desire for connection, whereas fear diminishes both individual and community. Bloch further differentiates between radical concrete utopia and a more reactionary version he describes as *abstract utopia*. Concrete utopia must emerge from a real possibility in the world. It cannot be mere wishful fantasy disconnected from material circumstances but must seek to understand what has been repressed or marginalized by hegemonic ideologies. For Bloch, the world is unfinished, it is something we are always in the process of making through our desires and actions: "Just as a Not-Yet-Conscious, which has never been conscious before, dawns in the human soul, so a Not-Yet-Become dawns in the world."[1]

The OA describes the power of the movements in very similar terms, as a method to activate something that truly exists within the material world—our capacity to be more generous, our ability to make positive social change, the possibility of resilience without bitterness despite unfair and traumatic experiences. As the OA explains to her recruited group, "The force of the movements, done with perfect feeling, opens up something that is already here." We see this in Part 1, for example, when BBA offers the $50,000 life insurance payment that she received upon her brother's death to prevent Steve from being forcibly taken to a military school. She becomes a new kind of teacher (previously she wanted him expelled), and he then newly dedicates himself to taking responsibility for his actions: he interrogates his feelings rather than responds by rote with violence, and later he initiates their resistance to the school shooter. Given the changes it enables for Steve as a person, it does not matter if the OA's story is literal or metaphorical: there is a more important kind of truth within her story in the affective capacities and possibilities she mobilizes in her listeners.

At the end of Part 1, we are left with a sequence that suggests her tale was mere fiction, an amalgam of folkloric religious ideas meshed with Homer's *The Iliad*. The OA joins the group in performing the movements at the school, but she is shot by the single bullet that escapes his gun as the police tackle him. As she is taken off in an ambulance, it is unclear if the OA has been able to journey to another realm or if she has simply been killed. Part 2 shows us that transit is possible as we follow the OA into a parallel life on a different world, and it concludes with her moving into yet a third realm, this time as a fictional version of Marling who is acting on a set that we recognize as the world of season two. Further parts were planned, but Netflix canceled the series before the narrative was completed. Based on the content of Part 2, these later installments would have further developed themes such as the commodification of our imagination and the importance of holding on to truths we intuit in a culture that insists they are delusions.

Although we did not get to see the completion of this narrative, *The OA* is more than just compelling entertainment. As has been the case with other beloved series, fans of *The OA* protested its cancelation, writing petitions and even marching in the streets to contest the premature end of a story that mattered to them. They sent its creators multiple videos of themselves performing the movements, demonstrating their perfect feelings of love not only for the series but also for the ethos it embodied. Marling and Batmangli set up a website (https://theoaisreal.com) to host this material and create a space for ongoing fan exchange about why *The OA* inspired such intense feelings. One of the fan-generated pages on this site is entitled, "Why *The OA* Matters." It argues, "Through *The OA*, we realized we weren't crazy, alone, broken. We realized that science and spirituality could co-exist. Most of all, we realized that hope is not naïve. We may be living in a dimension crumbling to violence and pettiness and greed, but that doesn't mean it can't be repaired if we all work together."[2] Fans further pledged to activate this ethos in their own lives, to form community with one another. The website demonstrates an experience of fandom that transcends the text, becoming a social force that transforms fans into social critics and activists.

The OA is about how stories build social worlds, one of the most important elements of speculative fiction. But more than that, *The OA* shows us that we can and have survived the unfair choices of this world, its uneven distribution of deprivation or plenitude, while also insisting that we should never give up the struggle to reduce such unevenness. It reminds us that we are more powerful together and that, through one another, we can find the faith to return to this world of struggle rather than to capitulate with cynicism to the world-as-apocalypse. OA stands for *original angel*, and near the end of Part 2 Prairie tells Hap that she prefers the difficult life she led as Prairie to the more affluent life of Nina, the version who lives in the alternative world. Nina lived a life of empty privilege, but Prairie was treated like dirt, "dust, pressed into a diamond by the weight of this world." And this, the OA concludes, is what an angel is—a refusal to be crushed by this broken world, the choice instead to pick one another up, to commit to hope and repair, and to open doorways to worlds of greater freedom and human flourishing.

Notes

1. Bloch, *Principle of Hope*, 623.
2. "Why Does the OA Matter?"

Bibliography

Bloch, Ernst. *The Principle of Hope*. Translated by Neville Plaice, Stephen Plaice, and Paul Knight. Three volumes. Oxford: Basil Blackwell, 1986.

Marling, Brit, and Zal Batmanglij. *The OA*. Performed by Brit Marling, Emory Cohen, and Scott Wilson. Netflix, 2016–2019, streaming.

"Why Does the OA Matter?" The OA Is Real. Accessed May 1, 2022. https://www.theoaisreal.com/why-does-the-oa-matter/.

8 Craig Laurance Gidney, *A Spectral Hue* (2019) / #OwnVoices and Intergroup Solidarity

Bogi Takács

> Iris remembered making the flowers out of tulle, silk, nylon and wire. Each microblossom was hand rolled and meticulously affixed to the center of a wool felt ball with tiny beads of glue. The work required precision, and she frequently pricked her fingers. But none of that mattered. The blood drops, or the pain. Because while she worked, she was in that dream sanctuary, in Fuchsia's presence.[1]

Craig Laurance Gidney's novel *A Spectral Hue* is a multifaceted gem of a book, hovering between genres: Is it fantasy, horror? Does it have a genre altogether? Is it contemporary or historical? *A Spectral Hue* doesn't fit into conventional categories, but those categories have always been dictated by the majority, and this book is unwavering about its commitment to itself, to a deeply felt queer Blackness that stretches across generations.

I felt this book in my whole body, even though I've never visited its setting, the marshlands of coastal Maryland. I'm a Jewish trans immigrant to the United States from Hungary and come from a different set of traditions altogether. I'm not Black. I am picking this book as one that has helped me survive; it might help you survive, too.

A Spectral Hue is about solidarity, a solidarity that comes from being firmly anchored within yourself and your place in the world. But how to show that, in the face of the Anglo-white juggernaut of the publishing industry that frames even "diversity and inclusion" in the context of extreme individualism?

The plot begins with the classic horror framing of someone from the big city visiting a small town with a mysterious past. Xavier is a young, queer Black man who studies art, and he has arrived in the (fictional) town of Shimmer, Maryland, to investigate a historical group of Black artists that worked in the area. But the story doesn't offer the usual horror theme of descent into the unknown, the exotic, the lethal—like Conrad's racist *Heart of Darkness. A Spectral Hue* gives readers something altogether different: a gift, not a curse. Right away we meet point-of-view characters who live *in* Shimmer, like Iris, a queer Black woman who uses Airbnb to rent out a room to Xavier. Lincoln is also Black and queer, and he had wandered into town from DC a while ago looking for a job, finding it at the local art museum. The story pushes against genre tropes even more by having a viewpoint for Fuchsia, a mysterious spirit tied to this land for generations—and not showing her as the unfathomable Other. The narrative starts with her, from her own point of view, as she wanders around in the swamp—calling out the names of animals and plants, trying to remember her own name. The mystery stems from her interactions with the world and her awareness of her environment, not from her own existence. She is written without obfuscation; her feelings are described in text.

The Shimmer artists Xavier investigates were invented for the purpose of the novel but feel very real. In the narrative, they all share a striking use of color in their works, all of them highlighting a specific purple, the color of salt marsh orchids. They work in a variety of unconventional media, from painted dolls to asemic writing. They do not have formal artistic backgrounds. They create their art alone, but they congregate: "So, it was a kind of . . . artists' salon they had there, out in Shimmer Marsh?"

All of the characters are drawn to the Shimmer group's art because of its spectral, possibly haunted nature. Is the artwork moving, twisting, glowing with an otherworldly light? What does all this have to do with Fuchsia, the marsh spirit?

Not everyone can see this light, and the artists themselves do not seek out an audience for it beyond each other. White visitors to the museum who dismiss the works as "art brut" or "outsider art" do not get to experience the magic; neither does Howard Lenski, the white curator, even though he might also be gay. Lenski even blocks the manifestations: Lincoln notices that "the artwork lay dormant when Howard was around, as if his presence suppressed the phantom energy."

Yet *readers* can see the magic, be they of any background. Readers can see the whole story all the way up to and including the mind of the marsh spirit herself. Everything is there for those willing to see, in minute detail. If there is any horror, it doesn't come from Othering and grotesquerie. It comes from the characters facing their own history, the transgenerational trauma of trans-Atlantic slavery—not a secret, not something hidden: "He's been on the journey from one end of the spectrum to the other. From outcast to acolyte. From darkest purple to hottest pink. The muse shows him the pattern, and in showing it, reveals her own journey. [. . .] She shows Linc the ship. The dark interior, like a belly, that devoured her father." This trauma can be reenacted, and while it does not go away, it can also be managed. Art can help with that, as it binds the different layers of reality together.

This kind of detail of the characters' internal lives generally only comes from lived experience—that of the writer, even when the writer and the main characters are not to be equated in any sense. Minoritized authors have perspectives that can be radically different from the viewpoints of the majority, and this readily comes through in literature. This is one of the reasons that #OwnVoices as a concept took the publishing industry by storm, became a buzzword, and even turned into something often misused. #OwnVoices refers to fictional narratives where the protagonist belongs to the same marginalized group as the author; the term was coined by Dutch author and disability activist Corinne Duyvis in 2015.

#OwnVoices acquired such resonance in part because the Anglo-American publishing industry often offers marginalization narratives by majority authors. As a striking illustration: according to the Cooperative Children's Book Center at the University of Wisconsin-Madison, in 2019, less than half of children's books with Black protagonists had Black authors.

The #OwnVoices approach has also faced criticism: for example, that it does not advocate for minority authors writing about whatever topic they want to tackle, and not only stories involving their own minority group. The issues in general stem from majority industry stakeholders glomming onto #OwnVoices as *the* one solution to the exclusionary nature of the field. (As far as I can tell, this was not how the term was intended; it was originally to highlight that narratives of marginalization are often written by outsiders, and that internal viewpoints are richer.) Another issue—less frequently mentioned—is that the discussions around #OwnVoices get combined with Anglo-American individualism.

There are two broader categories of possible relation to a narrative as a reader when it comes to identity: you either share the identities of the author or not. But these are not clear-cut boxes, as they are so often posited in these types of conversations; they are fuzzy categories. (How many kinds of queerness can you imagine? Even contained within this one book, there are a few.) Currently, most of the discussions around #OwnVoices center the former, the similarity: the emphasis that readers can see themselves in a book because their identities are similar to the author's. This aspect is both extremely important and is currently not institutionally provided for by the publishing industry writ large. For example, in 2019, American children's books had not only far more white protagonists, but also more animal or other nonhuman protagonists than protagonists of color, as measured by the Cooperative Children's Book Center. Furthermore, "books about white children, talking bears, trucks, monsters, potatoes, etc. represent nearly three quarters (71%) of children's and young adult books published in 2019"—out of the total, 41.8 percent white and 29.2 percent animal/nonhuman.[2] (I cite children's data herein because it is more available than comparable metrics for adult fiction.) Even publishing markets in non-Western countries are often dominated by translated English-language releases due to colonialism and imperialism; therefore, what happens in the United States—and more widely, in English-language literature—has repercussions throughout the globe.

This kind of self-representation is often provided as the first and foremost reason to increase diversity and inclusion in literature. But the emphasis on the individual—in general, characteristic of American public discourse—obscures another aspect of inclusion that is arguably just as important, the aspect of *community*. We want to see ourselves as marginalized people. But we also want to build solidarity—and solidarity generally works *across differences*. We wish to see ourselves, but we also wish to see each other. Neither the in-group nor the out-group is ever homogenous, and solidarity needs to be actively constructed: inside the group, outside the group, on the margins. Solidarity is a threat to the status quo, but it is invaluable to everyone working toward justice.

Especially for multiply marginalized people, an exact self-representation in fiction might be difficult. With the exclusion of each factor, something is changed. As Kimberlé Crenshaw pointed out, intersectionality is not additive: it is reconstitutive. Oppressions do not stack, they interact. Even when a very close match exists, individual experiences can be substantially different. When someone is held up as the singular representative of a group, someone else will be left out. For writers, it can be enticing to be "the first" or "the only," but it is often not true; and even when it is true, with a lack of simultaneous emphasis on community, it is easy to behave in exclusionary ways. We need to uphold each other—especially because the publishing industry won't do this for us. If someone can be presented as the first, the unique, that's a plus when it comes to marketability. Earlier examples—often obscure, small-press, self-published—are discarded. We can only count on each other, on community, memory, the traditions we ourselves build.

We need to emphasize both the individual and the community, and *A Spectral Hue* does just that. Community is represented by the Shimmer artists who work separately and yet together, the people who experience their art, the connection binding Fuchsia the marsh spirit and the artists together—a connection that is also recreated by the characters of the story in the present day—and also the many kinds of reader who come to this book. Individuality is demonstrated by many different and overlapping viewpoints within the text, showing that no group is homogenous. This allows the reader to discover their own commonalities while recognizing and acknowledging the differences and power imbalances, with a sense of deep respect and resonance.

I overlapped in carrying the transgenerational trauma of history (if a different one); the passion toward art; and more. Someone else might overlap in the passages involving Black hair with a loving queer gaze: "There stands Xavier. Short, cute as a button Xavier. His tiny pixie dreadlocks like the fronds of some undersea plant, his brow-line glasses." Someone might overlap in deeply knowing the coastal landscape of the Northeast and the desire for a violently uprooted people to be tied to the land.

I deliberately say "overlap in" and not "relate to" because we can potentially relate to everything even if we do not overlap in experience. We can feel a sense of relation, and the power of literature is at least partially in that.

Yet potentiality is not necessarily instantiated; we as readers do not necessarily relate to every single aspect of a narrative. I am sure that some of the details of the Black church experience mentioned are lost on me, for instance; I might not even recognize them for what they are, even though I have read this book multiple times. But still, the rich, internal viewpoints allow us to relate to the work *as a whole,* and to its many details—and through the work, to the experience Gidney wished to convey. We can experience the centering of queer Blackness that even appears in the smallest detail, like the little girl Ama on the slave ship talking about "the men" and "the pink men"; whiteness is not the default here. We can read and increase our understanding—and through this, our solidarity.

While some of my discussion certainly applies to Anglo-American readers, I would like to emphasize first and foremost solidarity that is between different marginalized groups. In *Decolonising the Mind*, Ngũgĩ wa Thiong'o describes the great Nairobi literature debate in the late 1960s: in what organizational structure should literature be taught in Kenya? When I first read Thiong'o's analysis in 2007, it really struck me that in the status quo, not only do non-Western literatures get viewed and discussed primarily in an Anglo-American context, but non-Western cultures also get exposed to *each other* through the mediating power of imperial and/or colonial forces. (After all, I myself was reading this argument in English, in a library in Austria.) Since then, I have been very aware of the need to recenter what has traditionally been considered the margin; starting directly from our own foothold in the world and then reaching out to each other as much without mediation as possible. We all have our different starting points: Kenyan, African American, Hungarian Jewish traditions are all marginalized in the Anglo-American hegemony in different ways, even without considering queerness or transness. But we can reach out to each other as directly as possible and find our points of relation and solidarity, without centering the hegemonic power. I don't claim to have a formula on how to do it: solidarity always has its frictions and difficulties, but that is part of the work.

Of course, reading a book of fiction cannot and should not be the totality of solidarity. One cannot just read a book and stop there; and one cannot and should not instrumentalize reading the books of marginalized authors as "the thing I have done for diversity" or even solidarity. That is both hurtful, and not enough. Solidarity needs to be grounded in direct action, every step of the way. But that emphasis on direct action is what the book itself says and demonstrates, with the fictional but deeply resonant example of the Shimmer artists.

Near the end of the story, we are offered a vision of artists, all marginalized in some way, and "all of the faces are some shade of brown." Linc sees this vision, but it is shared with us readers: "All of them are crafters, creating something. Dioramas, models, clothes, jewels. They work with glue, glitter, wire, nail and hammer, cellophane, mylar, gingham. Some of them write, their pens careening over yellow legal pads, vellum, the backs of envelopes, and even speckled composition notebooks. All of them create things—some ugly and primitive, some beautiful and precise—with their eyes closed. Their eyes, behind their shielding lids, move rapidly, as if they are dreaming."

The Shimmer artists worked together with each other, and also with the marsh spirit, to build a framework for reality. They worked for liberation; and we should, too. On the way, we might have to face our past, our present, all our differences and difficulties and clashes and hurts. We will need to lay down our preconceptions. We will need to work until we can reach that spectral awareness, in solidarity, as part of a larger whole that heals itself from untold pain: "The marsh populated by brilliant flowers. Flowers that became people who endlessly built the marsh out of yarn, paint, ink, tile. Tamar was one of their number, placing a bird in the flawless blue sky, shaping a cattail reed. The rush of euphoria filled her, then. She wanted to be there, forever."

Notes

1. Gidney, *A Spectral Hue*. Unless otherwise noted, all subsequent quotations are from the ebook version.

2. Cooperative Children's Book Center, "The Numbers Are In."

Bibliography

Cooperative Children's Book Center. "The Numbers Are In: 2019 CCBC Diversity Statistics." Cooperative Children's Book Center, School of Education, University of Wisconsin-Madison, June 16, 2020. https://ccbc.education.wisc.edu/the-numbers-are-in-2019-ccbc-diversity-statistics/.

Gidney, Craig Laurance. *A Spectral Hue*. Petaluma, CA: Word Horde, 2019.

9 Jonathan Hickman, *House of X* and *Powers of X* (2019) / Ecological Activism and Radical Sovereignty

David M. Higgins

Jonathan Hickman's 2019 relaunch of the Marvel Comics X-Men franchise begins from an all-too familiar premise: the future seems totally fucked. Actually, in Hickman's two interlinked miniseries—*House of X* and *Powers of X* (illustrated by Pepe Larraz, R. B. Silva, and Marte Gracia)—it's not just *one* future that's in trouble: a special mutant, Moira X (who restarts her life each time she dies) reveals that almost *every possible future* seems totally fucked.[1] "We always lose," she tells Charles Xavier, disillusioning him of his optimistic dream that hope and kindness will one day enable mutants and humans to overcome their differences and live together in harmony.

As Ramzi Fawaz argues, the X-Men have often (since their inception in the 1960s) embodied "the social and political aspirations of America's most marginalized groups, including women, racial and sexual minorities, and the working classes."[2] Being a "mutant," in other words, is often a metaphor for experiencing the world differently from those who enjoy various forms of uneven social and economic power: to identify with mutants is to imagine what it might be like to be hated and feared on the basis of one's gender, race, class, and/or sexuality.[3] Very often, X-Men stories have highlighted a tension between reconciliatory and militant visions of social, economic, political, and environmental justice. Typically, this has been expressed in the opposing perspectives of Charles Xavier—the Martin Luther King Jr. of mutantkind, who dreams of achieving a better world peacefully—and Magneto, the Malcolm X of mutants, who advocates for mutant empowerment by any means necessary (including, at times, violent domination).[4]

House of X and *Powers of X*, however, offer the sobering insight that *neither* reconciliatory *nor* militant visions—at least the ones we've seen thus far—may be adequate to address the challenges faced by marginalized groups in the twenty-first century (and beyond). Instead, Hickman's creative team uses the extrapolative power of science fiction to assess a spectrum of bleak prospective futures and to explore defiant possibilities for the utopian flourishing of marginalized communities. As Xavier and Magneto set aside their differences, drawn together by Moira's experience of multiple apocalyptic futures, they innovate new strategies for community survival that depend on political, juridical, economic, and social autonomy for the diverse and heterogeneous mutant community.

To begin with, *House of X* and *Powers of X* assert that a utopian future for marginalized peoples may crucially depend upon a foundation of legal and political sovereignty. As the story begins, Krakoa, a sentient mutant island, has become a protected homeland for all mutants (a nod to Thomas Moore's original island of Utopia). Krakoa's extraordinary flowers, when planted around the world (and beyond), can open teleportation gateways connecting faraway locations to Krakoa itself, offering fantastic possibilities for instantaneous communication and transportation. Furthermore, Krakoa's flora can create miracle drugs that extend the human lifespan, cure diseases of the mind, and serve as powerful adaptive antibiotics. The mutant nation of Krakoa, under the leadership of Xavier *and* Magneto, offers these valuable pharmaceuticals to the humans of the world in exchange for the unwavering acknowledgement of Krakoa's political sovereignty.

There is, of course, a catch: political sovereignty must include legal amnesty (or diplomatic immunity) for all mutants throughout the world, who must now face trial only in mutant courts. The scope of this mutant amnesty is tested when the Fantastic Four apprehend the violent mutant Sabretooth after he has killed a score of human security guards during a rampage in New York. Rather than engaging in a classic Marvel-style "X-Men vs. the Fantastic Four" battle to resolve who has jurisdiction over the villain, Cyclops simply allows Sabretooth to be taken into custody. Later, in court, Emma Frost successfully asserts Sabretooth's diplomatic immunity: if the world wants Krakoa's miracle drugs, then the nations that accept the drugs must honor the island's sovereignty. Ultimately, she escorts Sabretooth back to Krakoa for a mutant trial, and he is sentenced to permanent imprisonment deep within the island's vegetable roots.

On the surface, this scenario might seem entirely absurd: in Hickman's imaginary world, marginalized people can simply achieve legal autonomy with the help of magic flowers! Consider, however, the dramatic shift that has occurred within the key themes that have frequently driven X-Men narratives: no longer do we encounter Xavier trying to persuade the world to accept mutants on the strength of hope and optimism alone, nor do we find Magneto striking out against humanity from the self-perpetuating *ressentiment* of aggrieved victimhood. Instead, mutants are able to achieve political and legal independence because they have discovered a productive, nonviolent form of *leverage* they can utilize in the name of justice and equity.

Hickman's assertion that political and legal sovereignty might be acquired through the compassionate yet unyielding application of leverage counters the idealistic notion that social justice might be achieved through a straightforward appeal to the state for legal protection—especially if such an appeal is based on a supposedly universal discourse of human rights. As Glen Sean Coulthard observes in *Red Skin, White Masks* (2014), efforts of subjugated peoples to appeal to nation-states for legal and political recognition have often been doomed from the start: asking the state to recognize you as a rights-bearing human subject surrenders to the state the power to grant (or withhold) personhood in a manner that ultimately reinforces racist colonial power dynamics. Furthermore, Zakiyyah Iman Jackson argues that the very category of "the human" has often been produced through a racist mode of inclusive differentiation: it's less the case, she argues, that racism divides people between humans and nonhumans, and more the case that racism has always enforced hierarchies of purity that define certain humans as exemplars of civilization and other humans as abject, impure, and savage.[5]

Given these foundational problems, begging the state to recognize one's humanity and grant equal recognition to marginalized peoples might well be regarded as a fool's game (the state has *always* recognized different forms of humanity; it just unashamedly values certain kinds of humans much more than others). Jackson instead asserts that we must reject appeals for justice based on politics of recognition and problematize the very category of "the human" in more transformative ways. Similarly, Laura Harjo (a Mvskoke scholar and activist) proposes that subjugated peoples must work to achieve radical, real, or "holistic" sovereignty, a self-determination established from the ground up within one's own body and community relations, rather than granted from on high by the nation-state.[6]

Hickman's portrayal of Krakoa offers a speculative example of the radical sovereignty Harjo imagines: the mutants of Krakoa refuse to seek recognition of their personhood on humanity's terms, rejecting an Enlightenment conception of liberal-human selfhood that has always offered a promise of equity it relentlessly refuses to deliver. Instead, mutants build their sovereignty from the ground up: they begin from a radical and loving acceptance of their own bodies and abilities, and they work together as a conscious and inclusive community to create their own versions of science, language, economics, and culture. From this foundation, they develop the leverage that enables them to refuse to be prosecuted in systemically prejudicial human courts.

Although such a vision might seem fantastical, real-world examples of radical sovereignty have been appearing in the United States with increasing frequency, especially in the aftermath of George Floyd's murder in the summer of 2020. In Minneapolis (where I live), many citizens are demanding that racist law enforcement systems must be defunded and radically reformed, but some community organizers aren't waiting for change from the top down: groups like Security Latinos De La Lake, Little Earth of United Tribes, and the Minnesota Freedom Riders have formed local patrols to serve and protect members of their immediate communities.[7] Experimental autonomous zones have also appeared in cities like Portland and Seattle (provoking terrifyingly authoritarian displays of federal force in response). Hickman's portrayal of mutant amnesty thus raises provocative questions in the context of current efforts toward racial justice and equity: What might it look like if Black people in America, for example, could *only* be put on trial in Black courts, with Black lawyers, judges, and jury members? Hickman suggests that this wouldn't result in killers going free (Sabertooth is, after all, found guilty and punished); instead, justice might be served from *within* a community, rather than imposed from above by a prejudicial group upon a disenfranchised group.

What, then, is the real-world version of the magical Krakoan flower that might offer marginalized groups the leverage they need to create new forms of legal and political autonomy? As I was writing this essay during the summer of 2020, a certain revolutionary leverage was being achieved across the United States through the counterviolence of civil unrest. "If you continue killing us," many collectively asserted, "we will burn your cities." Hickman, however, imagines that leverage might instead be applied with a powerful economic carrot rather than through the stick of civil conflict. Peaceful leverage, Hickman argues, requires one to have something that others in the world want deeply enough that it is in their best interests to listen and negotiate.

In this regard, *House of X* and *Powers of X* echo Frank Herbert's *Dune* (1965), a novel in which the colonized Fremen of Arrakis rise up and achieve power by manipulating the Imperium's dependency on a vital economic resource—the spice called Melange (which makes interstellar travel possible). Interestingly, both *Dune* and *House/Powers* offer the insight that economic leverage for marginalized peoples might be achieved through a dramatic transformation in ecological sensitivity: if you improve your relationship with the natural world, Herbert and Hickman suggest, you may be able to access and leverage key natural resources that nearly everyone needs.

The mutants of Krakoa don't simply harvest the island for its miraculous pharmaceutical advantages; they (rightfully) regard the land itself as a living subject—a member of the mutant community that deserves to thrive like all the rest. "Krakoa is alive," Douglas Ramsey argues during a meeting of the Krakoan leadership to discuss laws and property rights. "Not a place, or a biome—a person. Fauna, not flora." The Quiet Council of Krakoa agrees, and they conclusively determine that no one will "own" Krakoa. Instead, the foundational law they decide upon is that Krakoa will be regarded as a sacred land that all mutants must strive to protect.

Hickman's utopian vision for marginalized peoples thus relies upon a generous and loving relationship with the earth itself. Rather than viewing the natural world as an inert material resource to be exploited for profit, Krakoan mutants agree to live in reciprocal relation with nature, regarding Krakoa as an ally and friend. This utopian ecological sensibility enables special access to natural resources (the pharmaceutical flowers) that offer mutants the economic leverage they need to secure legal and political autonomy.

Lest one imagine that Hickman's vision is entirely fanciful, it is worthwhile to remember that Western science has frequently pillaged the wealth of Indigenous scientific knowledges—as well as the inherent genetic resources of marginalized people—in order to reap extraordinary economic benefits. Numerous studies have demonstrated that the economic and technical value Western science and industry extracts from Indigenous knowledge traditions often depends upon the non-Western, noninstrumentalizing, ecologically reciprocal epistemological foundations of such knowledges.[8] Regarding the earth as a vibrant and living companion, in other words, can lead to valuable (and empirically valid) scientific insights that simply can't be achieved when you're determined to treat the world as passive territory that exists to be owned and exploited.

Hickman's insight, then, is that local and traditional knowledges (which are often based on different fundamental attitudes regarding ecological reciprocity and sustainability) are *already* the source of extraordinary economic value; why not claim this value for the benefit of one's own community and leverage it in the service of transformative change? The world desperately needs different ways of healing bodies and minds, alternative forms of energy, and social practices that deepen and enrich our connections (rather than isolating us and channeling us into violent antagonism). Perhaps, Hickman imagines, those very possibilities already exist within the traditional wisdom of certain communities, and they can be leveraged to both improve the world and create new opportunities for systemically disadvantaged people to flourish and thrive.

To be sure, there are flaws and limitations in Hickman's utopian vision. In some ways, his portrayal of a removed, autonomous mutant nation-state echoes the neoliberal fantasy (expressed by billionaires like Peter Thiel) of the right of the most powerful to withdraw into their own private protected enclaves, and the notion of radical sovereignty can too often be wielded as a blunt cudgel by reactionary "sovereign citizens" who simply don't want to pay taxes for the public services they enjoy. Furthermore, Hickman's conception of economic leverage as a utopian resource depends upon (and perpetuates) the notion that all social activity occurs within a competitive market with inevitable winners and losers—an economic paradigm that has often fueled racist violence under the guise of free market competition.

Despite these limitations, *House of X* and *Powers of X* offer a utopian futurological vision worthy of consideration: in the face of new forms of exploitation emerging from technologically mediated neoliberal globalization and new waves of hatred generated by reactionary ethnonationalisms, perhaps marginalized groups and their allies can achieve transformative change by innovating new forms of language and culture, by transforming their relationship with the natural world, and by demanding the power to be judged in their own courts (rather than in the structurally racist criminal justice system of the United States). *House of X* and *Powers of X* therefore offer valuable and uplifting lessons for what it might mean for marginalized communities to survive—and even thrive—in the face of the seemingly insurmountable dark futures that may lie ahead.

Notes

1. Hickman et al., *House of X/Powers of X*. This hardcover collects *House of X* issues 1–6 and *Powers of X* issues 1–6, all originally published in 2019.

2. Fawaz, *New Mutants*, back cover copy.

3. In "The Mutant Problem," Martin Lund observes that the drive to understand the X-Men as civil rights icons or as figures of "otherness" can often be overstated by both scholars and fans; such interpretations often encounter serious difficulties upon closer examination of X-Men comics from the 1960s. Despite this, it is nonetheless the case that in the contemporary popular imaginary, the X-Men almost ubiquitously serve as symbols for minority identity and minoritarian struggles. This interpretive tradition—even if it is more of an *imaginary* tradition than one that's historically precise—is the tradition in which Hickman intervenes within the pages of *House of X* and *Powers of X*.

4. Xavier and Magneto of course offer superficial (and literally whitewashed) allegories for the more complex perspectives embodied by King and Malcolm X; they represent a white American mainstream fantasy caricature of both figures. Yet, as Scott McCloud observes, comics often simplify (stripping away complex details) in order to amplify (to highlight certain key aspects and/or tensions; *Understanding Comics*, 31). This oversimplification of the attitudes of King and Malcolm X in the fantasy figures of Xavier and Magneto is arguably one of the strange foundations of their widespread popular appeal.

5. Jackson, *Becoming Human*.

6. Harjo, *Spiral to the Stars*, 62.

7. Fadel, "Armed Neighborhood Groups"; Burks and Martinez, "Little Earth Patrols"; "MN Freedom Riders."

8. See Scott, "Science for the West," and other essays in the same volume.

Bibliography

Burks, Megan, and Kathryn Styer Martinez. "Little Earth Patrols Might Be a Preview of a New Style of Policing." Minnesota Public Radio News, July 27, 2020. www.mprnews.org/story/2020/07/27/little-earth-patrols-might-be-a-preview-of-a-new-style-of-policing.

Fadel, Leila. "Armed Neighborhood Groups Form in the Absence of Police Protection." National Public Radio, June 3, 2020. www.npr.org/2020/06/03/868464167/armed-neighborhood-groups-form-in-the-absence-of-police-protection.

Fawaz, Ramzi. *The New Mutants: Superheroes and the Radical Imagination of American Comics*. New York: New York University Press, 2016.

Harjo, Joy. *Spiral to the Stars: Mvskoke Tools of Futurity*. Tucson: University of Arizona Press, 2019.

Hickman, Jonathan, Pepe Larraz, R. B. Silva, and Marte Gracia. *House of X/Powers of X*. New York: Marvel Comics.

Jackson, Zakiyyah Iman. *Becoming Human: Matter and Meaning in an Antiblack World*. New York: New York University Press, 2020.

Lund, Martin. "The Mutant Problem: X-Men, Confirmation Bias, and the Methodology of Comics and Identity." *European Journal of American Studies* 10, no. 2 (2015). https://doi.org/10.4000/ejas.10890.

McCloud, Scott. *Understanding Comics: The Invisible Art*. New York: Harper Perennial, 1994.

"MN Freedom Riders Working W/ Cops to Protect and Serve . . . Build Community Trust." TMZ, June 24, 2020. www.tmz.com/2020/06/24/mn-freedom-riders-working-with-minneapolis-pd-protect-peace/.

Scott, Colin. "Science for the West, Myth for the Rest? The Case of James Bay Creek Knowledge Construction." In *The Postcolonial Science and Technology Studies Reader*, edited by Sandra Harding, 175–197. Durham, NC: Duke University Press, 2011.

10 Rebecca Sugar, *Steven Universe Future* (2019–2020) / Camp Redemption

B. Pladek

On its own, *Steven Universe* would have been remarkable: a kids' show as emotionally intelligent as the best TV for adults; a deeply funny series whose laughs never punch down; a show boasting a queer understanding of identity as well as a broad cast of queer characters; and a solid Chosen One tale with enough intricate lore to satisfy its substantial fandom. Yet the show's coda, a twenty-episode special called *Steven Universe Future*, elevates it to a new level of narrative sophistication. The circle *Future* draws around its own generic limitations is key to its achievement. How do you talk to kids about the violence of colonization, while also signaling to adults that you know there are no easy solutions? *Steven Universe Future* offers one possible answer.

Steven Universe first aired on Cartoon Network in 2013. Its creator, Rebecca Sugar, was the first nonbinary person to helm a show there. Hailed for its storytelling and design work, the series was nearly canceled in 2016, when Sugar negotiated an extra thirty-two episodes to conclude it. A movie followed in 2018, and *Steven Universe Future* in 2019. The show tells the story of Steven, half-human son of Rose Quartz, one-time youngest royal in a rapacious and rigidly hierarchical empire of beings called Gems. Rose rebelled against the Gems' galaxy-wide colonizing project when it attacked Earth, a planet she'd grown to love. The show opens several thousand years after Rose's rebellion (Gems live a long time). Steven now lives with Rose's rebel companions, the Crystal Gems. *Steven Universe* chronicles his evolving understanding of his mother's history and his own. It culminates with the overthrow of the Gem empire and its triumvirate dictators, the Diamonds, who Steven convinces to cede their power and commit to a program of reparations before inducting them into his ever-growing found family. It's a victory won through love, not war.

Love is always the answer in *Steven Universe*. Its representation of queer love, a triumph that followed Sugar's years-long battle with network pressure, has earned it wide acclaim. The show was the first animated series to win a GLAAD Media Award and has been nominated for five Emmys; Sugar also made the Otherwise Award (formerly the James Tiptree Jr. Award) Honor List in 2015. More broadly, *Steven Universe*'s faith in solving problems by "sharing emotions"—as Steven jokingly puts it on the season 4 episode "Rocknaldo"—allows it to address a slate of complex issues with a deft hand, from mental health to abusive relationships. Steven himself is the engine of the show's conflict resolution, what Leah Schnelbach calls an *empathy superhero* who is always ready to put aside his own feelings and listen.[1] Airing during three years that saw an aggressive rise in movements allied with violent heteropatriarchy—from white nationalism to mass shooters to TERFs—*Steven Universe* offered a hopeful alternative in its portraits of a hero who embraces his softer emotions and a world where loving your enemies is a reliable way to resolve conflicts.

The show's faith in love is also its biggest narrative hurdle. Nowhere is this more visible than in the season 4 Thanksgiving special, "Gem Harvest." In this episode, Steven's uncle Andy, initially repelled by Steven's Gem family ("a bunch of weirdo, hippie, Martian immigrants"), learns to accept them through Steven's gentle coaching. Clearly written for a United States under Hillary Clinton, this redemption arc for *your one racist uncle* hit very differently than its writers had imagined when it aired on November 17, 2016, after Donald Trump won the US presidency. The episode remains painful to watch, a metatextual reminder that sometimes, love isn't enough. Racist uncles can't always be empathized into respecting your personhood. Millennia of colonial violence can't always be hugged out.

Can't they?

After the series' regular run ended, Sugar and the show's team, the "Crewniverse," wrapped up loose ends in *Steven Universe Future*. Set two years after the show's main action, *Future* considers the consequences of love saving the day for the child-hero whose burden it was to love. In *Future*, Steven finds he doesn't know who he is beyond his obligation to empathize. Frightened and furious, he lashes out, heartbreakingly confident that he's only worthy if he remains the same magic empathy boy. In the final episodes, he becomes a literal monster, his bottled anger and self-disgust exploding out of him in a set of Godzilla horns. Thankfully, love saves the day again—sort of. Steven isn't healed from his trauma (and the show does call it trauma: he's seeing a therapist by episode 20), but he's at least aware that he's allowed to try. *Future*'s thesis might best be expressed by the ex-Gem-slave Pearl, one of the show's most thoughtful mouthpieces for trauma. "How did you stop hurting?" asks another ex-slave in episode 4. Pearl replies, "I didn't."

Tucked into this storyline is a compelling claim about genre. Perhaps the biggest plot problem with *Steven Universe*'s commitment to love-as-answer is that it's offered in response to a dilemma whose stakes, beneath the colorful fantasy, are enormous. The Diamonds are colonizers who have committed galaxy-wide mass murder. They have done so for thousands of years. If Earth's dismal track record is any guide, repairing the Diamonds' damage would take millennia again; it might never be really possible ("I didn't," says Pearl).

Yet in *Future,* we learn that in less than two years, the Diamonds have dissolved their galactic empire, instituted social democracy, and embarked on a galaxy-wide program of reparations. Moreover, the three Diamonds have devoted the rest of their long-lived existence to personally healing those they've hurt, via magical inversions of their former Gem powers. Yellow Diamond, once a warlord, is now a surgeon gluing shattered gems back together. White Diamond, once able to control other Gems' bodies, is now a medium traumatized Gems can inhabit for talk therapy. Most pointedly, Blue Diamond's weaponized tears have evaporated into literal clouds of palliative happiness. "Before you came into my life, Steven, I wanted everyone to feel the pain I felt," Blue sighs in episode 17, "Homeworld Bound." "I realized I must make up for my *awful* behavior by bringing joy to others! And in that moment, my tears vaporized into these clouds, bringing *pure joy* to all those who came into contact with them!"

If this sounds a little over-the-top, it's because it is—which is enough to indicate that something deliberate is going on. As a franchise, *Steven Universe* rarely ridicules earnest goodwill. And the Diamonds are clearly earnest. We're meant to take their zeal seriously. What *Future* can't take seriously is their situation. Millennia of colonial violence can't be satisfactorily redeemed in twenty eleven-minute episodes, whose all-audiences mandate prevents them from even representing the reality of that violence in the first place. *Future* knows this. Yet we live in a media environment that embraces serious, high-stakes stories told through short-form children's animation. We've accepted that kids' cartoons can tackle fantasy colonialism (see *She-Ra* or *Avatar: The Last Airbender*). *Future* knows this too, and it takes that challenge seriously.

Its solution is to play the Diamonds' redemption as camp. *Future* does its best to offer a portrait of genuine reparation: massive social and governmental restructuring, coupled with good-faith commitments by abusers to spend their lives healing the communities they've violated. But it paints this picture with an exaggerated irreverence. The fact that the Diamonds are styled as, and voiced by, Broadway stars underlines this point. "What perfect timing, Steven!" coos White (Christine Ebersole), who sports a sparkly cape, big hair, and bigger makeup. "I've just gotten back from my latest *charitable escapade*. I've been going from planet to planet, giving *voice* to the *little Gem*." She's at once absurd and deadly serious. Likewise Yellow (Patti LuPone), the bitchiest Diamond, flutters her hand to her heart and cries: "Oh Steven! You startled me. I was just reversing one of my *awful* experiments." This exaggeration extends to setting. When Steven visits the Gem Homeworld, he encounters a historical tour of the Diamonds' former palace. "When you walk through these storied halls, it's easy to feel as if you have the power of a Diamond!" chirps the guide, as if the Diamonds had abdicated centuries ago, not just two years. "Now, if you'll follow me this way to the gift shop." The Gem empire's social revolution is simultaneously very real and deliberately performative.

It's also very funny, though we're not laughing *at* the Diamonds, precisely. "Camp taste identifies with what it is enjoying," proposed Susan Sontag in her famous 1964 essay, "Notes on 'Camp.'"[2] But what is amusing about Yellow Diamond, a former warlord, effusively dedicating her life to repairing the damage she's done? Doesn't this joke only work if we believe that such thoroughgoing redemption is a priori impossible?

And if so, isn't that kind of sad—I mean, funny?

As an aesthetic, camp does its best resistance work in context, write Helene A. Shugart and Catherine Egley Waggoner.[3] Since its collision with Pop in the 1960s, camp's lampooning of consumer culture has become hard to pry apart from consumerism itself. The kaleidoscopically interactive landscape of contemporary media has turbocharged that problem. How do you keep a campy dig at a media property from simply advertising that property, including whatever ideological horrors lurk in its basement? While there's no easy answer, camp's critique seems sharpened by a clear frame, a set of formal expectations on which to whet itself.

For *Future*, that frame is the show's idealism, a critical element of its generic identity. *Steven Universe* is a kids' show less because it imagines its audience as children and more because it clings, open-eyed, to hope. It's invested in selling a world where love really can save the day, where even deep evil is redeemable, and where reparation is seriously undertaken by those responsible for the original violence. *Steven Universe* knows its older audiences probably won't swallow this. Its wager seems to be that younger viewers might, and that training them to expect better of others (and themselves) is no bad thing. On their behalf, the series' regular run keeps the faith, and never drops its act. *Future* doesn't drop it either. But it winks. The critical edge of *Future's* camp springs from its rarity as a moment where an idealist-by-definition show allows itself a soupçon of cynicism. "After all the damage I've done," declares Yellow Diamond, "it's only *right* to use my powers for a little reconstructive work on the Gems I've hurt." She pauses, dramatically laying her hand on her heart, as if leaving space for the audience to sigh: *yeah, right. If only.*

The Diamonds' campy redemption mounts a glitter frame around the fantasy that underwrites *Steven Universe*, drawing our attention to it, asking us if we believe in it, already suspecting our reply. Yet because it's a kids' show, that suspicion is leavened by a hope that not every viewer will answer *no*. As Allan Pero notes, "camp is a form of critique" that, not unlike *Steven Universe*, "expresses its discontent with civilization in the name of love."[4] All camp finally turns its wink on the audience, reminding us that we believe, quite earnestly, in some pretty ridiculous things. The difficulty of genuine reparation is not ridiculous. But *Steven Universe Future* suggests—very gently—that maybe dismissing it as impossible is.

Surprisingly, this claim's strongest case is made by the Diamonds themselves. As warlords-turned-therapists, we might expect them to resent the apparent impotence of their new role. Camp, writes Andrew Ross, signifies defanged power.[5] Symbols of oppression (e.g., the British flag) are more easily camped when they're no longer seen as potent. By the same token, power feels threatened by camp because camp laughs at its future obsolescence. But the Diamonds never act threatened. They're in on the joke—or maybe outside of it, beyond it. They embrace their own ridicule with a maturity we don't normally expect from oppressors, whose egos can be breathtakingly fragile. "Isn't it great?" squeals the Gem Spinel of White Diamond's new ability. "Instead of taking control of other gems, now she can channel *our* thoughts into *her* body, so we can control *her* instead!" Spinel proceeds to pucker White's mouth and whip her through a Rockettes dance number. When White regains control, she bats her eyelashes and coos, "Oh! What *fun.*" The Diamonds haven't just accepted their new life: they love it. This is a resonant message for viewers who might grow up to wield power, and for those who already do. *Steven Universe Future* defines maturity in part as the ability to enjoy relinquishing control, to enjoy being camped. For the Diamonds, stepping down isn't the end of the world. It's the beginning of a new, better one.

Should we find that idea laughable? It depends on whether you believe that power, especially oppressive power, might be persuaded to welcome its own obsolescence. "Camp is generous," proposes Sontag, because it's "not a ruthless but a sweet cynicism."[6] If younger audiences take the Diamonds' redemption at face value, perhaps it's because to become sweet, cynicism must begin in idealism, in swallowing the fantasy of hope. For older audiences, *Future*'s camp redemption is a discontented but loving critique. It asks not, "Isn't it funny our show pretends this world is possible when we know it isn't?" but instead, "Isn't it funny we could make a world like this, and don't?"

Notes

1. Schnelbach, "*Hannibal* and *Steven Universe.*"
2. Sontag, "Notes on 'Camp,'" 291–292.
3. Shugart and Waggoner, *Making Camp.*
4. Pero, "Fugue on Camp," 29.
5. Ross, "Uses of Camp," 8–9.
6. Sontag, "Notes on 'Camp,'" 291.

Bibliography

Pero, Allan. "A Fugue on Camp." *Modernism/modernity* 23, no. 1 (January 2016): 28–36.

Ross, Andrew. "Uses of Camp." In *No Respect: Intellectuals and Popular Culture*, 135–170. New York: Routledge, 1989.

Schnelbach, Leah. "*Hannibal* and *Steven Universe* are the Same Show." Tor.com, August 3, 2020. https://www.tor.com/2020/08/03/hannibal-and-steven-universe-are-the-same-show/.

Shugart, Helene A., and Catherine Egley Waggoner. *Making Camp: Rhetorics of Transgression in U.S. Popular Culture*. Tuscaloosa: University of Alabama Press, 2008.

Sontag, Susan. "Notes on 'Camp.'" In *Against Interpretation, and Other Essays*, 275–292. New York: Farrar, Straus, and Giroux, 1966.

Sugar, Rebecca, writer. *Steven Universe*. Season 4, episodes 8–9, "Gem Harvest." Aired November 17, 2016, on Cartoon Network.

Sugar, Rebecca, writer. *Steven Universe*. Season 4, episode 18, "Rocknaldo." Aired February 24, 2017, on Cartoon Network.

Sugar, Rebecca, writer. *Steven Universe Future*. Season 1, episode 17, "Homeworld Bound." Aired March 27, 2020, on Cartoon Network.

Sugar, Rebecca, writer. *Steven Universe Future*. Season 1, episode 4, "Volleyball." Aired March 27, 2020, on Cartoon Network.

II Rupture

11 Edwin A. Abbott, *Flatland* (1884) / Unflattening Scientific Worldviews

Karen Lord

I am not accustomed to starting an essay with a personal note, yet I cannot overlook how many versions both the world and this piece have passed through over the last few months. I began to write with the knowledge that while scientists believe in progress, historians perceive cycles, and even a hundred-year-old text may be relevant to our present reality. But experience is a deeper kind of knowledge, and for me the differing approaches across the globe to the COVID-19 pandemic have painfully highlighted many old flaws of human civilization and governance. What at first felt heavy-handed in my earliest drafts became obvious and mundane on reread. We are living with the consequences of allowing false dichotomies: the familiar norms of the everyday versus the "elitism" of science; our personal viewpoints versus objective reality.

Flatland: A Romance of Many Dimensions was published in 1884 and is now a fixed point in time, a relic of its Victorian era. As such, it is easy to discuss and dissect, but the present is a moving target, and fiction can never be a dead artifact so long as it has living readers who grow and revise their thinking, seeing, and being. Now, more than ever, I see in this book the perils of complacency, the stagnating influence of philosophy boosted by propaganda, and the phobia of unwanted truths. I no longer view the text as a warning, but as a report on our contemporary condition. I realize how radically we must be challenged if we are to break out of the old, established ways of thinking, both the scientific paradigms and the social constructions.[1]

For the most part, there is not much about *Flatland* that is unrecognizable in the here and now. In the first part of the novella, Edwin A. Abbott satirizes the classism and sexism of Victorian society—like Jonathan Swift had more than a century and a half earlier in *Gulliver's Travels*—making the familiar unfamiliar and translating the follies of everyday life into a new landscape where they can stand out in sharper relief.

The narrator (whose title A Square echoes the sound and significance of A Squire in English society) is a professional and a gentleman in a world of sentient, two-dimensional shapes. Respectability and prestige are measured in the number of equal sides of middle-class equilateral triangles to a priestly class of polygons so multifaceted that they approximate smooth circles. Equilateral triangles beget squares, and squares beget pentagons, and thus each generation advances more or less inexorably up the social scale. The isosceles triangles of the working class have but a small, rare chance of similar advancement, by producing an equilateral triangle through careful breeding, intense training, and sheer luck. That newly middle-class offspring is immediately removed from the working-class family and adopted by equilateral triangles. As in real life, this limited advancement also serves as an excellent tactic for suppressing rebellion in the working class in two ways: by selecting a few as tokens of proof of an equitable system, and by educating those elevated exceptions away from the influences of their lower-class origins.

Women are straight lines, considered weak and unstable, but they are also dangerous because, like the criminal and vagabond classes with their sharply acute angles of one degree or less, they possess points that can be used as weapons. As such, they must be both protected and controlled. The Flatland social hierarchy grants them no path to advancement. "Once a Woman, always a Woman," the narrator quotes smugly, with much reference to the Decrees of Nature and Laws of Evolution that make this so.

The art and architecture of Flatland, the law and etiquette of its society, are all based on the norms of polygons with all sides equal, triangles with at least two sides equal, and straight lines. Irregulars deviate from the expected norm, and their ability to masquerade as a member of a higher class is feared. They are all but outcast as a result, treated as objects of pity and suspicion if the deviation is mild, and as candidates for sterilization or euthanasia if the deviation is severe.

Here we find two key similarities between Flatland's society and ours. First, there is always a rationale that places the blame for exclusion firmly on those excluded, or else one must invoke the ineffable—some law or pseudoscience—in order to renounce all personal and public responsibility for the state of affairs. Second, there is always an artificial process or structure imposed on the society to enforce these supposed innate tendencies and natural laws.

In the midst of all this inequality, the Square sits comfortably in the mainstream with his family—obedient wife, upstanding pentagonal sons and two noble hexagonal grandsons. He feels no need to question the system that has granted him a livelihood, prosperity, and a clear set of rules to define his physical and social realities. Three things come to disrupt the Square's certainty in life and expand his social hierarchies to dimensional hierarchies: a dream of Lineland (the inferior world of one dimension), his brilliant grandson's imagining of a cube (a square in three dimensions), and a visitation from Spaceland (the exalted realm of three dimensions).

In Lineland, the Square's one-dimensional counterpart describes and justifies the rules and etiquette of his own society in language very similar to that used by the Square. The Square's dream naturally echoes his own prejudices, as the Monarch of Lineland employs terms like *Law of Nature* to place societal order on the same level as physics and mathematics. The argument between Square and Line also foreshadows the Square's later encounter with the Sphere: the arrogance and condescension of the higher-dimensional being; the anger and denial of the lower-dimensional resident; and the misogyny, classism, and self-righteousness of both. The final, concluding dream of the sole inhabitant of Pointland, who assumes the external voice of the Square to be a manifestation of their own internal thoughts, reinforces the theme that it is near impossible to imagine that other dimensions and worlds exist so long as you remain within the dimensions of the world you know.

This is the paradox of *Flatland*: the shape of our world molds the manner of our lives, but the way that we live shapes our perception of the world. In Yoon Ha Lee's story "The Shadow Postulates," scholars internalize the concept that the universe is governed by a rule of three. Only by imagining a different perspective is the protagonist able to break through both her social and mathematical biases and find both the truth of her suppressed emotions and the solution to a long-lost mathematical proof. Similarly, in Abbott's novel, it is only by removing the Square completely from the plane of Flatland and transporting him to Spaceland that the Sphere is able to break through the Square's biases about the shape of the world. Seeing is believing for many; tangible evidence is sufficient to crack the shell of their old convictions. Unfortunately, there is no one to transport the Sphere to a higher set of dimensions, so his biases remain intact, and he rejects the Square's speculations of worlds of four dimensions and higher.

This paradox in turn creates a problem: in all known worlds, those whose sense of worth and meaning in life is tied to an arbitrarily hierarchical order react badly to anything that threatens that order. First there is laughter and mockery, then anger and denial. They question the intelligence and sanity of the source. They accuse them of being monsters from outside of the natural order, or women attempting to act beyond their station in society. Finally, when diminishing and discrediting do not work, they suppress the disruptive knowledge by erasing the source.

Such an emotional response shows that the failure to imagine realities beyond our observed and expected structures is caused not solely by restricted vision, but also by a restricted mind craving certainty, though that certainty comes with compromise. One does not need to be in the top tier to support the myths of supremacy and progress. The hope of advancement—if not now, then for a future generation—is enough. Even a Square can dream that his descendants will eventually reach the pinnacle of Many-sidedness, and he will vigorously defend the world order that allows this to be so.

In some cases, our prejudices may accidentally strengthen our ability to grasp new truths, however imperfectly. For a Square, the existence of Spaceland and the Sphere is affirmed by the Flatland belief that more means greater. If having more equal sides leads a polygon closer to divinity, more dimensions surely indicate a world closer to heaven. In the Square's worldview, Lineland and Pointland are clearly beneath him, but the higher-sided shapes and dimensions are something to aspire to. The Square is primed to incorporate Spaceland and the Sphere into his philosophy, and also to imagine yet higher dimensions—a hypothesis that the Sphere cannot admit to, lest his own standing be reduced.

When faced with a threat to order, most individuals do not have the power to fully suppress sources of inconvenient information. Self-delusion is an easy solution. The Pointland entity is an exemplar of that manner of coping; he hears the Square's words as an echo of his own thoughts because he cannot imagine that other beings might exist and have their own voice.

Societies have a similar approach. Gaslighting, or imposed delusion, can be seen in the duplicity of speech of Flatland men, who praise women to their faces and disparage them behind their backs, and speak not for communication, but for control: "With Women, we speak of 'love,' 'duty,' 'right,' 'wrong,' 'pity,' 'hope,' and other irrational and emotional conceptions which have no existence, and the fiction of which has no object except to control feminine exuberances; but among ourselves, and in our books, we have an entirely different vocabulary." The Square fears for the intellect of Flatland's young males, who must unlearn the values and vocabulary learned from their mothers to operate in the world of men. Further citing "the possible danger" of a Woman learning to read on the sly or being accidentally exposed to the logical idiom by an indiscreet or disobedient infant son, he suggests a return to the old system of basic education for women.

There is an assumption embedded in the Square's approach that the knowledge of women, educated or not, is not logical, not scientific, and therefore not worth knowing. But this too is a false dichotomy and needlessly gendered. Rosalind Franklin, famous for both her contributions to the discovery of the structure of DNA and the lack of respect shown to her from at least one of the codiscoverers, had this to say to her father in defense of science: "You look at science . . . as some sort of demoralising invention of man, something apart from real life, and which must be cautiously guarded and kept separate from everyday existence. But science and everyday life cannot and should not be separated."[2]

Can society create a more inclusive language, one that takes in both the scientific and the everyday? In her 1984 novel *Native Tongue*, set in a future where women no longer have any rights, Suzette Haden Elgin creates Láadan, a new language for women, free from the prejudices and skewed privileges of patriarchy and filled with the nuance of the lived experiences of women. The language project was both fictional and actual; the author hoped that her constructed language (conlang) would, if it were needed, be embraced as fervently as Klingon or Quenya. Although Láadan did not see widespread adoption, mainstream English has in its own way been interrogated and expanded to serve a wider range of people and experiences.

Individual denial can be distressing, and societal denial crushing, but the state has the power to entirely eliminate people whose presence or witness would disturb the public order. The Sphere's third, millennial appearance in the Council Chamber of Flatland, to declare the fact of three dimensions to the highest Circles of the realm, is suppressed, as on the previous two occasions, with ruthless efficiency. The Isosceles security force is sent for execution, and the Square clerk (our protagonist's own brother) is imprisoned, with the continuation of his life conditional on his silence.

Heralds are sent out into the streets to proclaim punishments for anyone daring to "pervert the minds of the people" with "delusions" or "revelations from other Worlds." The effect is immediate. When the Square tries to return to discussing the concept of the cube with that brilliant hexagonal grandson who first imagined it, the boy, wise beyond his years, hears the herald's warning outside and quickly pretends to laugh off the idea. Unable to silence himself for long, the Square tells all his dimensional adventures to the members of the Local Speculative Society and is locked up by the authorities—an inevitable end to a cautionary tale for all times.

After seven years of being a prisoner of the state, the Square adjusts his views on the lower classes and women, even coming to consider "that the Straight Lines are in many important respects superior to the Circles." He is less in awe of the aristocracy, and no longer assumes that the natural order and man-made order work to the same goals. The reordering of the Square's sense of his physical universe could be described as "a reconstruction of the field from new fundamentals,"[3] but, as Franklin reminds us, science and the everyday do not walk separately; they are intertwined. The Square's transformation goes beyond the merely mathematical to include his views on society and its so-called natural order of things.

Flatland is a depiction of any typical human society in any part of the world. On the surface, it is ordered and peaceful, with contented, law-abiding citizens. On closer examination, the idyll is at the cost of fascistic control of social mobility, gender roles, access to information, and freedom of expression. At the surface, perspectives are limited; at a higher vantage point, the inner workings are revealed with all their flaws and contradictions, and the revelation is shattering.

Thomas S. Kuhn notes that "like artists, creative scientists must occasionally be able to live in a world out of joint."[4] In the arts, in the sciences, in the everyday, those who seek to find order in chaos must do so creatively, flexibly, and with the courage to live in a world out of joint while tectonic shifts realign the borders and contours of our once-reliable maps. In the year 2020, and in the years to follow, such courage will be needed more and more as we learn to navigate the full dimensional range of our worlds and our lives.

Notes

1. On paradigms, see Kuhn, *Scientific Revolutions*; on social constructionism, see Berger and Luckmann, *Social Construction*.

2. Qtd. in Maddox, *Rosalind Franklin*, xx.

3. Kuhn, *Scientific Revolutions*, 85.

4. Kuhn, *Scientific Revolutions*, 79.

Bibliography

Abbott, Edwin Abbott. *Flatland: A Romance of Many Dimensions*. Reprint. New York: Dover Publications, 1992.

Berger, Peter L., and Thomas Luckmann. *The Social Construction of Reality: A Treatise in the Sociology of Knowledge*. London: Penguin Press, 1967.

Elgin, Suzette Haden. *Native Tongue*. New York: Daw Books, 1984.

Kuhn, Thomas S. *The Structure of Scientific Revolutions*. 2nd ed. Chicago: University of Chicago Press, 1970.

Lee, Yoon Ha. "The Shadow Postulates." *Helix*, no. 5 (July 2007). http://transcriptase.org/fiction/lee-yoon-ha-the-shadow-postulates/.

Maddox, Brenda. *Rosalind Franklin: The Dark Lady of DNA*. New York: HarperCollins, 2002.

12 Karel Čapek, *War with the Newts* (1936) / Comic Jeremiad Journalism

John Rieder

Karel Čapek's *War with the Newts*, published in 1936, one of the greatest pieces of science fiction of the twentieth century, is a prophetic work. When I say *prophetic*, I mean it has the gift of seeing the present for what it is—and not only seeing it but also telling the rest of us what we have been looking at. *War with the Newts* said to its contemporaries that their civilization was living on borrowed time; it explained how ultimately suicidal the shortsightedness and injustice of their way of living was. Eighty-five years later, after the Trump administration erased "climate change" from its official websites and the world digs furiously deeper into the pit of fossil fuel dependency, Čapek's apocalyptic vision has if anything become even more eerily, powerfully unsettling than it was in the context of Europe teetering on the brink of the Second World War.

At the same time, *War with the Newts* is also a very funny book. Čapek was a master of the light-hearted journalistic form called the feuilleton, which Webster's defines as "a part of a European newspaper or magazine devoted to material designed to entertain the general reader." *War with the Newts* originally appeared in a Prague newspaper as a series of feuilletons; the central section of the novel pretends to be a collection of haphazardly collected, wildly ludicrous newspaper clippings about the Newts. Čapek is certainly telling his readers about their own vanity, folly, and absurdity. But if *War with the Newts* is a jeremiad, it is the jeremiad as delivered by a stand-up comic.

It is definitely an odd novel, one with no central character, flitting across decades and continents at a frenetic pace. The plot concerns a species of intelligent, dam-building salamanders, the newts of the title, who are discovered in an isolated bay in the Pacific where their population is barely maintained against predation by sharks. The Dutch captain of a pearl-fishing boat gives them knives to combat the sharks; in return, they give him pearls. It turns out that the newts are not just handy at building dams and finding pearls. Once freed from their predators, they are also astoundingly prolific. Their numbers multiply from a few hundred to more than a million in only a few years. In fact, they turn out to be so prolific and such good pearl gatherers that within a few more years the entire Pacific pearl fishery has been depleted, and the market is glutted. With the pearl trade exhausted, the Pacific Export Company makes a momentous business decision: instead of using the newts' labor to supply them with pearls, they will market the newts' labor itself. Which is to say, they decide to go into the slave trade.

It really is a slave trade, not some sort of cattle industry, because the newts do not just build dams: they also speak, dance, read and write, and, eventually, become inventors and math professors and formidable technicians. They are not human, but they are definitely persons. It is difficult to understand how the analogy of the newts to colonized peoples could not have always struck readers as one of the most obvious features of the novel, but indeed literary critics for many decades managed to fail to explore the devastating power of Čapek's critique of colonialism. One of the main thrusts of Čapek's satire is to show, over and over, how the human world renders the newts into a kind of natural resource as laborers and simultaneously makes them invisible as fellow beings. All the while as the newts are being invaded and exploited in pursuit of the massive expropriation of natural resources, then bought and sold as slave labor, they are also being exoticized, fetishized, anatomized and experimented upon, forced into ghettos, and made into scapegoats. Indeed, detailing the various ways in which humans look at and fail to see the newts makes up most of the novel.

The second part of *War with the Newts*, titled "Up the Ladder of Civilisation," is made up mostly of a heterogeneous collection of newspaper clippings, including, in the order in which they appear:

- a "Newt Market Report" indicating that a million newts have been sold in the previous month, employed in titanic projects worldwide such as widening the Panama Canal and dredging the Torres Straits;
- "Thirty-Six Drowning Passengers Saved by Newts," recounting the newts' heroism in a Madras ferry boat collision with a steamship, commended

by the local authorities, although "the native population, on the other hand, is most indignant that the Newts should have been allowed to touch drowning persons of higher caste";

- a series of reports on the so-called S-trade, boasting that "if the slave trade in the past had been as well organized and as hygienically practiced as the present Newt trade, the slaves could have been congratulated";
- a follow-up on the illegal trade in newts, based on mass abductions, in which "it is estimated that on an average between 25 and 30 percent of the captured Newts survive transportation";
- reports on projects employing the newts, including the construction of a Greater Italy, "which would take up virtually the entire Mediterranean," new islands constructed by Japan and Germany, and "the world's first aircraft island" built by the United States "with a giant hotel, a sports stadium, a Fun Park and a cinema seating five thousand," all of which signify to the narrator that "man was beginning to realize that only now was he truly becoming the Master of the World, thanks to the Newts";
- a piece on the first scientific congress on newts, which reports a series of experiments concerned entirely with determining how much pain the newts can withstand and how little food and water is necessary in order to keep them alive; a magazine piece titled "Do Newts Have Souls?" with witty answers by luminaries such as G. B. Shaw, Toscanini, and Mae West;
- a summary of initiatives to devise a universal language to accommodate the worldwide spread of the newt population, though unfortunately "a different Universal Language was championed in each country";
- reports on the founding of an "international League for the Protection of Salamanders," which has ensured that "Newt work camps and hutments were surrounded by tall wooden fences to protect the Newts against all kinds of molestation, but mainly to ensure that the world of salamanders was sufficiently segregated from the human world";
- reports in the American press "of girls who claimed to have been raped by Newts while bathing," in consequence of which there has been a series of lynchings; an account of the emergence of a new religion, the cult of the Great Salamander, which "gained no adherence among the Newts at all, but it had quite a following among humans";

- a Communist Manifesto addressed to the newts, rendered incomprehensible by the censor's erasures; a summary of the opposing views that take shape regarding "the Newt Problem," one recognizing the newts as "a new working class," the other viewing them as "a dangerous competition to the human workforce"; the appearance of the first scientific paper written by a newt, "The Geological Composition of the Seabed near the Bahamas"; and, finally,
- a summary stating that the newts, now seven billion strong, "have joined the ranks of enlightened nations" to bring about an age of "unprecedented prosperity."[1]

Framing this riotous display is a parodic hymn to progress. There we learn that what makes the newtish Golden Age possible is an all-too-familiar form of short-range calculation: "Historical events could no longer be measured in centuries or even decades, as had been customary in world history until then, but by the three-month periods for which the quarterly economic statistics were published."[2] What may be lost in the long-term perspective, we are assured by the naive narrative persona, is made up for in efficiency: "Take the migration of peoples which used to drag on over several centuries: today, with our present organization of transport, it could be accomplished in three years; otherwise there would be no profit in it. The same is true of the liquidation of the Roman Empire, the colonization of the continents, the extermination of the Red Indians, and so on. All these things could have been accomplished incomparably more speedily if they had been put in the hands of entrepreneurs with a lot of capital behind them."[3]

The combination of the horrors of colonial history and the logic of the capitalist corporation in this passage is a key to the prophetic insight of the entire work. The not-so-funny joke at the heart of *War with the Newts* is our seemingly infinite capacity to place our faith in two self-contradictory fantasies: the capitalist fantasy of a constantly expanding economy, and the colonial fantasy of empty lands whose very reason for existing is to be occupied and exploited by the colonial masters. Thus, on the one hand, the newts are quickly set to work constructing artificial islands to satisfy the imperial powers' appetite for land. On the other, the narrator assures us in the triumphant conclusion to the second part of the novel that "say what you will, the Newts have brought enormous progress to the world . . .

The world's entire future lies in a continually increased consumption and production—so we need even more Newts to produce even more and consume even more."[4]

Perceptive readers, at this point, might say to themselves, "but remember what happened to the pearl fisheries." More is not always better. Of course, what Čapek is doing is ridiculing the quasi-religious orthodoxy with which this capitalist enthusiast embraces the belief that corporate profit is the fundamental goal of production—as opposed, say, to the material welfare of the society. He is also resurrecting as joke the apocalyptic logic of Marx's critique of capital, with the newts as the ever-growing proletariat destined to finally overwhelm and transform the capitalist system. Čapek is most often remembered in Anglo-American literary and science fiction contexts as the person who coined the word "robot," in the title and text of his 1920 play *R.U.R. (Rossum's Universal Robots)*—but what is not always remembered is that robot is simply the Czech word for "worker." The newts are in this sense Čapek's ultimate version of the robot.

The third part of the novel is titled "War with the Newts," an intentional misnomer both for this section of the narrative and for the novel as a whole, since the novel is almost entirely concerned for its first two thirds with humanity's undeclared war *on* the newts; then, at the beginning of the third part, with a war between human nations *with* the newts as cannon fodder; and finally, as the story reaches its conclusion, with a series of negotiations between humans and newts over the terms of a global restructuring designed by the newts to provide enough shallow shoreline waters to accommodate the now tens of billions of them thronging the oceans. The narrative ends with the redesigned coastline reaching Prague. How far this "war" between humans and newts is from a Wellsian war of the worlds or a space opera, Flash Gordon type of adventure is summed up brilliantly in some of Čapek's final words on the process. The narrator, here, is talking to himself: "Let me ask you this; do you know who *even now*, with one-fifth of Europe inundated, is supplying the Newts with high explosives and torpedoes and drills? Do you know who is feverishly working in laboratories night and day to discover even more efficient machines and substances to blow up the world? Do you know who is lending money to the Newts, who is financing this End of the World, this whole new Flood? 'I do. Every factory in the world. Every bank. Every country.'"[5]

When I first read *War with the Newts*, as a teenager, my main takeaway was that this novel is hilarious. Later, as a graduate student, I reread it mostly in the light of the Marxist critique of capital's self-contradictory and ultimately self-destructive logic. Still later, about twenty years into my career as an English professor, *War with the Newts* became one of my primary exhibits of science fiction's historical engagement with colonialism. When I read it before writing this essay, as the Trump administration's war on environmental regulations was grinding into its fourth year, I could not help but read Čapek's fable in the context of climate change. And so I ask, who, even now, in full knowledge of the global rise in temperatures, the melting of polar ice, the ever more furious wildfires plaguing California and Australia, is feverishly working to produce even more fossil fuel? Who, even now, is inventing new techniques and designing new equipment to drain every last drop of oil from the ground? Who, even now, is burning more coal and oil every year than the year before? Who, even now, is financing this despoliation of the environment?

What Čapek's jeremiad tells me these days is that the ironically appropriate outcome of the Anthropocene will be to impress the traces of *Homo sapiens* everywhere and upon everything in the world—while erasing *Home sapiens* itself. Let us hope that, instead, voices like those of Čapek will finally be listened to.

Notes

1. Čapek, *War with the Newts*, 124, 129, 133, 134, 145, 150, 154, 156, 159, 160, 165.
2. Čapek, *War with the Newts*, 121.
3. Čapek, *War with the Newts*, 122.
4. Čapek, *War with the Newts*, 166.
5. Čapek, *War with the Newts*, 237.

Bibliography

Čapek, Karel. *War with the Newts*. Translated by M. Weatherall and R. Weatherall. Evanston, IL: Northwestern University Press, 1996.

13 Ursula K. Le Guin, *The Tombs of Atuan* (1970) / Remaking the Bond

Sean Guynes

Like Ursula K. Le Guin's *A Wizard of Earthsea* (1968) before it, *The Tombs of Atuan* was meant for kids. Now we might call it a YA novel, though recent marketing schemes for the Earthsea series seem to aim more for the middle-grade crowd. Of course, the novels weren't written solely for children but for anyone, even if they happen to be quite marketable as children's fiction. But Le Guin certainly did right by her publishers' intended audience when she chose the setting: an underground tomb and labyrinth complex both frightening and exhilarating, an extension of Earthsea all the more exciting because it is so unspeakably mundane and exotic at once. What's more, she made it about those who dwell in the darkness of the eponymous Tombs of Atuan, the Nameless Ones, embodiments of the great Powers that children like me had imagined and feared are there. True, we've no proof, but we have heard stories and would rather not chance it. So we run, we shut the door tight, we turn the lights on, we pull the covers over our heads. Kids are primed to experience the Tombs.

The dark is a powerful fictive tool, taking on a life of its own, and Le Guin makes such beautiful art of it in *Tombs*, using the mythical storytelling mode of children's fear of the unknown to frame a story about the undoing, the challenging, and the freeing of oneself from the ideological forces we are made to participate in at the hands of our elders. This is the story of Arha, a child in the lands of the Kargad empire who is taken from her family before puberty and claimed as the new priestess of an ancient cult, whose Nameless Ones she is forced to serve in the darkness of the Labyrinth through the performance of half-forgotten rituals and obscure sacrifices. Out of the darkness in the Tombs of Atuan, and out of her struggles with the arch-mage Ged (who comes in search of a treasure in the Tombs) and with her own conscience in the dark of the underground Labyrinth, comes a powerful critique of ideology, of what it means to believe, and, more daringly, what it means to be oneself in a world where one is made to believe. These are important aspects of children's literature, in which protagonists often struggle to understand who they are, what the world is, and how they fit into the world as whoever they are.

Le Guin wrote *Tombs* as a publisher-requested sequel to the popular *A Wizard of Earthsea* after a road trip in summer 1969 to the part of Oregon that is unlike the Pacific Northwest (PNW) shown in movies and on TV. There, in the desert mountains of southeast Oregon, Le Guin discovered what the Kargish lands (the realm from whence came the warriors who attacked Ged's village in *Wizard*) must look like. No surprise, Le Guin's language is at its finest, its most artful, and its most loving in *Tombs* when her sentences luxuriate in the plainclothes description of thistle and juniper and frozen reeds by the banks of a desert river. Such sentences make me yearn again for the PNW, make me want to be the kind of person who knows plants of the forest by name and can return home days or months later, even, and write so vividly of the world that I am transported back to just for a moment.

So after writing *The Left Hand of Darkness*, Le Guin returned to the final lines of *Wizard*, to the prophetic note that Ged would one day recover the rest of the Ring of Erreth-Akbe from the Tombs of Atuan. She sat at the typewriter. She wrote a new novel—a pretty damn good feminist novel.

Le Guin let down a lot of folks when she couldn't imagine a girl-wizard becoming a powerful wizardess in her first Earthsea novel. She then made the rather startling decision, for narrative and continuity purposes, to write a sequel in which Ged, the protagonist of *Wizard*, appears only halfway through and in which he is never the protagonist. True, *Tombs*'s Arha is not a wizard and even lives in a land where wizards are barely more than a legend, but Arha is a priestess, *the* High Priestess born into her office, raised believing in her continued rebirth since time began. She is brought into service of the Nameless Ones who dwell below the Tombs of Atuan, who in her and the Kargs' beliefs have dwelt so since the beginning of time. Arha, in short, is powerful beyond measure. At least in *word*.

In *deed*, Arha is powerless, her office filled merely for the ritual of it. She has no real dominion over those who in theory serve her, neither over the priestesses of the Godking nor the priestesses of the Twin Gods. Her very name is no name at all, for it was ritualistically taken, rendering her as nameless as the Nameless Ones. Le Guin calls this loss of personal identity, this being folded into the belief that the young girl is the First Priestess eternally reborn, "eaten"—and so Arha is the Eaten One. This title gets at the heart of Le Guin's critique: namely that, in a patriarchal world, women with power hold power only insofar as they are made (by holders of actual power) to believe they are powerful.

Le Guin shows through Arha's story that power begets a sadistic, gendered ideology. Even the High Priestess of the Godking, Kossil, is implicated here. She holds power over Arha not just because she is older, and thus Arha's "remembering" of the First Priestess role is within her command as teacher of the role, but because Kossil attends to the rites and religious cult of one whose power is supreme in Kargad—the Godking, a human king whose ancestors (not unlike the pharaohs and caesars) declared themselves immortal gods. It is as Manan, Arha's servant who believes more fervently in the Nameless Ones than she does, says: in a society where belief in the Nameless Ones is waning and the cult of the Godking holds dominion, the High Priestess of the Godking could kill Arha in front of all the priestesses and go unpunished. But the High Priestess, a woman driven mad with the "power" she has attained through her position, lives at the Tombs along with all the other priestesses (and Arha) far away from Kargad civilization in a desert, where she performs her duties before a silent statue, and has no interaction with the world beyond the Tombs. Her power is as much a fantasy as Arha's. It is the Godking, he whom she and all Kargad worship, who holds power.

Yet—and here is where Le Guin deepens her gendered critical intuition—even the power of the Godking is illusory. After Arha escapes the Tombs with Ged, rejects the Nameless Ones, and takes a new name for herself, Tenar, she passes through what to her seems a gigantic city and thus represents the might of the Kargish Empire. The city is so grand she expects the Godking and his empire could crush Ged's lands to the west, but Ged gently quiets her naivete and lets her know that Kargad is but a small land, its cities small, its Godking barely more than a minor warlord. Indeed, the Godkings are petty men, so afraid of others having power that they both banished magic—understood in Earthsea as the ability to have power over other life through the knowing of true names—and labeled writing a dark art. Separated from the rest of Earthsea by geological happenstance, the

Godkings ruled the four islands of Kargad like British middle schoolers cast away on an uninhabited island.

Power, to the Kargs, is akin to godliness. It is something to be sought, not shared. Such was Ged's belief when he freed the Shadow in *Wizard*, a foolishness only unlearned through deadly struggle. In *Tombs*, we watch Arha's indoctrination into the cult of power-as-godliness. Why are Nameless Ones to be worshipped? They are old, they are powerful. And we watch her struggle with the idea of unfaith, occasionally exhibited by other priestesses, in different measures. We watch her become cleansed of the indoctrination and take the name Tenar, before disavowing the very existence of the Nameless Ones at the novel's climax, telling Ged that they are plainly dead. And from Ged she learns another lesson: simply unsaying what has been said does not make truth. The Nameless Ones *do* exist, but they are not to be worshipped as gods simply because they are powerful. No, they are an evil—and evil, however powerful, is still evil; worshipping it is folly at best and evil itself at worst.

Le Guin, not yet a feminist by her own words, used a children's fantasy novel to lay out what we might now call a deeply feminist understanding of power.[1] First, she implicated the relationship between gender and power through Arha's struggles with High Priestess Kossil and with her forced role as First Priestess to the Nameless Ones. Second, she implicated further the disempowerment of Kossil through her isolation and lack of material control over either her own life or over Kargad. Third, she implicated the Godking's own falsified establishment of power over not only Kossil (and Arha, and by extension the Nameless Ones), but over an entire nation. The fragility of the Godkings' masculinity abided neither wizards nor words, for both have power, both can see through the illusion of ideology.

For all the excitement of Le Guin's storytelling in the dark, with Arha going about the lightless Tombs, encountering Ged, and having her entire worldview challenged by one chance meeting, I love *Tombs of Atuan* most for the final two chapters. Having escaped the Tombs and traveling now with Ged across the Kargad lands she never knew, and then West across the seas to Ged's islands of Earthsea, the newly named Tenar discovers what it means to become free of the duties put to us by those who would have us serve their interests. The chapters are full of quiet wonder as Tenar discovers herself, the world beyond her once sharply delimited vision, and the possibilities of friendship and trust. I love these last chapters for what they say about power and ideology, how they remind me of my own coming into knowledge, that we need not believe what we are told simply because we are told—the dilemma of all who grow up, but also of all who have their unshaken beliefs finally shook. Sometimes what we are told is prudent, yes. "Fire burns!" Believe it not at your own risk. Other times, belief serves greater Powers, possibly even ones that those who taught us may not have known were being served. Belief births followers, but it also creates slaves (a highly loaded term Le Guin uses without racial cognizance).

To take Le Guin's critique further, *Tombs* suggests another type of power, that of the bond between people and across communities. In the story of Sparrohawk's (Ged's) life, the Tomb of Atuan is the setting of his great adventure to reunite the broken halves of the lost Ring of Erreth-Akbe. The novel itself ends with the ring being held aloft by Tenar as Ged's boat *Lookfar* glides into the harbors of Havnor to triumphant cheers in a scene reminiscent of Tolkien. (Sadly, Le Guin does not explain how her vision of power-sharing fits with the idea of kings and princes, still very much active in her pseudo-medieval fantasy world, but genius isn't all-encompassing.) Whether or not Erreth-Akbe's ring is a ring of power in the sense of Tolkien's rings, it symbolizes (and supposedly aids) the ability of leaders to bind together the people of Earthsea not under the autocratic submission of tyrants and princes, but in peace. The ring of Erreth-Akbe is sought because the rune carved on the ring, the Bond-Rune, was broken and lost along with the ring. Tenar and Ged reunite the runes through an act of solidarity and trust. Ged survives the Labyrinth because he trusts Tenar; she escapes the Tombs and her ideological enthrallment because she trusts Ged.

Trust and solidarity, despite differences: feminism today, thanks in large part to the interventions of radical thinkers of color and of queer folks, thrives on these conceptions of how we make a better world. The cult of power-as-godliness dies a hard death, its leaders fickle illusions and its followers unfairly or coercively duped. Power-as-solidarity breathes freely of the fresh desert air, basks in the image of a great and powerful wizard sleeping in the dirt, a thistle growing by his hand. Tenar refuses the life of both priestess and princess and chooses that of the goatherd's wife, as we see in Le Guin's fourth Earthsea novel, *Tehanu*. In this world of great wizards, monstrous unnamed powers of the dark, of empires and godkings, Le Guin shows us a way to the joy Tenar felt in the mountains outside of the Tombs. Solidarity. Trust. Friendship.

We may learn the rabbit's name—it is within our power—but to call him to us and to kill him is an evil. Better that we treat power, knowledge, as a gift and hold it in trust for the good of all. Better that we temper the temptation to rule over, that we learn to live with, side by side, as neighbors and goatherds' wives.

Notes

This chapter is adapted from an essay written for Tor.com as part of my Ursula K. Le Guin Reread series begun in January 2020.

1. See her interview with White, "Coming Back from Silence." It wasn't until writing *The Eye of the Heron* in 1978 that Le Guin began to engage feminist critique.

Bibliography

Le Guin, Ursula K. *The Books of Earthsea: The Complete Illustrated Edition.* New York: Gallery, 2018.

White, Jonathan. "Coming Back from Silence." In *Talking on the Water: Conversations about Nature and Creativity*, edited by Jonathan White, 99–120. San Antonio, TX: Trinity University Press, 2016.

14 Joan Slonczewski, *A Door into Ocean* (1986) / Peaceful Ecological Defiance

Gwyneth Jones

When I last wrote about Joan Slonczewski's Shora storyworld, at the turn of the century, I was a feminist SF writer and a women's human rights activist with Amnesty International who had become disgusted with the feminine exceptionalism that seemed to be invading feminism. "Don't celebrate feminine culture," I wrote. "It mows down individual women like grass . . . and has been happy to 'hold up half the sky' for the most brutal regimes the world has known."[1] Women in power *are not* by definition admirable. Women getting ahead, rich, or famous are *by no means always* shining examples of feminism's success. And in our harsh world, it's *women*, often and inevitably, who are the well-paid accessories and primary actors in our horrible, endemic sexual abuses against women and little girls.

Then I celebrated the Sharers of Shora, an alien species in Slonczewski's *A Door Into the Ocean*, as a marvelous breath of fresh air. For once I was invited to admire a science-fictional race of women who were exceptional *not* just because they were women, "making it" in a man's galaxy, or the innocent victims of male-ordered oppression (the Sharers don't do victimhood) or specially wise and gentle individuals (they're a mixed bunch) or specially civilized (though they are) or very good at building robust, utopian systems (though there's that too)—but because they absolutely excel at the intransigent but gentle art of nonviolent direct action (NVDA).

Introducing the Sharers

In Slonczewski's distant future, humankind is an empire of many planets, ruled by the military might of the Patriarch of Torr (an armored planet, possibly the ancient birthplace of humanity). Valedon and Shora are sister moons, orbiting a larger nonstellar body. Valedon, the "world of stone," is mainly dry land, and Valans are male-ordered, with women in traditional female roles. Shora is entirely ocean. Its people are exclusively female, and held to be of very ancient human lineage. One day, two Shorans, purple-skinned, hairless, and web-fingered, arrive at Chrysoport, a Valan spaceport and harbor town, and camp out in the marketplace. Their names are Merwen the Impatient and Usha the Inconsiderate (Shorans take ironic, disparaging second names at adulthood as a sign of self-knowledge). They are industrious, spinning and weaving Shoran sea-silk. They also wear the gorgeous fabric—awkwardly, as if they only just thought of wearing clothes—but the goods are not for sale. In marked contrast to the timid Valans, they show no fear when challenged by the imperial soldiers who police everybody's lives on this occupied planet. They explain that they have no weapons because they need none, except for "what is inside." When actively threatened, their response is eerie. Their purple skin drains of color, turning white as bone—suggesting to the paranoid onlookers that some horrible virus weapon is about to be deployed. Thereafter, the Shoran women are left unmolested.

To complete a vital mission, Merwen and Usha recruit Spinel, a good-willed, adventurous young Valan who is willing to come to Shora and learn their ways. And this is Merwen's mysterious response to the plague of Valan traders, who've established themselves on the ocean world's naturally occurring rafts of vegetation, which are also homes to the Shoran Sharers themselves.

It's an insidious, market forces invasion, eating away at the Ocean Moon's independence. But most Shorans find Valan trade goods attractive and the rates of exchange (for sea-silk and other treasures of the life-filled ocean) acceptable. They refuse to believe that a growing dependence on the mighty Empire's lifeless products is dangerous to their way of life. Of course, it's a pity that some young Sharers get addicted to the Valan gemstones that are also on sale (a purely psychic addiction, but it works like crack cocaine, destroying vulnerable minds and bodies). But the addicts are not *forced* to buy the poison . . .

The parallel to our own world is clear to read, and the advantage seems to be with the profit-driven aggressors, as usual, with the naive indigenes (as in Ursula Le Guin's *The Word for World Is Forest*) doomed to destruction either way: whether they fight back or whether they don't. But maybe not. From Slonczewski's opening gambit—the fearless purple women, suddenly appearing with their content-empty superpowers and their curious response to existential threat—the Shorans will remain a puzzle for the reader, as well as for the non-Shoran actors in the story, almost to the last page of *A Door into Ocean*. Are Sharers genuinely unarmed, except for their unshakeable courage? Or are they holding some kind of biological superweapon in reserve? What do they mean when they say they need to *find out whether the Valans are human*?

Eco/logical SF

The 1980s was a poor decade for science fiction that seeks ways *not* to destroy our living world and to avoid the dreadful future(s) we face today—at least on the shiny surface. SF's hipsters had banished the ecological concerns of "seventies feminism" and rebooted, for the digital age, the early genre's values of hard(hearted) science, cold equations, and H. G. Wells's exculpating finality in *The Time Machine*—in which an earthly paradise is for clueless saps, skipping about in their garden, unaware they're being reared for food. But the hope and goodwill of the feminist seventies hadn't vanished—nor become irrelevant to the genre. And the proof is in Slonczeweski's *A Door into Ocean*, one of the few science fiction works that I'm convinced everybody, of all genders or none, should be reading today.

The books Slonczewski cites as precursors were already unassailable classics, though neither is exactly feminist. Frank Herbert's *Dune* (1965), sometimes hailed as the first explicitly ecological SF novel, features a richly imagined desert world, Arrakis, that may have feasibility issues (a planet that's entirely desert can't really support an ecosystem) but is unequivocally a living and *lived* environment: a vast, complex web of interacting forces that human incomers have learned to understand, and to join, instead of replacing.

Herbert's marvelous desert ecology is embedded in a "golden age" style, rip-roaring adventure of lost heirs, magical nuns, a phenomenally desirable natural product (the *spice*); a far-flung galactic empire adorned with the costume and décor tastes of *Flash Gordon*; and strong female characters who get excited at the prospect of being called wives (as opposed to concubines). Slonczewski's other precursor, also set in a galactic empire, and featuring a planet with a unique selling point, is Ursula K. Le Guin's *The Word for*

World Is Forest (1972). In this slim fable, written in a white heat of anger over the US war in Vietnam and Cambodia, the small, green-furred—and to an extent female-ordered—posthumans of Athshe (a word that means world, but also forest) live in mystical communion with each other and in harmony with nature. But unlike the incomers of Arrakis, the gentle Athsheans are helpless against the evils of Empire. Goaded beyond endurance by brutally exploitative loggers from Earth (a.k.a., Planet USA), they regain their freedom only by resorting to violence—and at the cost of a moral, and spiritual, racial suicide.

Slonczewski describes *A Door into Ocean* as a *response* to both books, equally.[2] But *The Word for World Is Forest,* which at first impressed her immensely, had a deeply disappointing ending. Ironically, *Dune*, the highly romanticized, violence-glorifying, big-budget sci-fi adventure (two movies and a miniseries, so far), seems to have been the more positive influence. The forest-dwelling Athsheans, who seem only passively "in harmony" with nature and end up morally defeated, perhaps proved a very useful challenge to do something different.

The Sharers of Shora certainly aren't living in primal innocence. They don't fall from grace and mourn the Garden, either. Like the desert people of *Dune,* but with added science/fictional skills, rigor, and grown-up politics, they have become cocreators.

The Word for World Is Shora

Gloriously kitsch galactic empires have been a staple of science fiction for the genre's entire career: often mocked; just as often appropriated for grand schemes; even adapted to run on radical politics (as in Le Guin's Hainish universe, the setting for *Forest*); more recently rebooted as unstoppable, mass-market, money-spinning behemoths by the great franchises of Star Trek and Star Wars. But they can also seem disturbingly *familiar* in all their brutal pomp. In the Patriarch of Torr's empire, there are no doubt many worlds like Valadon, with soaring city architecture, designed for Ming the Merciless of Mars (or Donald Trump); voluptuous Kardashian interiors for cosseted wives; and jeweled uniforms for military commanders—while down the road the workers who fuel it all huddle in medieval poverty. And *of course* this gross inequality needs to be preserved, everywhere, by ruthless policing, and economic warfare. There can be no exceptions. The Sharers of Shora have enjoyed special status (never really explained: perhaps it's their ancient lineage; metafictionally, maybe they're the living descendants of seventies feminists!). But it seems to be time they were taught a lesson.

Merwen and Usha take Spinel back to Shora. While they argue the case for direct action with their Sharer sisters, he becomes the reader's guide. In Usha's bioengineering lab, his gut chemistry is adapted for the ocean world via a cobweb-fine tendril that painlessly penetrates his flesh. As a male, he can't be adapted by the same means to bear his own child, but the "breath microbes" (which will turn his skin purple and allow him to breathe underwater) don't even need to be infused: they're endemic now; he can't avoid them. With Lystra, Merwen's daughter, he meets the fearsome giant "starworm" that acts as the great raft's living engine and the "click-flies"—creatures "life-shaped" long ago to become a worldwide communications network. He learns that the women of Shora are not at all, as he had believed, weird but peaceful ocean-dwelling primitives—and he absorbs the Sharers' core belief that all force is reciprocal. Everything you hit hits back; everything you push pushes you. Everything is part of everything else. Even the ocean's enormous "sea-swallowers" (recalling the sandworms of *Dune*, but not so cuddly) are essential. If it wasn't for their rare, deadly rampages, the whole surface of Shora would be clogged with those natural rafts, and the ocean would die.

These naked purple women are extremely tough. For all their astonishing skills, they haven't *tamed* their wild world. They've chosen to become part of its wildness, and if they're now a sort of dominant species, shaping all other life, they still accept the one, essential component of life that nobody can change. *Shora* means *shore*: but the only shore on the ocean moon is the seabed, where everything that lives goes to die. They've named the world they love and cocreate *the place of death*.

It's something for any opponent going up against them to think about.

Moral Intransigence

While Spinel shares learning with Lystra (reciprocally conceiving the answer to that vital question about Valan humanity), Merwen succeeds in changing some minds. Women start peacefully occupying the Valan rafts, focusing on the evil of the gemstone trade. Eventually the traders, tired of throwing the women into the sea and seeing their livelihood suffer, offer to cut their prices and to sell no more addictive gems. But it's too late. More and more Sharers are joining the raft occupations, determined to defend their independence and defend the vital balances of Shora's ocean from Valan pollution. And so it begins: the grueling, relentless story of a war in which one side is heavily armed and increasingly dehumanized by stress, while the other is literally naked and absolutely indomitable.

Things escalate. The Shorans decide to boycott all Valan trade. Troops arrive from Valedon to put down an economic revolt that—however petty—must not succeed. An emissary from the Patriarch himself intervenes. He's a mech-bodied machine intelligence, and Merwen is pretty rude about that (in later Sloncsewski SF, AI actors are respected). He gets nowhere. The only actual resistance the women offer is the eerie "whitetrance" (which is not magic, it's just what happens when purple Shorans withdraw into deep trance, as a gesture of disgust, and aren't breathing). But the soldiers aren't scared anymore, and though not many Valans are sadists, there are exceptions. Women you've come to know and admire (or dislike) get beaten, burned, locked up in solitary, blown up, poisoned, tortured, killed—and *still* the Shorans won't resort to violence (although by now we know that they certainly could), and *still* they won't back down. Meanwhile the Valans, maybe still fearing that secret biological superweapon, hold back from hour to hour, from day to day, from genocide. And life goes on, in the chinks of the war machine.

It takes a while to realize that *A Door into Ocean* is the story of a war. But that's what it is, a war story like no other in science fiction: harrowing, uplifting, and, in a strange way, wonderful. And this is Slonczewski's "response" (you can't miss the references to *Dune*) to *The Word for World Is Forest*. Le Guin, though it surely wasn't her intention, depicted the peaceful people as weaklings, tragically destroyed by the temptations of violence. That's definitely not going to happen here. So how *does* it all end? I think I shouldn't tell you.

The ending of a story like this is never more than loose ends tied in a knot and a line drawn, anyway. But let me share a moment from the military occupation. A Valan soldier, standing guard over a Shoran science class, has accidentally started paying attention. Since he's a metallurgist in civilian life, he's able to supply the right answer to a cell biology question on the number of protons in an atom of Titanium.

And there it is. The binary opposition vanishes. Stone and life meet.

Afterword: Don't Hold Your Breath

But let's untie the knot, undo the line, for a postending paragraph (or two) and ask: What has been made of Slonczewski's *A Door into Ocean* as a serialized (if gendered) storyverse? In a sequel, *Daughter of Elysium* (1993), and two separate books set in this far future, *The Children Star* (1998) and *Brain Plague* (2000)—all three books entertaining and exceptional as biological science SF, if none of them quite yielding the same power as *A Door into Ocean*—the Sharers are still on Shora and still famous for their righteous recalcitrance, though not taken all that seriously.

And what of Shora as a transmedia storyworld? In the twenty-first century, with the SF genre basking in all the glory of IP franchises and cinematic universes, I'd love to see, for example, underwater photographer and visual artist Emma Critchley let loose on *A Door into Ocean*, to witness that politically and environmentally aware underwater video artist and fan of David Lynch's *Dune* try her hand at Shora. Better still, I'd love to see a big-budget *A Door into Ocean* miniseries. If there was ever a time for a visually stunning, emotionally harrowing, nonviolent direct action "war" to hit the small screens, that time is now. But I'm not holding my breath.

Notes

1. Jones, "Shora Revisited."
2. Slonczewski, "Study Guide."

Bibliography

Jones, Gwyneth. "Shora Revisited: Three Blog Posts on SF Feminism in a Time of War." In *Imagination/Space*, edited by Gwyneth Jones, 58–72. Seattle: Aqueduct Press, 2009.

Slonczewski, Joan. *A Door into Ocean*. New York: Arbor House, 1986.

Slonczewski, Joan. "*A Door into Ocean*: Study Guide." Joan L. Slonczewski (web page), January 4, 2001. http://biology.kenyon.edu/slonc/books/adoor_art/adoor_study.htm.

15 SCP Foundation (2008–) / Collaborative Canons

Andrew Ferguson

Yes, 4chan is an odd place to search for hope. After all, since its founding in 2004, 4chan has loosed several Pandora's boxes' worth of troubles upon the world, greatly augmenting the online spread of Gamergate, incel culture, swatting, white nationalism, mass shootings, and images of child abuse. And yet, as even Pandora herself discovered while her dubious gifts were bounding off to afflict humankind, there is nothing so toxic or so shallow that it does not contain at least a bit of its own antidote.

One of those potential antidotes is the SCP Foundation, an ever-growing collection of short horror stories focused on spooky objects or places and the quasi-governmental organization that exists to counter them. Although now established at its own wikified website (http://scp-wiki.net), SCP—short for *secure, contain, protect*—emerged out of 4chan's "paranormal" board in 2007. The project thus exists at the intersection between (1) a trend of born-digital horror (including so-called creepypastas) that emerged seemingly spontaneously across a variety of internet sites during the late 2000s and (2) the more specific "chan" culture that spawned 4chan, 8chan (later 8kun), and many other imitators and spinoffs. But ultimately, what the SCP Foundation is securing, containing, and protecting against is less the anomalies detailed in the more than five thousand stories in the archive and more the cynically antisocial and antidemocratic habits of thought that are privileged within chan culture.

Attempts to grapple with any product of the chans, or of internet message boards more generally, quickly run into the challenge that they really don't want you to. For those coming from the outside, the format itself is almost perversely hostile to navigate, and the content still more so. Initially, you're greeted with a long list of sub-boards, heavy on anime, gaming, and porn; the primacy of these interests is punctuated with a banner ad that often features *hentai* sex games or explicit pornography. The ad functions as an initial test of sorts: if you're the sort of person who objects to this or doesn't want it in your face constantly, you're better off leaving now. Those who stick around have already self-selected—a gatekeeping measure reflected in the community's own historical accounts, such as the one presently stored on Bibliotheca Anonoma, skewing heavily toward hyperdetailed documentation of ephemeral interboard rivalries told in the abrasive, recursive, slur-filled argot that is the site's lingua franca.

A further challenge is that the 4chan servers are designed to maximize ephemerality: threads are autodeleted seven days after they scroll off the main pages of each board, and the website itself forbids any automated external backups. With a few exceptions,[1] those individual posts that are preserved are in the form of screenshots. The word *copypasta* came into existence to describe this very thing: any post separated from its original context and reposted as a shorthand of sorts, encoding in itself for those in the know the entire history of the thread that produced it. Over time, even this knowledge fades as the original members drift away, but the decontextualized posts continue to be used by new board members who no longer have any connection to or often even awareness of the original meaning. It's not a phenomenon unique to 4chan—cutting and pasting is almost as old as textual encoding itself, and viral texts circulated on even the earliest bulletin boards—but there is a particular menace that attaches to 4chan copypastas, however innocuous (or not) they may appear on the surface level. To research a topic on the chans is to approach it through a mysterious and somehow disreputable fog, with the suspicion that whatever findings come of it will pose ridiculous and yet very real dangers.

Which is to say, such researchers find themselves in a similar position to the protagonists of a creepypasta. This mutant form takes such decontextualized digital artifacts as a starting point, injecting everything from video clips to game cartridges to TV shows with an inexplicable but undeniable malevolence. Creepypastas tend to obscure their origins as fiction, situating themselves within our own world in the manner of urban legends or found footage horror, rather than within any identifiably adjacent fictional world. While these types of stories are, again, hardly unique to 4chan, the term itself emerged there in 2007, echoing and repurposing *copypasta* from the year prior.

The chans proved to be fertile ground for born-digital horror, to the point that separate boards, designated /x/ for all things unknown or paranormal, had to be created to separate them from the general purpose or "random" board, or /b/—in part to keep them from clogging up the space, and in part to keep them from scrolling off too quickly. Since its inception, /b/ has been one of the primary sites for meme production across the internet. The speed is overwhelming, punishing, even hallucinatory: a sort of collective digital migraine. When 4chan's /b/ first went online in 2003, the clientele was formed largely of imports from the Something Awful anime subforum. It was meant to serve as an imageboard back channel for that fanbase, in particular providing hosting for images that were banned or frowned upon at SA; by day 2 of /b/'s existence, the site had been almost completely overrun by hentai porn, often involving depictions of children, torture, or both. One wonders, briefly, about the prevalence of wronged, abused, murdered, and above all vengeful children in the creepypasta form.

Regardless, the homegrown horror tales proved of sufficient interest to carve out a space away from /b/, to propagate fictions in which spiteful media processes lash out at the world around them rather than participate in the doxes and raids of the real thing. As a process whereby an unquenchable wildfire of aggrieved revanchism is directed with real-world consequences by anonymous agents at targets ranging from the eminently deserving to the completely random, 4chan is itself a sort of apotheosized creepypasta. The history of the site as it telescopes from the mid-2000s to today involves a scarcely believable trajectory that took it from an internet troll haven to . . . well, an internet troll haven, but one whose shitposts and conspiracy theories were regularly amplified by a former president of the United States of America. Along the way, an identifiable ideology develops, albeit one that goes under various labels (neoreaction, dark Enlightenment, accelerationism, Western chauvinism, Men Going Their Own Way, etc.) as it finds adherents in different venues, each with their particular emphases. The lodestar of these ideas is the belief that white, straight, able-bodied men are the natural legislators of society and that they currently are being prevented from filling this role not through any fault of their own—because how could they be at fault for anything?—but through the machinations of shadowy antagonists, the many names for which cannot obscure the misogyny, racism, or anti-Semitism upon which the ideology hangs. Obviously, 4chan did not originate this ideology, nor does it present that ideology with any overall coherency. What it did—along with a host of other chans (7, 8, 12, 420, 711, so on) and social media sites (Voat, Gab, Parler) that took up the slack once 4chan belatedly and half-heartedly decided to crack down on certain hostile or potentially illegal forms of expression—was provide a forum for conversation and radicalization, as well as a launching pad for coordinated attacks.

The separation of /x/ from /b/ back in 2007, long before the era of presidential retweets, might seem to constitute a conscious step back from such activities. But in effect, the establishment of a paranormal board on a site where everything in the world is there to be mocked and abused just means a board on which everything *except* the paranormal continues to be mocked and abused. Even today, /x/ remains one of the primary online outlets for a particular brand of extremely online horror—but as a cursory glance shows, it is loaded down with the baggage of the site as a whole, not least in the profusion of casually racist, ableist, and homophobic slurs, or the parade of anons available round the clock to aggressively belittle contributions that don't conform to their exact expectations. This, in addition to platform limitations such as the lack of archival capacity, led many in the nascent digital horror community to establish other, longer-term beachheads, such as Creepypasta.com (in 2008), the Creepypasta wiki, and the NoSleep subreddit (both 2010); while many genre-defining creepypastas start out on /x/, none of them have stayed there for long.

In this, if in few other ways, SCP is typical: after its initial mention on /x/, most likely posted by an anon using the name S. S. Walrus on June 22, 2007, the narrative quickly became a copypastable meme, with the post continuing to appear on various internet message boards up through mid- to late 2008. (Again, 4chan's aversion to archiving makes it difficult to ascertain authorship; while the S. S. Walrus post *appears* to be the originator, it may be more precise to say merely that it is the oldest version currently documented.)

It may not be surprising, given the complexity and sophistication of many latter entries in the corpus, that SCP-173 is not regarded particularly highly. By itself, a short story (flash fiction, really) of a statue that no one has ever observed moving but which poses a lethal threat to anyone around when it is not under constant observation is hardly a landmark horror tale—especially given its clear creative debt to the Weeping Angels from the *Doctor Who* episode "Blink," which aired only two weeks before the first known appearance of SCP-173. But what the entry lacks in refinement and literary sensibility, it gains back a hundredfold in terms of its suggestiveness and manipulation of its chosen platform. While many creepypastas, from Slender Man to Jeff the Killer, proved amenable to fanfiction, SCP cleverly opened itself to collaboration in at least three interlinking ways. First, by providing a number, SCP-173, for the "item" in question, the post invites speculation about the previous 172 numbered items, as well as the numbers beyond. Second, such a designation also implies the sort of organization that encounters sufficient such items that it would need to develop and maintain the numbering system in the first place. Third, and this is the element that would be most refined in the years to follow, the entry attempts to affect a dispassionate if sardonic scientific tone, asserting itself as impersonal third-person documentation (with a subject line reading "From the Files of Site 19") rather than the more traditional first-person encounter with a mysterious, cursed object. In a few short paragraphs, the author succeeds in establishing a subject, displacing it, and refocusing around the larger framing fiction.

After SCP-173 was posted, other authors immediately began extrapolating on the basic framework. These early tales haphazardly built out the mythology of the SCP Foundation—actually, several mythologies, with different posters setting up contradictory frameworks or attempting to make use of the same number for different artifacts. The creation of the SCP Wiki in early 2008 made the task of collaborative storytelling at once easier and vastly more complicated—easier because it reduced the number of duplications; more complicated because the sheer profusion of new entries quickly made it impossible to establish any sort of consistent canon, or often even to keep up with new contributions, especially after the appearance of additional formats such as the "Foundation Tales" that attempted to fill in the past and present adventures of the organization entrusted by "every major national government" with the documentation, assessment, and mitigation of these anomalies.

The overseers of the wiki wisely decided not to take on the impossible task of enforcing coherency, instead embracing the idea of *canons*, plural, as well as a necessary looseness of facts around the activities of a highly secretive paragovernmental organization. Multiple candidates for SCP-001? No problem. Clearly most if not all of them are decoys: fake files running interference for the real ones. Multiple contradictory timelines? Well, different perspectives can cause all sorts of discrepancies, whether from witness testimonies or quantum entanglement or anomalies that literally rewrite any document that attempts to describe them. As noted in a statement on canons that has remained largely consistent since being posted in 2013: "The idea that there is no canon is a bit silly at times. It's not that we don't have any. It's that we have a multitude which touch, cross, and dip into each other. It's up to you, as the reader, to decide what you believe and what you embrace as the heart of the universe. That doesn't mean, though, that authors lack intent or design, and collaboration is the heart of innovation."

Any adequate treatment of the foundation as a whole would require a book of at least this size to accomplish, so the preceding introduction will have to suffice as a jumping-off point. (Even just starting to rattle off some personal favorites here would result in this piece devolving into a listicle, like much other writing on the topic.) Instead, I'll close here by returning to SCP-173, its origins, and its final resting place, plus where in there we might locate glimmers of hope.

Like most of the stories posted on /x/ or other boards, or for that matter like most horror in general, SCP-173 does not depend on novelty for its effect. Horror does rather better when it takes something at least somewhat familiar and repackages it, perhaps with a shift in emphasis, to make it relatable to new audiences. Much of this brief story is borrowed from elsewhere, but the juxtapositions of these borrowed elements are calculated to appeal specifically to readers accustomed to the 4chan format, where the header image is at least as important as the title for convincing people to click. Meanwhile, the shift in that image toward the more contemporary installation work of Izumi Kato and away from the neoclassical sculptures animated in "Blink" marks a corresponding movement from *Doctor Who*'s primary concern with governing time to the SCP Foundation's task of managing space—specifically, constructing spaces that can contain impossibly rapid, murderous statuary, regardless of how they came to be there. In addition, it's a space that must be cleaned out periodically due to the inexplicable mixture of blood and feces that accrues on the floor.

This last detail might seem like a juvenile addendum—and it is—but it's also crucial to understanding how SCP positions itself within the 4chan environment: having clicked on the story and accessed the file, you have taken on the role and responsibility of a functionary charged with keeping this entity contained. Left to its own devices, it will mostly just scuffle around and produce gallons of liquid waste—but occasionally you still have to clean up after it, and just because it is pathetic and embarrassing does not also mean it's not extremely dangerous. The anomaly, in short, stands in for the general discourse on 4chan, from the aggressive attacks to the shitposting ambient; what is needed is someone who can reliably clean up while keeping the thing from getting out and menacing the general public. It's made clear, even at this early stage, that this containment must be a *collaborative* project, and also, as a fiction told through archives on a site without archival capacity, that for that collaboration to succeed, it must leave and establish some sort of separate place.

From the very first, SCP was an overture, an invitation to exit a toxic community (though not forget about it; still the anomaly must be monitored) and instead build something lasting. And now look how far this one project has come, leaving behind a website in which slurs and coordinated harassment continue to be the common coin of the realm for one with an established and explicit antiharassment policy. It's the treatment of canons, plural, that most stands out: the affordance of multiple potential points of intersection between the readers' interpretive horizons and the writers' creative projections—and, beyond that, the chance to move seamlessly between roles, to add your own materials for others to encounter. As ever, this collaborative partnership is not new to SCP, not even at the scale it is now, of a massive transmedia undertaking. But the emphasis on collaboration is refreshing, especially when that collaboration may very well have lasting effects on the universe being created. And if horror isn't quite your thing, then there's other recent examples as well that strive for and occasionally hit this synchronicity: many tabletop games, for one (especially with community contributions toward making the experiences and representation more diverse); digital construction sites such as are found on *Minecraft* or *Roblox* servers; maybe above all the browser game *Blaseball*, a gleefully queer, weird reimagining of baseball where the lore develops in a constant feedback loop between creators and fans.

In one sense, the SCP Foundation was never much of a creepypasta: its origins were more or less clear, it never pretended (until much later metatextual turns) to be an actual part of *our* universe, and it focused not on harm being done but rather the attempt to prevent that harm. And yet in other ways it functions as a creepypasta in reverse: providing starting points rather than obscuring them; exerting a beneficial effect on the real world while keeping respectfully separate from it; above all, encouraging people out of destructive communities through the offer of more constructive, collaborative uses of internet time. SCP by itself cannot undo the harm 4chan and similar sites have done. But it maps out an ethic that can be followed: to monitor those sites, to do everything possible (as seen in the aftermath of the Capitol-storming insurrection) to shut down the down the dangerously unpredictable alternatives such as Parler in favor of the more easily containable and protectable ones like Telegram, and, above all, to provide to those who will take it an alternative aspiration: Hey, there's a hell of a good universe next door. Let's go.

Notes

1. For example, the large /pol/ dataset gathered in Papasavva et al., "Raiders of the Lost Kek."

Bibliography

Papasavva, Atonis, Savvas Zannettou, Emiliano De Cristofaro, Gianluca Stringhini, and Jeremy Blackburn. "Raiders of the Lost Kek: 3.5 Years of Augmented 4chan Posts from the Politically Incorrect Board." In *Proceedings of the Fourteenth International AAAI Conference on Web and Social Media*, 885–894. Palo Alto, CA: Association for the Advancement of Artificial Intelligence, 2020.

16 Kléber Mendonça Filho, *Recife Frio* (2009) / Visualizing Disparity in Brazil

Alfredo Suppia and M. Elizabeth Ginway

Shot in 35mm film, *Recife Frio* (*Cold Tropics*, 2009) is Brazilian director Kléber Mendonça Filho's seventh short film. Presented as an Argentine television show covering unprecedented climate change in Recife, the capital city of the northeastern state of Pernambuco, Brazil, *Recife Frio* takes the form of a mockumentary. Popular for tourism because of its tropical climate and access to beautiful beaches, Recife suddenly and inexplicably takes on temperatures ranging from 14°C during the day to 6°C at night after a meteorite falls in the area. By speculating about this uncanny climate change, the film sets about turning the whole of society—and science—on its head. By the end of this twenty-five-minute film, the reporter-narrator of *Recife Frio* has addressed many of Brazil's endemic social problems, including poverty, homelessness, the lack of urban planning, real-estate speculation, social inequality, and the remnants of slavery present in the treatment of domestic help. By combining the tropes of science fiction with political concerns, the film's strategy is to present the impact of this "climate catastrophe" on the city's population, while also keeping viewers off balance with moments of cringy tongue-in-cheek humor. By closing with a song by the iconic figure of Lia de Itamaracá—whose work is considered to be part of Pernambuco's patrimônio vivo ("living heritage")—the film suggests that hope lies with the culture and resistance of its popular classes.

With more than fifty awards in Brazil and overseas, *Recife Frio* has become Brazil's most famous short film after Jorge Furtado's *Ilha das Flores* (*Island of Flowers*, 1989), and Mendonça Filhos's YouTube channel shows that his short has had over 185,000 views, while Vimeo counts over 39,000. In adopting a satirical documentary style, *Recife Frio* is part of a contemporary trend in world science fiction cinema, especially in its combination of

SF tropes and classic documentary cinema. Alex Rivera's short "Why Cybraceros?" (1997) portrays cyborg fruit pickers working remotely from Mexico. Using archival footage from the 1940s American Bracero program, Rivera makes room for speculation on the future of work in the age of cognitive capitalism and digital labor. In a similar mockumentary vein, Neill Blomkamp's "Alive in Joburg" (2005) portrays the tensions between aliens and humans in Johannesburg in an allegory of apartheid focused on race relations. Both directors used these shorts to develop full-length features, such as Rivera's *Sleep Dealer* (2008) and Blomkamp's *District 9* (2009). Over the last twenty years or so, piloting ideas in short films seems to have intensified in SF cinema, since mockumentaries have often served as a laboratory for more ambitious feature films. Similarly, *Recife Frio* serves as a pilot for Mendonça Filho's later full-length movies *O Som ao Redor* (*Neighboring Sounds*, 2012) and *Bacurau* (2019), which also further develop his use of fantasy and science fiction tropes respectively.

Set in a near future, *Recife Frio* opens as if it were the Argentine news show *El Mundo en Movimiento* (*The World in Motion*), and the voice-over is in Spanish, not Portuguese, lending an element of linguistic estrangement and drama to the film. The Argentine reporter-narrator Pablo Hundertwasser begins by reporting on a rescue team working on an isolated beach where the fatal meteorite has just killed three people. Through a sequence of shots, he reports on Recife's sunny tropical past, while embedding criticism of real environmental degradation of the Capibaribe River, noting that a stream of dark sludge now runs where water used to flow. Hundertwasser further explains that the average maximum temperatures, formerly hot and tropical, have permanently dipped and remain in the frigid range and that Recife has not experienced a single moment of sunlight during the past seven months. By using climate change to trigger the sense of cognitive estrangement, Mendonça Filho asks viewers to question the social structures that the tropical climate "minimizes," including the lack of shelter and services for the poor, the region's economic dependence on tourism, and even the layout of apartments designed to make the most of the sea breeze for the apartment owners while their maids are relegated to small stuffy rooms. As Barry Keith Grant has emphasized, films like *Recife Frio* depend on "cognitive estrangement" to unveil long-lasting contradictions by belaboring and overdramatizing catastrophe, especially by calling attention to the use of new of digital technology in the diegesis, which captures a general sense of postmodern anxiety promoted by "fake news," sensationalist media reports, and news exposés.[1]

At the same time, the film alternates in tone, combining concern for the victims of these uncanny events with amusing interviews with shop owners and popular singers, keeping viewers off balance, in the style of Michael Moore's 1989 *Roger and Me*. In *Recife Frio*, this uneven tone occurs when Hundertwasser begins by showing ominous shots of locals wearing hoodies, a landscape dotted by bonfires built by homeless, and a morgue where a large number of body bags line the hallway, which he then follows with more lighthearted stories. The street cameras, once deployed for surveillance indicating a high level of urban crime, now register only empty streets. This is explained in part by a segment later in the film, in which the reporter learns that many people who formerly strolled on the city streets now fill the hallways of a crowded shopping mall, which, decorated with Christmas winter motifs, now sports a skating rink. While this forms part of the film's critique of cultural colonization, we also note the abandonment of the city's public spaces caused by the rapid onset of climate change.

After this sensationalist and, at times, amusing critique, the most significant scene of the film is also the most realistic and documentary: an interview with an upper-class family, the Nogueiras, who live in a luxury apartment on the beachfront. Their well-ventilated apartment, designed for the tropical climate, with its wide windows and balconies, is now uncomfortable given the new conditions. Their spoiled teenage son, however, manages to escape the cold by moving into the maid's quarters at the center of the apartment. As the voiceover explains, this room is reminiscent of slavery; windowless and westward-facing bedrooms are traditionally designated as the maids' quarters. The parents explain that the maid is not happy, but she had to give in or lose her job. This scene provides a powerful and eloquent representation of class struggle and the persistence of oppressive social relations within the private spaces of contemporary Brazil.

The next segment serves as a utopian counterpoint to this scene. Hundertwasser continues his report by citing a book that was based on an actual master's thesis by Armando de Holanda about the architectural design for the tropics. Published as a book in 1976, Holanda's study offers a vision of modest structures on a more human scale than the high-rises that now dominate Recife's cityscape.[2] This alternative to modernist or "brutalist" architecture has now become a distant utopia given the preference by developers for verticalization and the privatization of space in Brazil. It is also a critique of real estate speculation in Recife and other coastal cities, where the cult of "modernity" has all but crushed the possibility of human interactions as streets are filled with cars and not pedestrians. Historically, during the first half of the twentieth century, informally constructed houses (known as mocambos) were found throughout the city, and lower- and middle- income neighborhoods used to be located side by side. With concerns for "hygiene" and tourism in the 1930s, the city's urban planners pushed the smaller businesses and lower-income populations to the periphery in the name of progress.[3] This is referenced in *Recife Frio* when a news segment reports that yet another historic building will be demolished for the construction of a tall (and lucrative) apartment complex.[4] The film's shots of desolate streets and tall buildings add irony to the elite's equation of progress with sterile architectural design and European culture, which is reinforced by the soundtrack playing Beethoven's Seventh Symphony.

In contrast to this bleak political landscape, popular culture provides a dose of humor, reality, and resistance. The film's first example is a singing "duel," known as repente, performed by the duo Pinto and Patativa, with each one trying to outdo the other by offering amusing canticles about climate change. They are on the street enthusiastically performing despite the cold. Another amusing segment on cultural imperialism is a report on a local mixed-race Santa Claus, Clodoaldo, who is the only character to welcome the climate change because he will no longer suffer from heat prostration and fainting spells, as documented in the archival footage inserted into his interview. He is now pictured with his family and grandchildren happily welcoming Christmas. Another example of resilience and adaptation is seen in the locally made, handcrafted wood and clay figures sold to tourists. A shopkeeper makes irreverent remarks about figurines of nude sunbathers and phallic keychains, remaining optimistic even though his shop appears to be empty. He enthusiastically shows how the new souvenirs are now reconfigured and adapted to winter motifs, including clay miniatures of domestic scenes that feature families around fireplaces instead of outdoor bonfires and small sculptures of tiny clay houses with the added novelty of chimneys.

The film ends with a tribute to popular culture, closing with a song known as a ciranda, led by the seventy-six-year-old Afro-descendant composer and performer Lia de Itamarcá in a segment that cross-fades over another cloudy and bleak TV weather forecast for Recife.[5] This final scene takes place on the beach, where Lia sings while a number of her fans and supporters, dressed in heavy winter outfits, dance in a circle. They all end up running toward a narrow sunbeam that eventually pierces the dark clouds. The last scene in the film sustains the overall irony and makes a nod to the hope that perhaps collective action may make a breakthrough, like the sun appearing through the clouds. It is key to note that Lia sings a ciranda, which is also a circle dance that originated on the street corners of Recife. According to Lúcia Gaspar, the ciranda symbolizes a sense of community without prejudice of race, class, gender, or age, welcoming all who care to join.[6] By holding hands, participants move counter-clockwise in the circle, raising and lowering their joined hands in unison to the song. By ending the film in this way, Mendonça Filho endorses the possibility of and need for collective action in a democratic public space—the beach—while illustrating the vitality of Brazilian popular culture.

As in earlier Brazilian science-fiction films, especially of the 1970s and 1980s, *Recife Frio* dissects the history of social inequality and protest in the guise of an ecodystopia.[7] Moreover, the most deep-rooted contradictions of Brazilian society, which are generally silenced to the point of invisibility in the media, consistently appear as central topics in Kléber Mendonça Filho's filmography. To tackle such issues, stories with a focus on Recife, his native city, or on the speculative real estate market end up being key in providing perfect settings and characters for an intense discussion of Brazil's history of violence, exclusion, oppression, and abuse of power. In this sense, *Recife Frio* can be seen as a blueprint or tutorial text for Mendonça Filho's whole film oeuvre, in as much as it condenses the intense interactions of people and the landscape. The director's interests—especially in genre film, irony, and satire—are part of his work with Juliano Dornelles, with whom he has made genre film mash-ups to tackle the enduring history of Brazilian inequality, including *O Som ao Redor* (*Neighboring Sounds*, 2012)—a social drama infused with fantasy and horror—and *Bacurau* (2019), a Brazilian western combined with science fiction. It is often the uncanny mash-up of genres that gives shape to Mendonça's cinematic vision, allowing outcasts—the excluded and silenced majority of the working-class people of Native Brazilian and/or African descent—to have the last word.

Notes

1. Grant, "Digital Anxiety."

2. See Holanda, *Roteiro para construir no Nordeste.*

3. Virgínia Pontual describes Recife during the 1920s, when a new class of urban proletarians began to demand rights to urban space, provoking the sugar barons and landowners who dominated politics at that time ("Tempos de Recife," 427). Dirceu Marroquim shows how authorities felt compelled to remove mocambos from the city landscape to promote tourism under Getúlio Vargas's New State ("Entre Sujeitos e Instituições," 78–79). More recently, Kaspar Loftin has noted how urban space in Recife continues to be disputed and politicized in the "Occupy Estelita" social movement, which began in order to save the historic wharf in Recife and reimagine public space as urban commons ("Occupy Estelita," 356).

4. Real estate speculation is the topic of Mendonça Filho's film *Aquarius* (2016), in which a woman who owns a beachfront home struggles against the powerful forces of those who wish to build a luxury apartment complex on her property. It can also be interpreted as an allegory for the legislative coup launched against former president Dilma Roussef.

5. Mendonça Filho also features Lia de Itamaracá in his 2019 film *Bacurau* as the late matriarch of the town and symbolic mother of all. She is thus a central figure in his conception of Brazilian identity.

6. Quoted in Fernandes, "Ciranda."

7. Among the best known of such films are Claudinê Perina's 1972 short *93º Tunnel*, José de Anchieta's 1978 *Stop 88*, Roberto Pires's 1981 *Nuclear Shelter*, and Bertoni's 1986 *Armadillo Blood*. See Suppia, "Breathe, Baby, Breathe."

Bibliography

Fernandes, Fernanda. "Ciranda: história e origens." MultiRio: a mídia educativa da cidade. 2 July 2021. http://www.multirio.rj.gov.br/index.php/leia/reportagens-artigos/reportagens/17261-ciranda-história-e-origens.

Grant, Barry Keith. 2013. "Digital Anxiety and the New Verité Horror and SF Film." *Science Fiction Film and Television* 6, no. 2 (2013): 153–175.

Holanda, Armando de. *Roteiro para construir no Nordeste* [Guidelines to build in the northeast]. Pernambuco: Universidade Federal de Pernambuco, 1976.

Loftin, Kaspar. "Occupy Estelita Puts Urban Rights in Motion in Northeastern Brazil." *NACLA Report on the Americas* 51 (2019): 356–363.

Marroquim, Dirceu S. M. "Entre sujeitos e instituições: turismo no Recife, 1939–1944." PhD diss., Universidade Federal de Pernambuco, 2015.

Pontual, Virgínia. "Tempos de Recife: representações culturais e configurações urbanas." *Revista de História Brasileira-São Paulo* 21, no. 42 (2001): 417–434.

Suppia, Alfredo. "Breathe, Baby, Breathe: Ecodystopia in Brazilian Science Fiction Film." In *Practicing Science Fiction: Critical Essays on Writing, Reading and Teaching the Genre*, edited by Karen Hellekson, Craig Jacobsen, Patrick Sharp, and Lisa Yaszek, 1–22. Jefferson, NC: McFarland, 2009.

17 Virginia Grise, *blu* (2011) / Queer Latinx Aesthetics of Apocalypse

Cathryn Merla-Watson

Recently, Black Lives Matter (BLM) protests erupted across the United States and the world, giving visibility to how structural racism upholds the world ending for people of color in the most brutal, obscene, and real sense. Climate change once again fomented ostensible natural disasters such as hurricanes and wildfires that disproportionately affect already vulnerable communities of color. Black and brown communities continued to bear the brunt of infection and death caused by COVID-19 while the sitting president proclaimed that the pandemic had already "turned a corner." The Texas-Mexico borderlands, for example, home to mainly poor and working Chicana/o/xs and Mexicana/o/xs and where one in three people live below the poverty line, became an epicenter of COVID-19 surges, morphing into "una herida abierta," an "open wound," in the words of philosopher Gloria Anzaldúa.[1] Our current moment, in sum, has shown how the catastrophic disproportionately shapes and normalizes social and real death for Latinxs and BIPOC communities. This naturalizing of apocalyptic Latinx lived experience is echoed in a 2010 episode entitled "Vatos" in the television serial *The Walking Dead*, in which a cholo remarks of his new dystopic, zombie-filled reality: "It's the same as it ever was." This line further underscores the mutually informing relationship between speculative art forms and the lived realities of Latinxs, as well as that this relationship is far from new in the United States. Indeed, it is telling that the colonization of present-day Mexico was described by the Aztecs in apocalyptic terms.

While less commercially successful than popular television serials, recent queer Latinx plays, such as Virgina Grise's award-winning *blu* (2011), have redeployed and reimagined the apocalyptic genre to bring to center stage and dramatize how the world ending and mundane collide within the intersectional lived experiences of Latinxs and queers of color. Queer Latinx playwrights have taken up the apocalyptic genre as more than just a mode to explore the catastrophic; they also have commanded it as a vehicle for social critique in addition to, concomitantly, imagining radical renewal and queer futures. After all, *apocalypses*—a term derived from the Greek word meaning "to reveal" or "to uncover"—not only incite destruction but also unveil social truths, catalyzing the possibility for new beginnings. Religious apocalyptic texts have also historically been penned by the disenfranchised and subjugated seeking to critique and end dominant regimes of power. It is these revelatory and visionary features of the genre that this emergent queer Latinx apocalyptic imagination mobilizes. This queer Latinx apocalyptic imagination is particularly suited to theater given that theater and performance offer a collective space in which to uncurtain social oppression and imagine and enact other possible presents and futures.

The play *blu*, winner of the Yale Drama Series Prize, exemplifies and explores the apocalyptic realities of queers of color and Latinxs, focalizing the affective, *felt* experience of the disastrous. While the play has only been produced a handful of times, including at the Ensemble Theater at CalArts School of Theater (2008), Cara Mía Theater Company in Dallas (2015), Company of Angels at the Alexandria in Los Angeles (2011), the Guadalupe Theater in San Antonio (2013), and Aaron Davis Hall in New York (2016), Grise has performed readings at various universities, social justice–oriented academic conferences, and cultural arts centers. The play is also increasingly taught in high school and university classrooms across the United States; in fact, in 2014, Donna High School theater director Victor Santos in the Río Grande Valley elected to have his students perform scenes from *blu* for the State National One-Act Play University Interscholastic League (UIL) competition. Inspired by Grise's own lived experience living and teaching on the Southside of San Antonio, Texas, as well as in Boyle Heights in East Los Angeles in the early 2000s, *blu* renders an intimate and harrowing portrayal of a queer Chicana/o/x familia surviving in the present-day barrio. While *blu* focuses on a queer familia, it importantly situates jotería or Chicanx queers within a web of complex relations that include heterosexual, cis-gender Chicana/os, within both the family and the present-day barrio community. As such, Grise enacts a clarion call to acknowledge how our futures are collective and intimately entwined.

Zeroing in on the daily lived experience of what Raúl Homero Villa calls *barrioization, blu* brings to center stage how external forces such as policing and surveillance, city zoning policies, and eminent domain delimit and constrain the lifeworlds of its denizens.[2] Framed through barrioization, the apocalyptic event is no longer singular, painted in broad strokes of history—nor is it even purely Western. Instead, it microscopes the granular affective experience of structural oppression and fuses Western and non-Western eschatologies, including those of the Aztecs. And while claustrophobia is a hallmark of the horror and apocalyptic genres, claustrophobia in *blu* is inflected by social difference and the focus of barrioization. *Blu* recasts the felt experience of barrioization as nothing less than apocalyptic, showing how Soledad, a mother and factory worker; her wife, Hailstorm; Soledad's incarcerated ex-husband, Eme; and their biological children, Gemini and her two brothers, Luna and Blu, navigate forces of social and real death. These forces include mass incarceration, homophobia, labor exploitation, domestic abuse and rape, gang violence, the military industrial complex, and a subpar public education system buttressing a school-to-prison pipeline. Structural inequality at every moment *feels* cataclysmic, inhering and inescapable.

The dreamlike, lyrical composition of *blu* dramatizes this "intimate terrorism," to borrow from Gloria Anzaldúa,[3] evoking a Greek tragedy, whereby the play puts to work the affective register of tragedy and elevates the plight of the characters. *Blu* concurrently elicits the theatre of the absurd through its claustrophobic ambiance and attendant leitmotif of immobility. Opening in medias res in a discombobulating way, the play reveals a constellation of shared memories of Soledad, Hailstorm, and Eme that map flashpoints of Soledad's life. These luminous bursts of memory—whose imagery is echoed in the characters' very names—relay the stasis in which the characters are effectively stuck. In one telling memory, when asked where she is going, Soledad pointedly answers, "Nowheres."[4] Soledad, like other Chicanas in the play, is horrifically immobilized in a choke hold of the interlocking grids of state-sanctioned racial violence as it overlays with gendered and sexualized colonial imaginaries, ensnaring Chicanas in binaries of virgin and whore.

The play's *time-out-of-joint* plot departs from the tight cause-and-effect plot structure of the typical or popular cultural apocalyptic narrative. Historically, white writers like Stephen King have temporally distinguished between terror and horror, with the former designating anticipation of the monstrous or horrific and the latter the actual encountering of the monstrous or horrific. However, as the contours of terror and horror in *blu* congeal into the mundane, they morph and assume different significations. The frenetic anticipation found in the dominant apocalyptic genre dissipates into one of being nearly numb, inured to state-sponsored terrorism.

Domestic abuse and rape, which US Latinas experience at high rates, figure prominently in *blu*. The middle of the play, moreover, unveils how Soledad was physically abused by Eme and that Soledad's mother was also physically abused by her father, highlighting intergenerational cycles of violence propelled through crushing systemic oppression. Recalling how her dad beat her mother, Soledad, using a grammar of the world ending, recollects how her father would "beat the shit out" out of her mother, making her feel as though "*the whole world stopped*, stopped spinning."[5] As well, a series of shared memories toward the end of *blu* recollect how Gemini is gang raped while her older brother Blu silently witnesses. Echoing the dismemberment of the Aztec goddess Coyolxauhqui, who was brutalized by her own brother Huizilopotchli, Gemini's speech becomes increasingly fragmented, staccato, as she remembers her assault: "closed my eyes. sky black. My body outside this body circling. Watched them. Group of homies. Move closer . . ."[6] Rape is articulated through the register of the apocalyptic as ominous imagery of a black sky elicits terrifying celestial imagery from the Book of Revelation, as well as that in Aztec eschatology. Subsequently, Gemini remembers how Blu had just "stood there, starin at me," giving insight into Gemini's multilayered trauma, as well as how the imaginary and spectral materializes into the horrifically real and apocalyptic.[7]

The barrio and the world itself feel as though they are slowly creeping and closing in on the characters, disremembering them, cutting them off from each other and their memories, the community and the land—and, in doing so, futurity itself. As if fleeing from spatial suffocation of barrioization, Gemini and her brother Lunatico often sit atop their house to peer into the sky ablaze in red and neon pink. Here they strive to gaze and imagine beyond the horizon. But even on the roof they are not safe. Like the flying beasts of Revelation, helicopters are omnipresent, what Eme refers to as "metal birds in the barrio" hovering above, signaling ceaseless surveillance.[8] Metal birds also recall the death of the titular character, Blu, who personifies Huitzilopochtli, the god of war who was represented in

Aztec art as a hummingbird or eagle. As the play's conclusion reveals, Blu perishes in a helicopter in the Iraq War, his death giving notice to how poor and working-class Chicana/o/xs and people of color exist as a captive population for targeted military recruitment, perishing at disproportionate rates to whites.

Blu additionally excavates how policing and prison industrial complexes intersect with the educational industrial complex in the catastrophic lockdown of brown men and people of color. Toward the middle of the play, Eme, Blu, and Lunantico share a memory wherein Lunatico is arrested at school and cuffed in front of his classmates for carrying a blue marker, which is apparently deemed contraband. As Lunatico sits cuffed in the back of the cop's car, Blu and Lunatico repeat together "I can't move," enunciating their indignation and rage at the prison industrial complex, their literal and figurative inability to do or say anything. Though the play was written and published before the horrific death of Eric Garner, who was murdered by a police officer who held him in a prohibited chokehold in 2014, "it's hard to breathe" and "i can't move" emerge as refrains that reverberate in and haunt *blu*. Within our own present milieu, this uncanny resonance amplifies anti-Blackness inherent in institutional racism and structural inequality in the United States and serves as a powerful reminder of how Black and brown identities and struggles are interlinked. It is no coincidence that Afro-pessimist Frank Wilderson describes anti-Blackness as a claustrophobic structural cartography offering no "way out" other than the apocalyptic destruction of the epistemological categories currently structuring human relations.[9] Like the piercing school bell marking the end of class, this shared memory provocatively concludes with the slamming of prison doors. Soledad's last lines in this memory—"i can't believe this is still happening"—signals how Latina/o/xs are trapped and immobilized by histories of catastrophic racial violence that continue to constrain the presents and futures of US people of color.[10] In this way, *blu* foregrounds the urgent need to collectively reckon with and dismantle structural inequality.

The denouement continues to perform systemic critique through its use of allegory and non-Western cosmologies. In a memory following her rape, Gemini pronounces that "hummingbirds are not meant to fly with helicopters" and that her brother Blu "carries [her] head in his hand. Has to let go of the hair by the roots."[11] While the hummingbird god Huizilopotchli, embodied by Blu, is associated with war, femicide, and toxic masculinity, his figure is also significant in Aztec and the Nahua peoples' eschatological beliefs. Gemini's prophetic words thus articulate social critique through a culturally particular vocabulary of the apocalyptic that powerfully refuses her own destruction and, by extension, that of all Chicanas and Latinas. Gemini, in other words, enacts the uprooting and ultimate obliteration of heteropatriarchy and neocolonial state-sanctioned violence.

Yet this queer and Chicana-centered apocalypse does not merely perpetuate violence in its upending of structural inequality and centering of radical critique. "Radical," as Angela Davis famously clarified, "simply means 'grasping things at the root.'" *Blu*'s apocalyptic vision is not simply divisive and destructive, but rather collective and regenerative through the creation of new, more liberatory apocalyptic mythologies, ones that provide for the "second coming" of its Chicana/o/x characters and community. Gemini further states, "i'm rewriting the myth . . . this time i do not die . . . gonna resurrect me,"[12] thereby decentering the singular patriarchal white-savior figure, and performs a collective resurrection of Chicanas and Chicanxs through reimagining the figure of Coyolxahqui. This collectivity is reinforced in the subsequent last shared memory where la familia constructs a Mexican altar—a sacred site for collective remembering and healing.

The play *blu*, which is representative of a larger and emergent queer Latinx apocalyptic imagination, refurbishes the apocalyptic to reveal the catastrophic affective realities of Chicanxs, as well as queer people and people of color, and how those lived experiences are incessantly shaped by neocolonial state violence. By tapping into the register of the affective, this provocative play shifts current conversations around structural inequality from the empirical, objective, and abstract to the felt, intimate, and visceral. This vital dramaturgical maneuver recenters and localizes knowledge and authority within the brown and queer body, momentarily muting and holding in abeyance heteronormativity and white fragility. Put simply, *blu* moves the audience to feel, to respond, to become responsible for ourselves and our perceived others; it incites compassion.

Latinx theater and performance holds the potential to intervene in concrete ways within the majoritarian public sphere by theatricalizing the affective realities of Latinxs, as José Esteban Muñoz underscores.[13] Extending upon this sentiment, Grise remarked during the Chicana Teatristas, Past and Present Symposium at Trinity University in the spring of 2019: "I believe that art lives in the unknown, in the questioning, in the imagining of the impossible, and the creating the conditions for the impossible to exist. As an artist, I want to create ambitious work that is transformative, that demands that we listen to our dreams, that we listen to ourselves and to each other, that incites movement. I want to make work that sets our people free." For Grise, performance is intimately tethered to the real and engenders a space of communal imagining. To that end, *blu* makes room for envisioning and enacting new, decolonial beginnings, concrete acts of social transformation and liberatory politics. This play, in tandem with an emerging queer Latinx speculative genre, pushes us to see and feel beyond the here and now and toward what the play's epigraph describes as "that place where the horizon meets the earth."[14]

Notes

1. Anzaldúa, *Borderlands/La frontera.*
2. Villa, *Barrio-Logos*, 4.
3. Anzaldúa, *Borderlands/La frontera.*
4. Grise, *blu*, 6.
5. Grise, *blu*, 32; emphasis added.
6. Grise, *blu*, 51.
7. Grise, *blu*, 52.
8. Grise, *blu*, 32.
9. Wilderson, "Blacks and the Master/Slave Relation," 30.
10. Grise, *blu*, 26.
11. Grise, *blu*, 56.
12. Grise, *blu*, 56.
13. Muñoz, "Feeling Brown."
14. Grise, *blu*, epigraph.

Bibliography

Anzaldúa, Gloria. *Borderlands/La frontera: The New Mestiza.* San Francisco: Aunt Lute Books, 2012.

Grise, Virginia. *blu*. New Haven, CT: Yale University Press, 2011.

Muñoz, José Esteban. "Feeling Brown: Ethnicity and Affect in Ricardo Bracho's *The Sweetest Hangover*." *Theatre Journal* 52, no. 1 (2000): 151–180.

Renck, Johan, director. *The Walking Dead*. Season 1, episode 4, "Vatos." Aired November 21, 2010, on AMC.

Villa, Raúl. *Barrio-Logos: Space and Place in Urban Chicano Literature and Culture*. Austin: University of Texas Press, 2000.

Wilderson, Frank. "Blacks and the Master/Slave Relation." In *Afro-Pessimism: An Introduction*, edited by Racked & Dispatched, 15–30. Minneapolis: Racked & Dispatched, 2017.

18 Claire Coleman, *Terra Nullius* (2017) / Aboriginal SF's Realities of the Imaginary

Allanah Hunt

On June 6, 2020, an estimated twenty thousand protestors marched in Brisbane, Australia, proclaiming support for Black Lives Matter.[1] The demonstration responded to the murders of George Floyd (a Black man killed in Minnesota in 2020) and David Dungay (a Dunghutti Aboriginal man killed in Sydney in 2015) by law enforcement, but it was also for all the Aboriginal people killed behind bars, while being arrested, or even shot in their own homes. In Australia, where Aboriginal people are referred to and identify as Black, the American-founded but now global Black Lives Matter movement has felt all too familiar and necessary. Not one policeman has been convicted in relation to these crimes in Australia. Chris Hurley became the first policeman to ever be charged over an Aboriginal death in custody, for the killing of Cameron Doomadgee, but was only charged with manslaughter.[2] Doomadgee died on the cell floor, his liver nearly cleaved in half; Hurley was subsequently acquitted by an all-white jury. In 2019, Zachary Rolfe became the first police officer ever charged with murder over the shooting of a nineteen-year-old Aboriginal man, Kumunjayi Walker.[3] It remains to be seen what happens in the future.

Aboriginal deaths in custody have risen 150 percent since the 1987 Royal Commission.[4] In the eight years between 2000 and 2007, 701 Aboriginal people died in custody, whereas roughly the same number died in similar conditions over the twenty years between 1980 to 2000. Today, Aboriginal people make up 28 percent of the prison population and 50 percent of the youth detention population, despite comprising only 3 percent of Australia's population.[5] With facts like these, it is hard not to worry about the future—especially for those of us with Black bodies. What percentages of my people will end up in prison in the future? Will I have to coach my future children to avoid policemen at all costs? This is a future I hope won't come to pass as Black voices are heard, as people learn from the present, think about the past, and reimagine the future.

Black Australia's past and present is captured in stories that need to be listened to. Our literature thinks of the future, too. One novel that does this exceptionally well is *Terra Nullius* (2017) by Noongar person Claire G. Coleman. The winning manuscript of the 2016 black&write! awards, *Terra Nullius* is a novel that appears to be realistically set in the early 1900s, when Aboriginal peoples were enslaved, their children were stolen, and they were considered by European settlers as flora and fauna. The character groups in Coleman's novel are only ever referred to as the Settlers and the Natives—which also seems historically truthful—but you get that feeling something is being withheld.

Despite its veneer of historical-fictional realism, the novel reveals itself halfway through to be full-on science fiction, and in the process it highlights the science-fictionality of the colonial apocalypse, of Indigenous-settler encounters. The Settlers, we learn, are actually an invading amphibious alien race colonizing the Natives of Earth to expand their empire. All throughout, Coleman weaves together with precision the similarities of this future alien colonization to the historical colonization of Australia by white settlers, from the massacres of the eighteenth and nineteenth centuries to the Stolen Generation of the twentieth, blurring the lines of past, present, and future.

Aboriginal Stories

Aboriginal literature often combats prejudiced views and shows Aboriginal cultures through their own lens rather than a Western one. These can often be hard stories to read because of the trauma depicted. They can be even harder stories to tell.

In the past, Aboriginal literature has often taken the form of literary and realist fiction, as well as memoirs. Memorable, astounding examples include *Steam Pigs* by Melissa Lucashenko (1997) and *Follow the Rabbit-Proof Fence* by Doris Pilkington-Garimara (1996). These stories are all the more powerful because Black voices have been muted in the past, as white Australia made up its own racist narratives on what it is to be Aboriginal. We have a lot of time to make up for, a lot of stories to tell, of the generations of genocide and injustice committed against diverse Aboriginal and Torres Strait Islander peoples. Unfortunately, the continued mistreatment of Indigenous people is still very much present in modern-day Australia, as evidenced by the Black Lives Matter movement and the Intervention, a modern-day Stolen Generation taking place at this very moment.

Terra Nullius adds to a growing chorus of Aboriginal and Torres Strait Islander writers, telling a story that is unfortunately very familiar: about brutal frontier wars, stolen children, abuse, and slavery, all under the guise of the best of intentions. However, *Terra Nullius* puts a twist on this narrative with its incorporation of science fiction. Aboriginal stories often use realist modes to share their understanding of the world with others, arguably because the stories being told *are* real. However, Aboriginal stories have started to use popular genres and culture as well to share their understanding of the world with a broader audience. This change in the use of genres by Aboriginal writers is significant for three reasons: First, Aboriginal genre stories reach a wider audience rather than an esoteric one. Second, they can create an emotional safety net in which someone can read and write about these stories if the other modes are too mentally taxing. And third, genre helps remove the danger of overrepresenting diverse historical experiences through a single type of story, as discussed by Chimamanda Adichie in her famous TED Talk.[6]

Aboriginal literature expanding into different genres helps speak to the variety of experiences and interests of Aboriginal peoples. As Ambelin Kwaymullina, an Aboriginal fantasy author, points out, there is no one experience of Aboriginality.[7] Coleman adds to this growing variety of storytelling in Australian Black literature, creating a novel that blurs both timelines and the distinction between real and unreal, possible and impossible. *Terra Nullius* is arguably about creating empathy and understanding, asking and answering the question, "How terrible would it be to experience this sort of invasion today?" and, potentially, "What did it feel like for our ancestors to experience the invasion when it first happened?" It feels surreal and impossible when reading the horror depicted in these pages. However, at the same time, it reminds the Aboriginal reader that this is an invasion we have already experienced and continue to feel the aftershocks of. It's a strong message, cleverly interwoven into a quintessential science fiction narrative, complete with plasma guns and invading alien races. But the genre conventions never detract from Coleman's message. Instead, the juxtapositions between this futuristic invasion and the past, actual one are striking.

What makes the futuristic setting all the more harrowing is the realization that colonial atrocities aren't so far in the past, nor is it an unrealistic thought experiment for the future. With the current climate of Interventions, where children continue to be taken from Aboriginal families, producing a modern "ongoing" Stolen Generation, *Terra Nullius* shows that this is still a reality for many Aboriginal families.[8] Bringing into factor the disproportionate rates of state violence still happening with Aboriginal deaths in police custody and incarceration, *Terra Nullius* starts to look less and less like science fiction, even as its science-fictionality is masked by its nod to this history. Because the fact of the matter is that this novel takes all of the horrors depicted in its pages from real-life experience, from the past—and after a while, you realize that some details come from the present too. Hopefully, they won't continue in the future. While movies have often depicted people looking at the skies, terrified of what is out there and the havoc alien races can wreak, *Terra Nullius* shows that, unfortunately, the Aboriginal nation doesn't have to look too far from home.

This blurring of fact and fiction is done exceptionally well in *Terra Nullius*. By way of example, consider two quotes. One, written by the Royal Commission in 1935, comes from the Moseley Report, infamous as the document that rationalized the systematic taking of Aboriginal children. The other quote is from *Terra Nullius*, taken from what the fictional Settlers have written about the Natives of this storyworld, the passages excerpted from Settler "papers" at the beginning of each chapter. Which is fact and which is fiction?

> The inmates of the compound are admitted for protection and education, and I found them living within a few hundred yards of a collection of useless, loafing natives.[9]
>
> Or:
>
> The only thing standing in our way, the main limitation to our growth is the depredations of the criminal, aggressive and intransigent natives.[10]

The two are uncannily similar. One is written seriously, the other a "fictional" example inspired by the actual treatment and attitude toward Aboriginal people in the past (reduplicated in this novel's future).

In Coleman's novel, the beginning of every chapter has a pretend "excerpt" from official Settler documents. When I first read the novel, these introductory passages felt so familiar to the racist documents I had read from Aboriginal history that I thought they were real. I believed Coleman had searched out quotes from the colonial administration and adapted them into fictional versions, to show the attitude that permeated (and still permeates) white Australia's imagination of Indigenous people. Though fiction, they are very much centered in the beliefs that rationalized the invasion and theft of Aboriginal land.

Coleman leaves no stone unturned when revealing the truth of Aboriginal treatment through this fictional setting. She heartbreakingly depicts the human children's treatment in alien missions where they are meant to have their souls saved by nuns. Coleman's Sister Bagra, for example, abuses the children in her care under the guise of religious zeal. If they so much as speak in their traditional language, she throws them in a tiny shack outside in the elements for two weeks as punishment. This kind of historical treatment was described to the letter in Moseley's report as well; while he hadn't liked that type of punishment, he praised the teachers and missionaries as doing a great social good by "training" the children.[11]

The documented history is so obviously, disgustingly racist that it is at times hard to believe the Moseley Report is anything but a fiction like *Terra Nullius*. Coleman's novel uses the same language, describing the aliens' view of oppressed human characters in her book as natives, savages that must be elevated: "Natives raising their own children to the primitive ways they lived before he [Devil] came was unacceptable." In one poignant moment, the character Devil (arguably a stand-in for A. O. Neville, the cruel chief protector in Western Australia in the early 1900s) is surrounded by letters from Black mothers, begging for their children back, as he stamps "Deny" on each one. He also receives a letter praising him for his wonderful work in taking the children away from their families to "educate" them; he feels proud that they would not have survived without him.[12]

What makes Coleman's novel so powerful is the story's juxtaposition with the reality of the situation for Aboriginal readers and those familiar with Australia's settler-colonial past. The story flashes to Jacky, one of the main characters, who has suffered greatly since being ripped away from his family. At the beginning of the novel, Jacky runs away after being severely beaten by the Settlers. The young man dreams of being reunited with his mother, but he never gets the reunion his heart bleeds for. At the end, he is murdered by the Troopers, along with a camp of "Natives" and one of the Settlers who had turned to the Natives' side, Johnny Star. The final words about their deaths together don't concentrate on how different they are, but instead on what a beautiful and powerful thing it was when they joined together, fighting for equality: "Among them, so scattered with the bones of Jacky Jerramungup it would have been impossible to separate them completely, lay the bones of Johnny Star."[13]

The reality of the situation, as opposed to the fictional good the Settlers dream up in their heads, is one of corruption, murder, and heartbreak. This is shown by the impact of those broken families on characters like Jacky, the true treatment of the stolen children by "saviors" like Sister Bagra, and the Troopers ruthlessly hunting down any runaway and partaking in a massacre. The Settlers killing a human infant in one of the attacks is one of the most gut-wrenching things to read, but again, it shows the truth of what is really happening, not the fantasy of "good intentions": "He saw a babe, taken from its screaming mother's arms, wailing as it was dashed against a rock with a sickening thud, its head spurting blood onto the stone, its still shuddering body cast onto the flames of its burning home."[14] This sort of violence seems so gratuitous that it must be false. Instead, Coleman describes with brutal accuracy what happened in the past. In Aileen Moreton-Robinson's iconic book *Talkin' Up to the White Woman*, she describes a scene very similar to this where babies were buried alive with just their heads above ground, then used as golf balls. With the recent stealing of children from the Intervention, a child in this true account describes how she is abused by her "carers" after being taken from her family.[15]

While *Terra Nullius* is meant to describe a science-fictional world, the scenes depict very realistic scenarios faced by Aboriginal peoples in their historical invasion. Science fiction is also meant to be a caution for the future. Let's hope that its message is heard loud and clear, that "good intentions" are often used as a cloak for more nefarious purposes. The Intervention, Aboriginal deaths in custody: we need to face the reality that these issues are not as much in the past as white Australia would like to believe. But the reality is that of pain: once again, Aboriginal people are the targets of a white supremacist, settler-colonial regime. We need to see past these layers, like with *Terra Nullius*, to the reality underneath.

Terra Nullius is a science fiction novel full of truths of Aboriginal past, present, and future. It educates, entertains, comforts, distresses, recycles, and creates. It is a paradoxical creation, with layers that give the reader a new appreciation on every read. It illuminates the past, makes the reader think in the present, and rewrites the future. Hopefully, it will be an inspiration for people to rewrite our own future, one that isn't another replica of the past for the Black Australia.

Notes

1. Moore, "'It Can't Just Be the Minority.'"

2. McCutcheon, "Qld Policeman Charged."

3. Anthony, "Kumunjayi Walker's Death Raises Questions"; Bamford, "Yuendumu Murder Charge Leaves Officers 'Feeling Unsupported.'"

4. Korff, "Royal Commission," 1.

5. SBS News, "Tens of Thousands of Protestors Have Attended Rallies."

6. TED, "Danger of a Single Story."

7. Kawymullina, "Telling the Real Story."

8. Gregoire, "Ongoing Stolen Generations."

9. Moseley, *Royal Commission*, 12.

10. Coleman, *Terra Nullius*, 55.

11. Moseley, *Royal Commission*, 13.

12. Coleman, *Terra Nullius*, 23.

13. Coleman, *Terra Nullius*, 286.

14. Coleman, *Terra Nullius*, 59.

15. Davidson, "Child Protection Cases More than Doubled."

Bibliography

Anthony, Thalia. "Kumunjayi Walker's Death Raises Questions about Policing in Aboriginal Homes." Australian Broadcasting Channel, last updated November 14, 2019. https://www.abc.net.au/news/2019-11-14/kumunjayi-walker-raises-questions-policing-aboriginal-homes/11702332.

Bamford, Matt. "Yuendumu Murder Charge Leaves Officers 'Feeling Unsupported,' Ex-Commissioner Says." Australian Broadcasting Channel, December 2, 2019. https://www.abc.net.au/news/2019-12-03/former-police-commissioner-says-police-feel-unsupported-yuendumu/11734478.

Coleman, Claire G. *Terra Nullius*. Sydney: Hachette Australia, 2017.

Davidson, Helen. "Child Protection Cases More than Doubled after NT Intervention, Inquiry Told." *Guardian*, June 19, 2017, https://www.theguardian.com/australia-news/2017/jun/19/child-protection-cases-more-than-doubled-after-nt-intervention-inquiry-told.

Gregoire, Paul. "The Ongoing Stolen Generations: An Interview with Grandmothers Against Removals." Sydney Criminal Lawyers, March 2, 2018. https://www.sydneycriminallawyers.com.au/blog/the-ongoing-stolen-generations-an-interview-with-grandmothers-against-removals/.

Korff, Jens. "Royal Commission into Aboriginal Deaths in Custody." Creative Spirits, last updated July 13, 2021. http://www.creativespirits.info/aboriginalculture/law/royal-commission-into-aboriginal-deaths-in-custody.

Kwaymullina, Ambelin. "Telling the Real Story: Diversity in Young Adult Literature." *The Conversation*, August 27, 2015. https://theconversation.com/telling-the-real-story-diversity-in-young-adult-literature-46268.

Lucashenko, Melissa. *Steam Pigs*. Brisbane: University of Queensland Press, 1997.

McCutcheon, P. "Qld Policeman Charged over Death in Custody." Australian Broadcasting Channel, last updated January 27, 2007. http://www.abc.net.au/7.30/content/2007/s1834538.htm.

Moore, Tony. "'It Can't Just Be the Minority': Thousands Raise Their Voices in Brisbane." *Brisbane Times*, June 7, 2020. https://www.brisbanetimes.com.au/politics/queensland/it-can-t-just-be-the-minority-thousands-raise-their-voices-in-brisbane-20200606-p5505u.html.

Moreton-Robinson, Aileen. *Talkin' Up to the White Woman: Indigenous Women and Feminism*. Brisbane: University of Queensland Press, 2000.

Moseley, H. D. *Royal Commission Appointed to Investigate, Report and Advise upon Matters in Relation to the Condition and Treatment of Aborigines*. Perth: Parliament of Western Australia, 1935. http://www.parliament.wa.gov.au/intranet/libpages.nsf/WebFiles/Royal+Commissions+-+Royal+Commission+Appointed+to+Investigate,+Report+and+Advise+Upon+Matters+in+Relation+to+the+Condition+and+Treatment+of+Aborigines/$FILE/Royal+Commission+Appointed+to+Investigate,+Report+and+Advise+Upon+Matters+in+Relation+to+the+Condition+and+Treatment+of+Aborigines.pdf.

Pilkington-Garimara, Doris. *Follow the Rabbit-Proof Fence*. Brisbane: University of Queensland Press, 1996.

SBS News. "Tens of Thousands of Protesters Have Attended Rallies across Australia in Some of the Largest Ever Demonstrations against Racism in the Country." SBS News, June 6, 2020. https://www.sbs.com.au/news/tens-of-thousands-call-for-end-to-violence-against-indigenous-people-at-black-lives-matter-protests-across-australia.

TED. "Chimamanda Ngozi Adichie: The Danger of a Single Story." YouTube video, October 7, 2009. https://www.youtube.com/watch?v=D9Ihs241zeg.

19 Liu Cixin (2000) and Frant Gwo (2019), *The Wandering Earth* / Deimperializing Empire

Nathaniel Isaacson

In this essay, I examine Liu Cixin's *The Wandering Earth* as a constellation of texts—a novella, a film, and the various discourses of fans and reviewers in the United States and China. In the novella, humankind learns that the earth is on the verge of being incinerated by our sun as it turns into a red giant sooner than expected. A globalized government decides to turn the planet into an interstellar spaceship driven by mountainous rock-burning plasma engines. Spaceship Earth then plots a course to our nearest star, Proxima Centauri. Half of the planet's population is left to die, while the other half is moved into underground cities, where these people will spend the next two-and-a-half millennia bound for a new solar system. The mission is nearly waylaid when the narrator's wife, Kayoko, joins a revolutionary junta that mistrusts the wisdom of the mission, but the revolution is put down and the technocrats are proven correct. This episode arguably allegorizes the Great Proletarian Cultural Revolution (1966–1976) and the ensuing era of one-party rule. A familiar theme—the errors of Maoism, and the comparative stability and prosperity of the present—lurks beneath the cloaking shield of the space opera genre.

Among some smaller alterations, the film differs from the novella in one key plot point, forgoing Kayoko's episode of revolutionary resistance, instead centering the core climactic action around the Earth getting drawn into the orbit of Jupiter so as to be nearly destroyed. Through some clever engineering, and a series of heroic sacrifices, the disaster is averted. Both the film and the book arguably fetishize China's achievements as an engineering state, lavishing attention on the "earth engines" as aesthetic objects.

The promotional poster shown in figure 19.1 crystallizes this fetishization of development, technology, and transportation. The top third of the

Figure 19.1
Promotional poster for Frant Gwo's *The Wandering Earth.*

poster is dominated by one of the massive Earth Engines used to propel the planet to Proxima Centauri. At bottom left sits the skyline of Shanghai's Pudong district, recognizable by the Shanghai Oriental Pearl tower, just in front of the second-tallest building in the world, the Shanghai Tower, and the Shanghai World Financial Center to its right. Between the towers and the earth engines, a massive rail system traverses the skies above the towers of the Pudong district. From bottom to top, the image presents historical progress as increasingly more massive developmental projects.

The film was well-received in China but fizzled in the international box office outside of the PRC. US audiences could see the film on Netflix shortly after its abbreviated run in theaters. I find *The Wandering Earth* and its reception to be problematic for a number of reasons. The story itself is troubling because both film and novella aestheticize fossil fuel consumption and development, masking burning the planet as a utilitarian solution to save humanity. Ahead, I share my consternation that *The Wandering Earth* fits into a long history of social Darwinism in Chinese literature. Beyond the question of evolution, I find it fascinating that Liu, hailed for his originality, actually deals in a very familiar set of tropes. Finally, I examine the troubling notion that a text that purports to be about utilitarian solutions for the human species is read in so consistently nationalistic, and Darwinistic, terms. In both the United States and China, popular discussion of the film fell into precisely the trap the film purports to offer solutions to: understanding a film about global cooperation in terms of national antagonisms.

Ying Zhu, writing for cultural website China File, summarizes the problematic ideological underpinnings of the plot: "Setting aside the question of whether a lifetime's slaving underground for the remote prospect of a new start for surface-dwelling humanity 2,500 years in the future is worth living for, the story of *The Wandering Earth* operates on the unchallenged premise that half the world's population is readily expendable for humankind to survive, leaving no time to explore the enormous moral implications of who gets to survive as the film hurries to get to the action and a happy ending."[1] The collective human effort at the heart of both versions of *The Wandering Earth* evades this dismal end, assigning responsibility for one holocaust to the impartiality of a lottery, while the opportunity to escape from a later natural disaster is apportioned based on age and the presumed number of prospective years the victims have remaining. *The Wandering*

Earth offers little consideration of the moral implications of these "cold equations"; half of humanity dies (no mention of other ecosystems), and we simply burn our way out of a planetary crisis. Both the plot and the circulation of the text in different media fit within a long-standing discourse of Chinese Darwinism.

Darwinian thinking was introduced to China as social Darwinism, a strain of thinking that saw strong expression in early Chinese SF and in Chinese utopian thinking at the turn of the twentieth century—and one that continues well into the twenty-first century. Yan Fu's translation of Thomas Henry Huxley's 1894 *Evolution and Ethics* was intended to spur national strength and competitiveness, deliberately emphasizing social Darwinism. Visions of social struggle permeated early Chinese science fiction, and social Darwinist strains reverberate across modern Chinese literature at large. In *Visions of Dystopia in China's New Historical Novels*, Jeffrey Kinkley argues that literary luminary Lu Xun "believed in progress, Darwin, and progressive modernity coming to the world."[2] Kinkley links China's turn-of-the-century reformist adoption of Darwinist thought to mid-century Maoism, which Frederic Wakeman Jr. argues "was just another variation of Social Darwinism: if not a teleology, then at least a scientific theodicy."[3] However, Kinkley concludes that in the contemporary context, Darwinian struggle is perceived in Chinese intellectual discourse as far from teleological, even evoking a sense of devolutionary regression by which "biology summons up images not of progress, but of secular and recurring decline, even regression."[4] While the motif of Earth as a planetary spaceship powered by massive plasma rockets is wholly unprecedented in Chinese literature, the ideological underpinnings of a spaceship ruled by revolution-canceling technocrats who in their "superior" judgement rid the ship of half its residents represent a long-standing and troubling adoption of Darwinian theory.

Beyond the Darwinian legacy, Liu's thematic canonicity can be seen in fan-generated content, which reveals the extent to which Liu Cixin's cosmic operas represent socialist-realist heroes who have traded in their Mao jackets for spacesuits. Fan-generated films using found footage, such as the found-footage version of Liu's *Xiangcun jiaoshi* (*The Village Schoolteacher*) and other shorts produced by fan-vlogger "Wenyue xiaoqiang," speak to the ways in which Liu Cixin's writing, even when adapted into different media, stands with one foot in China's canonical narratives of historical struggle and the other in global science fiction. In the short story of the same title, a group of rural schoolchildren save the earth from destruction by a silicon-based space federation because the children have memorized Newton's laws of motion. The online fan film splices film and television clips from earlier film and televisual texts such as Ah Cheng's *Haizi wang* (*King of the Children*, 1986; film: Chen Kaige, 1987), Yu Hua's *Huozhe* (*To Live*, 1993; film: Zhang Yimou, 1994), CCP hagiography *Jiandang weiye* (*The Founding of a Party*; film: Huang Jianxin, 2011), and finally, the eponymous biopic-miniseries *Jiao Yulu* (Li Wenqi, 2012), a Mao-era party devotee who died of cancer while struggling to ameliorate backward conditions in Henan's rural Lankao County. Memories of the traumas of the twentieth century—poverty, the suffering of women, and parochialism—comprise the principal struggle in the postsocialist historiography of educational and political movements, and the terrestrial half of Liu's original story "The Village Schoolteacher." CGI blockbusters and video games serve as the source materials for the portion of the plot set in outer space orbit above Earth. The visual repertoire of Hollywood space odysseys and battles, from films like *Apollo 13* and *Arrival* and from the Star Wars, Star Trek, and StarCraft franchises (the latter a video game series), serve as a new bottle for the old wine of a dialectic of enlightenment and parochialism.

Online and media critics' discussion of *The Wandering Earth* regularly focused on what the film as a *produced artifact* meant for China: not its thematic content, but its status as a CGI-driven blockbuster. These exchanges and related reviews hail *The Wandering Earth*'s release as marking "Year One" for Chinese SF film. Here, China's "new" mastery of the apparatus of cinematic production and distribution is taken as a sign of national might. This discourse focuses attention on the nation's achievement of a certain commercial brand of special effects and film spectacle, when in fact China had long since arrived as a global film player, in terms of both its audience market share and its ownership of production and distribution venues through the media-making efforts of corporations like Huayi and Wanda. These analyses often focus on *The Wandering Earth* in terms of PRC's cinema history, reading the film as indicative of national economic development rather than any transnational cross-cultural symbolic impact. While some critics have identified this discourse as a marketing ploy, acknowledging that Chinese SF film had already existed in territories like Hong Kong, in experimental films like Huang Jianxin's *Dislocation* (*Cuowei*, 1986), and in fan-produced work, this discourse generally ignored how fully imbricated in one another contemporary Sino-American film production and distribution are.

Online criticism and fan engagement with director Frant Gwo's 2019 Chinese film adaption of Liu Cixin's novella *The Wandering Earth*, both in the PRC and in the United States, is symptomatic of a broader trend in popular reception of Chinese science fiction that associates the rise of Chinese SF with the increasingly central role of China in global politics and economy and that recapitulates the discourse of Chinese national literatures as sites of social Darwinian struggle. This discourse hails China's technological and scientific prowess as the product of a Darwinian evolutionary process, while at the same time ignoring the prior existence of Chinese SF and SF cinema. Searching for evidence of China's might in the screen image and seized by a desire to label the film's release as Year One for Chinese SF cinema, fans and critics of the film in both the United States and China ignore a broader, less visible, cultural politics of Chinese literary SF and its adaptation into cinematic production.

Public debates regarding the quality of the 2019 Chinese feature film allowed for some criticism of how *The Wandering Earth* underscores the wisdom of the ruling technocratic party, which in the novella had appeared in the form of rioting masses unable to trust the scientific class—masses who in the film version have been removed entirely. One online critic posting under the pseudonym "fool's words" (yuyan, a homonym for both "fable" and "prophecy"), identifies two main categories of fans of the film, both of which recapitulate a social Darwinian view of international relations and cinematic production. This scathing critique of the film's nationalist content and reception was translated into English by online forum Chuangcn.org, a website dedicated to "analyzing the ongoing development of capitalism in China, its historical roots, and the revolts of those crushed beneath it." On the one hand, explains Yuyan, "young cyber-nationalists [xiao fenhong] are 20-somethings with a relatively low level of education, sitting somewhere in the lower rungs of the urban middle class. They believe that hostile forces from overseas are either the root of all evil in Chinese society, or at least are the main obstacles to be overcome, and they therefore think highly of China's rapid rise in military power and its hard diplomacy." The translators of Yuyan's analyses render the other group as Prometheans [gongye dang], "people in their thirties and forties who tend to have a higher level of education and compose the upper rungs of the urban middle class. They hope that China's industrial level can quickly surpass that of the West, and they revere the idea of a small intellectual elite ruling a country . . . It is, then, very easy for them to take pleasure in the fictional scenes of extreme cruelty in Liu Cixin's writing, because, in their opinion, such scenes of cruelty are simply a reflection of the dog-eat-dog reality of the world (domestically and internationally)." Yuyan concludes that "ultimately, both sides are volunteer propagandists for the state, deeply driven by the emotive power of narrow nationalism and a spirit of exceptionalism."[5]

Sometime in September of 2019, the Chinese-language version of the post was removed from its original location, Douban.com, leaving only a 404 Not Found error message in its place. However, this was not before the translations into English for Chuang.cn had been completed, and the post has indeed appeared on Zhihu and Douban—two other major platforms available in China. The critique has not been erased; internet censors merely papered over the debate when it got too hot on one particular platform. Meanwhile, the English-language translation plays into Western Orientalist notions of a totalitarian Chinese internet where dissent is eradicated. While Liu Cixin's story is one of collective human effort, viewers in both China and the United States interpreted the story and its reception in familiar terms as one of the "rise" of an oppressive Chinese nation-state.

On the US side, this is most prominent in the case of five US Republican senators who penned a letter to Netflix condemning Liu's support for CCP policy in Xinjiang. In September of 2020, when Netflix announced plans to adopt Liu Cixin's Three-Body Trilogy, I was surprised at the congressional outcry surrounding his comments about Uyghurs made in a June 2019 interview with Jiaying Fan for *The New Yorker*. A group of Republican senators penned a letter for the preemptive cancellation of the production, citing commentary Liu had made in support of Uyghur reeducation camps in China's Xinjiang Autonomous Region. My own naivete led me to be surprised by the irony that the signatories of the letter are among the most prominent critics of "cancel culture," which did not stop them from signing. While various fan groups criticized Hollywood's 2020 live-action remake of *Mulan* both on the grounds of Disney creating a bad adaptation *and* due to Disney thanking local officials in Xinjiang (where Muslim

Uighurs are said to be held in detention camps), to my knowledge Liu Cixin is one of very few Chinese media figures who have ascended to the level of congressional attention. The senators turned a glib comment from the author into a cause célèbre, but they clearly hadn't read Liu Cixin's work. The second book in the Three-Body Trilogy is titled *The Dark Forest*, a nod to a theory shared in the novel by a "cosmic sociologist" that the universe is a such a Hobbesian place—nasty, brutish, and really, really big—that the best thing to do is pretend your civilization doesn't exist, lest you be wiped out by the next civilization over. The trilogy, like *The Wandering Earth*, masks imperialism as scientific principle. Civilizations exist by and large to destroy one another. There is little room for altruism, or even for the apex predator whose dominance stabilizes an ecosystem.

It is disappointing, but perhaps unsurprising, that work so thoroughly steeped in a Spencerian mode of thinking would be read in antagonistic terms. Anglophone critiques occasionally indulged in Orientalist clichés, like in the case of a *Financial Times* article on the transnational success of Chinese SF. The article, written by Yale professor of modern Chinese studies Jing Tsu, presents an even-handed account of how Chinese SF has succeeded on an international scale in recent years, thus presenting an analysis of its texts' *cultural* power—but the editorial staff chose to frame it in a much more sinister fashion in terms of these texts' *political* power, titling it, "Why Sci-Fi Could Be the Secret Weapon in China's Soft-Power Arsenal." In similar fashion, a *New York Times* profile of prolific Chinese SF translator Ken Liu ran with the headline, "How Chinese Sci Fi Conquered America," again evoking the specter of the Yellow Peril. Popular media foisted a vision of cultural production as a social-Darwinian pursuit upon these writers' examinations of fan cultures and cultural diplomacy.

In closing, I would like to consider how Henry Jenkins's critique of scholarly anxieties regarding US hegemony can help us understand the polemic surrounding *The Wandering Earth* and its relationship to the PRC. *The Wandering Earth* offers a vision of a future where national borders have been transcended, but this transcendence has been achieved by abandoning the imagined islands of the nation-state and forging a spaceship earth. Fan engagement and popular discourse, which tends to see Liu's work in such starkly national terms, seems to indicate what a challenge this will be. Jenkins bemoans academic anxieties over cultural imperialism, which anticipate the threat of homogenization brought about by the ubiquity of

US mass media, for academics' failure to distinguish various forms of power. This attitude "blurs the distinction between at least four forms of power: economic (the ability to produce and distribute cultural goods), cultural (the ability to produce and circulate forms and meanings), political (the ability to impose ideologies), and psychological (the ability to shape desire, fantasy, and identity)."[6] This blurring occurs in both English-language and Chinese-language forums where analyses of Liu Cixin–related texts are shared. As the PRC consciously wields these forms of power in service of its own global status, it both contends with and strategically deploys indistinctions between hard and soft power.

Notes

1. Ying Zhu, "Same Old 'China Story.'"
2. Kinkley, *Visions of Dystopia*, 179; see also Pusey, *China and Charles Darwin*, 241.
3. Kinkley, *Visions of Dystopia*, 180; Wakeman, *History and Will*, 236.
4. Kinkley, *Visions of Dystopia*, 180.
5. Chuang, "Wandering Earth."
6. Jenkins, *Fans, Bloggers, and Gamers*, 156.

Bibliography

Alter, Alexandra. "How Chinese Sci Fi Conquered America." *New York Times*, December 3, 2019. https://www.nytimes.com/2019/12/03/magazine/ken-liu-three-body-problem-chinese-science-fiction.html.

Chuang. "The Wandering Earth: A Reflection of the Chinese New Right." Chuangcn.org, August 30, 2019. http://chuangcn.org/2019/08/wandering-earth/.

Gwo, Frant. *The Wandering Earth*. China Film Group Corporation, 2019.

Jenkins, Henry. *Fans, Bloggers and Gamers: Exploring Participatory Culture*. New York: New York University Press, 2006.

Jing Tsu. "Why Sci-Fi Could Be the Secret Weapon in China's Soft-Power Arsenal." *Financial Times*, May 29, 2020. https://www.ft.com/content/85ff1488-82ec-11ea-b6e9-a94cffd1d9bf.

Kinkley, Jeffrey. *Visions of Dystopia in China's New Historical Novels*. New York: Columbia University Press, 2014.

Liu, Cixin. "The Wandering Earth." In *The Wandering Earth*, translated by Ken Liu, 1–48. London: Head of Zeus, 2017.

Pusey, James Reeve. *China and Charles Darwin*. Cambridge, MA: Council on East Asian Studies, Harvard University, 1983.

Wakeman, Frederic, Jr. *History and Will: Philosophical Perspectives of Mao Tse-tung's Thought*. Berkeley: University of California Press, 1973.

Zhu, Ying. "The Same Old 'China Story' Keeps Chinese Sci-Fi Earthbound." *ChinaFile*, September 30, 2019. https://www.chinafile.com/reporting-opinion/culture/same-old-china-story-keeps-chinese-sci-fi-earthbound.

Interlude

20 Science Fiction Studies 3.0: Re-networking Our Hive Mind

Ida Yoshinaga

This essay is dedicated to John Rieder, with thanks for his intellectual generosity and superhuman kindness. Mahalo also to the students of my LMC 3206 and 3215 courses at Georgia Tech in fall 2021 and spring 2022, for helping me get a fresh perspective on the genre.

New Timescapes and Dangerous Actions

Now is the time to talk of science fiction and ethos. Science fiction and community. As knowledgeable gatekeepers, as proud nerds, we have spoken with each other about SF's qualifying traits, subjects and submotifs, categorizing schema. But our own communities, variegated in their embodiment and orientation, their (hi)stories and languages, their urgent political economies of place, have required a focus on more than mere genre classification.

The "Western SF and everything else" model of the science fiction *form*—where the former serves as star and the global legion of the latter are accommodated as orbiting exceptions to Darko Suvin's definition of a "literature of cognitive estrangement"—is over.[1] No surprise here. With multiple worldwide crises riddling the planet, largely facilitated by the irresponsible—in fact, immoral—use of scientific knowledge in the service of the technocratic class's capitalist masters, we have been inquiring: Who has been historically estranged, and by whom? And whose limited definition of cognition has driven the rest of the world to ruin?

Because modern colonial/industrial science is not holistic, stories about it isolate the operation of cognition—separate from intuition, ancestral memory, corporeal wisdom, environmental connection—to dare solve deep dilemmas of spiritual balance without interrogating the systemic. Because modern science is short-term, not futuristic, stories about it deploy stylized, estranging escapism (*This is us, now/here, in the real world; That is they, then/*

there, in the speculative novum)—rather than intertwining lived/imaginative storytimes together, evolving readers into skilled agents that can transform social relations going forward. Because modern science is not ethical, violence in stories about it is encountered in exploitative spectatorship—not as urgent trans-generational lessons or responsible cultural fables for justice, true security, peace. But with public and open science and community-engaged research—global technocultural approaches that aim to serve the people—come diverse stories that potentially nourish multitudes.

And so we have been expressing, experimenting with, fresh science-fictionalities (SFnalities). Our own "new suns"—as Susana M. Morris and Kinitra D. Brooks, editors of the Ohio State University Press's brilliant line of monographs, phrased it when cannily naming their series. Our deep desires to "destroy science fiction!"—as *Lightspeed* (and, later, *Uncanny*) *Magazine* would inclusively encourage community after community (people of color, women, queer people, people with disabilities, and so on) to reimagine the genre vibrantly.

Within the past few years, we enjoyed Suparno Banerjee's *Indian Science Fiction: Patterns, History and Hybridity*; *Star Warriors of the Modern Raj: Materiality, Mythology and Technology of Indian Science Fiction* by Sami Ahmad Khan; and Upamanyu Pablo Mukherjee's Science Fiction Research Association Book Award–winning *Final Frontiers: Science Fiction and Techno-Science in Non-Aligned India*. Three practitioners of Indian SF studies have dazzled with their historical and textual range, with their sheer scope of theoretical innovation. Highlighting reception, they reframe the genre's reader interpretation in terms of *local novums* including rhetorics of Indigenous narrative traditions, of regional Anglophonic literatures of the fantastic, of speculative fictions from other Asian countries, and of national technoscientific policies.

We hear whispers, over the horizon, suggesting that the notion of worldwide, sociohistorical *futurisms* (plural) will soon present a new galactic map as further Indigenous and international SF scholarship emerges. *Uneven Futures'* publication arrives around the same time as *The Routledge Handbook of CoFuturisms*, coedited by Bodhisattva Chattopadhyay, Grace L. Dillon, Isiah Lavender III, and Taryne Jade Taylor, a big bang of fresh formalisms. And we recall that almost a decade ago, diasporic Caribbean writer-scholar Nalo Hopkinson had pointed out that for much of the rest of the world beyond the United States and modern imperial nations, the rationalist distinction between science fiction and other fantastic genres, such as those engaging spirits and magics, does not exist.[2]

The timescape is shifting. To one where we are not so much (to paraphrase Damon Knight's memeable characterization) *pointing to something and saying it is SF*, but instead we take our cue from the fearless next generation, modeled by adrienne maree brown and Walidah Imarisha, who call themselves Octavia's Brood.[3] Through our social activism—which is intertwined with, not separate from, our storytelling—we are *doing SF*.

If the 1960s brought us an SF reflected in titles of editorial collections like *New Worlds* by Michael Moorcock and *Dangerous Visions* by Harlan Ellison, perhaps we are in a time of New Timescapes and Dangerous Actions. We are not so much world-building through literary visions as pragmatically enacting our own spacetimes and futurisms.

With so much at stake, this (mid)century's "science fiction that matters"[4] may have no pathway other than community-engaged justice. SF as an imaginative way of collectively organizing. As a contemporary aesthetic of interdependency. As a hybridizable modality—no longer blended with colonialism, capitalism, able-bodyism, cis-normativity, Anthropocenic planetary relations, and other structures of violence. But instead mixed with peoples' deep technocultural wisdoms about acquiring agency in the face of unrelenting, predatory biopolitical rule.

Multiformalisms from Communities of Practice

Now is the time to talk about form. Science fiction is the green-headed godchild of fantasy, which itself is both an age-old human survival strategy and a kinship system of modern artistic genres shaped by market forces. Fantasy's societal functions, comparative literature scholar Jack Zipes argues, are to furnish ordinary people with "spiritual regeneration" and to "contemplate alternatives to our harsh realities." When SF matters, it achieves both ends.

We now envision our storytelling traditions as less of a canonical *megatext* than *genealogies of people receiving/practicing/enhancing classical forms from the worldviews and poetics of different communities*. We send out community calls for fresh aesthetic experiments—in one example, for "alternative subjectivities," "dynamic temporalities," and "all manners of futural and historical thought" around the poetics of gender, as *The Routledge*

Companion to Gender and Science Fiction editors, Sonja Fritzsche, Keren Omry, Wendy Pearson, and Lisa Yaszek, have appealed far into the digital spaces of SF scholarship. The "we" of the global (still default-Anglophone) media community that enters into science fiction discourse is complicated and unequal—but I believe it productive to track one's own genealogies within its weave.

I am seeking a thread, a vibrance, that winds around Morris and Brooks; Banerjee, Khan, and Mukherjee; Chattopadhyay, Dillon, Lavender, Taylor, and Hopkinson; brown and Imarisha; and that finds Fritzsche, Omry, Pearson, Yaszek, and me—a *sansei* (third-generation Japanese settler) cisgender feminist—caught in its uplift too.

Now is the time to talk about multiformalisms, starting with literary production.[5] After the pulp era, when Western science fiction print literature began its genrification,[6] efforts to institutionalize science fiction as formal genre practice coalesced in the 1950s–1960s. In that era, members of the UK and US postwar SF writing, editing, and reading communities put together the first SFF creative writing workshops. As print fiction practitioners, publishing industry pros, and superfans of the fantastic genres, interest groups (overwhelmingly white and largely male) argued endlessly over form as they came to a working consensus. The Futurians of New York City, organizers of the original Milford workshops, and pre-Clarion attempts by writers-cum-editors-cum-critics such as Damon Knight and Judith Merril collectively hammered out an *industrial design*, a syntax, for SF's print literary aesthetics/thematics.

This creative template was matched with a parallel establishment of "classical" science-fiction theory—a methodological orientation of Global North university researchers (jump-started by Suvin in the 1970s based on his 1968 lecture).[7] A notable trait of this scholarly discourse has been its nonrecognition of this collective genre-making process as part and parcel of SF's own institutionalization. Its erasure of the earlier, culture- and gender-specific communities of practitioners that had developed the form through discourse: its inability to resolve tensions between aesthetics/thematics and social context, between SFnal form and SF history. A single, if universalizing, conceptualization emerged; cognitive estrangement led the way for formalist approaches to the genre for over three decades.

Let's call these two historical movements *Science Fiction Studies 1.0*, or "SF theory through professional creative and academic practice."

Influenced by diaspora and postcolonial studies, by SF-genre debates over Western/modern slipstream,[8] and by gender/queer studies of the 1990s, a wave of scholars in the first two decades of the millennium advanced what we might call "SF genre theory"—or, *Science Fiction Studies 2.0.* In part, this development stemmed from heterogeneous feminists—*experimental-artistic* (e.g., the fiction-writing "muses of slipstream" Emshwiller, Link, and Fowler[9]; the women behind the interstitial art movement;[10] story collections of Thomas and of Hopkinson and Mehan[11]), *technocultural* (scholarship on US postwar female authors by Yaszek, for instance[12]) and *intersectional* (such as the LGBTQ-centered collection of Pearson, Hollinger, and Gordon[13]), as well as *global* thinkers in the field (among them Ginway, Ferreira, and A. Banerjee[14])—who through creative and historical tools eroded the default Cartesian binaries and (national) genre origins and boundaries of SF.

In part, the genre theorists also comprised scholars who looked beyond commercial SF literature—to twentieth-century SF's Western literary precursors, to other media such as science-fiction film and TV, and to genre studies. A generation of mostly Marxism-influenced academics (theorists such as Kincaid, Bould and Vint, Dillon, and Rieder), shaped by but also responding to Suvin's analyses, recovered the sociohistorical specificities of science fiction from classical SF theory's oversimplification of the genre into a singular form.[15] Their lasting achievement was recentering SF's definition relativistically around diverse readers embedded in "communities of (genre) practice."[16] They opened the door to the current historical moment of broadly conceived SFnal expression put forth by wide-ranging global populations who seek justice through imaginative truth-telling.

Many genre theorists had heeded calls to decenter print literature as the taken-for-granted medium for SF. To respect longer community traditions of oral storytelling that had helped birth published literatures, as well as folkloric and contemporary technologies evincing Indigenous scientific literacies, as parts of SF's pragmatic heritage.[17] To rethink form in light of one hundred plus years of cinematic media that wielded a built-in fantastical element from the get-go in its sensorial apparatus, suggesting that cognitive estrangement was a meaningless boundary object for audiovisual media's science-fictionality.[18] And calls to move away from the narrative default: ludic gameplaying and interactive media (and many digital science fictions, more broadly[19]), science fiction fashion, and technoscientific conventions do not center on linear, preset stories, but rather centralize participation and reception contingencies in the making of their science fictions.

Toward a Science-Fiction Studies 3.0

Now is the time to speak of SF production. In 2009, William Merrin called for Media Studies 2.0, which urged his field to update its basic intellectual models in light of the information age. Access to means of mass communication has become, in the words of convergence-culture herald Henry Jenkins that same year, "spreadable" and distributive rather than "sticky" and exclusive. We no longer live in a limited accessibility, solely studio film/network broadcast/print publishing era.[20] People can produce their own stories for mass distribution, not just receive (i.e., purchase, passively ingest) them. Reflecting the ensuing "productive turn" in media studies, this orientation, toward makers and practitioners, makes up the heart of what I call *Science Fiction Studies 3.0*.[21]

As a teacher, I have students analyze the cinematic SF of film, TV, and streaming texts in the first half of the term, then write science-fictional modes into their short original screenplays in the second half. I deeply hold that science-fictional expression must be treated as a core imaginative literacy in classrooms of this century, so I build student storytelling skills to combat the consumerization of humanity planned by large fantasy factories such as Disney, Warner Bros., Universal, and Netflix.

This think piece comes from my need to explore new rubrics of form.

SF as . . . Keeping Kinship Circles in Respectful Relations of Balance

If science fiction is an ethical, a just, action, then SF Studies 3.0 asks, What goal might this behavior entail, as we make our science-fictional art? The simplest (and perhaps hardest) aim would be to reconsider how we enact community with others, including with the planet, in respectful kin relations (not capitalist production relations)—taking our cue from First Nations and Aboriginal practitioners of their science fictions. Here I draw upon Indigenous Futurisms theorist Grace Dillon's ideal of going back to a sense of spiritual, cultural, and community balance, or, in her Anishinaabe language, *Biskaabiiyang* (which she translates as "returning to ourselves").[22] And upon the scientific visions of Native artists and artist-scholars Jason Edward Lewis, Noelani Arista, Archer Pechawis, and Suzanne Kite, who emphasize that what Indigenous Futurisms offer is often lacking in colonial/capitalistic cultural approaches to technology (in this case, AI). Namely, "how to treat these new non-human kin respectfully and reciprocally" in a "circle of relationships" of communities that encompass the living and nonliving, "from network daemons to robot dogs to artificial intelligences."[23] These two lived practices of social justice, of balanced self-care and of maintaining reciprocal, respectful kinship circles with others, eclipse the consumption of any single SF text; they may be intergenerational, as Dillon has emphasized about stories of Indigenous scientific literacies, as well as intertextual/intermedial.[24] With such future outcomes in mind, I envision one way to rethink science-fictional artistic expression across media:

> [Science fiction as a verb, a doing.]
>
> *Science-fictional modality* is a hybrid and cross-media exercise of critical consciousness and epistemological self-reflexivity that technocultural communities of practice imaginatively enjoy/deploy toward finding balance with the nonhuman (and other humans) in their network of kin relations.

SF as . . . Necessary Immaterial Labor for Building the Knowledge Infrastructure

If science fiction is a perspective or orientation that aims to comprehend the world, SF Studies 3.0 asks, What does that ontology open us up to? What cultural work do science-fictional arts perform? For this, we can learn from theorists of color researching the genre. Joy Sanchez-Taylor's bracing *Diverse Futures: Science Fiction and Authors of Color* (from the previously mentioned New Suns series), pairs the "double consciousness" of Black sociologist W. E. B. Du Bois with Suvinian estrangement in her evaluation of the imaginative (what Hardt and Negri might call *immaterial*) labor performed by writers of color whose narrative SF work challenges the genre's Eurocentricity. Performing "double estrangement," the dual creative labor of both inventing narrative situations following traditional (European/US) SF conventions and of depicting within that storyworld everyday patterns drawn from the real world in racialized ways that embody (for instance) African American readers' experiences, these writers accomplish a deeper, more stimulating politics of recognition than do mainstream SF authors. Through this latter descriptive technique, writers of color produce *ethnoscapes*, Sanchez-Taylor says, utilizing Isiah Lavender III's concept.[25] Sanchez-Taylor sums up Lavender's notion of the ethnoscape as a "racialized science fiction environment that both highlights and reconceives depictions of race to unpack the assumptions about race and ethnicity often made in science-fictional writing."[26]

My belief is that the substantial immaterial labor of this SF art, while producing ludic, ontological (sometimes existential) outcomes for readers, is pedagogically essential work aimed at creating a sophisticated knowledge infrastructure to help diverse communities in the future withstand and survive the talons of capital and empire. SF as a hybrid modality engages not only racial but also regional, class, gender, embodied, and other ontologies, which we sift against each other to eke out social meaning, sometimes empirically but often intuitively and integratively. This allows us to apprehend the functions of SF artistic production as such:

> [Science fiction as the infrastructural product of knowledge labor, or a noun.]
>
> *Science fiction* is the cultural recalibration of existing knowledge systems through innovative genre play, toward the ethical transformation, or community-informed regeneration, of historical modes of production.

Or at least that's how I've come to view it.

SF as . . . ?

What is *your science fiction* that spiritually refreshes you, that can help you imagine social relations alternative to our harsh realities?

Now is the time to get started.

Notes

1. To be fair, in the 2014 postscript to his original 1972 "Enlightenment and Cognition," Suvin reflected that the main limitation of his 1960s–1970s definition was "its innocently and naively Formalist horizon" and that "I seem to have felt I could freeze or even freeze out history, as all pursuits of aesthetics do: transcending the moment. I was wrong."

2. Hopkinson, "Introduction," xii–xiv.

3. See brown and Imarisha, *Octavia's Brood*, for the inspiration behind this movement.

4. I am adapting a phrase from Zipes, "Why Fantasy Matters Too Much": "fantasy that matters."

5. I borrow the term *multiformalisms* from postmodern poets Finch and Schultz (see *Multiformalisms*).

6. To apply a concept from genre theorist Altman, *Film/Genre*, 49–68.

7. Also see Scholes, *Structural Fabulation* and Delany, "About 5,750 Words." Relatively recent scholars such as Roberts, in *Science Fiction: The New Critical Idiom*, try to capture the SF form in literary studies' traditional tension between metaphorical and literalized narrative modes. Others such as Csicsery-Ronay, in *The Seven Beauties*, evolve SF formalism to be less one-dimensionally exclusivist by speaking of multiple reader effects, playing with the concepts of SF modalities and science-fictionality (which thus can be hybridized with other genres or used nonexclusively in non-SF texts).

8. I adjectivize what many think of as the slipstream subgenre as "Western and modern" because as Dillon says in a 2021 interview, mixing traditional and experimental forms and calling it "slipstream" existed in North American Indigenous SF communities of literary practice well before Bruce Sterling "discovered" the subgenre (Dillon and Marques, "Taking the Fiction out of Science Fiction").

9. As boundary-breaking SF writers Carol Emshwiller, Kelly Link, and Karen Joy Fowler were anointed by Kelly in "On the Net: Slipstream."

10. Fenkl's "Introduction" explains Delia Sherman and Theodora Goss's interstitial writing/arts project.

11. See for example, Thomas in the first volume of *Dark Matter*; Hopkinson and Mehan in *So Long Been Dreaming*.

12. See Yaszek's *Galactic Suburbia*.

13. See, from Pearson, Hollinger, and Gordon, "Introduction: Queer Universes."

14. That is: Ginway's *Brazilian Science Fiction*; Ferreira's *The Emergence of Latin American Science Fiction*; and A. Banerjee's *We Modern People: Science Fiction and the Emergence of Russian Modernity*.

15. See, for example, Kincaid, "On the Origins of Genre"; Bould and Vint, "There Is No Such Thing as Science Fiction"; Dillon, "Imagining Indigenous Futurisms"; Rieder, "On Defining SF, or Not."

16. See again Rieder, "On Defining SF, or Not," citing Bowker and Starr, "Sorting Things Out," 203–206.

17. Again, Dillon's "Imagining Indigenous Futurisms" is a prime example.

18. As per Butler, *Fantasy Cinema.*

19. See Frelik, "Introduction: Digital Science Fiction(s)."

20. Merrin's original 2009 "Media Studies 2.0," 17–34; Jenkins, Ford, and Green, "Introduction: Why Media Spreads."

21. Merrin, *Media Studies 2.0,* 146–154.

22. Dillon, "Imagining Indigenous Futurisms," 10

23. Lewis et al., "Making Kin with the Machines."

24. Dillon and Marques, "Taking the Fiction out of Science Fiction."

25. Sanchez-Taylor, *Diverse Futures,* 3. See also Lavender, "Ethnoscapes," 189.

26. Sanchez-Taylor, *Diverse Futures,* 3.

Bibliography

Altman, Rick. *Film/Genre.* London: British Film Institute, 1999.

Banerjee, Anindita. *We Modern People: Science Fiction and the Making of Russian Modernity.* Middletown, CT: Wesleyan University Press, 2013.

Banerjee, Suparno. *Indian Science Fiction: Patterns, History and Hybridity.* Cardiff: University of Wales Press, 2020.

Bould, Mark, and Sherryl Vint. "There Is No Such Thing as Science Fiction." In *Reading Science Fiction,* edited by James Gunn, Marleen Barr, and Matthew Candelaria, 43–51. New York: Palgrave, 2009.

Bowker, Geoffrey C., and Susan Leigh Starr. *Sorting Things Out: Classification and Its Consequences.* Cambridge, MA: MIT Press, 1999.

brown, adrienne maree, and Walidah Imarisha, eds. *Octavia's Brood: Science Fiction Stories from Social Justice Movement.* Oakland: AK Press, 2015.

Butler, David. *Fantasy Cinema: Impossible Worlds Onscreen.* London: Wallflower Press, 2010.

Chattopadhyay, Bodhisattva, Grace L. Dillon, Isiah Lavender III, and Taryne Taylor, eds. *The Routledge Handbook of CoFuturisms.* London: Routledge, forthcoming.

Csicsery-Ronay Jr., Istvan. *The Seven Beauties of Science Fiction*. Middletown, CT: Wesleyan University Press, 2008.

Delany, Samuel R. "About 5,750 Words." In *The Jewel-Hinged Jaw: Notes on the Language of Science Fiction*, 1–15. Middletown, CT: Wesleyan University Press, 2009.

Dillon, Grace L. "Imagining Indigenous Futurisms." In *Walking the Clouds: An Anthology of Indigenous Science Fiction*, edited by Grace L. Dillon, 1–12. Tucson: University of Arizona Press, 2012.

Dillon, Grace L., and Pedro Neves Marques. "Taking the Fiction out of Science Fiction: A Conversation about Indigenous Futurisms." *e-flux* 120 (September 2021). https://www.e-flux.com/journal/120/417043/taking-the-fiction-out-of-science-fiction-a-conversation-about-indigenous-futurisms.

Fenkl, Heinz Insu. "Introduction." In *Interfictions: An Anthology of Interstitial Writing*, edited by Delia Sherman and Theodora Goss, i–viii. Boston: Interstitial Arts Foundation, 2007.

Ferreira, Rachel Haywood. *The Emergence of Latin American Science Fiction*. Middletown, CT: Wesleyan University Press, 2011.

Finch, Annie, and Susan Schultz, eds. *Multiformalisms: Postmodern Poetics of Form*. Cincinnati, OH: Textos Books, 2008.

Frelik, Paweł. "Introduction: Digital Science Fiction(s)." *Science Fiction Studies* 43, no. 1 (March 2016): 1–3.

Fritzsche, Sonja, Keren Omry, Wendy Pearson, and Lisa Yaszek, eds. *The Routledge Companion to Gender and Science Fiction*. London: Routledge, forthcoming.

Ginway, M. Elizabeth. *Brazilian Science Fiction: Cultural Myths and Nationhood in the Land of the Future*. Lewisberg, PA: Bucknell University Press, 2004.

Hopkinson, Nalo. "Introduction." In *Whispers from the Cotton Tree Root*, edited by Nalo Hopkinson, xi–xiv. Montpelier, VT: Invisible Cities Press, 2000.

Hopkinson, Nalo, and Uppinder Mehan. *So Long Been Dreaming: Postcolonial Science Fiction and Fantasy*. Vancouver: Arsenal Pulp Press, 2004.

Jenkins, Henry, Sam Ford, and Joshua Green. "Introduction: Why Media Spreads." In *Spreadable Media: Creating Value and Meaning in a Networked Culture*, 1–46. New York: New York University Press, 2013.

Kelly, James Patrick. "On the Net: Slipstream." *Asimov's Science Fiction* 27, no. 12 (December 2003), 10–13.

Khan, Sami Ahmad. *Star Warriors of the Modern Raj: Materiality, Mythology and Technology of Indian Science Fiction*. Cardiff: University of Wales Press, 2021.

Kincaid, Paul. "On the Origins of Genre." *Extrapolation* 44 (Winter 2003): 409–419.

Lavender, Isiah III. "Ethnoscapes: Environment and Language in Ishmael Reed's 'Mumbo Jumbo,' Colson Whitehead's 'The Intuitionist,' and Samuel R. Delany's 'Babel-17.'" In *Science Fiction Studies* 34, no. 2 (July 2007): 187–200.

Lewis, Jason Edward, Noelani Arista, Archer Pechawis, and Suzanne Kite. "Making Kin with the Machines." *Journal of Design and Science*, July 16, 2018. https://jods.mitpress.mit.edu/pub/lewis-arista-pechawis-kite/release/1.

Merrin, William. *Media Studies 2.0*. London: Routledge, 2014.

Merrin, William. "Media Studies 2.0: Upgrading and Open-Sourcing the Discipline." *Studies in Communication and Culture* 1, no. 1 (2009): 17–34.

Mukherjee, Upamanyu Pablo. *Final Frontiers: Science Fiction and Techno-Science in Non-Aligned India*. Liverpool: Liverpool University Press, 2020.

Pearson, Wendy Gay, Veronica Hollinger, and Joan Gordon. "Introduction: Queer Universes." In *Queer Universes: Sexualities in Science Fiction*, edited by Wendy Gay Pearson, Veronica Hollinger, and Joan Gordon, 1–13. Liverpool: Liverpool University Press, 2008.

Rieder, John. "On Defining Science Fiction, or Not: Genre Theory, SF, and History." *Science Fiction Studies* 37, no. 2 (July 2010): 191–209.

Roberts, Adam. *Science Fiction: The New Critical Idiom*. London: Routledge, 2006.

Sanchez-Taylor, Joy. *Diverse Futures: Science Fiction and Authors of Color*. Columbus: Ohio State University Press, 2021.

Scholes, Robert. *Structural Fabulation: An Essay on Fiction of the Future*. Notre Dame, IN: Notre Dame University Press, 1975.

Suvin, Darko. "Estrangement and Cognition." *Strange Horizons*, November 24, 2014. http://strangehorizons.com/non-fiction/articles/estrangement-and-cognition. Reprint of "On the Poetics of the Science Fiction Genre." *College English* 34, no. 3 (December 1972): 372–382. Citations refer to the online edition.

Thomas, Sheree R. *Dark Matter: A Century of Speculative Fiction from the African Diaspora*. New York: Warner-Aspect, 2010.

Yaszek, Lisa. *Galactic Suburbia: Recovering Women's Science Fiction*. Columbus: Ohio University Press, 2008.

Zipes, Jack. "Why Fantasy Matters Too Much." *CLCWeb: Comparative Literature and Culture* 10, no. 4 (2008). https://doi.org/10.7771/1481-4374.1392.

III Transformation

21 Ursula K. Le Guin, *The Dispossessed* (1974) / Permanent Feminist Revolution

Kim Stanley Robinson

One origin for Ursula Le Guin's *The Dispossessed* is a question she ran across while reading William James, in which James wondered what we would do if living in a society that was perfect in all respects, except that this perfection relied on the misery of one poor child, imprisoned in a dungeon under the city. A fairy-tale situation, in effect, in that James gave no reason for why the child's imprisonment should create or indemnify the city's goodness. It's not a smart thought experiment, I must say. It's like asking "What if everyone were purple?" and then expecting an intelligent discussion to ensue.

Nevertheless, Le Guin wrote "The Ones Who Walk Away from Omelas," in which a small trickle of people leave this good city because they can't abide the mistreatment of the sacrificial child. I've always disliked this story for its self-righteousness and failure to suggest resistance. This trickle of departing people don't go to the dungeon and release the child; they walk away. How very pure of them. They are led apparently by a political/religious leader named Odo, who later in Le Guin's fictional world helps to start a new society on the habitable moon Annares; in *The Wind's Twelve Quarters*, Le Guin describes the great Odo as "one of the ones who walked away from Omelas."

That the great novel *The Dispossessed* arose from this unpromising beginning is surprising to me, but Le Guin says that's how it happened, so I have to believe her. And maybe the method she uses in both cases is the same: take a postulated situation—a political fairy, tale so to speak—and then examine it in a fiction. But this time, in *The Dispossessed*, by bringing the full weight of her novelist's skills to bear, rather than tossing off a fable in an afternoon, she created something very fine. It's a great novel, and it makes you think about political economy; maybe those two things always go together, but seldom is that so obvious as here.

The Dispossessed provides no answers. It is not self-righteous or pure. It tests many parts of what one might call the *anarchist proposal* by way of writing scenes in which one aspect or another of the proposal is dramatized. In a state of anarchy (and note the possible contradiction in this phrase, because Le Guin sure does), when two people get in a fight, what happens? When a child is born, how is it reared? What happens when teenagers want to have sex? And who does the dirty work?

All these questions are staged as dramatic scenes by Le Guin. Early on in the novel, the clanking of the stage machinery can sometimes be heard. Sometimes a scene takes life; other times it's like a textbook prompt dutifully fulfilled. But Le Guin was a great novelist, and as her characters catch her up, and she gets absorbed in her protagonist's biography, the thing takes off and flies. It's an ambiguous utopia (her subtitle) because it's a novel about a revolutionary moment, in which two different political economies are put under existential stresses at the same time. Because classical utopias were previously somewhat like blueprints for societies, and novels are always somewhat like soap operas about individuals, the idea of a "utopian novel" is unwieldy, not to say bizarre; but here, some 450 years after More's *Utopia*, we get the first really great utopian novel.

Le Guin manages this feat partly by way of a basic compare-and-contrast exercise between Annares and Urras. Urras is the main world, with a rich biosphere and a long human history. At the time of our story, its society much resembles Europe in the late nineteenth century, with all that era's unsustainable tensions: rampant inequality leading to great luxury and great poverty, a violent state apparatus working for the rich, helicopters with machine guns to suppress mass demonstrations of discontent, and revolution brewing. Classical capitalism, yes, although the resemblance to our own neoliberal moment is also strong: capitalism is always capitalism, in every period of its development.

The socialist state said to exist elsewhere on Urras is never visited and has no part in the story. We can recall the Sovietesque state in *The Left Hand of Darkness* if we are curious to know what Le Guin might think of such an arrangement. She wasn't impressed with that version. And we can see that lack of enthusiasm in this novel, too, because Annares, the contrasting political economy to Urras, turns out in many respects to be a kind of socialist state.

I say this because Le Guin has here interpreted anarchism to mean not the absence of law, but the absence of rulers. The Greek word *archy* admits either meaning, and which meaning one chooses makes for a crucial distinction (although both also would be an option). For Le Guin, it means an absence of rulers. As for absence of law, Annares is, like Urras, a technological civilization with a large population. Therefore, it has laws. That people could exist without laws in a crowded high-tech society is implied to be impossible. Le Guin suggests this subtly at first, by way of a pun, which is very characteristic of her; she loved jokes and word play. And so on Anarres there is a thing called the DivLab. It stands, we learn eventually, offhandedly, for Division of Labor; and her joke is that this Division of Labor exists to handle the Anarresti society's division of labor. Which means there is a system of laws here, which all members of this society have agreed to live by. So how anarchic is that?

Well, there's the absence of rulers. Annares is cooperative and communalist, and in theory everyone shares the same amount of power. In that specific sense, it's an anarchism, and a real achievement as such. And when it comes to reconciling the contradictions of anarchism and the state, there is a political economy or philosophy called *anarcho-syndicalism*, which Le Guin sometimes spoke of approvingly, that pushes toward this kind of horizontalization of power. In anarcho-syndicalism, the laws, and the institutions created by those laws, still organize the efforts of a complex modern society, by way of a division of labor that people agree voluntarily to abide by. Some individuals volunteer or are drafted to do the organizational work of dividing the work up, but that doesn't give them as individuals any extra power in the system; they are only performing the roles called out by the system, and after a while they will be replaced in their roles, with no personal benefits having accrued to them.

Thus the theory—but in her novel, Le Guin shows how quickly such a system can lead to temporary misuses of power given temporarily to temporary operators of the system. Here her natural skepticism, or her feel for human behavior, meaning a kind of ad hoc psychology or sociobiology, or what Hemingway called the novelist's "bullshit detector," comes into play, as she imagines in dramatized scenes various aspects of this proposed political system, all strung out along the life of Shevek, her protagonist.

He's an individual in a society. All the individuals have to cooperate for any one individual to survive. The cooperation is crucial—especially in a world of scarcity, this story seems to be saying—but no matter what the exterior situation or the political set-up, the consciousness of the individual is inescapably individual. Even if given a collectivist upbringing from birth, an existential moment is going to arrive in which the individual wants what she wants, and this desire may conflict with what some other individual wants, or what the society needs. And neither the structure of the society nor whatever kind of upbringing one has been given is going to be enough to erase such conflicts. The social order may provide ways of mediating them, but they won't go away. And maybe it isn't a law equivalent to Newton's law of gravitation to say "power corrupts," but it does seem safe to say, given all the historical evidence now accumulated, that "power tends to corrupt." Even just a little power, as, for instance, that wielded by a temporary bureaucrat, can lead to a little bit of corruption.

And so, because in a technologically complicated society there is a need for a division of labor, there is also a need for a Division of Labor. As a result, little pockets of power exist all over the place, and thus little opportunities for, or even incitements to, corruption.

So it turns out that anarcho-syndicalism, which is mostly a political strategy within capitalism, an imagined stage on the way to a better system, is not really what obtains on Anarres. Once anarcho-syndicalism takes over an entire political economy, what results is a bureaucratic state that much resembles democratic socialism. It's not a complete political solution solving all problems, if that is one's definition of *utopia*; indeed, it can get quite oppressive and dark, at least for individuals who want to do something sharply individualistic.

These are some of what I take to be Le Guin's conclusions, such as they are. She doesn't express many explicit conclusions in this novel, but it's true that you can usually tell which behaviors she likes or dislikes, and the opinions her protagonist Shevek expresses seem to meet with her approval: he says, by the choices he makes, something like "as an individual I get to do what I want, and in a society devoted to principles of anarchism, that should be fine; no one gets to stop me. I'm living by the real law of our society, which is that no one gets to rule me; and by living that way I'll help the society more than by any other way I could live."

This almost sounds libertarian; but I don't think Le Guin means libertarianism as the cri de coeur of some privileged members of a capitalist economy. On Anarres, there is no child in the dungeon. This is a sad symbol, so let's just say there is no oppressed working class on Anarres, doing the unseen work necessary to make the prosperous so prosperous. There is no private property beyond your clothes. So Annares is not a capitalist state; thus, no one in it can be libertarian. Annares is merely living out the contradictions of democratic socialism. The state exists; people have to share the necessary work, voluntarily if possible, but if a biospheric emergency strikes, then a kind of low-level conscription will have to be brought to bear. You have to pitch in to help; it's required. No one gets to shirk the dirty work. If, after pitching in on that work, you want to do something more, you should be free to do that. In a just and equal society, self-assertion could be appropriate, but as a kind of tack-on activity, after putting one's shoulder to the collective wheel. At that point, it might even be the best way to help that society. This is what Shevek says with his life story, and in living the life he does, he underlines the elements of a gift economy on Anarres and in socialist societies. People give what they have to give, in part because they want to.

The novel seems to end on a cliff-hanger, but because it exists in Le Guin's Hainish story universe, we actually can deduce from the rest of her work a little bit of what happens after the last chapter of *The Dispossessed*. After the last page, in the next chapter that remains unwritten, Shevek must in some way be welcomed home because in the rest of Le Guin's work, there is this device called the *ansible*. This is a sign of Shevek's eventual success. By the end of this novel, he has done the theoretical work needed to take advantage of that aspect of reality that quantum mechanics calls *nonlocality*; although objects cannot be moved instantaneously through space (as the physicists on Urras are hoping to do), information can be. But in this book the machine to do that has not yet been built. Later, in other novels, we see the ansible working, so we can conclude that Shevek has been allowed to proceed with his work in physics, collaborating with people on Urras, people on Terra, or with the older Hainish civilization, who presumably get the machine built.

So, Shevek is not stoned to death on his arrival home; we can know that. And one can trust that therefore he is reunited with his partner Takver, and lives on with her in a life that includes interactions with their child, their friends, and their fellow citizens. A happy ending is thus portended by the existence of the ansible in Le Guin's other books, some written much earlier than this one; this is a lovely move for a novelist, one of the best narrative payoffs that I know of for having created a story universe or novel cycle—and maybe also a little example of the ansible in question, as information about the device has jumped across Le Guin's time.

Ultimately, there's enough cross-cutting and complication in this novel that it isn't always easy to see what Le Guin believes in, or even what she's saying here, except in this one crucial respect: the great achievement of Anarres, as Le Guin presents it, is its feminism. This is one part of a general lack of hierarchy in all forms, yes; power having been spread out to all, the result is a different structure of feeling. This changed structure of feeling is valorized in many incidental scenes showing solidarity among fellow citizens, some of them as fine as anything Le Guin ever wrote (the conversations in trucks and trains, the small gifts of needed help). Lack of hierarchy leads to a general feeling of solidarity and fellowship; and by far the most important of the missing hierarchies on Anarres is patriarchy, the exertion of power by men over women. In the foregrounding of Shevek's disorientation at the patriarchy he sees still in Urrasti society, and the valorization of his easy equality and deep bond with "the partner"—their equality being the precondition for the depth—and in the complete absence of gender discrimination in Annaresti society, we see Le Guin straightforwardly plumping for feminist values and gender equality.

That the protagonist of the novel is a man might obscure this somewhat, but I think Le Guin's point here might be that the badness of patriarchy disfigures men too. Only when patriarchy is overthrown will men be freed of the guilt, denial, and disconnection from reality that upholding the master-slave system entails. In a post-patriarchy, in a feminist state, men will be freed from participation in a general criminal conspiracy and finally have the chance, like Shevek, to become real people at last, without guilt and fully alive; and women will be freed from the oppression of a subalternity that ranged from condescension to slavery. The erasure of gender as a power determinant, which we saw also depicted in *The Left Hand of Darkness*, will be an unreservedly good thing. The society that results might still be ambiguous, but it will be better than what we have now, which for me is the best working definition of *utopia*. Having seen in this novel how that different world might feel, by reading and thus imagining it, Le Guin can kick us out the door with her cliff-hanger, back into the reality we live in; with empty hands, like Shevek, but also living where we do (on Urras!), with a spur in our butts. Change!

Bibliography

Le Guin, Ursula K. "The Day Before the Revolution." In *The Wind's Twelve Quarters*, 232–246. New York: Harper & Row, 1975.

Le Guin, Ursula K. *The Dispossessed*. New York: Harper Perennial Modern Classics, 2014. First published 1974.

Le Guin, Ursula K. "The Ones Who Walk Away from Omelas." In *The Wind's Twelve Quarters*, 224–231. New York: Harper & Row, 1975.

22 Joanna Russ, *We Who Are About To . . .* (1976) / There Is No Planet B

Farah Mendlesohn

We are dying. We are dying as individuals and we are dying as a species. We just aren't very good at accepting it.

In *We Who Are About To . . .* (1976), Joanna Russ steps into a politics of radical extinction. The novel is about the self-regard that leads us to assume humans are vital and that infuses both radical and conservative politics. The narrator, Elaine, comes to understand and reject this attitude, which has underpinned her experiences both as an activist and as a castaway. This narrative of her individual failure and death thus becomes analogous to the failure and death of the human system, or the human episteme.

When *We Who Are About To . . .* was published, no subgenre within the field was more optimistic than planetary colonization novels. Among these, no story type was more committed to the survival of the species as an unquestioned good than the robinsonade, the stranding of a spaceship full of people on a new planet where, as exemplified in works such as Marion Zimmer Bradley's *Darkover Landfall* (1972), everyone, particularly women, would be assumed to abandon all sense of self-identity to settle and reproduce.

Although the novel initially met with some hostility and, later, relative critical indifference, in the past decade its rising critical esteem reflects clearly the understanding that, in the words of the T-shirt, there is no Planet B; and that the human desire to survive at any cost—both as individuals and as a species—threatens both the environment and other species with which we share the planet. A novel that once felt nihilistic today feels both realistic and moral.

The plot of the novel is straightforward: eight people crash-land on a marginally habitable planet. Seven of them decide to colonize it, to save the human race and human civilization; the eighth, the narrator, refuses.

The seven colonists are a professor (the group's low-grade agent of authority), a young woman on the way to being trained as a spy, a young waitress and dancer who trades on her looks, a young man trading on his size and strength, a very rich woman, her boy-toy husband, and the child she bought because the child needed millions of dollars of medical intervention (the book is profoundly ableist). These characters are exemplary types of beings and ways to live in the world. The narrator-protagonist, Elaine, is a refusenik: a music scholar whose scholarly life has been a refuge after the failure of her youthful activism, which disguises her decision to opt out of the notion of a human future.

The eight land, bringing with them the ecotechnological shadow of Western civilization: all the equipment they have has but limited time to use and reflects a culture in which the right to repair has been rejected. Everything is sealed; nothing can be repurposed. The narrator rejects the decision to reproduce, runs from an attempt at rape, kills four in self-defense, and murders two. She then settles in to die, recording all the events and her own feelings and thoughts on a "vocoder," which she seals so that no one will be able to read it in the very unlikely event it is found.

Critics today have reevaluated *We Who Are About To . . .* as a conscious attempt to demolish both what Kurt Vonnegut in *God Bless You, Mr. Rosewater* called science fiction's fantasies of an "impossibly generous universe"[1] and Zimmer Bradley's coercive fantasy of forced reproduction. In the past, Marilyn Hacker had judged it as "a bald book—it is about failure and death"[2]; Jeanine Cortiel similarly assessed the novel as without any link to activism or agency, minimizing its impact: "The only effect of androcide in this story is that the narrator can die in peace and in the process soliloquize the story of herself and the would-be colony."[3] And in her recent analysis, Gwyneth Jones argued that the surface plot about death has been lost to a secondary narrative about failed activism, refusal, and the rejection that human continuity is at stake.[4]

The book showcases a multitude of radical-extinction events: the rejection of robinsonade enthusiasm; the limitations of a society in which technology becomes, in John W. Campbell's famous phrase, "the magic that works"[5]; the examination of capitalism's values holding true only as long as its constructed order is accepted[6]; the absence of anything that could be considered a natural sisterhood; and the willingness of men to re-exert the patriarchy.

This is a book about how and when to die well.

Elaine embodies the no-holds-barred approach of Russ's politics: "There can be no excuses, no exceptions; niceness is not a mitigating factor in the structures of oppression. Difference isn't enough. Niceness merely pads the cell. Only rage is enough."[7] Both as an activist and as a survivor in this narrative, Elaine challenges the storifying that would be imposed by male readers—challenges their romantic interpretation of the robinsonade.[8]

We Who Are About To . . . is not a plague novel or an apocalyptic novel. It is not about the end of humanity. It is about the realization that the people in the text have stepped outside of humanity/the human story; that their assumption, that the world narrative is about them, is wrong. The story is, in its own way, the end of the affirmation of the myth of the human-centric planet. In one of the novel's most-quoted passages, Elaine thinks about Earth: "Oh, sure. Think of Earth. Kind old home . . . Think of smallpox and plague and earthquakes and ringworm and pit vipers . . . Amoebic dysentery. The Minnesota pioneers who tied a rope from the house to the barn in winter because you could lose your way in a blizzard and die three feet from the house." The other passengers believe themselves at the center of the planetary narrative. Elaine knows they are not: that a tagged planet may not contain compatible proteins, or that it may be able to provide food but not essential vitamins and minerals; "that if we could eat the local macro-life, the local micro-life could eat us," she realizes. Elaine rejects the anthropocene, the human-centered narrative in which everything belongs to us (or a subsection of us). In this world, the planet has a story, and in that story, humans aren't even bit players.

Elaine is not a harbinger of doom in the usual sense. As she notes, civilization is doing just fine; humans just aren't part of it: "We died the minute we crashed. Plague, toxic food, deficiency diseases, broken bones, infection, gangrene, cold, heat and just plain starvation. I'm just a Trembler. My God, you're the ones who want to suffer: conquer and control, conquer and control, when you haven't even got stone spears." Elaine is a prophet, advocating "for the declaration of human life through the cessation of reproduction . . . and the absolute end of perception that apprehends all living organisms and relations through anthropocentric-signifying systems."[9] And one by one, Elaine kills the signifiers by killing the humans.

For Russ, death is utterly material: it is a losing of oneself, of deciding to record all the poetry one remembers, then not doing it. Loss of civilization renders meaning not only from life, but from dying and death. We are not our physical corporeality, but our memories and our culture: "If history were not fantasy, then one could ask to be remembered but history is fake, and memories die when you do and only God (don't believe it) remembers. History always rewritten. Nobody will find this anyway or they'll have flippers so who cares." Elaine reminisces about her radical youth as a neo-Christian—Joanna Russ was Jewish—writing what is effectively a deathbed confession of a radicalism that was all sound and fury and "just petered out." She records what she has seen around her, the almost-classic planetary report, then calmly chooses to starve, reflecting that she is "fasting like a desert father."

In Elaine's narration and Russ's description of how the protagonist encounters this ending, this neo-Christian radicalism has left its trace. For the movement that calls itself Nobody has produced a woman who understands herself as no one. Death is not frightening; it is boring. Elaine cannot understand those who cling to life at any cost, for whom death is something ordered from a hospital bed, medicated for, denied. When one character says, "I don't want to die," the protagonist responds, "You won't"—the unreasonable reassured by the unpromisable.

Elaine's starvation serves to intensify the awareness of life. In her last stages, the music (Handel) comes back, solitude turns the walls and textures of the rock cave vivid so that she experiences "extraordinarily beautiful and rich . . . full arrangements of colour and shape . . . everything fits; if it didn't fit it couldn't exist on this world or any other."[10] Elaine's final accounting of the world has narrowed from planetary exploration to the intense detailing of the cave, the stream, the pebbles. The elegy for the loss of humanity (not its end) is muted by the reality of misery, hatred, self-indulgence.

Elaine's remaining anthropocentricity is minimized, framed as self-deprecating humor. Perhaps recalling the occultist Robert Cochrane, who did just this in 1966, she notes: "Plan: to kill myself on the exact, glorious day of the summer solstice but I won't know what day that is until several days afterward." The solstice of course doesn't care: there is no one left to understand this as significant. Can you even have a religious ritual of just one person?

She starves, she hallucinates, she dreams a trail. In the phases of death, she hears those she killed calling her a coward. When Elaine hears the voice of one of the deceased female colonists calling her an incompetent bitch, she responds, "*What else can you do but die?? It's the only thing you're good at. Exiled to this place? It was made for you; if it hadn't existed you would have created it.*"

The threats, the put-downs, are all in terms of whether humans have a place: the colonists assume that humans always have a place, that not having a place is somehow an indictment, a failure to be fully human. As Elaine grows weaker and the hallucinations more vivid, the people she killed march out of the cave. Another female colonizer turns in the last moment to thank her "for killing me."

In the last stages, Elaine sings to the vocoder, conjuring the strains of Handel and Bach, singing to the "silver haired plants and alien hills" as St. Francis once preached to the birds. "They all sat in rows and listened." The very landscape now feels alive: "I started up The Messiah but you have to be quite careful about *Every valley* because I'm near one and might get ideas."[11]

At last, deciding it is time to die, Elaine can only think about how it's "instant, euphoric, religious, sleep trancelike—really, nowadays you'd think one was shopping for couch covers . . . I can muster up a jump. I can roll off the cliff . . . The natural method. . . . Get it all over, that dying. Long dying: long, long dying, forty-two years, that's too much and I really wish."[12]

We Who Are About To . . . is a novel of refusal: a refusal to present a false narrative, to center either the human individual or the human species. In Patricia MacCormack's *The Ahuman Manifesto*, in the section titled "The End as Affirmation," MacCormack demands, "We must live the life we theorise or desire, even if it seems utopic, deluded or extreme." MacCormack calls for "A manifesto of 'radical compassion'" and says that "addressing our own privilege as humans can unveil a devastating awareness of what human compulsions have wreaked, with which we are all complicit."[13]

It is with this rallying cry that *We Who Are About To . . .* resonates, both in its politics and in its poetics. It is a demand that we decenter both the individual and the wider human experience, that we rethink the human experience holistically with all its indignities and horrors, and accept both individual responsibility and, at one and the same time, individual ineffectiveness. In a world in which individual and mass campaigning appears to achieve little against the actions of a tiny but immensely wealthy and powerful minority, it may also be a reminder that our final, most human act may be to choose the manner and affect of our passing. The world will go on without us. It may even go on better.

Notes

1. See Delany, introduction to *We Who Are About to . . . .*
2. Qtd. in Cortiel, *Demand My Writing*, 76.
3. Cortiel, *Demand My Writing*, 208.
4. Jones, *Joanna Russ*, 102–108.
5. Campbell, "Place of Science Fiction," 5.
6. Delaney, introduction.
7. Delaney, introduction, ix.
8. Delaney, introduction, viii.
9. MacCormack, *Ahuman Manifesto*, 129.
10. Russ, *We Who Are About To . . .* , 129.
11. Russ, *We Who Are About To . . .* , 163, 165.
12. Russ, *We Who Are About To . . .* , 168.
13. MacCormack, *Ahuman Manifesto*, x, xi.

Bibliography

Campbell, John W., Jr. "The Place of Science Fiction Today." In *Modern Science Fiction, Its Meaning and Its Future*, edited by Reginald Bretnor, 3–22. Chicago: Advent Publishers Inc., 1979.

Cortiel, Jeanne. *Demand My Writing: Joanna Russ/Feminism/Science Fiction*. Liverpool: Liverpool University Press, 1999.

Delany, Samuel R. Introduction to *We Who Are About To . . .* , by Joanna Russ, v–xv. Middletown, CT: Wesleyan University Press, 2005.

Jones, Gwyneth. *Joanna Russ*. Urbana: Illinois University Press, 2019.

MacCormack, Patricia. *The Ahuman Manifesto*. New York: Bloomsbury Academic, 2019.

Russ, Joanna. *We Who Are About To . . . .* London: Women's Press, 1987. First published 1976.

Vonnegut, Kurt. *God Bless You, Mr. Rosewater*. New York: Dell, 1979.

23 Eleanor Arnason, *Ring of Swords* (1993) / Queer-Feminist Peace Work

Veronica Hollinger

It is the future, and there are faster-than-light drives. So what happens when two space-faring and aggressive species run up against each other in the course of territorial expansion? This very old SF plot is perhaps most familiar to readers (and movie-goers) as the background to Robert A. Heinlein's hyperbolic revision of military SF, *Starship Troopers* (1959). It is also the setup to Eleanor Arnason's far more progressively political *Ring of Swords* (1993), which traces the fraught interactions between humans and the alien fur-covered *hwarhath* (always italicized in the novel). *Ring of Swords* is an entertaining queer-feminist defamiliarization of standard military SF that poses a serious challenge to the idea that war is inevitable in the encounter with radical difference.

If you happen to inhabit the violent world of *Starship Troopers*, you will respond to the alien with maximum force and you will continue to fight until the "Pseudo-Arachnids" (the "Bugs") are wiped off the face of the universe. In the storyworld of *Ring of Swords*, however, "you" becomes an unstable signifier because the narrative focus is shared equally by both species: humans are faced with the imminent threat of the alien *hwarhath* and the *hwarhath* are faced with the imminent threat of the alien humans. Each must try to wipe the other out unless they can learn to recognize each other as "persons" with whom they can come to reasonable and rational terms. War between humans and Bugs is an inevitability in Heinlein's universe because the Bugs are inconceivably different and humans are defending themselves against the insatiable and irrational violence of the truly alien. War between humans and the *hwarhath* in Arnason's universe is a distinct possibility because *hwarhath* and humans are so obliquely alike. Arnason's universe is ambiguous and uncomfortable for both species because dearly held beliefs about insurmountable differences become difficult to sustain in the face of growing familiarity. In *Ring of Swords*, military SF is transformed into the novel of manners (quite literally): the tragedy of war becomes the comedy of diplomacy.

The question of what it means to be a "person" and what it means for a species to be considered "people" rather than "animals" is at the center of the diplomatic negotiations that provide most of the "action" in *Ring of Swords*. In significant contrast to military SF in general, there are no individual heroes in *Ring of Swords*, nor is there a single scene of violent warfare. Instead of battles, Arnason puts her characters through interminable meetings: they spend most of their time talking. The necessity of honest and open communication, in fact, is the whole point of this novel about two equally violent, paranoid, and technologically advanced species who must struggle to "recognize" each other. As the human xenobiologist Anna explains to the *hwarhath* women, "We expected to find aliens who were different from us, really different. We didn't expect to find aliens who are very similar with some striking differences. It has us off balance." Or, as the alien commander Gwarha observes, "It's interesting how similar you are to us, except in the areas where you are different."[1] These areas include, most crucially, supposedly natural traits such as gender roles and sexual orientation.

The most serious stumbling block for both species—once the military hotheads on both sides have been sidelined—is sex. *Ring of Swords* thus models one of the most contentious areas of human social life, defamiliarizing it through the metaphor of the alien. *Hwarhath* society enacts a radical separation of women and men, given their conviction that male violence is natural and inevitable. Women live with children on the home planet, while the only role for men is in the military; all are posted to various off-world stations, forming the "ring of swords" that protects the home world. Women and men take same-sex lovers, and sex between women and men is a perversion. Procreation, for the most part through artificial insemination, is carefully arranged by women for maximum political advantage among families.

From the estranged perspective of the *hwarhath*, heterosexuality is a demonstration of the animal nature of humans who cannot maintain the "proper" distinctions between women and men. Unsurprisingly, many of the human characters have difficulty with *hwarhath* sexuality, which they tend to read as if it were no different from human homosexuality. While it is all too easy, in light of human history, to assume that violence is hardwired into human nature, for many of us it is much more difficult to accept what we consider to be "unnatural" social relations. In Brian Attebery's ironic terms, both human and *hwarhath* sexual difference "is enforced with the special vigilance reserved for instilling what culture believes to be natural."[2] Even more than in many human cultures, the restrictions on *hwarhath* sexual expression are absolute, something that the human characters must simply accept as one of the irresolvable differences between themselves and the aliens. We might consider that although both humans and *hwarhath* have quite definite ideas about appropriate sexual behavior, the universe that throws them together is much queerer than they bargained for.

It is a happy coincidence that *Ring of Swords* was published in the same year as Judith Butler's influential queer-feminist theorization of gender performativity, *Bodies that Matter: On the Discursive Limits of Sex*. While second-wave feminist scholars, especially during the 1970s, focused on critiques of gender—associating gender with "culture" and sex with "nature"—the 1990s were a productive period for the queering of feminist theory, given the growing awareness that it is impossible to separate gender, conventionally the purview of feminist theory, and sexuality, conventionally the purview of gay and lesbian studies. Butler goes so far as to argue, counterintuitively, that gender, as the citation of social norms, is the privileged term: "If gender is the social construction of sex, and if there is no access to this 'sex' except by means of its construction, then it appears not only that sex is absorbed by gender, but that 'sex' becomes something like a fiction . . . retroactively installed at a prelinguistic site to which there is no direct access."[3] In other words, gender is not simply the expression of a preexistent sex(uality); rather, the regulatory norms of gender in any given society strongly constrain sexual behavior. From this perspective, both Arnason's humans and her *hwarhath* are subject to the constraints posed by their respective sociocultural environments.

In Butler's terms, humans and *hwarhath* find each other's sexualities "culturally unintelligible": each is what the other has repudiated through a process of disidentification that tends to abject what is different.[4] Like humans, the *hwarhath* essentialize sexual and gender relations as natural or unnatural, perverse or proper: "that is something else that the humans can't keep clear. They don't seem to understand the difference between having sex and having children. Nine billion of them! Are they crazy?"[5] If humans are indeed animals, no matter how intelligent-seeming they are, then the *hwarhath* rules of war—women and children are sacrosanct, for example—need not be followed; indeed, humans have already demonstrated their ignorance of such rules in previous skirmishes with the *hwarhath*, as well as their lack of cultural refinement in how they mix the lives of women and men together even in the military: "There is no way to have a decent war with creatures like these."[6]

Ring of Swords is a charmingly didactic novel about learning to accept the queerness of a universe in which "there is more than one way to be."[7] Arnason mines science fiction's capacity for defamiliarization to the fullest, reflecting critically on human short-sightedness through the "gaze" of the aliens. This is demonstrated very clearly in the novel's treatment of sexualities and genders, not only through the equal weight given to both *hwarhath* and human sexual mores, but more intriguingly through the relationship between Defender-of-the-Hearth-with-Honor First-Ahead Ettin Gwarha and Nicholas Sanders. Gwarha is the leader of the *hwarhath* negotiating team; Nicky, the "traitor," was captured years earlier by the *hwarhath* in one of their skirmishes with humans and is now Gwarha's lover and a go-between for the *hwarhath*. Arnason highlights the confusion of the other humans, who are puzzled because there is nothing about homosexual activity in Nicky's past military record. Nicky appreciates the complexities of the relationship: "We don't belong to the same species, First-Defender. We have not had the same kind of sexual experience. Even now we don't have the same kind of experience."[8] Only the very useful category of *queer*—which refuses fixed identities and fixed ways to perform gender and to express sexuality—seems adequate to accommodate this completely unexpected partnership: "There's something pleasant about the idea of inventing a new form of sexuality."[9]

Attebery notes how the masculinities in the novel are "manifold and contradictory," challenging the gender essentialisms of both species.[10] This holds true as well for the *hwarhath* women who are protected by the ring of swords and spend their lives for the most part to the home planet. While the divisions between women and men are absolute, *hwarhath* society is not at all a replication of human patriarchy. Ruling from the home planet, *hwarhath* women, "broad and blunt-featured and covered with fur," are in charge of social organization, government, and family alliances, and it is they who take over negotiations with the humans when the situation seems most dire.[11] Among the most important of the human negotiators is the xenobiologist Anna Perez: when we first meet her, she is on an Earth-like planet studying the alien pseudosiphonophores, aquatic "animals" that may or may not be intelligent life-forms. This not only foreshadows the dilemma faced by the *hwarhath* when they encounter humans, but Anna's aliens also function as a third way to remind us not to yield to the temptations to reduce the complex negotiations between *hwarhath* and humans to a simple binary opposition.

Anna has been commandeered both for her professional expertise and because she is a woman with whom the *hwarhath* women—"These terrifying women"—agree to deal.[12] Anna becomes not only an intensely involved participant observer, but also the "object" of intense study by the *hwarhath* women: "The aliens had plenty of facts. Now they wanted an explanation. How could humanity be this way? What did it feel like to be a human? What was it like to be a woman on Earth?"[13] It is the *hwarhath* women's study of Anna, Nicky, and the other humans that leads them to conclude, however reluctantly, that humans are people, but people with a completely different moral system. As Nicky explains, "If humans exist, who knows what other ugly surprises are waiting for the People among the stars? Maybe the next set of aliens will be even more disgusting. The People have to find new ways to think about morality and war."[14]

Recalling both Heinlein's over-the-top masculinist military fiction and Butler's theoretical arguments about gender as performance, it is delightful to discover that the *hwarhath* soldiers are wearing "space warrior" uniforms designed by their Art Corps so that they can "perform" the kind of masculinity that will impress the human negotiators.[15] They typically wear shorts and sandals, but Nicky admits to Anna, "I told the general that the humans might find it hard to take people wearing shorts seriously. So we had the Art Corps design space cadet uniforms. . . . I especially like the high shiny black boots, though I can't imagine what they would be for."[16]

There are other suggestions in *Ring of Swords* that gender may not be as relatively simple and natural as common sense—both *hwarhath* and human—would like it to be. After all, it is impossible to separate "nature" from "culture" when everything we can say about "nature" is spoken by "culture" and when so much about a particular culture has evolved to conform to what it already considers to be natural. Nicky speculates that the *hwarhath* belief that men are inherently violent "is a crock; but there is no question that *hwarhath* males are socialized to be intensely competitive and to think that violence is no big deal."[17]

The novel's interest in gender as performance is nicely supported by its parallel interest in theater. As the mention of the *hwarhath* Art Corps might suggest, men and women have rich but separate cultural traditions. Theater is particularly valued. *Hwarhath* males write "hero plays," tragedies in which the protagonist is caught in an insoluble situation for which the only solution is death, echoing everything from classical Greek to French neoclassical tragedies. Women prefer comedy and plays, often obscene, about sly animals. The promising young playwright Eh Matsehar is smitten by Shakespeare's *Othello*: "It would make a terrific hero play [. . .] the kind about the dangers of heterosexual love."[18] His crowning achievement is a revised version in translation of *Macbeth*, which in his hands becomes a magnificent story about an ambitious mother and her warrior son, trapped by "greed and bad manners" ("Can you think of a worse host than Macbeth?").[19]

Ring of Swords rejects the conclusions and resolutions of tragedy in its recognition that real life is "a mess."[20] If Nicky were the central character in a hero play, as he points out to Anna, he would have to kill himself because of his tangled human and *hwarhath* loyalties. Instead, the novel welcomes the (ir)resolutions of comedy, dramatizing the reciprocity of ongoing cultural exchange and suggesting the deep entanglements that are already transforming each species. One of the *hwarhath* women is going to name her daughter Anna. To solidify the still fragile détente, Anna herself is invited to attend a theater festival on the home planet. Eh Matsehar's production of *Macbeth* will be the centerpiece of the festival.

Arnason's earlier novel, *A Woman of the Iron People* (1991), won the inaugural James Tiptree Jr. Award (renamed the Otherwise Award in 2019) for its contributions to the exploration of gender in science fiction. *Ring of Swords* continues this exploration and is itself the centerpiece of a wonderful series of *hwarhath* stories that Arnason published between 1993 and 2012.[21] In a 2013 essay in *Strange Horizons*, Arnason emphasizes the necessity of maintaining optimism in the face of uncertain futures, and she is particularly appreciative of Kim Stanley Robinson's utopian-inflected science fiction "because he thinks about politics and economics and the process of change."[22] On more than one occasion, Robinson has claimed that "we are now living in a science fiction novel that we are all writing together."[23] This is as good a way as any to describe what *hwarhath* and humans are collectively undertaking in Arnason's novel, as each must now incorporate the other into its politics, its culture, and its future.

We might do worse than to take *Ring of Swords* as a model for how to write the future in collaboration with our human and nonhuman others. Unlike the characters in Eh Matsehar's *Macbeth*, it is both generous and well-mannered. Its plot models its conviction that the most important first step in dealing with difference—among individuals, among nations, among cultures, among species—is the respectful acknowledgement that "there is more than one way to be." Everything follows from that first uncertain step, that utopian inflection point aimed at an open-ended future of queer diversity. Arnason leaves it up to her readers to imagine what might come after.

Notes

1. Arnason, *Ring of Swords*, 250, 316.
2. Attebery, *Decoding Gender*, 130.
3. Butler, *Bodies that Matter*, 5.
4. Butler, *Bodies that Matter*, 2.
5. Arnason, *Ring of Swords*, 270
6. Arnason, *Ring of Swords*, 271.
7. Arnason, *Ring of Swords*, 168.
8. Arnason, *Ring of Swords*, 235.
9. Arnason, *Ring of Swords*, 253.
10. Arnason, *Ring of Swords*, 123.
11. Arnason, *Ring of Swords*, 141.
12. Arnason, *Ring of Swords*, 305.
13. Arnason, *Ring of Swords*, 335.
14. Arnason, *Ring of Swords*, 345.
15. Arnason, *Ring of Swords*, 362.
16. Arnason, *Ring of Swords*, 139.
17. Arnason, *Ring of Swords*, 283.

18. Arnason, *Ring of Swords*, 195.

19. Arnason, *Ring of Swords*, 333.

20. Arnason, *Ring of Swords*, 363.

21. Collected in Arnason, *Hwarhath Stories*.

22. Arnason, "Me and Science Fiction."

23. Robinson and Canavan, "Afterword," 255.

Bibliography

Arnason, Eleanor. *Hwarhath Stories: Transgressive Tales by Aliens*. Seattle: Aqueduct Press, 2016.

Arnason, Eleanor. "Me and Science Fiction: Hope for the Future." *Strange Horizons*, March 11, 2013. http://strangehorizons.com/non-fiction/columns/me-and-science-fiction-hope-for-the-future/.

Arnason, Eleanor. *Ring of Swords*. New York: Tor, 1993.

Attebery, Brian. *Decoding Gender in Science Fiction*. New York: Routledge, 2002.

Butler, Judith. *Bodies that Matter: On the Discursive Limits of "Sex"*. New York: Routledge, 1993.

Robinson, Kim Stanley, and Gerry Canavan. "Afterword: Still, I'm Reluctant to Call This Pessimism." In *Green Planets: Ecology and Science Fiction*, edited by Gerry Canavan and Kim Stanley Robinson, 243–260. Middleton, CT: Wesleyan University Press, 2014.

24 Margaret Atwood, MaddAddam Trilogy (2003–2013) / Interspecies Coalition-Building

Alison Sperling

It's often remarked upon how Margaret Atwood's speculative futures, as imagined in her novels, come eerily to pass in the world.[1] Her MaddAddam trilogy is no exception.[2] As Atwood writes in her acknowledgements of the third book: "Although *MaddAddam* is a work of fiction, it does not include any technologies or biobeings that do not already exist, are not under construction, or are not possible in theory."[3] The trilogy is therefore unsurprisingly read alongside developing scientific practices of gene-splicing and CRISPR technologies, and it purposefully troubles the ethical futures of already existent or underway biotechnologies.

Set in a near future with few survivors left from a man-made plague let loose by evil genius figure Crake, the last humans must learn to live not only with each other, but alongside various genetically created animal and humanoid others. In this short piece, I think once again about the most discussed of these genetic creations (after the Crakers), the pigoons—transgenic pig hosts engineered to grow multiple regenerating organs that could be harvested for implantation into humans in need of them. Pigs are, in fact, one of the most popular animals in science and speculative fictions across media, especially in what is considered "genetic science fiction," because of their likeness in DNA and organ structures to those of humans and for their sentient and intellectual capabilities.[4] They are regularly experimented upon in apocalyptic scenarios struggling to imagine a future for humankind. Pigs in many non-Indigenous science and speculative fiction narratives coming out of the United States therefore often serve as figures of futurity without having themselves a future. They are harborers of scientific fantasies about the survival of some form of humanity in a future that requires their own annihilation. In what follows, I will think briefly about the vision of futurity offered by the pigoons, alongside recent horrific developments in the conditions for pigs (and other domesticated animals) in the factory farming industry, particularly in the United States.

Very early in the first book of the trilogy, readers are introduced to *Oryx and Crake*'s main character, Jimmy, by way of his "earliest complete memory." "Bonfire," as the second short section of the novel is titled, describes Jimmy's experience at a culling and mass burning of farm animals who had been killed because they contracted (or were purposely infected with) hoof-and-mouth disease:

> The bonfire was an enormous pile of cows and sheep and pigs. Their legs stuck out stiff and straight; gasoline had been poured onto them; the flames shot up and out, yellow and white and red and orange, and a smell of charred flesh filled the air. It was like the barbeque in the backyard when his father cooked things but a lot stronger, and mixed with it was a gas-station smell, and the odour of burning hair . . . he thought he could see the animals looking at him reproachfully out of their burning eyes. In some way all of this—the bonfire, the charred smell, but most of all the lit-up, suffering animals—was his fault, because he'd done nothing to rescue them.[5]

Atwood scholarship has often drawn on this recollection as being central to Jimmy's character development eventually into the postapocalyptic "Snowman" figure in the trilogy.[6] The animal bonfire that Jimmy witnesses in childhood is thus an early example (both in the novel and in Jimmy's life) of the ways in which we are cultured through systems of consumer capital to disregard certain lives or to exploit certain bodies for the supposed benefit of greater humanity. The importance of this memory to Jimmy and to the plot demonstrates the ways in which the recovery of (and from) memories like this become one route toward a physical and psychical healing that is necessitated by the horrific events of "the waterless flood."

Indeed, scholarship on the trilogy has been invested in the larger ethical dilemmas presented by the pigoon project. Gerry Canavan has written, for example, that "the entire plot of the book unfurls through the recovery of Jimmy's buried traumatic memories of the unhappy hypercapitalist system." Slawomir Kozial recently argued that the trilogy's treatment of animals, and especially pigs, demonstrates the ways in which humans value systems of rationality over the category of life itself. Koziol argues that the trilogy encourages engagement not only with animal studies and animal justice scholarship, but also with critical race studies and postcolonial thinking, which have long thought about expendable bodies and labor in relation to race, class, and settler-colonial relations. Silvia Camporesi has additionally pointed to the ways in which the trilogy demonstrates how especially nonhuman species are exploited as expendable labor, revealing the privileging of economic and medical efficiency for the very few over, for example, environmental concerns.[7]

Recent events related to the ongoing global pandemic caused by the COVID-19 virus have made some of these relations painfully visible in forms of violence that continue to emerge in response to new crises of hypercapitalism that the pandemic brings into sharp relief. Strangely, it wasn't the loosing of the virus in the MaddAddam trilogy that called the current pandemic to mind as suddenly urgent (again) in 2020. Rather, it was the news that started to filter through in the spring about the "depopulation" of farms of their livestock due to the mass closures of meatpacking plants as hotspots for the transmission of the coronavirus. Jimmy's haunting memory of the bonfire kept coming to mind as I imagined farms across the United States "backlogged" with pigs, once designated to be butchered and packed, with nowhere to go. Farm owners reported to having to resort to the mass killing of their livestock, largely by way of ventilation system shutdowns or carbon dioxide gassing. The *New York Times* reported on May 14, 2020, that some six hundred thousand pigs in Iowa, the nation's largest producer of pork, would be backlogged (i.e., mass killed) over the next six weeks, while ninety thousand hogs in Minnesota had already been killed and disposed of in the previous month alone.[8] *Reuters* reported a single farm in Minnesota that euthanized sixty-one thousand egg-laying hens through carbon dioxide poisoning.[9] A surplus of animals apparently means slaughter without the follow-up packing stage; "senseless" killing (as if other forms of killing are somehow more sensical, but more on this in a moment) on an alarmingly mass scale. While the mass slaughter of animals for factory farms has already long proved animal abuse, especially in the United States, and has been rampant and unchecked, this killing of animals because of the collapse of industry is for some reason especially hard to fathom.

An article in the *Guardian* echoes the sentiment across media sources on the issue: the "closure of meat plants due to coronavirus means 'depopulation' of hens and pigs with methods experts say are inhumane, *despite unprecedented demand at food banks*."[10] On one level, this notion is that the killings are tragic because they are wasteful—people are starving; but in actuality, this rehearsed response to these slaughters misses the mark entirely. The claim that the animals are slaughtered "without purpose," as if their killing is tragic because it is wasteful, is of course to already miss the point of the tragedies of factory farming, which kill on far larger scales than this on a daily basis across the world. Wastefulness is unjustly framed as the tragedy, rather than systems of consumption and the abuse of nonhuman life.

In Atwood's trilogy, this relation is explored at length with regard to the pigoons. While the pigoon project has no problems exploiting them by splicing human genes into their DNA and reaping their extra human-compatible organs, the project also must simultaneously assure consumers ("to set the queasy at ease") that pigoon flesh would never be rendered into edible products: "No one would want to eat an animal whose cells might be identical with at least some of their own."[11] Certain forms of violence are excused, while others border on the limits of what humanity is willing to do to survive. At the end of the third book of the trilogy, the pigoons, humans, and Crakers find a way to communicate psychically. They ultimately agree to do no harm to one another and to respect species/cultural differences. While it's interesting to consider speculative modes of communication or other forms of attachments to nonhumans that might serve to engender coalition building, it is also perhaps important to maintain certain distinctions between human and nonhuman animal here. Too easily collapsing the boundaries between species and their ability to communicate or "understand one another" might suggest that practicing nonviolence against nonhuman animals necessitates their humanizing or intellectualizing.

Soon after the memory of the bonfire, the narrator recounts Jimmy remembering when he first learned of the pigoon project: "All of this was explained to Jimmy when he was old enough." But Snowman interjects: "Old enough . . . such a dumb concept . . . Old enough for what? . . . what can it be called? This situation. He'll never be old enough, no sane human being could ever." Looking back after the near annihilation of humanity, Jimmy-turned-Snowman asks at what point in a human life, at what age one is able to comprehend such atrocities. "Old enough for what? To drink, to fuck, to know better?"[12] In other words, what acts or rites of passage could possibly be understood as parallel to being able to receive certain difficult truths?

It may seem difficult to consider the fate of pigs and other domesticated animals in what is already an extraordinarily tumultuous political and social moment worldwide, when so many human lives are urgently endangered by racism and fascism and capitalism, paired with the general incompetence of many of those in power around the world. But I would suggest that the MaddAddam trilogy's pigoons remind us of the ways in which it is consumer capitalism and its inherent relation to speciesism, racism, and classism, made even more evident in a pandemic-changed world, where the current practices of meat production and consumption must be addressed in any coherent plan for radical social justice and change.

Notes

1. See, as examples, Mulkerrins, "Elisabeth Moss on *The Handmaid's Tale*"; Schwartz, "Freaky Prediction."

2. The trilogy comprises *Oryx and Crake* (2003), *The Year of the Flood* (2009), and *MaddAddam* (2013).

3. Atwood, *MaddAddam*, 275.

4. See Hamner, *Editing the Soul*, for a description of this subgenre.

5. Atwood, *Oryx and Crake*, 17, 18–20.

6. Canavan, "Hope, but Not for Us."

7. Canavan, "Hope, but Not for Us," 142; Kozioł, "From Sausages to Hoplites"; Camporesi, "CRISPR Pigs."

8. Corkery and Yaffe-Bellany, "Meat Plant Closures." For other reports about the mass murder of farm animals, see Gawthorpe, "Pandemic Highlights Gruesome Animal Abuses"; Scully, "Coronavirus Pandemic."

9. Polansek and Huffstutter, "Piglets Aborted, Chickens Gassed."

10. Kevany, "Millions of US Farm Animals to Be Culled"; emphasis added.

11. Atwood, *Oryx and Crake*, 27.

12. Atwood, *Oryx and Crake*, 26.

Bibliography

Atwood, Margaret. *MaddAddam*. London: Virago, 2013.

Atwood, Margaret. *Oryx and Crake*. London: Virago, 2003.

Atwood, Margaret. *The Year of the Flood*. London: Virago, 2009.

Camporesi, Silvia. "CRISPR Pigs, Pigoons, and the Future of Organ Transplantation: An Ethical Investigation of the Creation of CRISPR-Engineered Humanised Organs in Pigs." *Etica e Politica* 20, no. 3 (2018): 35–52.

Canavan, Gerry. "Hope, but Not for Us: Ecological Science Fiction and the End of the World in Margaret Atwood's *Oryx and Crake* and *The Year of the Flood*," *Literature Interpretation Theory* 23 (2012): 138–159.

Corkery, Michael, and David Yaffe-Bellany. "Meat Plant Closures Mean Pigs Are Gassed or Shot Instead." *New York Times*, May 14, 2020. https://www.nytimes.com/2020/05/14/business/coronavirus-farmers-killing-pigs.html.

Gawthorpe, Andrew. "The Pandemic Highlights the Gruesome Animal Abuses at US Factory Farms." *Guardian*, August 3, 2020. https://www.theguardian.com/commentisfree/2020/aug/03/coronavirus-animal-abuse-us-factory-farms.

Hamner, Everett. *Editing the Soul: Science Fiction and the Genomic Age*. University Park: Pennsylvania State University Press, 2017.

Kevany, Sophie. "Millions of US Farm Animals to Be Culled by Suffocation, Drowning, and Shooting." *Guardian*, May 19, 2020. https://www.theguardian.com/environment/2020/may/19/millions-of-us-farm-animals-to-be-culled-by-suffocation-drowning-and-shooting-coronavirus.

Kozioł, Sławomir. "From Sausages to Hoplites of Ham and Beyond: The Status of Genetically Modified Pigs in Margaret Atwood's MaddAddam Trilogy." *Papers on Language and Literature* 54, no. 3 (2019).

Mulkerrins, Jane. "Elisabeth Moss on The Handmaid's Tale: 'This Is Happening in Real Life. Wake up, People.'" *Guardian*, May 5, 2018. https://www.theguardian.com/tv-and-radio/2018/may/05/elisabeth-moss-handmaids-tale-this-is-happening-in-real-life-wake-up-people.

Polansek, Tom, and P. J. Huffstutter. "Piglets Aborted, Chickens Gassed as Pandemic Slams Meat Sector." Reuters, April 27, 2020. https://www.reuters.com/article/us-health-coronavirus-livestock-insight/piglets-aborted-chickens-gassed-as-pandemic-slams-meat-sector-idUSKCN2292YS.

Schwartz, Ariel. "A Freaky Prediction about Pigs in a Popular Sci-Fi Trilogy Is Starting to Come True." *Business Insider*, June 7, 2016. https://www.businessinsider.com/margaret-atwoods-pigoons-are-starting-to-become-reality-2016-6.

Scully, Matthew. "Coronavirus Pandemic: The Human Cost of 'Culling' Livestock and 'Depopulating' Farms." *National Review*, May 7, 2020. https://www.nationalreview.com/2020/05/coronavirus-pandemic-human-cost-of-culling-livestock-depopulating-farms/.

25 Buried without Ceremony, *The Quiet Year* (2013) and *The Deep Forest* (2014) / Mechanics of Resolution

Brent Ryan Bellamy

In fall 2019, I joined a group of university students to instruct them on critical worldbuilding. The students formed small groups and considered objects gathered before them: colorful pencils, a blank sheet of paper, a deck of cards, a set of tokens, and a rule booklet. They were preparing to play two related role-playing games published by Buried without Ceremony. Some groups would define the struggles of a community living after the collapse of civilization in *The Quiet Year* (2013), solo-written by Avery Alder. Other groups would instead imagine the trials faced by the monsters who inhabit a place previously occupied by invading humans who have now been driven off in *The Deep Forest* (2014), cowritten by Alder and Mark Diaz Truman. In both games, players take turns adding details to the collaboratively created map, including abundant and scarce resources, locations of interest, community relationships, and even other communities. These games' unique approaches to resolving conflict register the urgent social struggles of the day, inviting players to join in such representational and resource-oriented struggles together. They also offer a chance for those who have not felt the pressure of making good decisions for the betterment of a community under duress to work through such feelings.

Students initially delight in the imaginative play of creating a lived-in place from scratch. To play these games feels like anything might happen. But players soon realize two things: a turn in the game is short, and the other players may have different, occasionally conflicting, impulses. At the crossroads of imagination and compromise, these games introduce mechanics for collaborative play to mediate collective decisions about a shared imaginary space. Rather than considering the procedures and rules as external to the game (e.g., as the background to the gaming experience provided by the publishers themselves and into which players have little to no input), *The Quiet Year* and *The Deep Forest* demonstrate how the game mechanics or the way in which we play the game (whether through rolling dice or drawing a card) define what is possible and what is important. How one follows the rules, and the kind of story that produces, become the site of knowledge, of affect, and of struggle. This self-reflective turn makes players aware of the game world's social construction; both games teach us that the future is always under negotiation, even though we have too little time to discuss it. These games provide space and time for people to gather and work through tensions produced by their own expectations, as their narrative mixes collaborative storytelling, drawing and mapmaking, and role-playing through turn-based mechanics.

A game's mechanics shape its political possibilities. In both of Buried without Ceremony's games, a small group of people role-play a community during one quiet year sheltered between catastrophes. In *The Deep Forest*, for instance, the script tells players: "For a long time, our monstrous home was occupied by invading humans. Now, finally, we've driven them off, and we're left with this: a year of relative peace. One quiet year, with which to dismantle their settlements and reclaim our lands."[1] At the end of one in-game year, a force from outside the community arrives to end play. Players confront disaster's wake together, negotiate genre and tone, and socially channel their responses to the oracle deck's week-by-week prompts. Players put pencil to paper, drawing characters and events on a shared canvas.

The Quiet Year and *The Deep Forest* make it possible for players to realize collectively their fractured assumptions about the fun, the good, the necessary, and the just. The mechanics are designed in such a way that players will reach resolutions or they won't, and that both outcomes are intriguing from ethical or sociopolitical standpoints. Each turn consists of first drawing a card, which will prompt a decision. For instance, one prompt from *The Quiet Year* asks, "There's another community somewhere on the map. Where are they? What sets them apart from you? or . . . What belief or practice helps to unify your community?" The active player will then choose the question and choose how they wish to answer it. For instance, "There is a community that calls itself the Sovereignty of Ire and they have a deeply held spiritual belief in expressing their anger through displays of physical daring. They are located in the mountains here." That player might then draw an angry mountain on the map. Next, the player will choose to start a project, hold a discussion, or announce a discovery. Projects take several weeks to complete; the players negotiate the duration and indicate it with a six-sided die. Discussions compel the airing, but not the addressing, of grievances. *The Quiet Year* rulebook explains, "A discussion never results in a decision or summation process. Everyone weighs in, and then it's over. This is how conversations work in communities: they are untidy and inconclusive affairs."[2] The mechanics of these games, when manipulated by the players, shape the kind of story that emerges. Time is limited and disagreements emerge easily. Finally, announcing a discovery allows a player to add something of interest to the map. For instance, a player might invent that a community member discovers an ancient library full of political writings. That player would then draw a small scroll or codex on the map. It is now up to the other players to decide to pick this thread up or to pursue their own plans.

In this way, a community is formed. It will slowly be populated with interesting characters and hooks for new discussions, discoveries, and projects. Although players might imagine predominantly taking on the role of one community member, the rules encourage players to keep the whole of the community in mind, to play from the perspective of the community itself. *The Quiet Year* rulebook explains that the game "will falter" should the mechanics be used to "tell a story about any one of these individuals," adding that players should use "named characters to support that larger, bird's eye view—and not the other way around."[3] Unlike other collaborative storytelling games or role-playing games, players share the role of the community, and no one controls or represents an individual character.

In *The Deep Forest*, rather than decide on scarce and abundant resources at the outset of the game, players are asked to consider what remains of human settlement to adopt and which to consider taboo. Likewise, during a turn, the active player may start a project, uncover something old, or agree on something. The mechanics here subtly shift the emphasis from colonially loaded language, *discover*, to neutral language, *uncover*. The world of monsters is old. Similarly, the language of *discussion* has been revised to *agree on something*, where the rules explain "everyone else then gets to weigh in once, sharing their agreement with your statement or describing what their silence looks like."[4] *The Deep Forest* subtly adjusts the mechanics of *The Quiet Year* and thus creates a distinct gaming experience.

The Quiet Year and *The Deep Forest* offer a compelling play experience if players have the right collective mindset. The first time I played, I could tell my interests diverged from one of the other players. The most recent time I played, two of the players got in a heated argument about how things should go. Both fractures had the potential to be interesting. Was this what each group set out to create, though? No. It wasn't. If players agree on a loose location, mood, theme, and tone, the potential for shared engagement rises. Groups that do not reach consensus might discuss the spoken disagreement or unacknowledged tensions that arose in gameplay after the game is finished. More importantly, players might discuss the topics they don't wish to discuss. In gaming communities, these discussions might introduce the "x card," a safeword mechanic whereby anyone who feels they do not want to continue can touch or point to the card, or even say "x card," to have play stop or be redirected. They may also discuss players' hard lines on some topics (e.g., child endangerment) and subjects that can be addressed but not explicitly played through the metaphor of placing a veil over explicit discussions of the subject (e.g., implying sexual scenes and then describing the scene fading to black). The addition of a frank conversation at the outset sets players up for generative frustrations later on.

The game makes resolution through discussion challenging by design. Players are encouraged to make decisions on their own for the sake of the community. Play doesn't stop so that players can share their vision. The group moves on to the next prompt; some agendas are taken up, while others are passed over in silence. If a group manages to use the limited mechanics for decision-making to reach consensus, they should congratulate themselves! If they cannot reach consensus, the game offers a mechanic called *contempt*. If a player feels they were not "consulted or honored" during decision-making, they can take a contempt token. For instance, in a recent game, a player decided to build a deep-sea oil platform; another player took contempt as an outlet for "expressing disagreement or tension."[5] The rule booklet makes clear that a player cannot speak to their contempt. Instead, the token sits in front of them as a visible sign of disunity. The player may later return the contempt, but only in a situation where they wish to either act in their own interests or to diffuse tensions. The token may be later discarded to justify behavior that will negatively impact the community (e.g., training the community's dolphin allies to throw themselves at the oil platform in assault and protest, thereby undermining the community's agreed-upon decision to build the platform). This action may result in others taking contempt tokens. Conversely, if someone does something to repair relations and demonstrate their trustworthiness—for instance, if the oil-hungry player had somehow canceled their project—the player who took contempt may then discard it to move past old disagreements. Players need to have contempt (in the literalized form of the token) in order to act selfishly or else to communicate resolution of intracommunal conflict. If a player has no contempt, they cannot justify a destructive course of action nor rebuild trust with the community. Counterintuitively, providing a system for players to register their disagreement allows the game to progress. Contempt signals to the offending player that their actions have created a rift, and, crucially, it provides the chance for other players to notice and the possibility for them to agree by taking their own tokens in a show of solidarity in strife. The mechanics of resolution diverge from other competitive and cooperative tabletop games: they encourage an emergent sense of what is worth taking contempt for that will vary by game and thus from community to community.

I first encountered *The Quiet Year* listening to a live play on the podcast *Friends at the Table*. The conceit spoke to me immediately, as did the model for collaboration and shared storytelling. Yet what made intuitive sense to *Friends at the Table* stumped the tabletop gaming reviewers on *Shut Up & Sit Down*. While I heard Austin Walker of *Friends at the Table* make marvelous, collaborative fun in *The Quiet Year*, Quintin "Quinns" Smith of *Shut Up & Sit Down* argues that the play is "willfully antisocial." Quinns complains that each player has control one at a time, making the game "maddeningly hands-off for everybody else." For Quinns, *The Quiet Year* presents a counterintuitive roleplaying experience.[6] But *The Quiet Year* is only counterintuitive when compared to the bulk of roleplaying games, where the model has been to play an individual and leave the map-drawing to the game master or storyteller figure. *The Quiet Year* is comparatively iconoclastic, willfully divergent. Quinns's comment assumes that the intuitive thing is the individualist expectations of most tabletop role-playing games, that each player will control, develop, and enact one character under the purview of a seemingly all-powerful storyteller. By contrast, *The Quiet Year* meaningfully places the players in negotiation over what exists, what happens, and, crucially, how the community feels about it. Meanwhile, Alder and Truman's *The Deep Forest* pushes beyond colonial tropes in *The Quiet Year* and many other role-playing games that pit antagonistic monsters against heroes, tending to differentiate, other, and racialize monstrous creatures at the level of the mechanics themselves.

The Quiet Year and *The Deep Forest* provide a model for collective decision-making, negotiation, and consensus-building that pushes back against the individual-as-actor model of politics that many have internalized. For those who have felt the crush of settler-colonial violence, grief of anti-Black racism, or damaging expectations of a gender-normative and patriarchal culture, *The Quiet Year* and *The Deep Forest* offer a space where recognition of these and other intersecting injustices may be possible through a unique mechanics of resolution that supports the recognition and airing of grievances. It is here, in the year-long community building experiments each game provides, that contempt may be openly modeled and expressed, where players will be able to determine whether or not that is enough to build and maintain communities, and where they will learn to act in ways that address the need to make amends and recognize the grievances our comrades bear.

Notes

1. Alder and Truman, *Deep Forest*, 4.
2. Alder, *Quiet Year*, 6.
3. Alder, *Quiet Year*, 7.
4. Alder and Truman, *Deep Forest*, 11.
5. Alder, *Quiet Year*, 7.
6. Alexander and Smith, "RPG Review."

Bibliography

Alder, Avery. *The Quiet Year*. The unceded territories of the Sinixt and Ktunaxa: Buried without Ceremony, 2013.

Alder, Avery, and Mark Diaz Truman. *The Deep Forest.* The unceded territories of the Sinixt and Ktunaxa: Buried without Ceremony, 2014.

Alexander, Leigh, and Quintin Smith. "RPG Review: *The Quiet Year.*" *Shut Up & Sit Down,* August 14, 2013. http://www.shutupandsitdown.com/rpg-review-quiet-year/.

Walker, Austin, host. "Marielda 01: The City of Light Pt. 1." *Friends at Table* (podcast). July 14, 2016. Accessed February 24, 2022. https://friendsatthetable.net/marielda-01-the-city-of-light-pt-1.

26 Undead Labs, *State of Decay* (2013) / Crafting Community at the End of the World

Cameron Kunzelman

The video game *State of Decay* begins the same way every time: two friends return from a camping trip. They approach a site around a ranger station, and trouble breaks out. There are groaning, moaning *creatures* there. The player knows what's up, of course: the world has been overtaken by zombies. It's two buddies against a world gone undead, and they're going to need to recruit and craft and plan their way out of this whole awful thing.

It's familiar to the point of exhaustion.

What's slightly different about *State of Decay*, and what I want to get at here in this piece, is that this is not a game that revels in the violent reclamation of the world. Instead, it is about playing your way through how community functions. At its base, *State of Decay* centers on recruitment, expansion, and supply management within Trumbull Valley, the little *Dawn of the Dead*–ish place we play in.

It is a place both apocalyptically abandoned yet teeming with activity. There are named factions, like the local booze-creating family or the remains of a trucking company, and also procedurally generated people just living their lives in single-family homes. These people, whom the game groups under the broad term *neighbors*, all have relationships with their own people that are represented via a reputation system.

In between all of these things are the zombies; yes, you've gotta make your way through them, but they are not the point. What *State of Decay* is focused on, above all else, is thinking about care and community after everything's gone to shit.

That's different from the majority of "zombie media," especially in games. The inclusion of the living dead in a video game often feels more like a justification of mechanics than it does an artistic statement. They look human, but they are not, which allows game developers (and other media creatives) to construct scenarios in which you can shoot and carve your way, relentlessly, through swaths of beings. They seem born from a fundamental question: What kind of world would allow you to chainsaw through your enemies? And from this, the zombie game was born.

In these more traditional games, like *Dying Light* or the Dead Rising series, you represent the last bastion of humanity. You're alive in a sea of the dead; you have a mission to accomplish. The player character allegorically stands in for all good people left alive. Your goals are the goals of these blessed few. A moral universe is restored with every headshot you land.

By contrast, in *State of Decay*, the player character cannot stand in for anything because there is no central player character. When you pick up a controller and begin interacting with the game, you are not deciding to play as one single person, experiencing their narrative ups and downs. Instead, you can freely float between all of your active community members, choosing which one to control at any given time. To put it another way: this game contrasts with so many others because you do not have a singular character that makes its way through the game. You play as the *community itself*, the very concept of willfully gathered individuals. In doing so you experience the variety of the human condition after the end of the world (or at least as much of it as can be imagined by the game's dev team).

In the video game zombie apocalypse, playing a community rather than a specific character, you're put into an arrangement quite unlike any other. In his essay on Georges Bataille's concept of community, Maurice Blanchot claimed that every community is "enjoined to death." All people are bound together by the fact that they all die in the same way, what he called an "impossible communion."[1] When you play *State of Decay*, your characters will die. The former football coach and the park ranger are torn apart in the same way. The movie lover and the alcoholic can crash cars and crawl from the wreckage only to be chased down and torn apart on the side of the highway. These people are differentiated, but they are united in that they live to be controlled and they die when their hit points are reduced to zero.

In the hours before death, however, you get to know them. They have character information sheets that tell you about their former jobs and hobbies, and you understand how those interests are transformed when they make the leap into this new condition. One person might have been a brewer in the time before, meaning that they have some skill in cooking.

Another might have played golf, so they have additional stamina for carrying supplies across the map. Some of these are useful in moment-to-moment gameplay, and some, like a counseling trait, only happen when they're not being controlled at all. Part of the play of the game is tactically leaving people alone to process their trauma, or to cook, or to simply rest. Learning to play is learning when to call on your people.

Cycling through these characters, some of whom are procedurally generated and some of whom are authored specifically to interact with the game's plot in some way, is what allows you to understand what happened to the world. They each have their own perspective that appears in conversation, and in doing missions with them you learn about where they were when the zombie plague broke out. Bit by bit, the individuals' stories stitch together into a tapestry of suffering, infection, and breakdown. And it's more than a little uncanny to play right now.

As I write this, we're sitting in a worldwide COVID-19 pandemic. The United States is climbing into a "second wave" of infections that will likely eclipse the first. The state I live in has made a tactical move to "open up," the vast majority of people refuse to wear masks, and many seem committed to pretending that things are "back to normal." It has become mind-annihilatingly clear that whatever ideas we had about cohesive social structure and the common good are wrong. Between a massive campaign to mystify the numbers of deaths and a complete lack of leadership from governmental officials, it seems clear that a substantial number of people are simply okay with letting themselves, their families, their friends, and many in the general population die of a preventable disease. And that's saying nothing about those who are held in border camps or those who are imprisoned, each locked in with the disease without any legal recourse.

If I were to paint a sunny picture of the relationship between *State of Decay* and this current nightmare, I would say that it provides a kind of road map. It gets you out of the idea that we're all individual heroes. It pulls you into the recognition that the reality of life is that we're social creatures, that our lives depend on the labor of others, and that playing as a community might shake free some of our most destructive ideological beliefs. It might be the dose of hope that we need in a time when the most basic tenets of the social contract have atrophied down to their thinnest sinews.

But the reality, as I see it, is much starker. Against all think piece logic, I think that video games will not save us. No media object will, at least in the sense that all a piece of media can do is gesture toward a potential world to come without doing all that much to instantiate it. No video game is going to change the material conditions of the world of its players.

At best, I think what *State of Decay* can provide us with is a cornerstone for thinking about how we might preserve specific values for some time to come. Félix Guattari often referred to the 1980s as "the winter years," demarcating them from the relatively radical 1960s and 1970s, and in doing so he gave a flavor to the chilling of thought that happened when the right wing took power across Europe and in the United States during the 1980s. Like a virus or a seed, Guattari saw himself closing up to save his energy, holding onto it for the time where it could take root.

Rather than a chance for projective politics, for thinking about orientations of future affairs, I think that *State of Decay* might be an opportunity for the cultivation of the self, a kind of meditative practice of making oneself into a seed. It is a reflective game that gives players a chance to consider what it might mean to manage threats to community values in a way that refuses to define a community by perceived threats to it. The zombies are out there, sure, but they're not the problem. They can be managed. They can be detoured. What we cannot defer is our own nourishment, our own self-development; nor can we avoid reflection about our own practices of how we connect and form coalitions with others.

Because there are times in *State of Decay* when you have to save your neighbors. Remember, that's what the game calls all of the other factions who are trapped in Trumbull Valley with you: neighbors. Like your community, they are threatened by zombies. Like you, they have to fight. And also like you, they get in jams, and they'll call over the radio to help. In these instances, you have a choice to make: Do I risk my own people to help? Do I use my ammunition, my melee weapon durability, to assure that my neighbors will continue to have a healthy life? Do I value them in that way, or is this an opportunity to let them become extinguished so that I can take over their property?

These are questions about the limits of care, and they call attention to the limit points that we draw around what we consider a community. *State of Decay* presents a world in which you play your community, where you *are* your community, and you have to take care of those people. At first glance, that communal function is your roster of controllable characters that live in the compounds that you build. They're the people you ride out the end of the world with, in close proximity, helping each other find food and building materials and a sense of safety.

But if we put it in Bataillean terms, when we play as the community, we're really playing as everyone in the valley. The player is every living soul in that place because they are all tending toward death. They are all one community, bound up by the same limits, and the small actions that characters can take on small supply run missions can have large impacts on the livability of the world. You're not the world spirit on horseback; you're a little piece of living being in a beat-up car.

And, of course, you feel that sense of larger community when you fail at the tasks of maintaining the other characters. A neighbor calls for help, and you're across the map. You have time to get there, you think, so you first do a short supply run. Then you rescue another neighbor because she's closer. When you finally make time for the broader community, you pull up in your truck. The windows of the store your neighbors lived in are broken. You go inside and there's no one to talk to. You check your map again, and their icon isn't there. And if you're like me, you have this guilt that wells up with no outlet. There's no going back. There's just trudging forward.

Nothing here is an allegory for face mask wearing or social infection. It doesn't give us a grip on the absolute despair that is electoral politics, and there's no vision of hope or change on the horizon. *State of Decay* simply decenters the individual zombie protagonist into community, and then it doubles down by troubling how we understand community. And my perspective here in the summer of 2020, deep in the US South, is that these things need to be troubled at every turn so as to turn back the oncoming winter.

Note

1. Blanchot, *Unavowable Community*, 10, 11.

Bibliography

Blanchot, Maurice. *The Unavowable Community*. Translated by Pierre Joris. Barrytown, NY: Station Hill Press, 1984.

State of Decay. Undead Labs, 2013.

27 Hideo Kojima, *Death Stranding* (2019) / Reconnecting in the Time of Climate Change

Darshana Jayemanne, Brendan Keogh, and Ben Abraham

Since its first trailer in 2016, digital game *Death Stranding* primed audiences with a strange aesthetic imagery: photorealistic Hollywood celebrities stand on a beach of oil-spilled tar and stranded whales; a naked Norman Reedus carries an unborn baby in an artificial womb; a World War II battlefield writhes with monstrous tentacles; undead US Marines emerge from the black blood of the planet itself, only to be set aflame by a cigarette-smoking Mads Mikkelsen. In the public's first vision of this massively anticipated title—auteur Hideo Kojima's first game since his messy departure from long-time publisher Konami—*Death Stranding* promised to encapsulate the pressing issues of our time. These range from climate and ecological catastrophe to life and death in the Anthropocene to, most uncanny of all, the challenges of staying connected in a socially distanced world.

The eventual 2019 release was in many ways even stranger than the selective marketing glimpses suggested. An event known as the "death stranding" has muddled together the realms of the living and the dead, while spectral "Beached Things" (BTs) haunt parts of the world. When BTs, comprised of what looks like tarry oil and exhaust fumes, attack a living person, a massive supernatural explosion called a "voidout" occurs. The risk of voidouts and other supernatural effects have forced the world's survivors into underground bunkers, unable to move around the world (an uncanny prefiguring of the 2020 COVID-19 lockdowns). Society becomes dependent on the few "porters" that trek across dangerous remnants of the world, delivering food, resources, and messages between outposts.

As is common for video games directed by Kojima (best recognized for his work on the long-running Metal Gear series), *Death Stranding* is a heady cocktail of experimental and generic gameplay styles, grim seriousness, soapy drama, fourth-wall breakings, on-the-nose metaphors, magical militarism, an incomprehensible number of neologisms and abbreviations, and sophomoric sexual and scatological humor. Although much more goes on in *Death Stranding* than could even be glossed over in a single essay, it teaches us about living through the end of the world—both through and *after* climate catastrophe—and the double-edged sword of "chronic connectivity."[1] The latter gets players to question our pervasive internet connections, gamified social-media platforms, and the forms of social interaction they mediate. *Death Stranding* shows us how we might live on in our time of unevenly distributed collapse.

Death Stranding is also, like many of the texts in this collection that teeter on the edge of utopia/dystopia, fatally compromised—as much as any other video game, anyway. Like all digital games, *Death Stranding* requires a hardware platform notorious for devouring conflict minerals and spewing e-waste—sucking real energy to create pleasing illusions and potentially diverting our attention from vital concerns. Certainly in many possible end-of-the-world scenarios, video games will be among the first cultural texts to become illegible and unsupportable.

But these endemic compromises are what makes the game instructive: *Death Stranding* sits at an inflection point in science fiction storytelling and digital gaming, one pushing back against mainstream gaming's often unreflexive apocalypticism with a more critical climate fiction imaginary shot through with dim rays of hope. As the product of a globally dispersed production team (with locations credits including Santa Monica, Tokyo, Amsterdam, and London, among others) helmed by Kojima, a creative director who has an almost uniquely auteurist status in the industry, *Death Stranding* operates at an intensive contemporary nexus of independent aesthetic vision supported by the extractive potentials of game tech conceived both as "experience machine"[2] and attention economy or platform. While the auteur notion is as important to scrutinize and problematize in digital games as elsewhere, the uniqueness of this case can be gleaned from the studio established by *Death Stranding*'s creator after Kojima's public departure from Konami: Kojima Productions. Kojima ranks among the few game developers that could have negotiated access to the jaw-dropping resources necessary to produce such an idiosyncratic vision.

With explicit themes of human extinction and a visual language that hints at climate catastrophe in our fossil-fueled era, the game captures something of the contemporary zeitgeist. As another lesson along these lines, *Death Stranding* teaches us, by working through its own conditions of possibility, the importance of the contingency or "banality" of infrastructure in the face of our quilted apocalypses.[3]

Uneven Apocalypses

In *Death Stranding*, players take on the role of Sam Porter-Bridges, motion-captured and voiced by actor Norman Reedus. Sam is tasked by President Bridget Strand with tracking the path of her daughter Amelie, who had led a failed expedition to "make America whole again" in the wake of the catastrophe. Mirroring the colonialist path of the Westward Expansion of the 1800s, players steer Sam west across what was the United States of America, reconnecting isolated outposts to the "Chiral Network" (a combination high-speed internet and power grid) to physically rebuild a fragmented country as the United Cities of America. Players route him through "the Beach"—the timeless oily limbo from which issue the returned dead (the aforementioned Beached Things). With the Chiral Network capable of miraculous information transfer and matter manipulation, as players bring outposts into that network, they gain for themselves access to another network: that of the game's online servers that allow players to share the infrastructural pathways across the world.

Perhaps the most innovative, and polarizing, aspect of *Death Stranding* is the design decision to make simply traversing the environment a central feature. Through Sam—that is, all the Sams of *Death Stranding*'s globally dispersed player base—traversal is not treated as a sovereign right of neocolonial conquest wielded by "the player," guaranteed through vast cycles of playtesting and iteration, but instead is facilitated by the connection to an ad hoc community and the infrastructure it maintains. This muddles the normative game-design truism that it is a cardinal sin for players to become lost, not knowing where to go next nor how to get there. Identifying a novel path to new outposts through the apocalyptic landscape presents a tedious task. Mundane, real-world logistics, such as balancing cargo weight while walking, become key to gameplay. Attempt to carry too much or unevenly distribute your items' weight, and the chance of a fall that scatters precious cargo is increased; carry too little, and the grueling trek becomes less worthwhile relative to the dangers of the environment and players' time.

This future is topologically uneven in a way that spatially reflects the extreme temporalities of diachronic timefall and the synchrony of the Beach. Steep slopes, ravines, and rocky terrain risk unbalancing Sam, and make the going slow; players can hold the trigger buttons on the controller to have Sam hold onto his load more tightly to prevent toppling, but this slows him down to a walking pace. Cliffs, ravines, and even other tamer environmental obstacles like gentle slopes and rocky ground that would be unproblematic in any other game here become formidable obstacles requiring delicate maneuvering and appropriate equipment.

Once Sam has connected a region to the Chiral Network, however, this task not only becomes much easier but also is suddenly and dramatically *synchronized* to the experiences of other players and "porters" in their own games. The Chiral Network maps repetition and difference in strange ways: bridges and ladders established in one player's world will appear in another, and the regular foot-traffic of players along certain routes create pathways that smooth out uneven ground, making it much easier for Sam to move through the worlds.

Playing *Death Stranding* online means accessing a support network of other players who help make the aggressively tedious terrain more navigable and the lonely disconnected world more communal. One player may place a bridge across a fast-flowing river, or leave a rope dangling over an otherwise unscalable cliff. The placement of these objects in the world also reflects the very ordinary needs of other humans, not conforming to (or dependent on) the rigid, regular order of centralized planning. Upkeep of these objects requires the contribution of materials to restore them to their prime condition, relying on decentralized donations and the generosity of other players, rather than a centralized collection and distribution scheme. In a quirky turn, players can show their thanks by rewarding other players' infrastructure in the world with "Likes"—operating not as a pretext for extractive competition and scarcity simulation characteristic of (capitalistic) attention economies, but as an endless and renewable resource of gratitude that gradually builds a grassroots sense of community.

Extinction Entities

In *Climate Leviathan*, political scientists Geoff Mann and Joel Wainwright offer an analysis of the political space for governance structures to adapt to climate change in the near future. They figure the space for adaptation exists between poles of capitalist/anticapitalist responses to climate change, as well as along an axis of planetary sovereignty. They argue for a future that is hard to imagine, only the faintest of glimmers of which are evident today, a world-future they describe as Climate X, which is not "Support for Green Keynesianism . . . climate finance . . . and the elite politics of adaptation . . . distractions, dissipaters of energy for change."[4] Instead Climate X takes the form of grass roots, decentralized and highly local focused actions adding up to a revolution in the way we inhabit planet Earth. *Death Stranding* shows some of the benefits of this kind of devolution of power and planning with public, shared infrastructure that is determined not by central government but by individuals, created and maintained according to need and the greatest utility. As with most video games, however, these principles are not simply explored by *Death Stranding*'s scripted narrative but are unearthed systematically through the very act of playing, in engaging with the game system's affordances and constraints. The act of playing *Death Stranding* exemplifies Mann and Wainwright's Climate X vision of a world built on the principles of equality, "the inclusion and dignity of all," and "solidarity in composing a world of many worlds."[5]

The game's two overarching themes—climate apocalypse and the always-on internet—are not as distinct as they might first appear. In 2001, at the peak of enthusiasm for the empowering, democratizing, and participatory power of "Web 2.0," Kojima helmed *Metal Gear Solid 2* (*MGS2*), a game deeply cynical and pessimistic of the impacts of the internet and its ability to spread misinformation through society. In recent years, many have looked back at *MGS2* as anticipating the current age, in which fake news, bots, and meme farms support unbelievable conspiracy theories and authoritarian world leaders, while the private platforms we depend on for our social world stand by and do nothing. Climate change, in particular, has been emblematic of the insufficiency of "facts" to allow the imagining of climate change's nonhuman (but accelerating) timescales—or, for that matter, alternative, sustainable futures.

If *MGS2* warned of how the internet would destroy society, then *Death Stranding*, released eighteen years later, muses over how the internet *has already* fragmented society: how a nonexploitative vision of the social is critical to our response to the uneven apocalypses with which we are faced. This quality of the game's vision is clearly tied into the specific violence of US colonialism. Immobilized President Bridget and her expeditionary daughter Amelie are (we learn at the end of the game) the same person: a physical body subject to terminal cancer, and an atemporal, ageless ideal of a recolonized United States of America that exists in the timeless Beach. Together, they form an "Extinction Entity"—beings responsible for mass extinctions, which emerge from the tarry, oily mass of the Beach.

Sam, heading west to reconnect and recolonize the American continent, we learn toward the end of the game, was saved by this Extinction Entity, sent back to the world of the living after his untimely death as a baby. This explains, within the game's internal logic, Sam's ability to traverse multiple worlds: both fictionally, through the Chiral Network, and in reality through knotting together multiple players' labor, their painstakingly created infrastructures of support. Sam, as a being whose death was incomplete, is something akin to Meillasoux's notion of the *essential specter*—a paradoxical being that enjoins us to be open to radical contingency (such as a bridge appearing from another world).[6] But perhaps more apropos is a figure that has emerged in a new light during the coronavirus pandemic that is the most proximal crisis as of this writing: Sam as *essential worker*. "Essential work extends beyond health care. Although some people have been able to shift their jobs to their homes, millions of workers have jobs that cannot be done at home—not only custodial staff and orderlies in hospitals, but also teachers and child-care workers, grocery clerks and supermarket workers, delivery people, factory and farm workers, and restaurant staff, often without adequate PPE."[7] Essential workers reveal both the colonial infrastructure of everyday life and the reality of technological capabilities as constrained by the politics and culture of empire, and they do so through overexposure to contingency.

Death Stranding thus offers different answers than Kojima's prior directorial efforts on the perspective of daily labor serving empire. In *MGS2*, "magical militarism" was used to explore the formation of the subjectivity of *soldiers*: individual workers who have been shaped and traumatized by the state to project colonial force. In *Death Stranding*, however, the considered balance of realism and fantasy in *MGS2* gives way to the far more oneiric tonality of the death-stranding event. It is true that Sam can equip the armor and guns beloved of mainstream gaming, but combat encounters are so rare amid the drudgery that these iconic objects are most of the time *just more cargo*. In another of Kojima's uncanny anticipations, the hazardous conditions of the game's world means that the PPE of the essential worker is far more important than the hyperspecialized equipage of the super soldier. This decenters player action itself, such that player activity comes to resemble the "quality assurance" hours that go into creating such a virtual world. Often outsourced and precarious, this form of labor resembles "essential" and banal infrastructural work beneath the glitzy surface of game industry culture and products.

As a focal point for both players' interactivity in the game and the shift from soldier to essential worker, as a protagonist of a game born of a dysfunctional relationship between the games industry and one of its marquee creators, Sam reveals the game's autocritique of the delirium of big-budget video games: "virtual reality" not as speculative science fiction trope or marketing flimflam, but as it really exists in the everyday domesticity of game consoles, personal computers, and mobile devices. In linking this critique to its engagements with both fictional and real social medias, *Death Stranding* plays with the idea that the technologies shaping human communicative and creative powers could be developed not by extractive interests but with a view to "solidarity in composing a world of many worlds."[8]

Notes

1. Gregg, *Work's Intimacy*, xi.
2. Nozick, *Anarchy, State, and Utopia.*
3. Anand, "Banality of Infrastructure."
4. Mann and Wainwright, *Climate Leviathan*, 173.
5. Mann and Wainwright, *Climate Leviathan*, 175–176.
6. Meillassoux, "Spectral Dilemma."
7. Lancet, "Plight of Essential Workers."
8. Mann and Wainwright, *Climate Leviathan*, 176.

Bibliography

Anand, Nikhil. "The Banality of Infrastructure." *Items: Insights from the Social Sciences*, June 27, 2017. https://items.ssrc.org/just-environments/the-banality-of-infrastructure/.

Gregg, Melissa. *Work's Intimacy*. Boston: Polity, 2013.

Kojima, Hideo. *Death Stranding*. Kojima Productions, 2019.

Lancet. "The Plight of Essential Workers during the COVID-19 Pandemic." *Lancet* 395, no. 10237 (May 23, 2020). https://doi.org/10.1016/S0140-6736(20)31200-9.

Mann, Geoff, and Joel Wainwright. *Climate Leviathan: A Political Theory of Our Planetary Future*. New York: Verso, 2018.

Meillassoux, Quentin. "Spectral Dilemma." *Collapse* 4 (2018): 261–276.

Nozick, Robert. *Anarchy, State, and Utopia*. New York: Basic Books, 1974.

28 Toshi Reagon and Bernice Johnson Reagon, *Octavia E. Butler's Parable of the Sower* (2020) / Links to Our Future-Present

Ayana Jamieson

The Future-Present

Octavia E. Butler warned us. Octavia Butler *warned* us. *Octavia Warned Us.*

Almost every day since spring 2020, this phrase has bounced around my head as a statement of fact, or a response to another devastating piece of news, or the belated recognition of some folks who have only *just* realized the detailed specificity of her cautionary tales. "There's a new day coming! . . . Where you gon' be standing when it comes?" Lauren Oya Olamina challenges her father Reverend Olamina on stage. Through Olamina, Butler speaks directly to us: "I've never felt that I was making any of this up—not the name Earthseed, not any of it." Instead, Olamina's found belief system is "discovery rather than invention, exploration rather than creation," and observable through patterns, chaos, and cycles.[1]

Olamina, a fifteen-year-old Black girl from Robledo, California, writes in her journals that comprise the speculative future novel. Crafted through Butler's meticulous research in the late 1970s, 1980s, and early 1990s, the novel takes place from 2024 through 2027. On April 26, 2025, Olamina writes: "All I do is observe and take notes, trying to put things down in ways that are as powerful, as simple, and as direct as I feel them."[2] Born in 2009, Olamina is twelve years old in our current moment. I imagine that she is hearing and seeing everything happening now, taking note, and gearing up to write *The Books of the Living,* the shape her Earthseed verses and principles will take.

One need not have read the novels to feel the pull of African American sacred music over the last two hundred plus years, but it helps to interpret what we all experience at the time. In a 2000 interview with *Essence,* Butler didn't claim prescience about our present calamities: "All I did was look around at the problems we're neglecting now and give them about 30 years to grow into full-fledged disasters."[3] But it has taken us only twenty years to get to our present calamities of climate change, global pandemic, xenophobic racial oppression, and teetering on the brink of economic collapse. The pandemic has shined a light on the unsustainability of early twenty-first-century capitalism, false diversions from healing the planet, and tangible human contributions to our collective survival.

When people ask me how I (as a Black person, or mother of sons, or academic, or scholar, or trauma survivor, or human) am doing with "everything that's going on," I don't always know what to say. Who can be succinct about ongoing inequality, recording of Black death, the carceral state, or poverty? Instead, I place a pin on the map of this reality of rupture we are all trying to navigate, carving out the edges of an existence that is tenuous and tentative. What follows is an attempt at charting the landscapes of Change by giving an accounting of events, joyful and painful, large and small, personal and communal, public and private, that unpack Octavia E. Butler's warnings. It is necessary to take both Olamina's and Butler's approach, to write things as simply and directly as possible; to take up Butler's own personal praxis of "Learning to Fly," dreaming aloud: "It comes to me when I struggle—when I twist on my own personal hook and try to pretend that nothing unusual is happening."[4]

Lauren Oya Olamina is named after Oya, the Yoruban deity of rupture via Change, winds, violent storms, life and death. Change is a proper noun the way Butler wrote it in the Parables. It is an archetype, an organizing pattern. I first learned about archetypes as a theatre student. *Archetypes* are versions of things that are familiar to human beings, acted out in culture and in private throughout history, across time, via cultures in different guises, and represented in socially constructed norms and resistance to those norms. Archetypes are not things or people in and of themselves; they're indicated by what is observed. A person cannot be an archetype, but a character or event can represent the way the pattern unfolds, like ripples of water moving out in all directions. I tell my ethnic and cultural studies students that an archetype is the opposite of a stereotype. If a stereotype is the lowest common denominator, or the fewest number of characteristics or behaviors assigned to identify someone within a group as representative of the whole group, then what is an archetype? An archetype is all of the possible iterations—positive, negative, known, unknown, hidden, expressed, revealed, suppressed, and so on. Like Change, archetypes are speculatively open-ended and come in many forms.

Octavia E. Butler's Parable of the Sower, an opera with music and lyrics written by Toshi Reagon and Bernice Johnson Reagon, and directed by Eric Ting, is a fulcrum that marks the transition from a before-COVID-19 time, to now, and to whatever cycles exist afterward. Transforming Butler's fiction into a theatrical production by Reagon and Reagon, *Parable Opera* brings archetypal patterns into conversation, most notably beginning with Change. The theatre production with its specialized seating, memorized words and music, performers and audience are another kind of rite of passage steeped in the rituals of Black church. Toshi and her castmates, designers, musicians, and community partners tap into the energy of Change, and we are forever altered by the show, a profound act of forging transformative community. Poet, queer Black feminist, and Black love evangelist Alexis Pauline Gumbs notes that the opera brings Lauren's journal entries and the novel's character to life through Black congregational sound.[5] As members of the audience, we are drafted into this space of ritual as we watch and are called to actively participate in what we are *withnessing* (witnessing *with*).

The Recent Past

On March 4, 2020, both the California governor's office and the county and city of Los Angeles declared official emergencies. The novel coronavirus that causes the COVID-19 disease had reached American shores with 129 cases confirmed, including fifty-three in California. At the same time, people were converging from all over the country for the Los Angeles premier of the *Octavia E. Butler's Parable of the Sower* opera and for events scheduled in the area in conjunction with the production. Toshi was returning to the southland in preparation for the performance in the spring as part of an artist's residency, as the third or fourth visit among other events. An artist, in Toshi's view, has a responsibility to community. A kind of *community-accountable scholarship*, as Gumbs terms it.

Toshi's method of doing the Parable opera as an independently produced and financed large-scale production is one of being in right relationship with the communities where the show will be performed, by investing time and attention within communities surrounding Boston, Chapel Hill, Philadelphia, St. Paul, and elsewhere while highlighting local expertise already in existence beforehand and afterward.[6] Like Lauren Oya Olamina's gathering of members of Earthseed and Mary Larkin's Pattern in Butler's *Seed to Harvest* (Patternist) novels, Toshi brings together communities of artists, activists, organizations, and venues to facilitate important work that is already ongoing, or newly sprouted from Butler's writing. Everything is intentional, from preshow programming to educational opportunities and other ways to leverage the resources that the show generates for the benefit of marginalized people in community. The "sharing" of resources, responsibility, pain, and joy are all intertwined and highlighted throughout the production. We share warnings through the call and response of "Don't let your baby go to Olivar," the oppressive company town. The personification of hyperempathy syndrome takes shape in another song: "If I feel all you feel, would you know me better? If I share all your pain, would I know you better? If I take flight in your joy, would I know you better?"

Toshi describes the theatrical performance as a navel, a belly button that is central to a network of systems that create an entire body of communities around the globe. This navel is more like a marsupial pouch, incubating little ponds of activity before birthing an entire oceanic continent. Free and affordable tickets at a range of prices mean that when audiences gather, they see themselves reflected in the performers onstage, as well as in the seats all around them. Theatre as Toshi enacts it returns to her griot-as-liberation-theology grassroots activism. The music of the show flows from Toshi's own multigenre folk music,[7] from her mother Bernice's life as Freedom Singer, scholar, "songtalker," Sweet Honey on the Rock, and more, the sacred music of Black folks, DC Black Repertory Theatre, and workshopping the Parable novel in a class at Princeton for Toni Morrison.[8]

My own work as the founder of the Octavia E. Butler Legacy Network follows this same community-accountable engagement, a method of horizontal, rather than hierarchical, collaboration. This method requires that I talk about, write, teach, and highlight Butler's life and work, along with ongoing efforts around the globe that do the same. While Butler's writing is globally recognized and lauded, it also needs to be rooted in the understanding of what is also local and specific about her life. In other words, my message hinges on the fact that Butler needs to be understood as the individual, as well as the archetypes she invokes.

In the days leading up to the production, it is decided that I will join Toshi and other artists on stage afterward for the question and answer session. On Saturday, March 7, 2020, we gather as a group of nearly two thousand people enveloped in an ornate performance space. Toshi remarks, "Octavia don't play!" and that this historic performance near to Butler's birthplace and place of upbringing of Pasadena, California, is meant to happen. We participate with a sense of hope, that we are not isolated in the ongoing acts of resistance for equality, but that there are hundreds of people who feel compelled to fight, strategize, stay together, and demand equal rights. In the moment, I am overwhelmed when Corazon "Cory" Olamina and Reverend Olamina sing "I Won't Crumble if You Fall" after he brutalizes their son Keith for wanting to go outside. (Later, when the versions of the show are rebroadcast on the internet, this song is missing, and Keith's words foreshadow our new normal, locked inside, isolated from one another.) We formed a chosen community—a congregation—without knowing it would be the last in-person gathering of that size permitted under the "Safe at Home" orders. Had the performance been scheduled a day or week later, it would have been prohibited and canceled! We are still blissfully ignorant of what is to come.

The image of the navel resounds throughout the evening. Toshi sits in the center of the stage as conductor and musical director. A row of musicians sits behind her on another higher-raised platform. There are two Black women on either side of her, who along with Toshi form the "Talents," a kind of chorus of Fates that infuse the entire space. Sometimes they bring current events into the room; sometimes we watch their joy or anguish as they draw us into the present. Besides each of these women, and extending out on the floor, the cast sits in a half-circle of chairs opening toward the audience, through the proscenium arch. We complete the circle. Behind them, we notice two rows of people in seats watching the action. At first, it isn't clear whether these are actors or audience members. They are dressed like the cast members who mostly look like regular contemporary folks. These people are most likely UCLA theatre students who are privileged and tasked to *withness* the action up close, crammed in the middle of the action, unable to move, silent participants.

Along with these students, Toshi lures us into the action as narrator, guide, artist, folksinger, and clarion, along with the Talents. We are all part of the performance. There is no separation, no safety beyond the proscenium arch, no fourth wall to be broken. Instead, Toshi pierces our illusions of separateness and independence, enlisting us in writing ourselves in, to use Butler's method—experiencing joy along with despair and hope along with *interdependent* righteous anger and calls to action. Toshi herself says, "I found something missing in the future," as she addresses us: "A folksinger!" As we chuckle, she explains that she sees herself in a coffee shop, on a stoop or porch, serving tea, bartering acorn bread in exchange for a song.

I have driven to the show with my mother, Peggy Kathryn, who is the same age as Ruby Bridges, the first child to desegregate a school in Louisiana in 1960. Our beloved left-coast state has always had racism without racists—more Jim Crow laws than any other state. My grandmother, a nurse, would have to fight with the school board over a decade later in Southern California to allow my mother and her sister to attend a school across the street from the house instead of being bussed to the Black school in the 1970s. My mother sits on my right while horror author and filmmaker Tananarive Due sits on the other side of my mother. I pass facial tissues down the aisle when I realize that one of them is also weeping during the show. When Lauren Olamina sings, "Have you seen my father?" in a spotlight at the center of the stage, her voice is a time crystal, slicing through from the future to let us know we will be mourning our lost loved ones and unable to be with them when they transition.

On the other side of Tananarive, Donna Oliver, Butler's longtime childhood best friend (since kindergarten!) sits, our assigned seats randomly placing us all together. I wonder how this world appears to her after more than seventy years on this planet. What else besides the reminder that "it don't rain no more" and "all struggles are essentially power struggles" can such a long life teach us? Before and after the show, we all embrace and take photos and try to metabolize our feelings about what we've shared together. We mourn Butler's passing as we mourn the truth of the words she wrote, the unfinished work that we must commit ourselves to doing. As we say our goodbyes, our existence is affirmed without the need for the pastor to say, "Turn to your neighbor and tell them that the only lasting truth is Change!" We are certain that we are a "harvest of survivors" and we deserve to thrive. Performances of the opera are rooted in the text, but also speak to ongoing issues depicted in the novel that continue to arise.

On Thursday, March 12, 2020, at 12:51 p.m., my public schoolteacher husband sends me a message while he is at work: "They're going to close the schools. Tonight, or tomorrow." The next day, Friday, March 13, 2020, his message says: "Schools are closing starting Monday—confirmed," and my preschooler and I pick up my third grader from school for the last time. School closures bring us closer to the world in the *Parable of the Sower*. After an extended spring break, teachers and students are supposed to participate in some form of crisis schooling. Like the uneducated hordes of people who live outside the walls of Lauren's Robledo cul-de-sac, thousands of children do not have access to the internet, transportation, and adult supervision when schools and daycares close. Migrant children are still being incarcerated and denied healthcare; unarmed Black folks continued to be murdered with impunity.

In the largely immigrant, working-class school district where I worked while I was in graduate school, students are supposed to pick up photocopied packets of worksheets to complete, but many are unable to do that. Teachers, postal workers, grocery store workers, and those in the supply chain for goods are all deemed essential workers, along with the doctors and nurses working in healthcare to stem the spread of the virus. We are asked to wear masks, especially when we are indoors conducting essential business to protect one another and store employees. Millions of workers' jobs disappear overnight along with their incomes, benefits, and livelihoods. Disabled workers decry the sudden availability of work-from-home options that many have advocated for and been denied in the past. And still others must work from home and care for school-aged children and/or elderly dependents simultaneously, all while trying to stop the deadly virus under mandatory lockdown.

The Present-Future

Now that so much time has passed, it is hard to recall the feeling of elation and optimism we experienced that March 7. The world feels more and more like the Parables. Access to healthcare, education, resources, and the ability to stay home and shelter in place varies widely. As the death toll climbs, disproportionate numbers of low-income men, women, and children from marginalized ethnic groups die from COVID-19. After the filmed suffocation death of George Floyd by Minneapolis police officers on May 25, 2020, sparked worldwide protests, it feels as if Earthseed is spreading as Black Lives Matter. Toshi sings, "The whole world's gone crazy / except for you and me," and we believe her.[9]

At the time of this writing, another complication depicted in *Parable of the Sower* brings Butler's writing and the Reagons' renderings into high relief. Wildfires are burning all up and down the West Coast. Whereas the environment had just begun to heal itself from the ravages of human-caused pollution, global warming, dry, hot conditions, and fire-prevention measures canceled due to COVID-19 have made a recipe for disaster. I live in one of the foothill communities under evacuation warning. There are helicopters and aircraft flying over my home, dumping water and blood-red fire retardant on the nearby San Gabriel Mountains, as the over 115,000-acre Bobcat Fire continues to burn day and night. I develop a painful new understanding of what it means to live with fire, smoke seeping into the house each night and being poised to wonder what it might be like if we need to leave. We are all completely naïve about what this will actually mean and how quickly things will escalate. Over seven hundred thousand people have died of COVID-19 in the United States alone, and loved ones have frequently been prevented from gathering to lay the deceased to rest.

I am comforted by the fact that there are vulnerable elders being protected, artists like Toshi who continue to sing and encourage us all to "vibrate in our bodies in any way we can," even from a distance over the internet. I look at my ten-year-old, my five-year-old, and other children in this crisis and imagine multiple possible Lauren Oya Olaminas. Olamina is the same age as my mother was when she attended Little Zion Missionary Baptist Church in Compton, California. The time-traversing evocation of my mother's former life and the ones the children of today might live overlap in our memories of the performance. I know for certain that Olamina, twelve years old in our current moment, is hearing and seeing everything as it occurs, taking note, and gearing up to write *The Books of the Living* because "We are Earthseed."

As wind, as fire, as water, as life, God is Change.

Notes

1. Butler, *Parable of the Sower*, 78.
2. Butler, *Parable of the Sower*, 78.
3. Butler, "Rules for Predicting the Future," 165.

4. Butler, *Parable of the Sower,* 1. Olamina opens the novel by recalling a recurring dream. The dream becomes Olamina's first song in the opera.

5. Gumbs, "Hundredfold."

6. See brown, "Vulnerability."

7. For a discussion of Toshi's roots, see "Folk Musician Pete Seeger, As Remembered by His Goddaughter."

8. See "About Dr. Reagon" for a history of her musical background.

9. CAP UCLA, "Toshi Reagon—Whole World's Gone Crazy."

Bibliography

"About Dr. Reagon." Bernice Johnson Reagon. Accessed September 21, 2020. https://www.bernicejohnsonreagon.com/about/.

brown, adrienne maree. "On Vulnerability, Playfulness, and Keeping Yourself Honest." *Creative Independent* (blog), July 11, 2019. https://thecreativeindependent.com/people/adrienne-maree-brown-on-vulnerability-playfulness-and-keeping-yourself-honest/.

Butler, Octavia E. "A Few Rules for Predicting the Future." *Essence,* May 2000, 165–166, 264.

Butler, Octavia E. *Parable of the Sower.* New York: Four Walls Eight Windows, 1993.

Butler, Octavia E. *Seed to Harvest.* New York: Warner Books, 2007.

CAP UCLA. "Toshi Reagon—Whole World's Gone Crazy." YouTube video, February 3, 2020. https://www.youtube.com/watch?v=Wie63mAbm8s.

"Folk Musician Pete Seeger, As Remembered by His Goddaughter." *All Things Considered,* National Public Radio, January 24, 2014. https://www.npr.org/2014/01/28/267797309/folk-musician-pete-seeger-as-remembered-by-his-goddaughter.

Gumbs, Alexis Pauline. "A Hundredfold: An Experiential Archive of *Octavia E. Butler's Parable of the Sower: The Opera.*" In *The Routledge Companion to African American Theatre and Performance,* edited by Kathy A. Perkins, Sandra L. Richards, Renée Alexander Craft, and Thomas F. DeFratz, 307–310. London: Routledge, 2018.

IV Revolution

29 Pauline Hopkins, *Of One Blood* (1902) / Antiracism and the Counternarrative of the Black Fantastic

Dexter Gabriel

Beginning in the fall of 1902, *Colored American Magazine* began publishing a series by writer Pauline Hopkins titled *Of One Blood, or The Hidden Self.* Set sometime after the Civil War, the story centers on young Boston medical student Reuel Briggs. Raised on the racism so pervasive in early twentieth-century America, Briggs has come to accept notions of Black inferiority and has little concern about a Black past—a heritage that he, quite literally, hides from the world. This changes when he embarks on an expedition to Africa, where he finds both a lost Black civilization and the roots of his own hidden identity.[1]

Hopkins's story was extraordinary, as a narrative by an African American writer using an imagined African setting, drawing on historical romance, lost world mythos, science fiction, fantasy, and mystery. But Hopkins intended her work to be more than storytelling, and rather an expose exploring the fallacies of racism and its deleterious effects.[2] Three years later, she self-published a 1905 pamphlet titled *A Primer of Facts Pertaining to the Early Greatness of the African Race and the Possibility of Restoration by Its Descendants.* Using Biblical ethnology and available sources, Hopkins traced the descendants of Ham—in particular, the eponymous Cush—as the founders of a vast "Ethiopian" civilization stretching from Babylon to Egypt to Sudan, thus making them the progenitors of western Civilization.

Hopkins argued that knowledge of a glorious past, albeit a romanticized one, would counteract the psychologically damaging racism of the age. Pamphlets with collected facts were one tool, but as a writer Hopkins also believed that narrative literature could serve a similar purpose. As she would later explain, she wrote not just for notoriety, but to "raise the stigma of degradation from my race."[3] *Of One Blood,* with its tale of lost cities and reconstituted pride, imbued the Black imaginary with purpose: an inherently political act, intended to challenge, and in some ways overthrow, white supremacy's claim to historical hegemony.

Of One Blood revolves around three central characters: the protagonist Reuel Briggs, his friend Aubrey Livingston, and a young woman, Dianthe Lusk. The relationship between the two men is particularly interesting as Aubrey knows Reuel's racial origins, and though Aubrey is a Southerner and son of a plantation owner, he agrees to keep Reuel's secret. But the two eventually come into conflict over Dianthe: a young singer who performs with a Black troupe from Fisk University. When Dianthe is brought unconscious to Reuel's hospital, he uses his medical prowess to save her life, though at the cost of her memory. While Reuel successfully courts Dianthe, Aubrey seeks to possess her. This plot drives much of the narrative: two Black characters denied the ability to enact their own agency due to the power-hungry desires of Aubrey, who sees Dianthe as an object to be owned.

Such issues of race, identity, and sexuality were matters of social and political importance in early twentieth-century America. Just years earlier, in 1898, the Black journalist Alexander Manly's editorial on interracial sex—most pressingly, the explosive contention of illicit affairs between Black men and white women—had been the ruse for a massacre and a political coup in Wilmington, North Carolina. This was contemporaneous with the passage and enforcement of new antimiscegenation laws throughout the South, a compliment to Jim Crow in the era of conservative redemption. But Hopkins appeared determined to reverse this trope, presenting Aubrey as the white predator in contrast to the "Negrophobia" common in her day.

This desire to challenge popular narratives on race and sex appears also in Hopkins's use of "passing" as a plot device. Both Reuel and Dianthe pass for white. Reuel does so consciously. With her memory loss, Dianthe becomes an unknowing participant—passed off as Reuel's white fiancée so he can maintain his own facade. An air of uninterrogated colorism underpins these characters. Yet through them Hopkins also exposes the absurdity of race: a concept so malleable that Reuel and Dianthe easily slip between its allegedly immutable boundaries. Dianthe even befriends and lives with Aubrey's well-to-do fiancée, Molly. But there is a price. While Dianthe's racial transformation is unwitting, Reuel has purposefully shed his Blackness like a useless skin. In a world where whiteness marks status, advancement, and success, it is a sensible but also damning choice. If racism is absurd in its fallacies, Hopkins alludes, it is also detrimental to Black self-worth and identity.

Although written over a century ago, Hopkins's concerns and critiques resonate in our era when we speak of "representation" and question if certain "voices" are being marginalized. Diversity is posited in social justice circles as an antithesis to racism and bigotry, forging a more tolerant society. Of equal if not greater importance is the negative impact a lack of diversity has on the marginalized themselves. In a society where racism is systemic, how might the erasure of nonwhite faces and voices, from our history books to our cinematic screens, diminish feelings of self-worth and identity? For Hopkins, then, as we say now, representation mattered. And in her work, she sought its remedy.

It is perhaps a writer's flair for irony that casts Aubrey as the catalyst for Reuel's racial self-awakening. He encourages his friend to leave on an expedition to Africa—in search of ancient Meroe, where he might unearth treasure to secure a stable financial life. While Reuel is abroad, however, Dianthe's memories return. Aubrey threatens to expose her heritage if she does not submit to him. He even plots and carries out the murder of his own fiancée, Molly, in a staged boating accident, while simultaneously falsifying Dianthe's death: spiriting her away to his Livingston family home, where he forces her to marry him.

Unsuspectingly manipulated by his friend's duplicity, Reuel arrives in East Africa and journeys to Sudan—referenced by Hopkins as Ethiopia, in accordance with Biblical writings that informed a growing Black Atlantic Ethiopianist movement—and the ruins of ancient Meroe.[4] Despite Reuel's own hunt for treasure, the expedition has a loftier purpose: to work against race prejudice by establishing "the primal existence of the Negro as the most ancient source" of human civilization.[5] Upon reaching Meroe, Reuel for the first time gazes on ancient temples and pyramids adorned with images of once-powerful Black sovereigns. When Reuel's white friend Charlie Vance exclaims, "You don't mean to tell me that all of this was done by niggers," one of the expedition's scholars affirms "Ethiopians" as the founders of human civilization. "Undoubtedly," he tells Charlie, "Your Afro-Americans are a branch of the wonderful and mysterious Ethiopians who had a prehistoric existence of magnificence." Another listener comments, "It is hard to believe . . . from what a height must this people have fallen to reach the abjectness of the American Negro."[6]

As he charts this heroic quest to self-awareness, Reuel's main antagonist turns out to be the only other Black man on the expedition, Jim Titus. Secretly working for Aubrey, Jim harries Reuel at every turn—as if to keep him from his destiny. Hopkins names Jim "a Negro of the old regime" who believed "the Anglo-Saxon was appointed by God to rule over the African" and obsequiously referred to whites as "Massa."[7] If reaching Meroe is how Reuel finds (and recovers) his racial self, Hopkins represents Jim as an antiquated expression of the Black self that must be similarly vanquished—the antithesis of the "New Negro" Alain Locke will call into being two decades later. And there are uninterrogated questions of class and color here that Hopkins never broaches.

Still, like Aubrey's treachery, Jim provides a catalyst for Reuel's journey. When Jim brings deceptive news of Dianthe's death, a distraught Reuel goes wandering through Meroe's ruins. It is there that he stumbles upon lost Telessar—a place of ancient wonder, rich with the use of telepathy, a futurist technology based on crystals, bountiful agriculture, suspended animation, and more: an early vision of Wakanda over half a century before Marvel's conceptions. Populated with "the direct descendants of the inhabitants of Meroe," the people of Telessar range in complexion "from a creamy tint to purest ebony," a seeming way for Hopkins to represent the diaspora within her fantastical African past and to imbue it with relevance to the present state of Black America.[8]

This question of the diaspora's place in space and time troubled the poet Countee Cullen two decades later, musing, "What is Africa to me . . . ?" It has never been answered in full and remains a complicated and vexing query of truncated identity, sought for in slave ship records, oral histories, cultural legacies, and DNA tests—each limited in the answers they provide, at times simultaneously serving to highlight the gaping silences of history wrought by slavery and colonialism. Hopkins bridges the unknowable through speculation, creating a past that slavery's descendants can latch onto. In Telessar, Reuel is heralded as the "son of a fallen dynasty, outcast of a sunken people" and at once a long-lost king: a reclamation of glory as reparations for all those who suffered the psychic terror of the Middle Passage and the natal alienation of slavery's social death.[9] "Upon Reuel a strange force seemed to be working," Hopkins writes of this moment of self-discovery. "If what he heard was true, how great a destiny was his!"[10]

But if Hopkins flirts with a return to a veritable African Eden, she troubles this with the inescapable realities of the present. Through the arcane sciences of Telessar, Reuel learns to his shock that Dianthe is alive and of Aubrey's treachery. Near the same time, Jim and Charlie stumble upon Telessar. To escape its guards, Jim is mortally wounded and with his dying breath confesses his misdeeds. Most starkly, he reveals that Aubrey is Reuel's brother and that Dianthe is their sister. We later learn that the three share the same mixed-race enslaved mother, who bore three children for her owner, with Aubrey being switched at birth to be raised as white.

Stories of passing often end in misfortune as the perpetrators are unmasked for their duplicity: a common archetype of the tragic mulatto. And certainly, there is tragedy here. Reuel returns to America just in time to witness Dianthe's death. Simultaneously, a guilty Aubrey is induced by the arcane powers of the men of Telessar to take his own life. Yet in this rendition, Hopkins offers that the true villains are not Reuel or Dianthe, nor even, in the end, Aubrey. Instead, it is the evils of slavery and its legacies that bear the blame: white supremacy and all its deleterious effects. If racism has caused Reuel to be divorced from his racial identity, it has similarly cast Aubrey down his own debased path. Here, Hopkins makes a salient point about oppression: that individual actions cannot be divorced from systems of power. Her work also displays the pluralities through which marginalized people at times strategize to counter oppression—namely, by calling for racial pride while at the same time condemning the fallacies of race, a seeming answer for those still unable, or unwilling, to grasp the antiracist conceptual framework of a phrase as simple as "Black Lives Matter." The illogic of race, in fact, is never far from Hopkins's understanding. "The slogan of the hour is 'Keep the Negro down!'" she writes, "but who is . . . to decide who hath black blood and who hath not?" Quoting then from the Biblical Acts 17:26, she references the namesake of her work: "Of one blood have I made all races of men to dwell upon the whole face of the earth. . . . No man can draw the dividing line between the two races, for they are both of one blood!"[11]

In 2014, in the wake of Ferguson, activist and writer Walidah Imarisha called for a new sense of "visionary fiction," where artists used "science fiction, horror, and fantasy genres to envision alternatives to unjust and oppressive systems." Speculative fiction, she asserted, was "a perfect testing ground" to explore alternatives to the current state of racism and systemic repression.[12] *Of One Blood* took up this challenge over a century earlier, providing a medium for Hopkins to explore multifaceted contemporaneous issues ranging from white supremacy to colonialism to slavery's numerous legacies.[13] Evoking a romantic African past into her present, she offered a counternarrative to the racist ideologies that permeated African society. Some elements of Hopkins's politics are undoubtedly antiquated for a twenty-first century readership.[14] Yet this struggle she takes up, of deconstructing whiteness in all its suppositions and unspoken assumptions, remains important and vital work. And though it is incomplete work, it reminds us of the long history of resistance to racial oppression—that we follow in the footsteps of those who have faced similar uncertain tomorrows. In the bleakest of moments, Black writers like Hopkins turned to literature to confront racial terror and the internalized trauma it could induce. As we seek to comprehend the challenges that face us today, looking back to *Of One Blood* may prove instructive. Facing systemic oppression now, as then, may require us to journey beyond the mundane and explore new imaginative ways to give voice to our resistance.

Notes

1. Hopkins, *Of One Blood*, vi–vii.

2. Wallinger, *Pauline E. Hopkins*.

3. Hopkins, *Contending Forces*, 13.

4. For discussions of Hopkins's place in the Ethiopianist movement, see Fiorelli, "Hidden Cities, Hidden Selves"; Nurheissein, "Hand of Mysticism"; Robey, "Excavating Ethiopia."

5. Hopkins, *Of One Blood*, 87.

6. Hopkins, *Of One Blood*, 99.

7. Hopkins, *Of One Blood*, 78.

8. Hopkins, *Of One Blood*, 112-115.

9. Wallinger, "Voyager into the Heart of Africa."

10. Hopkins, *Of One Blood*, 125.

11. Hopkins, *Of One Blood*, 178.

12. Interviewed in Hansen, "Science Fiction and the Post-Ferguson World."

13. For a comparison of Hopkins's work to and the influence it had on more recent Black women SFF writers, see Allen, "Kindred Spirits."

14. On Hopkins's vision of a "postracial fantasy," see Daniels, "Limits of Literary Realism."

Bibliography

Allen, Marlene D. "Kindred Spirits: The Speculative Fictions of Pauline E. Hopkins, Octavia E. Butler, and Tananarive Due." *CLA Journal* 61, no. 1–2 (2017): 95–108.

Daniels, Melissa Asher. "The Limits of Literary Realism: *Of One Blood*'s Post-Racial Fantasy by Pauline Hopkins." *Callaloo* 36, no. 1 (Winter 2013): 158–177.

Fiorelli, Julie A. "Hidden Cities, Hidden Selves: Lost-Race Romance in Pauline Hopkins's *Of One Blood* and Walter McDougall's *The Hidden City*." *Modern Fiction Studies* 63, no. 3 (2017): 452–474.

Hansen, Mary. "Science Fiction and the Post-Ferguson World: 'There Are as Many Ways to Exist as We Can Imagine.'" *YES!*, December 4, 2014. https://www.yesmagazine.org/social-justice/2014/12/04/science-fiction-post-ferguson-world-walidah-imarisha.

Hopkins, Pauline. *Contending Forces: A Romance Illustrative of Negro Life North and South*. Boston: The Colored Co-operative Publishing Co., 1900.

Hopkins, Pauline. *Of One Blood, or The Hidden Self*. New York: Washington Square Press, 2004. First published 1902.

Hopkins, Pauline. *A Primer of Facts Pertaining to the Early Greatness of the African Race and the Possibility of Restoration by Its Descendants, with Epilogue: Compiled and Arranged from the Works of the Best Known Ethnologists and Historians*. Cambridge, MA: P. E. Hopkins, 1905.

Nurhussein, Nadia. "The Hand of Mysticism: Ethiopianist Writing in Pauline Hopkins's *Of One Blood* and the Colored American Magazine." *Callaloo* 33, no. 1 (Spring 2010): 278–289.

Robey, Molly K. "Excavating Ethiopia: Biblical Archaeology in Pauline Hopkins's *Of One Blood*." *Studies in American Fiction* 43, no. 2 (2016): 183–206.

Wallinger, Hanna. *Pauline E. Hopkins: A Literary Biography*. Athens: University of Georgia Press, 2005.

Wallinger, Hanna. "Voyage into the Heart of Africa: Pauline Hopkins and *Of One Blood*." In *Black Imagination and the Middle Passage*, edited by Maria Diedrich, Henry Louis Gates Jr., and Carl Pederson, 203–214. Oxford: Oxford University Press, 1999.

30 Alan Moore, David Gibbons, and John Higgins, *Watchmen*, no. 11 (1987) / Autonomous Collectivity against the State

Gerry Canavan

There may still be no superhero narrative more influential than *Watchmen*, published in twelve issues between 1986 and 1987 by DC Comics and remaining a perennial best seller ever since. *Watchmen* is neither the first nor the last story to explore the seedy underbelly of US superhero fantasies, but it is viewed by many as the definitive articulation of the possibilities and pitfalls of the genre, revealing crimefighters as hypocrites, perverts, and violent megalomaniacs rather than paragons or exemplars. Since its publication, the novel has functioned almost as a curse on the genre: however much later creators try to wriggle out of its grasp and return to some earlier state of innocence for the superhero, somehow the stories always return to the unhappy terms laid out by Moore, Gibbons, and Higgins in *Watchmen*. Do heroes destroy more than they save? Does the violence they deal out unevenly across class, race, gender, and ethnic lines serve any goal other than the wretched reproduction of the status quo? What would it take for the superhero to be radical rather than reactionary, to envisage utopian possibility rather than the antiutopian confirmation that the only true moral authority is power? Since their formation in the World War II era, comics in the United States have positioned the superhero as a figuration for state power, both at the level of the beat cop (Mr. Fantastic using his amazing powers and brilliant intellect to catch bank robbers rather than cure cancer; Batman burning his billion-dollar inheritance on more and more complex ways to beat up the unhoused and the mentally ill) and at the level of the national imperial imaginary (Superman's "Truth, Justice, and the American Way"; Captain America punching out Hitler on the cover of *Captain America*, no. 1). *Watchmen* suggests this path is a moral and political dead-end; instead, we must reject the superhero, the book argues, and in turn reject the traditional forms of authority the superhero has always represented. In this way, *Watchmen* positions itself as the last superhero story: certainly not the last one ever published, but perhaps the last one you ever need to read.

Watchmen tells an alternate history of the twentieth century, with two points of divergence from our own situation. First, the debut of Superman in *Action Comics*, no. 1 (June 1938) and the subsequent explosion of superhero narratives in the medium led to the emergence of real-life imitators, masked vigilantes whose brutal methods matched the retributive violence of Superman himself in those early stories. (Confronted with these real-life crimefighters, the comics industry in the *Watchmen* universe quickly grew bored with the subgenre; there, they read pirate comics instead.) Second, a fluke radiological accident in 1959 created the world's first *true* superhero, Dr. Manhattan, whose powers make him nearly godlike in both his ability and in his detachment from human suffering; the events of Manhattan's creation mirror the creation of the Hulk in *The Incredible Hulk*, no. 1 (May 1962), but this time the man of science becomes monstrous not through inhuman rage but through inhuman objectivity and hyperrationality. Dr. Manhattan's powers allow the United States to win the Vietnam War, which in turn allows a triumphant Nixon to remain president until the 1980s over an increasingly brutal and corrupt United States, desperately clinging to its military superiority over the Soviet Union through the ongoing ministrations of Dr. Manhattan.

The main story of *Watchmen* explores a rash of vigilante slayings being investigated by Rorschach (Walter Kovacs), loosely based on the Steve-Ditko-created characters The Question and Mr. A, and functioning as a parody of the extreme right-wing politics that dominated Ditko's later life and work. Scandalized by the March 13, 1964, murder of Kitty Genovese—an event that happened in both the *Watchmen* timeline and our own—Rorschach makes his trademark black-and-white mask out of a party dress Genovese never picked up and becomes a vigilante avenger. In particular, *Watchmen* draws strongly on the myth of Genovese as misreported by the media at the time: the notion that she died screaming for help amid a sea of neighbors who did not intervene. That Kitty Genovese's neighbors did not really let her die without trying to get help[1]—and that if anything the police neglect and outright persecution of people like Genovese contributed more to her death than her neighbors[2]—only strengthens the book's critique of the superhero, as we will see.

Rorschach positions himself as a moral absolutist, the last honest man, brutally punishing the wicked and indeed growing more hyperviolent as his career goes on. But his sense of moral vice and virtue is shot through with an infantile nostalgia for an earlier moment in American history and hero-worship of an absent father; his vicious attacks on rapists and drug dealers rapidly blur into a near-universal contempt for women, homosexuals, racial minorities, "liberals, and intellectuals and smooth talkers," and so on. (Indeed, the father Rorschach never knew is expressly related on the first page of the book to President Truman, who inaugurated the very cycle of nuclear war that the book suggests has since doomed humanity.) Even after vigilante crimefighters (called "masks") are banned by the state, Rorschach continues his obsessive work, enforcing his own twisted version of the law for the "benefit" of a general populace he finds nearly as loathsome as the criminals he pursues.

At the end of issue no. 6, the exact midpoint of the series, following his arrest, Rorschach reveals in an interview with police psychologist Malcolm Long that this commitment to moral absolutism is itself a reaction to an ultimate nihilism, an attempt (like the Rorschach test from which he derives his superhero branding) to impose order on a universe that is actually an arbitrary assortment of meaningless patterns: "'Born from oblivion; bear children, hell-bound as ourselves; go into oblivion. There is nothing else. Existence is random. Has no pattern save what we imagine after staring at it for too long. No meaning save what we choose to impose. This rudderless world is not shaped by vague metaphysical forces. It is not God who kills the children. Not fate that butchers them or destiny that feeds them to the dogs. It's us. Only us.'"[3] It might almost be a heroic confrontation with the abyss, a moving demonstration of the way nihilism (properly understood) actually calls on us not to simply *give up* but rather to construct a value system that can sustain our collective lives and spirit—if only Rorschasch weren't a fascist.

Physically and mentally repugnant, with political opinions the famously left-wing anarchist Moore undoubtedly intends for us to be disgusted by, Rorschach is nevertheless the only character in the book who is willing to stand up to the comic's surprise antagonist, his former superhero teammate Ozymandias (Adrian Veidt), who has manufactured a deeply traumatic alien-invasion hoax in Times Square to unify and disarm a world standing on the brink of nuclear Armageddon and ecological catastrophe, at the small cost of only three million or so lives. In issue no. 12, when Rorschach is summarily executed by Dr. Manhattan, the other heroes agree to accept Ozymandias's devil's bargain, and the story ends on the cusp of Ozymandias's utopia—with only Rorschach's journal the last outstanding piece of evidence that could unravel the new dawn. The book thus ends with a renewed and reinvigorated America—Veidt's multinational is now selling "Millennium"-branded perfumes instead of "Nostalgia"—with a bloody secret lurking at its core, at risk of exposure and return to our own apocalyptic status quo at any moment. Thus the final judgment of *Watchmen*: our worship of heroes—all the politicians, agents, the entire superhuman crew—leads us in the end to a miserable forced choice between two equally unacceptable nightmares, with neither governmentality (Ozymandias) nor ungovernability (Rorschach) pointing toward anything like truth or justice (to say nothing of what we might euphemistically still call "the American way").

That's the end of the series. But at the end of the penultimate issue, issue no. 11, we see the possibility of a different line of flight out of this conundrum. As Rorschach and his companion Nite Owl confront Ozymandias at his Antarctic retreat, still incorrectly believing they can stop him in time, the narrative takes a brief moment to consider the decidedly mundane, nonvigilante characters who have populated the background of the series since issue no. 1. We have seen these characters in different contexts across the book: street-level cops, a lesbian couple doing outreach work for the political activist group Gay Women Against Rape (GWAR), a devoted fan of pirate comics bantering with the owner of a local newsstand about whether or not he's ever going to buy anything. The background characters converge by chance in Times Square, where they witness a moment of domestic violence between two women on the street; in a more optimistic psychic replay of the Kitty Genovese myth that inspired Rorschach's grim, brutal retribution, these characters autonomously and collectively decide to intervene, working together to stop the violence before it spirals out of control. One of these characters is none other than Malcolm Long, whose own life has spiraled out of control since he first encountered Rorschach; disturbed, distracted, and on the brink of divorce, he finds himself nonetheless called to help. This moment, I would argue, is the moral heart of the entire series; as Long explains to his wife, who is begging him to just stay out of it: "Gloria, please! I have to. In a world like this . . . I mean, it's all we *can* do, try to *help* each other. It's all that *means* anything."[4] His disillusioning encounter with Rorschach and his disturbing vision of the ultimate meaninglessness of all things has called on him to try to craft a new moral order out of the chaos of the universe, like Rorschach does—but without Malcolm simply becoming yet another Rorschach. He can heal rather than hurt.

The ordinary, selfless heroism of these characters in this moment stands in very stark contrast to those of superheroes across the novel (all of whom stand in as barely disguised allegories for the forces of US imperialism, state violence, and callous business elites); indeed, in this precise moment, the failed heroes Rorschach and Nite Owl are already in Ozymandias's Antarctic compound, where they confront but fail to stop the hero-turned-mass-murderer, whose twisted project of world transformation Nite Owl will ultimately endorse. In issue no. 11, Malcolm and the other background characters offer a rare, genuinely utopian glimmer for the book, coming together without technocratic leadership or police coercion to simply try to help the world where they can, how they can—at which time they are all promptly murdered (along with millions of other New Yorkers) as the necessary collateral damage of Ozymandias's grand plan for a better tomorrow.

The familiar three-by-three panel construction used nearly uniformly across the rest of *Watchmen* breaks in this moment as the book's famously vivid coloration washes out to black and white and finally to pixilation (figure 30.1)—calling our attention to the importance of this singular moment in the text. The shadow imagery recalls the "Hiroshima lovers" referenced elsewhere in the novel—which themselves mirror the last embraces recorded by heat and ash after the dropping of the nuclear bomb. It's ordinary acts of love and decency, of kindness, that the unbounded megaviolence of the hero form ("good men like my father, and President Truman") finally snuffs out.

The Times Square subplot—the book's only positive gesture toward the possibility of any moral order that is neither murderous utopianism or murderous nihilism—has been largely invisible in expansions and transmedia extensions of the *Watchmen* franchise. In Zack Snyder's critically derided 2009 film adaptation, Long's scenes interviewing Rorschach after his arrest are included in the film but significantly truncated, and the moment in Times Square is reduced to a single ponderous glance before the attack; the notion that Long dies alongside other normal, street-level New Yorkers

Figure 30.1
Nothing beside remains. *Watchmen*, no. 11, 28.

trying to help prevent violence through nonviolent intervention and mediation is completely eliminated. Neither Long nor any of the other ordinary New Yorkers merit a *Before Watchmen* comic prequel, coming in after the supervillain Moloch, the pirate-themed *Crimson Corsair*, and even a one-shot devoted to joke character Dollar Bill (a superhero who does floor security for a national bank chain, and who is asphyxiated when his cape gets caught in a revolving door). Long is referenced only once in HBO's 2019–2020 sequel series, also called *Watchmen*, in an online supplement; instead, the series defaults into exactly the sort of pro-cop narrative the original comic outright rejected, in which the answer to white supremacist bad cops is a demographically diverse alliance of good cops. (Even Ozymandias himself gets a redemption arc, swooping in at the last moment to save the neoliberal consensus from a less murderous version of his own revolutionary genocidal act!) Only the 2017–2019 comic sequel *Doomsday Clock* takes real note of Long's subplot and tries to do anything with it, putting his and Gloria's surviving son, Reggie, behind the mask as Rorschach II—though the series ultimately loses interest in the character and treats Malcolm only as a figure for grief rather than as an inspiring vision of what a different sort of heroism might look like. Instead, *Doomsday Clock* argues, the only possible solution to the problem of superheroes is more superheroes: Superman's red boot stomping on a human face, forever.

If *Watchmen* is in some basic sense the last superhero narrative, the final disproof that this cultural celebration of beneficent Übermensch offers anything useful for us either politically or ethically, it is noteworthy that both fan response and the numerous highly problematic attempts to expand the *Watchmen* narrative to prequels, sequels, transmedia extensions, and other homages/rip-offs have nonetheless been utterly fixated on the flashy superpowered badasses who occupy the foreground of the story and successor franchises like the Arrowverse and the MCU. Their quippy violence remains the splash, the headline, the billion-dollar boffo box office; alas, there isn't much in the way of Malcolm Long fandom or cosplay. But it is only the blighted and prematurely clipped possibility of *Watchmen*'s ennobled background characters—murdered, precisely, by a man who claims to know how to save the world through yet another remorseless application of the violence that has doomed it—that offers any way out of the alienating and disempowering trap that capitalism, meritocracy, patriarchy, and the state have laid for us. Perhaps it's not all that surprising that a superhero media-industrial complex that has been compulsively reenacting *Watchmen* for the last thirty-five years has managed to miss its antisuperhero moral lesson—and, as the center left in the United States lurches from antifascist revulsion toward Trump toward renewed national greatness liberalism under the Biden-Harris administration, perhaps we could all use a reminder. Neither Nixon nor Redford. Neither Rorschach nor Ozymandias. No cops. No presidents. No gods. No masters. Only us—trying to help.

Notes

1. See Lemmann, "A Call for Help."
2. See Johnston, "Don't Look Now."
3. Moore, Gibbons, and Higgins, *Watchmen*, no. 6, 26.
4. Moore, Gibbons, and Higgins, *Watchmen*, no. 11, 20.

Bibliography

Before Watchmen. New York: DC Comics, 2012.

Johns, Geoff (writer), Gary Frank (penciller), Rob Leigh (letterer), and Brad Anderson (colorist). *Doomsday Clock*, nos. 1–12. New York: DC Comics, 2017–2019.

Johnston, Angus. "Don't Look Now." *New Inquiry*, March 27, 2014. https://thenewinquiry.com/dont-look-now/.

Lemann, Nicholas. "A Call for Help: What the Kitty Genovese Story Really Means." *New Yorker*, March 3, 2014. https://www.newyorker.com/magazine/2014/03/10/a-call-for-help.

Lindleof, Damon. *Watchmen*. DC Comics and Home Box Office, 2019–2020.

Moore, Alan (writer), David Gibbons (artist), and John Higgins (colorist). *Watchmen*, nos. 1–12. New York: DC Comics, 1986–1987.

Snyder, Zack, director. *Watchmen*. Warner Brother, 2009.

31 Tobias Buckell, *Sly Mongoose* (2008) / Inhabiting Hostile Futures

Nicola Hunte

The dust jacket of Tobias Buckell's novel *Sly Mongoose* proclaims: "Welcome to Chilo, a planet with corrosive rain, crushing pressure, and deadly heat. Fortunately, fourteen-year old Timas lives in one of the domed cities that float a hundred thousand feet above the surface, circling near the edge of a monstrous perpetual storm." The upbeat tone describing a hostile environment and the silver-lining view of the central character's living conditions may just be a way to pull readers into this story. (After all, the possibility of these inhabited cities falling into the all-consuming storm below has to be a reasonable consideration for such an engineered landscape.) But the world Buckell creates in this novel is both terrifying and hopeful—much like the dust jacket promises.

In *Sly Mongoose*'s universe, humanity has become an interstellar diaspora—everyone is a planetary immigrant, a refugee among the stars. Furthermore, all humanity has been enslaved by nonhuman beings. Unlike the idyllic first contact story of *Star Trek*, the alien response to humanity's technological progress toward space travel is a far-reaching colonial empire founded on the premise that humans are destined to be chattel. Nonetheless, humanity manages to break free of its imperialist slavers (tellingly called the Satraps of the Forty-Eight Worlds), to forge their own "home" worlds.

Unsurprisingly, given a chance at new beginnings on other planets, humanity manages to rehearse its legacy of exploitation and inequity, finding new ways to preserve social hierarchies. The nature of this inequity runs along familiar lines: between the haves and the have-nots. The inevitable social tensions resulting from this division, exacerbated by the impossibly hostile physical environment, seem to take a back seat to the more immediate threat of space-hardy zombies who have targeted Chilo and its many floating cities, among them Eupatoria and Yatapek, for invasion. Buckell places on a collision course the Aeolians of Eupatoria (the haves), the people of Yatapek (the have-nots), and the Swarm (the space zombies) against the backdrop of larger agendas for control played out between the interplanetary organizations of the Satrapy, the League of Human Affairs, and the Ragamuffins. The Satrapy are aliens who, individually, exercise psychic control over an organic collective of aliens and humans. The League, born out of a galaxy-wide human uprising against the Satrapy, are dedicated to the consolidation of humanity under one governing body aimed at the complete destruction of all forms of alien imperialism. The Ragamuffins, once the merchant traders that brought predominantly islander refugees from Earth to two of the new worlds, become the space-faring guerillas who protect these newly settled planets from all external threats—alien or human.

Alongside the typical elements of a science fiction adventure tale, such as aerial dogfights between spaceships, wormhole travel, and cybernetically enhanced humans, are sobering observations that hit fairly close to present-day realities for so-called third world developing nations. The dystopic nature of Yatapek society offers an obvious illustration of resource-poor, land-scarce, densely populated countries existing as satellites to materially wealthy nations. In particular, Yatapek's relationship to its Aeolian neighbors, like Eupatoria, reads like that of the Caribbean to North America and Europe: almost completely dependent on imported technology, viewed as an exotic tourist site, and only able to exercise face-value autonomy in its economic and political negotiations, Yatapek symbolizes the Caribbean's vulnerability as a region based on colonial economies.

Dystopia as a genre is not usually associated with the Caribbean—rarely depicted as a "bad place" (for white settlers), it is also not typically portrayed as one set in the future, at least in SF circulated outside the Caribbean, except in rare instances like Buckell's or Nalo Hopkinson's writing. Fundamentally, the Caribbean is familiarly offered up as an idyllic place pleasantly frozen in the here and now. Nonetheless, this novel connects to the region through its title, which references a Caribbean folksong and its trickster figure, as well as through its space-travelling freedom fighters, the Ragamuffins. The narrative clearly points to the region as historically important to its conceptualization of the future because those who have traveled to the stars "came from a piece of the Caribbean that had picked itself up from the mother planet and held together for centuries now."[1] It is also possible to see how the power dynamics across the various groups that populate this far-flung space suggest the region's present and implications for its future.

In looking at the condition of the contemporary Caribbean and its transition beyond its centuries-long legacy of colonialism, Aaron Kamugisha starkly proclaims that the region languishes in a "state of tragedy and crisis" that has been simplistically understood as the product of neoliberalism. He states: "The term *neoliberalism* flattens the complexity of the Caribbean's current moment. Rather, in the Caribbean we see an amalgam of neocolonialism, postcolonial elite domination, *and* neoliberalism, which have undermined the conditions of possibility for any kind of social democracy."[2] In keeping with this dire outlook, he refers to Jamaican economist Norman Girvan's "Existential Threats in the Caribbean," with its apocalyptic view of a Caribbean future due to "a constellation of economic, social and environmental pressures that threaten the viability of our societies as functional entities in any meaningful sense."[3]

The narrative of dire survival within a heavily stratified society facing apocalyptic conditions that only promise a hostile future for the many who become expendable units of labor for the wealthy few—the stuff of dystopic fiction—has, in fact, been the historical legacy of Caribbean countries built on plantation slavery. The apocalyptic nature of neoliberalism is already foreshadowed in the marginalization, predation, and dependence of the resource-exporting colonial economies of the Caribbean. Buckell's imagination therefore renders Yatapek as a poverty-stricken, socially divided, environmentally vulnerable city vertically organized to illustrate how those with privilege and access literally rise to the top. In this society, Timas, who is essentially a child-miner, can leave the crowded human warrens below by riding an elevator to "the dizzying top, where the parks and farms basked under the sun's warmth, protected by the city's globe above them."[4]

But to maintain this hierarchy of access comes at a high human cost. For instance, only Timas can live on the upper level because he is xocoyotzin, the label given to those in Yatapek, usually children, who are the only ones "young, thin, and small enough to fit inside the groundsuits designed to fit svelte outsiders, not adults from his city."[5] Buckell's nod to the Aztec empire with the use of this term suggests the society's ingrained adherence to human exploitation because, to mine the planet's surface, these children effectively become revered sacrifice. To be xocoyotzin is to don an ancient suit weighing over fifty pounds with failing technology in order to walk on the surface of the planet under ninety-nine times normal pressure, through acid rain, hurricane-like winds, and eight hundred–degree temperatures, all to maintain an antiquated mining machine. The dangerous short-sightedness of this approach becomes apparent with the realization that not only are the Aeolian cities, also floating above Chilo, able to mine for resources in much safer ways, but also those on Yatapek continue this practice because they have inherited an ideology that says they are unable to make use of technology. Essentially, very little that is technological is made, enhanced, or maintained in Yatapek.

From Timas's perspective, not only are this society's failures evident, but so are its maneuvers to maintain this detrimental status quo. The squalor of the lower levels, the exploitation and abuse of children, have become validated as necessary and inevitable sacrifice. We need look no further than the vulnerability of Caribbean tourist economies, brought into stark view by the COVID-19 pandemic, to observe a similarly dangerous short-sightedness. The region is placed in the position of having no choice but to offer up the bodies and general welfare of its people in order to stay afloat. As Kamugisha points out, Caribbean state managers have long been using tax-funded educational and cultural programs to trumpet tourism service as a fundamental pillar of the region's cultural identity, but "if this same effort was made to assess the needs and aspirations of Caribbean citizens the Caribbean might, as the old cliché goes, actually be a better place to live."[6]

The complexity of Yatapek's society is further troubled by the involvement of the Satrapy, the Swarm, and the League. The imperial mandate of the Satrapy is clear: absolute human subjugation—for the good of humanity. With the end of the "three-hundred-year peace under the Benevolent Satrapy" by human revolution, the last remaining Satrap conceives a long-term plan to revive imperial rule, beginning with Chilo. The Satrapy, in this way, comes to embody the haunting presence of neocolonialism.

The Swarm's attack on the planet manifests as "groaning, stumbling, . . . old-school zombies," which spreads as a contagion that turns the infected into members of its zombie collective.[7] This novel's adaptation of zombified bodies to a science fiction setting includes their ability to speak and the sharing of a hive mind (like an organic version of Star Trek's Borg).

The Swarm promises, like the Satrapy, universal freedom and peace as a result of being folded into their collective: "We can offer you an infection that does not degrade your individuality," they claim.[8]

But the effect of zombie recruitment is reminiscent of how George Monbiot metaphorically describes neoliberalism, as "the God that failed. But the zombie doctrine staggers on, and one of the reasons is its anonymity. Or rather, a cluster of anonymities." Exemplifying this blind, purportedly collective faith is the Swarm's bid to convince one of the Ragamuffin that he too should experience this freedom. However, as Monbiot astutely perceives, "The freedom that neoliberalism offers, which sounds so beguiling when expressed in general terms, turns out to mean freedom for the pike, not for the minnows."[9] The individual bodies of the Swarm, when convenient, are sacrificed for the agenda of a behind-the-scenes agent. This agent—the pike—remains hidden until near the end of the novel. What is less obvious is the danger posed by the once-oppressed League of Human Affairs. The League's desire to rid the universe of alien masters is undermined by selfish, if hypocritical, tactics. Less concerned about the welfare of human (and other) societies and more obsessed about losing control, the League appears like the realization of what Kamugisha had called "postcolonial elite domination," for which the "nature of democracy and citizenship in polities still structured in dominance" proves questionable.[10]

The first response to this triumvirate of collective domination comes in the form of the Ragamuffins, embodied by Pepper, the centuries-old cyborg. Pepper works to mobilize the people of Yatapek and the Aeolian cities against the attack by the Swarm and the coercion of the League. At every confrontation that demands the sacrifice of sovereignty and freedom, allegedly in exchange for survival or progress, Pepper's response is an unambiguous refusal. As a founding father of the Black Star Liner Corporation, he is responsible for the exodus of Caribbean people into the stars. The significance of the corporation's name is, as Andrea Shaw Nevins explains, an acknowledgement of the "postslavery efforts of regional leaders such as Marcus Garvey and organizations like the Universal Negro Improvement Association (UNIA) to foster black economic independence. The UNIA founded the Black Star Line, intended to facilitate trade and movement across the African diaspora."[11] Pepper's embodiment as living history and his rejection of compromised agency are consistent with one of the core tenets of the UNIA from the early twentieth century: "that any limited liberty which deprives one of the complete rights and prerogatives of full citizenship is but a modified form of slavery."[12]

The second response comes from the Aeolians in the form of a technodemocracy. The Aeolians of Eupatoria and the inhabitants of Yatapek treat each other as outsiders: the resource disparity between them is such that Yatapek behaves more like a satellite of Eupatoria than of Chilo. However, as the narrative later reveals, both cities are populated by refugees from planets formerly under alien control, with a great deal of the settlers to both floating habitats coming from the same planet. The distinction between them stems from the decisions made by their ancestors in response to the legacies of oppression and domination that forced them to seek refuge around Chilo.

Whereas those who settled on Yatapek decided to obscure their past, those who became Aeolian sought to confront it. As such, the Aeolians were able to redirect the use of technology away from its abusive application by aliens and toward their benefit, while Yatapek turned themselves away from such technology altogether. Unwilling to examine the scars of the past and their effects, Yatapek society fell back into an exploitative, hierarchical system that shadowed their people's past. The decision of the Aeolians to learn from past failures leads to the use of technology to develop a technodemocracy. Cybernetic optical implants and high-speed communication networks are tools that facilitate a significant ideological shift to self-governance. As one Aeolian character explains: "Better yet to make the government vanish: run by monthly volunteers and automated frameworks. . . . We all serve. We all vote. We're the government."[13]

Both Yatapek and Eupatoria, therefore, can function as versions of the Caribbean, or at least Caribbean responses to its multidimensional constellation of pressures that constantly work to "run over its people." Eupatoria tries to look to a future where inhabitants of a place are, as one of the characters declares, not just property but *citizens*—that is, individuals with rights.[14] The technodemocracy of the Aeolian Consensus employs technology for the benefit of social welfare—the well-being of *all* citizens. This socially conscious framework with its focus on community that can act collectively, by consensus, not coercion, removes the use of technology for the sake of Big Brother totalitarian tactics like those expressed by the Satrapy, the Swarm, and, to some extent, the League. The Ragamuffins' anticolonial ethos and the futuristic Aeolian approach come together to offer the beginnings of a genuine self-governing collective instead of returning to another version of group control. The novel ends with the Ragamuffins spearheading an alliance across aliens and different human societies to form an interstellar collective called the Xenowealth.

The world Buckell creates in this novel is both terrifying and hopeful: even as it acknowledges despair and deprivation, it suggests that we have it within us to recuperate from these losses, as seen in the following observation by Shaw Nevins: "By titling his series 'Xenowealth,' Buckell [gestures] . . . toward a recovery of the region's history, because these Caribbean nationals have a counterpart community to the oppressive history of slavery and colonization associated with the paradoxically titled British Commonwealth."[15] This recovery of history is a way of looking at the lessons of the past in order to think about how we might collectively move beyond long-standing inequities that, as is all too well known for the Caribbean, promise an uneven future.

Notes

1. Buckell, *Sly Mongoose*, 49.
2. Kamugisha, *Beyond Coloniality*, 1.
3. Qtd. in Kamugisha, *Beyond Coloniality*, 63.
4. Buckell, *Sly Mongoose*, 23.
5. Buckell, *Sly Mongoose*, 12.
6. Kamugisha, *Beyond Coloniality*, 58.
7. Buckell, *Sly Mongoose*, 46.
8. Buckell, *Sly Mongoose*, 280.
9. Monbiot, "Neoliberalism."
10. Kamugisha, *Beyond Coloniality*, 43.
11. Shaw Nevins, *Working Juju*, 113.
12. Qtd. in Kamugisha, *Beyond Coloniality*, 63.
13. Buckell, *Sly Mongoose*, 113.
14. Buckell, *Sly Mongoose*, 158.
15. Shaw Nevins, *Working Juju*, 107.

Bibliography

Buckell, Tobias. *Sly Mongoose*. New York: Tor, 2008.

Kamugisha, Aaron. *Beyond Coloniality: Citizenship and Freedom in the Caribbean Intellectual Tradition*. Bloomington: Indiana University Press, 2019.

Monbiot, George. "Neoliberalism: Ideology at the Root of All Our Problems." *Guardian*, April 15, 2016. www.theguardian.com/books/2016/apr/15/neoliberalism-ideology-problem-george-monbiot.

Shaw Nevins, Andrea. *Working Juju: Representations of the Caribbean Fantastic*. Athens: University of Georgia Press, 2019.

32 Tochi Onyebuchi, *Riot Baby* (2019) / Black Lives Matter SF

Isiah Lavender III

The violence inflicted upon Black bodies by white people in such a terrifyingly uniform manner smoothly fuses together the past, present, and future of race relations across time—in fact, so seamlessly that we can no longer distinguish where it begins and where it ends. This hyperreality, after Baudrillard, defines the racial tensions Black Americans have always lived with in the United States on a daily basis.[1] That is, the seeming desire for an imaginary white ethno-state, itself masquerading as a color-blind world, generates the actual death of Black people in the pursuit of a false reality. And it is this illusion which masks our existence as a *hyperreality*—a blended representation of reality undermining our social world. The unreality of such an existence feels downright science-fictional. Unabated pseudoscientific racist beliefs immortalize damaging stereotypes about Black people being overtly criminal, oversexed, or lazy, among others. For the sake of profit and control, dating back to 1619 at the very least and the beginning of American exceptionalism, Black bodies must be absolutely labeled as dangerous commodities. A white overseer whipping a Black slave to a bloody death in the past feels remotely fantastical as a part of history, but what of a mirror-shaded cop gunning down Black people with no provocation in the present?

Nothing has really changed.

Our present reality normalizes, if not mythologizes, racial violence: Ahmaud Arbery, a Black man, chased, hunted, and murdered by two white men for jogging in a suburb on the Atlantic Coast of southern Georgia on February 23, 2020; Breonna Taylor, a Black woman, murdered by narcotics police who raided her apartment in Louisville with a "no-knock" search warrant in the early morning hours on March 13, 2020; and George Floyd, a Black man, murdered by a cop kneeling on his neck while he was face-down and handcuffed on a street in Minneapolis for nearly nine minutes pleading for air on May 25, 2020. This is our reality in 2020—a science-fictional Blackness endlessly looping through the centuries. As viscerally demonstrated—Emmett Till, Trayvon Martin, Alton Sterling, Sandra Bland, Layleen Polanco, Tony McDade, and countless other Black lives ended—time and again, Black lives count for nothing when a white man's power is questioned, which forms the crux of the hyperreal violence loop. And former president Trump (Orange Hitler, as I think of him) promised to quell nationwide nonviolent, peaceful protestors demanding racial justice with the full might of the US military, as well as with secret police that snatch lawful citizens off the streets in an instant to protect the imaginary suburban lifestyle dream he tweeted about nonsensically. The world watched America as its deferred dreams exploded yet again.

Listen, I wonder if the daily stress racism causes me when I leave the house each morning will be my own end. In fact, most Black Americans *do* speculate on this very thing every day. It's the "total surround" Samuel R. Delany talks about in his definitive essay "Racism and Science Fiction."[2] And, naturally, I simply don't know, nor did Ahmaud Arbery, Breonna Taylor, or George Floyd. However, I do know that reading Black-authored, Indigenous-authored, Latinx-authored, Asian-authored, queer-authored SF, and reflecting on the alternative futurisms they provide, is where we can find answers. Then we can hope, we can be brave, and we can talk about racism as we stand together.

The unending visceral reality of racial violence in the United States, stretching across centuries, defines the simulated reality of racism in which we now live. People, both Black and white, cannot distinguish what is real, and, for different reasons, they inhabit the hyperreal world despite the physical, emotional, and cultural consequences. We live more in tune with digital space, streaming services, and technology than the physical world. In fact, we can only perceive and access the real world through antiracist thinking, where racial equality and collective community learning generate action in the fight to equalize "racial distinctions in ethnicities, bodies, cultures, colors, classes, spaces, genders, and sexualities."[3] That Black US history has been science-fictional itself is now beyond question. With that said, part of what makes these acts of state and cultural violence—like the Karens calling the cops on innocent Black people BBQing in the park or bird-watching—feel so unreal *is* exactly the advanced technoscientific level our society is enjoying historically. This moment surely must imply an equal sophistication/advancement of social and spiritual ethos. Embedded in that distinction—between ages, generations, genders, and historical circumstances—collective Black agency does not require permission from the past, only an awareness of it, in this nation-spanning movement of our age—something special cataloged in twenty-first-century Afrofuturist storytelling.

A case in point: the Nigerian-descended American SF writer and former civil rights attorney Tochi Onyebuchi employs his legal experience to create a dystopian world where two Black superpowered siblings, Ella and Kev, get racial justice against the backdrop of recent racial history as they grow up, beginning with the 1992 Los Angeles Riots. Onyebuchi creates a powerful narrative in *Riot Baby* that confronts the mass incarceration of Black and brown people in the United States to free us from the death grip of American racial history and to give us a colored future in which to ponder as these two siblings' parallel narrative arcs lead up to revolution. In other words, Onyebuchi directly taps into the same energy and frustration that sparked the Black Lives Matter movement in 2013 in response to the social injustice, continuing racism, and police brutality perpetually faced by Black Americans. He dares to imagine what Black vengeance, justice, and agency look like simultaneously in writing a hyperreal Afrofuturist tale to engage and expose the hyperreal situation.

Riot Baby fundamentally concerns white supremacy and Black vengeance, and it does not have a white audience in mind. Set in South Central, Los Angeles, the first part introduces us to Ella as she rides a Compton school bus that is pulled over by Bloods in a lowrider angry at the young kids flashing Crip gang signs at them out the bus windows. We immediately recognize this past because of the prevalence of gang culture in the news media and rap music. We also witness the first manifestation of Ella's powers, "her Thing," as precognition, where she sees the death of Jelani, one of her classmates, in a drive-by shooting years before it happens.[4] Later, Ella will ask her grandma why Black people are so angry and whether it has something to do with Rodney King being beaten by the police, and she knows something bad will happen. She and her grandma get caught up in the rioting that erupts after the not guilty verdicts for the police officers, although they are picked up by a friend rushing Ella's mother to the hospital while in labor. Kev, the titular riot baby, is born to single mother Lanie during the height of the rioting.

The second part of the novel picks up in Harlem, New York, where Ella tries to look out for her baby brother while dealing with her burgeoning psionic powers, like telekinesis—she makes a rat's head explode in their tenement—and teleportation—she literally disappears after watching the news of Sean Bell's murder by the NYPD on November 25, 2006, to prevent endangering her mother and brother in her anger—as well as weather manipulation—making the hot apartment cold and materializing a snowball out of thin air to throw at Kev. Yet Ella fails to prevent her brother from hanging out on the street corners where he witnesses firsthand the police brutality solely enacted on young Black males simply playing the dozens. These young Black men display their wit by jokingly responding to Kev's telling them how he was studying George Washington Carver in history class with lines like Carver "woulda made C-4 outta peanuts."[5] Of course, the NYPD show up and show out by throwing one of the young kids face-down on the sidewalk while handcuffed for questioning before releasing the belligerent Black youth and backing away because of the presence of video cameras in the crowd. Kev later gravitates to this crowd. By the end of the second part, an older teenaged Kev gets arrested for attempted armed robbery, becoming another statistic while his sister is gone trying to master her powers.

The third part entails Kev's time at the infamous Rikers Island, Ella's mastery of her powers, and a jump into the near future of "aerial mobile suits and crabtanks and Guardians tall as apartment buildings."[6] Ella learns telepathy, astral projection, and invisibility but is powerless to help her brother, who must do his time and simply survive because "she doesn't want to reduce the entire compound . . . to dust."[7] We also get a glimpse of Kev's nascent powers when he reads his cellmate's eyes and tells Ricky to stay out of the fight in the yard that will land Kev in solitary confinement for six months after throwing a correctional officer (CO) through the air with his mind in the smoke and confusion. His nose bleeds and his head aches just like Ella's when learning to use her powers. In the outside world, augmented officers patrol the streets in mini tanks, and "metal orbs float along the sidewalks above the streetlamps," watching and recording everything.[8] His mother dies and he inadvertently shakes the prison building, but Ella stops him from tearing the place down in his grief and anger. Kev's time in prison comes to an end as he reflects on his eight years behind bars: "fights with inmates . . . COs attacking us, COs trying to rape us, beating us in the showers, us fighting back. . . . More time in the Box."[9] Finally, Kev is able to see Ella use her powers on COs to convince them that Kev is a model inmate.

Upon his release, Kev chooses to go west to Watts in the fourth part, where he joins a sponsored community picked by the patrol board through a computer algorithm. His thumb is microchipped by a private company and functions as a geotag. They know Kev's whereabouts at all times. Likewise, the company also administers anxiety-dampening chemicals through the chip. He works as a welder and makes prosthetics, but begins to perceive the sponsored Watts community as a prison since outsiders are not allowed inside and he's cut off from the internet and all forms of social media. But Kev can sense his sister's building rage at the "mechanized cops programmed with this supposedly race-neutral algorithm" and all of the murder they commit in the outside world as she visits various American cities.[10] Ella visits her mother's old church in Harlem and in speaking to the pastor about the Charleston church shooting, realizes that she does not need permission to end the violence against Black people. What Ella comprehends is that younger generations of Black people don't need permission from older generations to do things their own way in the fight for racial justice, in the fight for equality, in the fight for the future of humanity itself. That's a powerful realization held up against the color-blind hijacking and co-optation of the civil rights movement by white America. That's what being woke is all about.

Not for the first time, Onyebuchi explicitly connects his novel to our current moment of racial strife, beginning with the beating of Rodney King and the LA Riots and continuing to the murders of Sean Bell and Freddie Gray by overzealous police in New York and Baltimore respectively. In addition to these moments, we learn that Ella "had Traveled," using one of her many powers, "straight to the site of the killing, and she'd touch the ground, breathed in the air, and sucked that history deep into her body."[11] Onyebuchi even references the McKinney, Texas, pool party incident of June 2015 that became a viral sensation on YouTube within hours of Black teenager Dajerria Becton being violently restrained by a white police officer while in her bathing suit. Not only does this history of injustice fuel Ella's mounting rage, it unleashes Onyebuchi's ability to write with anger and love in seeking justice.

With this powerful moment of self-recognition, Ella teleports herself to Kev and informs Kev that everything he has built in the community factory has gone to augmenting the cops in "working to make the police invincible" and that he was "never free" of the prison-industrial complex.[12] Kev rips the chip out of his thumb with his mind, freeing himself. With Kev's powers fully manifested, he and Ella will use their abilities to completely obliterate the American police state and begin anew with freedom. *Riot Baby* explores the meaning of Black vengeance against the carceral and white supremacist American state and the bonds of filial love as the superpowered Black siblings take racial justice into their own hands.

Onyebuchi does three important things in *Riot Baby* with respect to the hyperreal violence loop. First, he entrenches the recent history of violence against Black people in his novel, beginning with the Rodney King beating and the LA Riots, and shows his audience what the prison-industrial complex looks like from the inside perspective of Kev in order to unpack the harm it causes. Second, he disrupts this narrative with the multiply psionically gifted sister and brother protagonists as they navigate life in the defamiliarized but recognizable United States of America. And third, he provides an alternative understanding of our social world to better imagine what racial justice could look like through antiracist thinking—the reason behind telling this story, to counteract color-blindness and the apathy toward Black people it causes when violence occurs. In *Riot Baby*, Onyebuchi effectively combines antiracist activism with science-fictional world building.

Onyebuchi utilizes science fiction to confront an American truth so terrible yet so plain in *Riot Baby*. White America will not abandon the structural advantages it has over all other races and ethnicities and would annihilate everyone to maintain this privileged status. Not without a fight! White society doesn't even acknowledge the psychological harm, physical pain, and cultural suffering it has continually inflicted on Black (and brown) people in America; violent oppression continues against its most vilified and vulnerable citizens. The embedded hatred for Black people in the United States runs so deep in our country's fabric that we may never overcome it as a citizenry. Guilt, fear, and anger by whites at Black excellence live in our politics and produce racial inequality. In eulogizing the recently deceased Black civil rights icon Representative John Lewis, former president Barack Obama says it best: "Bull Connor may be gone. But today we witness with our own eyes police officers kneeling on the necks of Black Americans. George Wallace may be gone. But we can witness our federal government sending agents to use tear gas and batons against peaceful demonstrators."[13]

Onyebuchi's novel functions as a second testimonial that indicates how a righteous anger can ignite the necessary hope for change to end this enduring dystopian nightmare for Blacks in the United States of America. Ella's conversation with the pastor as previously mentioned concerned the forgiving of the white supremacist Dylan Roof, who murdered nine African Americans in cold blood during a Bible study at the Emanuel African Methodist Episcopal Church in Charleston, South Carolina. Through her epiphany, Ella concedes the futility in forgiving this evil and decides that she herself is the answer to her people's prayers against the augmented police and the biased computer algorithms they use. Black lives matter to her!

In this respect, whites have always radicalized in response to Black progress. We see it in the colonial era, the antebellum era, the Civil War, Reconstruction, the Jim Crow era, the Civil Rights era, the age of affirmative action, and the especially short-lived post-Black era of the nearly unbelievable yet extraordinary two-term Obama presidency. Thus, the hyperreal violence loop has always been the engine driving the social movements most impacting Blacks in America from the beginning: like abolition to end slavery, like civil rights to end Jim Crow segregation, like Black Lives Matter to end police brutality and the school-to-prison pipeline of disadvantaged minorities caught up in a racist legal system. Onyebuchi asks the relevant question of what contemporary American society might look like if policing, criminal justice, and the incarceration of Black and brown people in lieu of white nationalism continues. And Onyebuchi answers: it definitely *explodes*.

The self-replicating nature of the hyperreal violence loop has produced a variety of powerful written responses from Black Americans across time: Ida B. Wells-Barnett's *The Red Record: Tabulated Statistics and Alleged Causes of Lynching in the United States* (1895), Octavia E. Butler's *Kindred* (1979), Michelle Alexander's *The New Jim Crow: Mass Incarceration in the Age of Colorblindness* (2010), and now Tochi Onyebuchi's *Riot Baby* (2019). Arguably, as the first conscious BLM science fiction novel, it belongs in this group. As an Afrofuturist, I take a deep interest in Onyebuchi's vision of our struggle to simply exist as full-fledged human beings seeking equality and basic rights, something historically and culturally denied us.

Afrofuturism challenges a uniquely American racial paralysis, which devalues Black life as alien humans—a de facto science-fictional Blackness.[14] Consequently, everyone should be reading *Riot Baby*! It's powerful. It's prescient. It's now. In fact, it *is* truth—powerful, powerful truth! Onyebuchi does not care about the strange SF/literature divide, where white SFF writers want to protect their perceived territory—the future and the fantastic. Rather, Onyebuchi appropriates a few science-fictional motifs—near-future setting, psionic powers, and cybernetics—to illustrate the current dystopia of Black existence—continual technological surveillance, police brutality, and prison—and to better challenge the ongoing systemic oppression of white America. Like other Black American SF writers, he shows us the ugly face of America in the mirror of Afrofuturism.

Notes

1. Baudrillard, *Simulacra and Simulation.*
2. Delany, "Racism and Science Fiction," 84.
3. Kendi, *How to Be Antiracist*, 226.
4. Onyebuchi, *Riot Baby*, 9.
5. Onyebuchi, *Riot Baby*, 34.
6. Onyebuchi, *Riot Baby*, 57–58.
7. Onyebuchi, *Riot Baby*, 65.
8. Onyebuchi, *Riot Baby*, 89.
9. Onyebuchi, *Riot Baby*, 120–121.
10. Onyebuchi, *Riot Baby*, 156.
11. Onyebuchi, *Riot Baby*, 110.
12. Onyebuchi, *Riot Baby*, 170–171.
13. *Washington Post*, "Barack Obama's Full Eulogy."
14. See my recent book, Lavender, *Afrofuturism Rising*, for a look at the long history of Black science-fictional responses to American racism.

Bibliography

Baudrillard, Jean. *Simulacra and Simulation*. Translated by Sheila F. Glaser. Ann Arbor: University of Michigan Press, 1994.

Delany, Samuel R. "Racism and Science Fiction." In *The Atheist in the Attic*, by Samuel R. Delany, 72–94. Oakland: PM Press, 2018. First published 1998.

Kendi, Ibram X. *How to Be an Antiracist*. New York: Random House, 2019.

Lavender, Isiah, III. *Afrofuturism Rising: The Literary Prehistory of a Movement*. Columbus: Ohio State University Press, 2019.

Onyebuchi, Tochi. *Riot Baby*. New York: Tor, 2019.

Washington Post. "Barack Obama's Full Eulogy at John Lewis's Funeral." YouTube video, July 30, 2020. https://www.youtube.com/watch?v=V1pKoCq1bn0.

33 Rosaura Sánchez and Beatrice Pita, *Lunar Braceros: 2125–2148* (2009) / Imagination against Resistance

Lysa Rivera

> The imagination is a tool of resistance.
>
> —Ytasha Womack, *Afrofuturism: Black Sci-Fi and Culture*[1]

Gloria Anzaldúa once wrote that "nothing happens in the 'real' world unless it first happens in the images in our heads."[2] Such a simple sentence with such far-reaching implications, especially for people of color in the age of late capitalism. It reminds me of something Walidah Imarisha wrote nearly thirty years later: "Whenever we try to envision a world without war, without violence, without prisons, without capitalism, we are engaging in speculative fiction."[3] Educator, activist, and science fiction visionary, Imarisha has spent years traveling around the United States empowering students by validating and energizing their imagination. Along with her coeditor adrienne maree brown, she leads workshops on zine making, worldbuilding, and community-building for students interested in learning how to organize for change. There is something profoundly possible when the imagination meets marginalization, when writers of color in this age of entrenched neoliberalism dare to imagine alternatives, an elsewhere that disrupts and ultimately transforms the dangerous status quo. This chapter unpacks this possibility as it emerges in a short science fiction novel called *Lunar Braceros: 2125–2158*. In it, Chicana visionaries Rosaura Sánchez and Beatrice Pita imagine a future in which late capitalism has ravaged the earth to the point that the moon, a new "spatial fix for capitalism," now serves as an extraterrestrial landfill. Yet within this imaginary dystopia, Sánchez and Pita also dare to envision scenarios of resistance and survival. They refuse to foreclose on the possibility for change by exploring imaginary oppositional spaces that can, and must, inspire the next generation of writers and SF visionaries.

The dystopian force driving the future in *Lunar Braceros* is the aptly named New Imperial Order (NIO), a multinational consortium of corporations that has undermined most of the world's already capitalistic nation states through a combination of economic and paramilitaristic force. Much of the world's population, the majority people of color, have been reduced to grunt laborers.[4] Hence the title of the novel: lunar braceros are laborers who toil on the moon, which has become a large repository for the debris and refuse of capitalist excess.[5] At ground zero of this nightmare are the US Southwest and Northern Mexico, fused into a new geopolitical territory called Cali-Texas that manages several heavily armed, highly secured labor camps known as "Reservations," where the unemployed are forced to live while they work at menial, dehumanizing jobs.[6] Essentially high-tech gulags named after the mass dislocation of the Indigenous peoples of North America in previous centuries, the Reservations provide multinational corporations with an endless stream of cheap, affordable, and ultimately expendable labor. As one of the "Reslifers" puts it, the Reservations offer the corporate elite a "controlled laboratory labor force" and function as nothing less than a "disciplinary society . . . useful to the state."[7]

I read these nightmarish Reservations as extrapolations of what Sánchez and Pita see as today's "new enclosures."[8] Emerging originally out of Marx's theory of primitive accumulation, industrial enclosures began to manifest after the forced expropriation of peasant communities from their land (and, by extension, their own means of production) to industrialized urban centers, such as London, where they toiled under new forms of waged and factory labor. As Sánchez and Pita see it, today's capitalist enclosures continue to serve capitalist accumulation, but on a much larger scale, meeting the needs of "global capitalist interests" by maintaining and policing a constant supply of cheap labor by absorbing and housing "workers in the global South."[9] Citing the pressure coming from agribusiness, US industries, and NAFTA, which have prompted the displacement of workers now forced to migrate to the border for work in the maquiladoras, Sánchez and Pita view today's new enclosures as yet another "neoliberal tactic for the dispossession of the commons and the creation of a waged labor force."[10] I argue that their reality makes the Reservations of the novel uncannily familiar. In centering the traumatic experiences of the Reslifers themselves,

Lunar Braceros effectively excoriates global capitalism by imagining it from the perspective of those whose labor, often invisible and always essential, makes it possible.

Sánchez and Pita bring these dystopian conditions to life with a series of stunning calacas (skeleton images) that are interspersed between some of the nanotexts in the novel. Illustrated by Chicano artist Mario Chacon, these calacas are effective in underscoring the deathly consequences of neoliberalist labor practice. Macabre and mischievous, las calacas have enjoyed a long history in both Mexican and Chicanx contexts. Journalists, activists, and cultural critics have used las calacas to satirize political corruption and to criticize "government and corporate policies that cause death on a local, national, or global level."[11] Following suit, las calacas in *Lunar Braceros* exclusively and directly correspond with the oppressed, standing in at times for the novel's various laborers, including those who live on the Reservations. In one of the most chilling images, for instance, Chacon depicts two school-aged Reslifers riding bikes along the perimeter of a Reservation (figure 33.1a). In front of the children is a barbed-wire fence, behind them a menacing control tower. Together, fence and tower signal how these Reservations do more than simply house the under- and unemployed; they imprison the Reslifers, who refer to the camp as a type of "panopticon prison" for the chronically unemployed.[12] In other illustrations, Chacon's calacas signify resistance and resilience. For example, in the image that adorns both the text's cover and its first page, Chacon depicts one of the eponymous lunar braceros whose points of view drive the narrative (figure 33.1b). In it, the lunar bracero looks directly at the viewer while appearing to be floating in outer space with a raised fist in the air. This raised fist, I contend, signals that amid oppression and exploitation, there remains space for resilience and survival. Because without that space, change becomes impossible. Without that space, the oppressor triumphs.

In fact, this space—for hope, agency, and transformation—animates the broader realm of Chicanx speculative fiction at the turn of the century, generally speaking. Lunar Braceros joins a slew of other similarly focused texts—a type of Chicanx cyberpunk—that also seek to confront, resist, and ultimately transform systemic oppression in the neoliberal age. This is precisely what prompted Catherine Ramírez to include "survival" in her groundbreaking introduction to *Chicanafuturism*, an umbrella term that refers to Chicanx cultural production that recasts the icons and ideas of

a b

Figure 33.1
Details of Chacon's calacas art from *Lunar Braceros.*

technoculture within Chicanx contexts. According to Ramírez, Chicanafuturism is a type of Chicanx cultural practice that "articulates colonial and postcolonial histories in indigenismo, mestizaje, hegemony, and survival" within a speculative or science-fictional idiom.[13] In other words, Chicanafuturism draws from and often incorporates traditional forms and practices while recasting them into the present and while it "dares to imagine new ways of being for the future."[14] Similarly, Chacon's illustrations are also inspired by tradition, but they simultaneously recast those traditional images in a futuristic context, merging both the progressive histories of Mexican and Chicanx political protest movements and the trappings of science fiction.

In doing this, they speak to the ways in which any attempt to imagine a future of resilience and resistance is, in and of itself, a type of science fiction. After all, the calacas in *Lunar Braceros* are illustrative stand-ins for the lunar braceros themselves, laborers who defy the odds and manage to escape their horrid working conditions. Scrappy, smart, and resilient, the lunar braceros imagined in the novel eventually join with a collective underground resistance movement that "represents a rejection of everything that is hegemonic and dominated by capital relations."[15] In other words, las calacas signify both the histories and conditions of oppression, *as well as* narratives of futurity and the potential for transformation, not only being from the future, but also often positioned as contemporary agents of resistance, as the image in figure 33.1b makes clear.

What, then, does resistance look like in *Lunar Braceros*? What is this blueprint for survival, and how does it ultimately work? One response to these questions can be found in the imaginary community of Chinganaza, "one of the few places in the world . . . where communal farming is the primary practice."[16] Described as an "alternative space" and "little oasis," Chinganaza figures as the only life-affirming livable space for the laborers of the future, the vast underclass, the majority of whom are people of color.[17] According to one of the lunar braceros, Chinganaza emerged after a hemispheric war known as the Indigenous War of 2070, when Indigenous tribes scattered across the Americas took up arms to fight "against the dispossession and exploitation of the remaining indigenous peoples" of the Global South.[18] Chinganaza replaces the latter's repressive, capitalistic police state, which uniformly subjugates people of color and poor whites through mass incarceration and habitual debt slavery, with an intentional community where "the land belongs to those who work it; everything is shared and there are no bosses."[19]

To fully appreciate the deep historical significance of Chinganaza, it is important to consider its name. Readers familiar with Chicanx and Mexican literary and cultural history will clearly catch the allusion to la Chingada, a term often associated with the iconic Mexican figure la Malinche, a "faceless and voiceless" Indigenous Mexican slave who was given to the Spanish during the conquest and who has become a symbol for the mestiza/o race (European and Indigenous) in Mexico. The "unfortunate" name of Chinganaza, then, refers not only to the individual story of Malinche herself, but of the brutalities of Indigenous labor under conquest as well. Chicana feminists, however, have rewritten the story of Malinche by transforming her narrative from one of victimization into one of agency and survival. Gloria Anzaldúa, for example, reminds us that Malinche was more than just a victim of Cortez's seductive ways. Likewise, in *Lunar Braceros*—a text written by two Chicana feminists—la Chinganaza transforms la Chingada into a figure of agency and survival, prompting an apt comparison between it and the figure of Malinche that Chicana writer Carmen Tafolla describes this way: "Not tricked, not screwed," but who "saw a dream" and "reached it."[20] Chinganaza therefore represents a historically grounded and forward-looking imaginary space. It draws directly from a colonial past, yet it also signals a sense of futurity and possibility, offering as it does a model for change in the grim future Sánchez and Pita imagine for their readers.

At the heart of Chinganza's transformative ethos is the belief that only collective action across differences leads to real (material, tangible) change. As one of the lunar braceros puts it: "Only participation in collective action ever gave me a sense of freedom, a sense of being more than a caged animal, whether on the Reservation, in prison, or up on the Moon."[21] Chinganaza, after all, is a coalitional space made up of several Indigenous tribes from many nations. It is a hemispheric community, not a national one. Moreover, in the novel, the seven lunar braceros whose stories drive the narrative eventually join forces with a multinational, multiracial, and multicultural anticapitalist movement that has clandestine underground networks scattered throughout the world. Diffuse, stealthy, and decidedly committed to undermining the machinations of the NIO from the ground up, this collective movement seeks to align communities that might be culturally and ethnically diverse, yet share a common position in relation to the NIO and devastating late capitalism. What is more, this underground network often appropriates the same technologies often used to oppress its members, including and especially the various computer surveillance technologies the novel imagines elsewhere in the narrative. As Sánchez and Pita describe it, this is a new "global movement that synchronized local cells through alternative internet systems that piggybacked clandestinely on the worldwide communication grid."[22] Through these means, the powerless in Cali-Texas's menacing Reservations could "reach even the farthest village in Peru and Brazil as well as some in Africa and Asia" and together forge a united front of resistance.[23] If this sounds familiar, it is because it was "inspired by the Zapatista Movement in Chiapas [Mexico] many years before."[24] In a clever and deliberate move, Sánchez and Pita imply that the future of resistance already has a prototype: the 1994 uprisings against the ratification of NAFTA, itself a symbol of Mexico's transition to a neoliberal state. What is more, like the EZLN's[25] signature cyberculture tactics, the future of resistance imagined in *Lunar Braceros* will also center Indigenous rights, promote collective action, and appropriate information technologies to disseminate its messages. After all, the novel's imaginary "alternative internet systems" cited earlier clearly resonate with the EZLN's push for an "intercontinental network of alternative communication that will search channels so that words may travel all the paths that resist" and so that "distinct resistances communicate with one another."[26]

Texts like *Lunar Braceros* signal an important departure from the type of science fiction stories that currently dominate the United States's mainstream cultural imaginary: the superhero franchise. In these narratives, it is often a lone hero (or an extraordinarily elite, members only club) that saves the day. Heroes like Batman, Spider-Man, and the Avengers, exciting and sexy as they may be, promote narratives of heroism that do not rely on community-building and coalitions across a multitude of differences. They may depict outsiders and underdogs subverting the powers that be, but they often imply that said subversion can be a single man or monocultural enterprise. By contrast, texts like *Lunar Braceros*—like real-life Indigenous-centered movements such as the EZLN—point to a collective and coalitional approach to resistance. What is more, they throw into relief how striving for alternatives to a powerful status quo requires the courage to imagine those alternatives in the face of great adversity. As Walidah Imarisha has aptly put it, "all organizing is science fiction" because collective organizing not only requires building communities that do not yet exist, but also requires striving for futures that do not yet exist, imagining ways to make the world a better place for those whose realities often resemble those imagined in dystopian science fiction—in a world often beleaguered by alienation, estrangement, and unspeakable violence.[27] Ultimately, texts like *Lunar Braceros* remind us that for a long time, writers of color have turned to science fiction to imagine alternatives to the dystopian status quo in which they find themselves, worlds marred by xenophobia, rampant poverty, and total marginalization from all necessary spheres of life. Practitioners of what Imarisha calls *visionary fiction*, they have availed themselves of a subversive form of science fiction that weds the power of the imagination with the grit of social justice. To effect real change, one cannot exist without the other. Imagination put in the service of heroism can only take us so far. Imagination put in the service of community building and coalition politics? That is the future of change.

Notes

1. Womack, *Afrofuturism*, 24.

2. Anzaldúa, *Borderlands*, 109.

3. Imarisha, "Introduction," 3.

4. Sánchez and Pita, *Lunar Braceros*, 11.

5. Sánchez and Pita, *Lunar Braceros*, 16. "Bracero" is Spanish for "he who works with his arms," or "manual laborer."

6. Sánchez and Pita, *Lunar Braceros*, 8.

7. Sánchez and Pita, *Lunar Braceros*, 14.

8. Sánchez and Pita, "Rethinking Settler Colonialism," 1043.

9. Sánchez and Pita, "Rethinking Settler Colonialism," 1043.

10. Sánchez and Pita, "Rethinking Settler Colonialism," 1043.

11. Herrera-Sobek, *Celebrating Latino Folklore*, 422.

12. Sánchez and Pita, *Lunar Braceros*, 35.

13. Ramírez, "Afrofuturism/Chicanafuturism," 187.

14. Ramírez, "Deus ex Machina," 82.

15. Sánchez and Pita, *Lunar Braceros*, 25.

16. Sánchez and Pita, *Lunar Braceros*, 177.

17. Sánchez and Pita, *Lunar Braceros*, 25, 114.

18. Sánchez and Pita, *Lunar Braceros*, 85.

19. Sánchez and Pita, *Lunar Braceros*, 87.

20. Tafolla, "La Malinche," 198.

21. Sánchez and Pita, *Lunar Braceros*, 81.

22. Sánchez and Pita, *Lunar Braceros*, 34.

23. Sánchez and Pita, *Lunar Braceros*, 34.

24. Sánchez and Pita, *Lunar Braceros*, 95.

25. EZLN stands for the Ejército Zapatista de Liberación Nacional, which translates as the Zapatista Army of National Liberation in English.

26. Ruggiero, *Zapatista Encuentro*, 53.

27. Imarisha, "Introduction," 4.

Bibliography

Anzaldúa, Gloria. *Borderlands/La frontera: The New Mestiza*. San Francisco: Aunt Lute Books, 2012.

Herrera-Sobek, María. *Celebrating Latino Folklore: An Encyclopedia of Cultural Traditions*, edited by María Herrera-Sobek. Volume 1. Santa Barbara: ABC-CLIO, 2012.

Imarisha, Walidah. "Introduction." In *Octavia's Brood: Science Fiction Stories from Social Justice Movements*, edited by adrienne maree brown and Imarisha Walidah, 3–5. Oakland: AK Press, 2015.

Ramírez, Catherine. "Afrofuturism/Chicanafuturism: Fictive Kin." *Aztlán: A Journal of Chicano Studies* 33, no. 1 (2008): 185–194.

Ramírez, Catherine. "Deus ex Machina: Tradition, Technology, and the Chicanafuturist Art of Marion C. Martinez." *Aztlán: A Journal of Chicano Studies* 29, no. 2 (2004): 55–92.

Ruggiero, Greg, ed. *Zapatista Encuentro: Documents from the First Intercontinental Encounter for Humanity and Against Neoliberalism*. New York: Seven Stories Press, 1998.

Sánchez, Rosaura, and Beatrice Pita. *Lunar Braceros: 2125–2148*. National City: Calaca Press, 2009.

Sánchez, Rosaura, and Beatrice Pita. "Rethinking Settler Colonialism." *American Quarterly* 66, no. 4 (2014): 1039–1055.

Tafolla, Carmen. "La Malinche." *Infinite Divisions: An Anthology of Chicana Literature*, edited by Tey Diana Rebolledo and Eliana S. Rivero, 198–199. Tucson: University of Arizona Press, 1993.

Womack, Ytasha. *Afrofuturism: The World of Black Sci-Fi and Fantasy Culture*. Chicago: Lawrence Hill Books, 2013.

34 Boualem Sansal, *2084: The End of the World* (2015) / Resisting Censorship

Ouissal Harize

Imagine university teachers freely spewing the following statements to their students: "God created man for himself and the woman for the man," "Women gaze down as men gaze at them." Now imagine the outraged students being permanently dismissed from the same university for mocking these teachers on Facebook. Does it feel oppressive? Dystopic? Unreal? These, unfortunately, are real incidents I lived through and witnessed as a college student in Algeria. The nature of this essay warrants inaugurating it with such a conjunction between dystopia and reality. By reading Boualem Sansal's controversial novel *2084: The End of the World* (2015) against the contexts of contemporary Algerian life in particular and Arab life here in general, I examine how languages, genres, and the processes of defamiliarization and desensitization from religious oppression can become combative tools of resistance. The personal account in this essay is not merely a subjective intervention, but rather a testimony to larger political and societal concerns.

I was born in 1992 in Algeria amid the rampant mayhem of what is now known as the Black Decade: a decade of (un)civil war between the democratic government and the fundamentalist party Islamic Salvation Front—a decade of blood, corruption, utter terror, and despicable woes. Sansal's novel frames a question: What makes terror even more pernicious than its initial violence? For me and for many Algerian millennials, there are two answers: reliving the same terror again, and not understanding what had happened to begin with. Whereas the first is a globally shared concern, the latter is a form of trauma bestowed upon us by the state's malicious censorship during that time (and to this day). We do not really know who was opening fire and who was the victim; we do, however, know it as a time of national, irrational hysteria.

Growing up in Algeria, I was particularly struck by the endless attempt to infuse different languages with certain ideologies. Eventually, this gave birth to bizarre stereotypes of the Islamist Arabophone and the Westernized Francophone, ironically rooted in the long history of European Orientalism and imperialist ambitions in the Middle East and North Africa (MENA). Then, with the enthusiasm of liberating ourselves from colonial histories attached to the French language and to the Islamic one etched on Arabic, English became a linguistic harbor to millennials.[1] Using language as a tool for evading censorship can therefore be thought-provoking; I believe that Sansal strategically wrote his novel in French and within the genre of science fiction to evade the harsh censorship of both communities of readers and the state.

Contemporary Arab science fiction writers and researchers like Basma Ghalayini suggest that the paucity of technological innovations and scientific research in the Arab world, which are partially due to the Arab world's history under colonization, constitutes one reason for the scarcity of SF works.[2] Ian Campbell also notes in *Arabic Science Fiction* how the serviceability of science fiction to imperialism and colonialism led to a general distaste among literary elites for Western SF. However, there has been a remarkable upsurge in SF works after the Arab Spring to demarcate a current disillusionment with revolutions, especially using the genre to depict postcolonial discontent with social movements. From a postcolonial/anticolonial perspective, this turn to science fiction, speculative fiction, and dystopian fiction can be seen as a form of resistance to a genre that has hitherto excluded the postcolonial Other. Cast as aliens in their homeland, the postcolonial Other has always been a monstrous terror awaiting the white man as he descends from his explorative ship. In Sansal's text, however, SF is a way to confront and criticize the self without focusing on any one cultural or philosophical Other.

2084's narrative is about a future, not necessarily a distant one, where only one religion reigns supreme on the entire globe: a new religion of a god called Yolah, and Abi, his delegate and prophet. The protagonist Ati wakes up doubting everything one day, which leads him on a quest to discover the geopolitical borders surrounding the fictional kingdom of Abistan, as well as metaphorical borders between good and evil. It is important here to clarify that Arab SF works predominantly focus on utopic/dystopic cautionary tales; the novel presents itself as a cautionary tale that allegorically explores issues of agency, intentionality, and free will. Although the narrative is set on a future earth, it explores a binary impetus of religious terror and resistance in the past and present. The imaginary future of the novel therefore generously lends itself to assessing, criticizing, and perhaps changing the real future; the course of the made-up Abistan offers echoes for the paths of Algeria, MENA, and the world.

Algeria's real history with Islamist terrorism has been largely restricted to the civil war from 1990 to 2000, known as the Black Decade. The war remains mysterious due to massive media disinformation during that era, as Western media was restricted in terms of firsthand, on-site coverage and as the Algerian media was, at that time, not privatized yet, limiting the availability of non-government-issued news reports. Only the official (state) TV channel L'ENTV and a few newspapers such as *Al-Khabar* were covering the news. Moreover, with the systematic targeting of journalists during that time, coverage of terror stories became a hazardous path avoided by many reporters. Clashing theories about the truth behind the Algerian civil war continue to this day, as more government officials are coming out with their testimonies about governmental operations that targeted civilians to defame political Islam.[3]

In Sansal's book, distance—the temporal and spatial distancing of speculative fiction—allows the author to criticize people's readiness to submit to, to follow, religious worldviews and their politics without any doubt or questioning. Such submission, in the language of Islam but applicable across religions, can make man a defeated victim and a villainous terrorist at the same time. The novel opens with a note that mocks the gullible reading board responsible for cultural censorship in Algeria: "Warning: This is a work of pure invention: the world of Bigaye that I describe in these pages does not exist and has no reason to exist in the future, just as the world of Big Brother imagined by George Orwell, and so marvellously depicted in his novel *1984*, did not exist in his time, does not exist in our own, and truly has no reason to exist in the future. Sleep soundly, good people, everything is sheer falsehood, and the rest is under control."[4] Sansal's dark humor helps situate the novel in time and in genre contexts; like the Orwell novel, his is at once a sheer criticism of both past and present, and a call to hope for the future. It is significant to emphasize that the terror described in this novel is in no way imagined; it is historical terror merely displaced onto an imagined realm.

Themes of erasure of history and memory, which dominate the novel, are deeply rooted in colonial endeavors to erase Indigenous cultures, histories, and languages. However, the novel suggests that this intensified process of forced memory erasure, leading to memory's twin facet, amnesia, is deeply linked to massive wars of utter destruction. Focusing on politics of fear, the anticipation of a massive war was the second belief implemented into the people's memory, after the unquestionable belief in God [Yolah]: "The battle to end all battles' just like those real or imagined battles that had come before and would come again, century after century. There was no hierarchy among martyrs, nor ever any end to the holy war; it would only be proclaimed once Yolah crushed Balis, in accordance with the promise."[5]

Scenes like this take me back to upsetting memories of outspoken racism and hatred expressed by prominent university teachers—just one situation in Algeria that Boualem is no doubt drawing on in his novel. Utterances like "Jews are parasites that destroy any society that hosts them" and "Jews master the art of weeping to get what they want," and the unrelenting warning of future wars with a Jewish enemy, were regular lessons—yet our teachers said them without fearing repercussions. We students had no authority to report these incidents. Just like the novel, and like a nightmare, we felt a suspension of morality within the realm of the university; we had no power to fight it except through essays in which we criticized the politics of fear and the injustice of racial othering without directly confronting the teachers.

Similar to our strategic use of a general criticism of racism to castigate particular instances of antisemitism, Sansal's novel deploys the theme of enforced cultural and historical amnesia to create an effect of defamiliarization. The following passage, for example, stages a visit to the Louvre after the global reign of terror: "Finally they ended up in a huge green expanse, in the middle of which stood a magnificent white building surrounded by an impeccable lawn. Ati would learn later from Toz himself that the building was the fifth copy of an ancient, prestigious, gigantic museum called the Louvre, or the Loufre, that has been ransacked and razed to the ground during the first Great Holy War and the annexation of Abistan by the Lig."[6] In addition to presenting us with a destroyed Louvre—a horror to many due to the museum's lasting, if complicated, value to the global art and cultural world—the passage also reminds us of ISIL's destruction of ancient artifacts and sculptures in the Museum of Mosul in 2014.[7] It is important here to explain that horror and terror are complementary: *horror* is a reaction to an unbearable atrocity, and *terror* is the fear of experiencing that horror again and the anxious anticipation of that experience. This push and pull between horror and terror is represented by the defamiliarization of terror in the novel.

In addition to Sansal's rhapsodic prose, the peculiarly metaphysical and ritualistic passages of the novel engender a feeling of displacement. Concentrating on seeing religious rituals through the distance of defamiliarization, the novel desensitizes us to reconsider our acquiescence to everyday rules, perhaps internalized through colonial convention. The following is a blistering example of how a passage by Sansal encouraged such self-reflection: "In some regions it had become customary to gather once a year in huge crowds for mass self-flogging with studded whips, amid a joyful uproar, to show that suffering was nothing compared to the happiness of awaiting the Bidi."[8] This self-immolation passage can also be a tool to disguise dissent; it in fact compelled me to recall the time I had to apologize for saying the word *rape* in the classroom because a censorious teacher had found it "unscrupulous." To me, my apology—instead of speaking up and explaining to him that the only shame is in the draconian censorship he was imposing on us—felt like an illusory ritual of self-flagellation to avoid worse chastisement by the institution.

In *2084*, the author reflects on the consequences of total obedience through characters who fail to rely on their critical agency but who instead submit to the established order. The satirical criticism even suggests that higher officials within the religious state apparatuses had their brains removed at birth in order for them to do their jobs efficiently: "These massive guards were selected at birth, painstakingly trained by the apparatus, and they obeyed no one else; nothing could distract them, divert them, unsettle them; no compassion could restrain their cruelty. No one knew whether they were actually human; their brains had been removed at birth, which would explain their terrifying stubbornness and haunted gaze."[9] Thus, the novel in many ways points an accusatory finger at the religious state and that state's ideological apparatus for systematically suspending morality to oppress the nation.

The novel criticizes the manner in which personal acts and intimate thoughts are regimented and meticulously supervised by the state or religion. In a globalized world, where borders are conceptually becoming more fluid, Sansal's novel explores the literal and allegorical serviceability of borders. Hence, in addition to the geopolitical border in the novel, there are many abstract borders between the storyworld's obedient believers and its readership's critical thinkers, and between those subjugated to power and those in power. Sansal expands the discussion on borders to a more philosophical level. The novel is concerned not only with geographical borders, but also the borders between material logic and metaphysics and between the private and public spheres. For example, in the novel, the Committee of Righteousness is tasked with monitoring people's everyday behavior in general, and commitment to religious rituals in particular; this is very similar to the Committee for the Promotion of Virtue and the Prevention of Vice in Saudi Arabia, a governmental organization tasked with the social policing of people to make sure everything is done according to Islamic Sharia law.

The novel thus shows us how personal loyalties and relationships are under the punitive control of the state in its satirical attack against dictatorial censorship. While comparing the published text of Boualem Sansal and my experience in academia (in Algeria), the Algerian university stands out not only as a system of censorship but also, more generally, as a fiercely repressive, even oppressive, institution. Of course, some students also experienced singular cases of benevolence in which teachers allowed us to think and express our views freely, but I will offer my critique that these individual allowances of free speech, when occurring side by side with oppressive classroom teaching in the same institutions of higher education, can easily become part of a larger system of educational repression simply because they usually do not criticize the wider practice of censorship among teaching colleagues. This normalization of censorship, by teachers in the university system who do not address their colleagues' ongoing silencing of students, can support dominant structures of oppression.

The land of Abistan in the novel and my university alike are microcosmic representations of the power dynamic between censorship and dissent. Sansal's strategic use of science fiction creates an illusory distance between reality and the imaginary. His novel, which is not taught in the Algerian university, opens our eyes to how the state manipulates religion, customs, and politics to oppress and suppress the population. This novel is one among several Arab SF novels that together form a new direction of resisting sociopolitical tyranny. SF not only evades censorship: it mocks it, denuding it to frailty. This is why I believe academic research has to step in and cement the combative role of Arab SF, to present a coup against the intellectual hegemony proliferating in our universities.

It is important to expand our understanding of the speculative beyond the textuality of novels and films; any dream of a different future, any praxis of futurism, fits within the scope of speculative fiction. To the colonized, independence was a form of speculative fiction. To the victims of a brutal civil war, peace was speculative fiction. Today, to my generation, which led the first peaceful revolution in the history of Algeria, the thought of having a civil state is speculative fiction. The novel *2084* is particularly interesting because it is a cautionary tale stating, *we must not allow what happened before to happen again*. As Toni Cade Bambara said, the mission of a writer "is to make revolution irresistible"; Sansal's novel was a great incentive to doubt, to ask questions, and to dare and revolt. It is therefore clear that within oppressive regimes, science fiction and speculative fiction are tools of evading censorship, but also tools for resisting it.

Octavia E. Butler famously wrote in *Parable of the Sower*: "All that you touch you Change. All that you Change Changes you. The only lasting truth is Change. God Is Change."[10] This notion of eternal churn and generative transformation permeates the novel. In the face of radical change, its chief protagonist, Ati, succeeds in protecting the essence of his humanity and his free thinking, like we Algerian students who, in the face of an indoctrination, managed to sharpen our free thinking instead of bending to the system. The Algerian nation has survived colonization, civil wars, Islamist terrorism, and neocolonization, with its indefatigable spirit of resistance ever more determined not only to dream but also to pursue its dreams. Both the novel and Algeria's history of resistance show the relationship between science fiction and survival: our dream is a seed of change that can only be described as speculative fiction; activism is the pathway we take toward making that dream come true. The 2019 Algerian Revolution of Smiles, which toppled ex-president Abdelaziz Bouteflika's regime, is the best evidence of a nation that survived and even thrived through speculative fiction—by dreaming of change.

Notes

1. The argument here is not that English as a language is decolonial, but that it has no painful history in Algeria.

2. See Ghalayini, *Palestine +100.*

3. For more, see Souaïdia, *La sale guerre.*

4. Sansal, *2084*, 12.

5. Sansal, *2084*, 34.

6. Sansal, *2084*, 221.

7. For more, see Shaheen, "ISIS Fighters Destroy Ancient Artefacts."

8. Sansal, *2084*, 25.

9. Sansal, *2084*, 29.

10. Butler, *Parable of the Sower*, 3.

Bibliography

Butler, Octavia E. *Parable of the Sower.* New York: Open Road Media, 2012.

Campbell, Ian. *Arabic Science Fiction.* New York: Palgrave, 2018.

Ghalayini, Basma, ed. *Palestine +100: Stories from a Century after the Nakba.* Manchester: Comma Press, 2019.

Sansal, Boualem. *2084: The End of the World.* New York: Europa Editions, 2017. First published 2015.

Shaheen, Kareem. "ISIS Fighters Destroy Ancient Artefacts at Mosul Museum." *Guardian*, February 26, 2015. https://www.theguardian.com/world/2015/feb/26/isis-fighters-destroy-ancient-artefacts-mosul-museum-iraq.

Souaïdia, Habib. *La sale guerre.* Paris: La Découverte, 2001.

35 The Russo Brothers, *Captain America: The Winter Soldier* (2014) and *Captain America: Civil War* (2016) / The Patriotism of Raising Hell

Sarah Marrs

In 2010, the actors that formed the face of the nascent Marvel Cinematic Universe gathered at San Diego Comic Con to officially announce *The Avengers*, an unprecedented crossover uniting three multifilm franchises into a fourth, team-based franchise. Nerds everywhere rejoiced because only a few years before, such a thing seemed impossible. But here was visible proof that there could be an interconnected universe of films telling in three dimensions the stories generations had grown up with on two-dimensional pages of comic books. There was, however, a question looming over the whole proceeding: How in the world was Marvel Studios going to make Captain America, that fuddy-duddy symbol of American Übermensch left over from the less morally complex time of World War II, relatable to twenty-first century audiences? In 2010, Captain America was understood to be the vitamin we must choke down in order to unite the Avengers on the big screen. He was not the most popular character even among the B-list Avengers, but we would tolerate him for the bigger, trendier, flashier characters he brought with him. And to appeal to international markets, where American patriotism is often not as welcome, his first film was subtitled "The First Avenger" instead of repurposing one of Cap's less neutral nicknames, such as "The Sentinel of Liberty" or "America's New Hope." Cap was a tough sell—but by 2019, when *Avengers: Endgame* marked the high-water mark of Marvel Studios' grand narrative experiment, Captain America, as portrayed by Chris Evans, had grown to be one of the most popular and beloved of the MCU's Avengers. He had transcended every possible scale of popularity to become a recognizable symbol worldwide, and for a generation of young fans, their de facto Superman. How did it happen? With six words: "This isn't freedom. This is fear."

In 2014, Captain America made his third on-screen appearance in *Captain America: The Winter Soldier*. In many ways, this was the real test of the character's appeal to twenty-first-century audiences. His first film, *The First Avenger*, set in World War II, aligned Cap with a long tradition of Nazi-punching good guys in American cinema. The conflict of World War II offers a moral purity behind Cap's will to fight, lending urgency to his declaration, "I don't like bullies." There is no greater twentieth-century bully than Adolf Hitler—and here is a comic-book hero created explicitly to punch Hitler in the face. Everyone can get on board with that. But bringing him into the twenty-first century meant integrating Cap into a very different US military, one engaged in "forever wars" aided by dubious—at best—homeland security policies and apparently permanent overseas occupations. The public had become weary of conflict, growing ever more cynical about our US foreign policy with each passing year of the 2010s. It was one thing to buy into Cap as a defeater of Nazis, something else entirely to buy into him as an upholder of a system that was exhausting everyone daily.

But in *The Winter Soldier*, Cap is not gung-ho about his day job with S.H.I.E.L.D., an intelligence organization even more shadowy than the CIA. He's lonely, adrift, unhappy, and struggling with PTSD—recognizable as any generation of soldier coming home but explicitly aligned with current through post-9/11 cohorts of veterans who have served in Iraq and Afghanistan. This is a smart way to engender audience sympathy for a character that is basically a Greek god—Athena, by my reckoning—but it also lays the foundation for the six words he's about to utter and completely shift his relationship with the US military-industrial complex and the public perception of American patriotism. Captain America is the great patriot of Marvel comics. His flag-themed uniform would do Betsy Ross proud; he's always talking about duty and honor; and he is not only a super soldier because of his physical strength, but because of his pure dedication to fighting for the little guy and upholding American values of courage and sacrifice. But in *The Winter Soldier*, the directing duo of Joe Russo and Anthony Russo tapped into the comic book tradition of associating Captain America with dissent. That line runs from Jack Kirby and Joe Simon creating Cap in 1940 to fight Nazis, at a time when America was officially neutral as World War II began in Europe, to the 1970s, when writer Steve Englehart imagined Cap taking down Richard Nixon. In the 1980s, writer J. M. DeMatteis had Cap supporting the vulnerable even when the US state did not, for a range of social issues, including domestic violence against women, Native American rights, and LGBTQ+ identity. This narrative formula, a rich tradition of Cap breaking with the US government and going his own way, was mined by the Russo brothers to make Cap relatable to contemporary audiences.

The role of dissent, and its close compatriot, rebellion, are often debated in US politics. Is it more American to support your government blindly, trusting that it is acting in good faith and the public's best interests? Or is it more American to dissent, to protest, to rebel? And what does it mean when the language of rebellion is adopted by a global media conglomerate to serve its own corporate interests? Captain America is coded as a patriot because he dissents, but Cap's dissent is also a way to make the entire Marvel apparatus palatable to audiences who might not be so keen to support a hero wrapped in the American flag. *The Winter Soldier* deliberately kept Cap's main conflict centered on a science fiction stand-in for widely unpopular American foreign policy, especially the use of citizen surveillance and drone strikes, which makes him a superhero not for one country, but for anyone skeptical of the US military-industrial complex itself. He is easier to embrace because he shares the same skepticism, and acts on it, a particular kind of anti-American foreign policy wish fulfillment.

A happy accident occurred in 2013—or rather, an unhappy accident. As production on *The Winter Soldier* proceeded that spring, NSA contractor Edward Snowden leaked to the public the existence of government-sanctioned domestic surveillance programs. Film production normally moves too slowly to plan for something like this, but it turned out that the bad guy in *The Winter Soldier* was a corrupt politician with a domestic surveillance program. The Snowden leak gave *The Winter Soldier* unintended relevancy, but *The Winter Soldier* had cast Cap as a rebel, and his rebellion as a symbol of patriotism, before that. It's all laid out in his costumes in the film. Throughout most of *The Winter Soldier,* Cap works in a version of the "stealth suit" from the comic books, in which his red, white, and blue uniform is blacked out. But when Cap decides to take on S.H.I.E.L.D. and its surveillance program, he breaks into the Smithsonian to don his old patriotic uniform instead. He is visually at his most demonstrably patriotic and American when he destroys an agency of his own government.

Thus, the un/happy accident was underway: just as segments of the public were turning against the US surveillance state that metastasized after September 11, 2001, Captain America donned his flag uniform and punched the American surveillance state in the face. The MCU has never quite followed through on the radicality of this moment; the antistate politics of *Winter Soldier* were quickly undone when S.H.I.E.L.D. remade itself on the television show *Agents of S.H.I.E.L.D.*, and no voice was given to Sam Wilson, who follows Cap into battle because he is so dazzled by Cap himself. Sam would be a natural mouthpiece for antisurveillance as both a veteran of the war in Afghanistan and a Black man whose community is targeted by surveillance and overpolicing. But Sam's involvement was framed merely as an almost starstruck desire to help Captain America. There was no acknowledgment that he might have his own motivations for wanting to see an apparatus of surveillance destroyed, or that if things go wrong, Sam will almost certainly face a different standard of jurisprudence than Cap. *Winter Soldier*'s accidental politics were even further undermined when Tony Stark invented E.D.I.T.H., an AI-infused satellite targeting system that Peter Parker, a teenager, used to almost murder a classmate in a fit of pique. Because Cap never rejects America itself, only what it has become, Captain America is a convenient vehicle to interrogate America's governmental surveillance state—but when Tony Stark: Private Citizen does basically the same thing as S.H.I.E.L.D./HYDRA, he gets a free pass.

Indeed, no Iron Man film, or any other entry into the MCU, is devoted to deconstructing the issue of military privatization (the Iron Man films explicitly endorse it), even though the United States government has, in reality, off-loaded much of the military apparatus to private contractors, often with disastrous consequences. *Captain America: Civil War* from 2016 might have provided the perfect opportunity to interrogate this aspect of the American military-industrial complex as the Avengers were in trouble in the first place due to another out-of-control Stark project that turned into a murder bot: Ultron. But Stark is never held accountable because he *means well*, something *Civil War* and the MCU writ large buy into. Stark believes in what economist Michael Munger calls *unicorn governance*, the assumption that political actors will always act in good faith, for the good of the people—and the MCU adopts the same position, attributing good intention to Stark and assuming, by default, that E.D.I.T.H. could never be as bad as state-sponsored surveillance, even though it operates in the exact same way. Another missed opportunity arose in 2021's *The Falcon and the Winter Soldier*, in which Sam Wilson contracted as the Falcon with the US

Air Force. Sure, Sam is an Air Force veteran, but he is also an Avenger, and at no point does anyone question if having Avengers explicitly working for the US military is a good idea. This seems like the exact circumstance Cap was trying to avoid in *Civil War*, but as with Tony Stark, the assumption is that individual action is always well-meaning, regardless of larger context or outcome.

But even if the rest of the MCU does not support Cap's cynical view on civilian surveillance, at least for this one film the Snowden coincidence gives *Winter Soldier* cultural cache not usually enjoyed by superhero films; that is, it took a stance often deemed too political for anodyne superhero entertainment. It also firmly entrenched the comic book tradition of Cap's dissent into the cinematic version of the character, and throughout the rest of his tenure in the Marvel Cinematic Universe, Cap would repeatedly buck authority and reject politicized oversight—most notably in *Civil War*, in which he takes an individualistic stance based on skepticism of political agendas. Cap is a film character designed to be globally appealing and to conform to heteronormative "family values" that will also play in any quadrant of audiences in US theaters; "skepticism of political agendas" is a uniquely appealing, broad stance. It will work for anyone, from those suspicious of actual foreign policy to the wildest conspiracy theorists. Cap is branded as a dissenter, but he's just mutable enough to retain mass appeal.

And this view of Cap as a professional rabble-rouser was widely embraced by fans; his popularity absolutely exploded following *Winter Soldier*. Fan works frequently depict Cap as a New Deal Democrat transported to the twenty-first century and imagine him at protests ranging from the Obama-era gatherings of Occupy Wall Street to the Trump-era women's marches and immigration rallies; there is an entire subgenre of fanfiction devoted to Cap taking down Fox News, which is especially interesting as the overall popularity of Marvel films means that everyone watches them, including the Fox News audience. Another half-serious, half-satirical memetic work from the 2020 election imagines Joe Biden as Captain America, heroically staring down Trump/Thanos, aided by a host of Democratic Avengers ranging from Barack Obama to Nancy Pelosi to Pete Buttigieg and Alexandria Ocasio-Cortez. Captain America, once considered boring and almost problematically retrograde, has been embraced as a symbol of dissent by a restless and ever more protest-prone sector of Americans, even as the character remained palatable to those who actually support citizen surveillance. And his dissatisfaction with his own government translates well to foreign audiences critical of US foreign policy, even as he doubles as a symbol of both American greatness and American decency.

It's quite a hat trick for a character that is, ultimately, a corporate puppet. The science fiction element in the story provides plausible deniability for those who simply do not want to see correlations to the US drone program, where giant flying gunships are meant to obliterate civilians from the sky. They're not drones! They're flying aircraft carriers and those don't exist, so this is all a slick fantasy! Even deliberate, pointed references to real-world issues like policing in Black communities are instantly undone by the sci-fi escape hatch. In *Winter Soldier*, Nick Fury, played by Samuel L. Jackson, has a snarky exchange with a couple of white DC metro police officers that is a direct call-out of police harassment of Black citizens. But the moment, crystal clear in its intent and execution, is betrayed when the "cops" are immediately revealed to be HYDRA, not police at all but members of a super-nazi death cult. If you don't want to see the sociopolitical criticism in *Winter Soldier*, you don't have to, because the sci-fi escape hatch is always there. But the fact that Cap's shield emblem became a frequent spot at real-world protests speaks to how many people *did* make that correlation and come to associate Cap with criticism of the military-industrial complex and, by extension, US foreign policy, even if the larger MCU did nothing to back up that stance.

Captain America can be described as a "traditional American." He's a tall, handsome white man, an officer in the US Army, a hero regarded for his courage and moral fortitude. But as Barbara Ehrenreich writes in her essay "Family Values," "dissent is also a traditional value," which when applied to the films solidifies the image of a patriotic poster boy, who, by virtue of being conventionally traditional in presentation, must therefore be dissident in action.[1] Cap's greatest, and arguably most traditional, expression of patriotism is his refusal to serve as a mouthpiece of government and embracing the role of a political dissident. In the watered-down ideological landscape of global corporate entertainment, Cap is only recognizable as a patriot *because* he dissents. But it's also important that he only does it the one time, as if once his bona fides are established, they need not ever be revisited; and that these ideals only apply to Steve Rogers, and not to Isaiah Bradley and Sam Wilson, the Black men who come in his wake.

The Falcon and the Winter Soldier presented Isaiah Bradley as a Korean War–era super soldier who undertakes the same kind of orders-defying mission Steve Rogers did in World War II to save fellow soldiers trapped behind enemy lines. But where Steve became a hero on the back of these events, Isaiah Bradley was instead imprisoned for thirty years and scrubbed from history. And Sam Wilson, who goes from Cap's friend and sidekick in *The Winter Soldier* to the new Captain America in *The Falcon and the Winter Soldier*, does not undertake any significant acts of dissent. His Cap-making moment came in the form of an impassioned speech delivered to politicians, entreating them to "do better," an especially toothless moment when contrasted with Steve's active antiauthoritarianism. *The Falcon and the Winter Soldier* touched on the shortcomings of Captain America's legacy and how it is entangled with the US government's own failings toward communities of color, particularly the Black community, but apparently has no room for Sam to be the kind of antiauthoritarian figurehead Steve became.

After *The Winter Soldier*, the MCU became increasingly more high-concept, and the parallels with the real world separated until they vanished altogether. As a defender of humanity at large, there was no need to interrogate Cap's place within the US military-industrial complex. Even *Civil War* is removed from that context, as the fight is framed as an interpersonal office conflict that comes with laser robots and flying magic people. *Civil War* likes Cap the rebel but does not engage with the political ramifications of the literal poster boy for the US Army rejecting government oversight, and later installments like *The Falcon and the Winter Soldier* refused to allow the new, Black Captain America the same kind of dissenting action. The double standard applied to the new and old Captain Americas highlights the double standard in how real Americans protest, that Black protestors are more likely to be overpoliced while protesting and more often arrested during protesting activities than white protestors. The stakes are literally higher for Sam Wilson to show open dissent, but instead of engaging and exploring what it would mean for Sam to be the kind of active dissident Steve was, *The Falcon and the Winter Soldier* tied everything up in a neat speech that ultimately reinforced support for the system.

Undermining the (accidental) tones of dissent in Captain America feels like betrayal of more than just Sam Wilson, though, because the idea of dissenting patriotism transcends purely American values. Democracy, after all, is much older than the American republic. No one has a corner on democratic ideals, and Cap's prodissent values translate easily into modern culture around the globe. Cap's shield iconography can be seen in Hong Kong's prodemocracy protests, proving the power of his message of patriotic dissent, and Cap's brand of patriotism echoes through the digital space. The image of Cap the rebel is enhanced by fan works that depict Cap as an idealized ally, a member of the dominant group who unfailingly shows up to support his marginalized peers. This fan depiction of Cap as someone who embraces all causes for equality and social justice became so prevalent that it burnished the cinematic character, who never actually delved into the social justice space, an impression further enhanced by Chris Evans's real-world political activism. The opportunity then exists for the image of Cap to evolve as the mantle is assumed by Sam Wilson and Cap becomes a member of a marginalized group whose fight for justice and equality is intimate and personal, not just conceptual. Through 2021, however, this potential has not been embraced.

The Captain America films may be political for superhero films, but they're still products of the Disney Corporation, a global megaconglomerate whose corporate interests will always supersede the political will of any creators, even favored sons like the Russo brothers. But for the audience consuming the film, an idealized mythos can be a way of expressing progressive ideas. Thanks to the Snowden coincidence, Cap provided that idealized mythos for those arguing against America's post-9/11 security policies. Cinema can be a unifying cultural language, and here is a pop-culture icon fronting an enormously popular film franchise, communicating to the biggest audience possible that it is okay to disagree with your government—patriotism is *not* blind faith in unicorn governance—and it is okay to actively fight back against those things to which you object. At least, it's okay to fight back if you're white. The double standard at play in *The Falcon and the Winter Soldier* makes it clear that dissent is not an option for a Black Captain America, even though in 2021 it would be fitting for Sam Wilson to be a figurehead for social change. But the shift from depicting Cap as a rebel to Cap as a stern lecturer seems like a corporate clampdown on a character massively co-opted by fans.

In co-opting Cap as a symbol of resistance, fans took ownership over what Cap disapproved of, increasing his rebellious quotient with each transformative work. The films were content to mostly aim Cap at state overreach and alien invaders, but fans dropped him into pride parades—even as the films flatly refused to give into the fan desire to see Cap and Bucky Barnes settle down in romantic bliss—and racial justice rallies, aligning him with far more progressive values than the films ever demonstrated (though one wonders how long that implied progressivism lasts if Sam Wilson is never allowed to be as demonstrative as Captain America as Steve Rogers was). The recurrence of Cap's iconography at protests indicates that the film version of Cap worked well in transmitting disapproval for authoritarianism and fascism in all its forms, even as that image is shadowed by Disney's corporate control.

And it all starts with those six words, "This isn't freedom. This is fear." With those words, Cap answered a question that had been growing in the American consciousness over the last decade: Were the sacrifices of our civil liberties worth it? Was an illusion of safety worth the loss of personal privacy? Cap, with his mien of disapproval, said no. (That's another popular subgenre in fanfiction: Cap, appalled at the lack of privacy in the modern world.) His disapproval turned to violent dissent, and in the process he became a symbol in a wave of pro-protest sentiment in American pop culture. The idealized mythos at play, Cap is specifically American in symbology, but his early distrust of twenty-first-century American policy made him appealing to those not interested in more American hegemony.

The Winter Soldier gave Cap a moral authority that spoke to twenty-first century concerns, particularly in areas where Americans betrayed their ideals for political expedience. Captain America, originally a symbol of American military might and moral uprightness, used all the impetus granted to him as a symbol to object to the state's overreach. He is the most rebellious Avenger, constantly dissenting—sometimes violently—to injustice, often perpetrated by his own government—though notably, this penchant for rebellion is not extended to other, nonwhite characters who assume the mantle of Captain America. In the preceding decade, patriotism was used to bludgeon the American public against questioning its leaders. To publicly dissent was to *not* "support the troops" (see also the Chicks' blacklisting from country music following public criticism of George W. Bush's war policies). Then, as public sentiment soured on that particular brand of patriotism, here came a hell-raising Captain America to reinvigorate the popular image of the patriotic dissenter. Ehrenreich ended her essay with a powerful line: "Dissent, rebellion, and all-around hell-raising remain the true duty of patriots." Captain America codified that belief into popular culture for a new generation.

Notes

1. Ehrenreich, "Family Values," 11.

Bibliography

Ehrenreich, Barbara. "Family Values." In *The Worst Years of Our Lives: Irreverent Notes from a Decade of Greed*, 3–14. New York: Pantheon Books, 1990.

Russo, Anthony, and Joe Russo, directors. *Captain America: Civil War*. Marvel Studios, 2016.

Russo, Anthony, and Joe Russo, directors. *Captain America: The Winter Soldier*. Marvel Studios, 2014.

36 Princess Nokia, "Brujas" (2016) / Santería's Decolonial Futurisms

Taryne Jade Taylor

Princess Nokia's "Brujas," from her debut album *1992*, begins with an invocation of Yemaya. Although the song then transitions from this invocation to a more traditional hip-hop track, the invocation to Yemaya situates the song as a powerful invocation of decolonizing radical self-care. "Brujas" is a prayer to and for women of color, urging us to decolonize our minds, spirits, and bodies by invoking the power of Santería. By centering Santería as a tool of decolonization, Nokia imagines a path to a decolonial, Latinx future. Nokia's centering of Santería as a tool of decolonization is Latinx Futurist. The first image we see in the video is sacred: we see an Afro-Latina santera standing in a body of water, dressed in light blue, white, and silver—colors associated with the Orisha Yemaya. As the forty-six-second invocation begins, the video pans to show four young Afro-Latinas standing in the water facing her, dressed in the traditional white of Santería acolytes. Yemaya is one of the main Orishas in Santería—a mother goddess figure associated with creation, the ocean, the protection of women, healing, and self-love.

The invocation to Yemaya is sung in Lukumi, a dialect of Yoruba, and makes up the first forty-six seconds of the short song. The invocation begins: "Kai Kai Kai—Yemaya Olodo/Kai Kai Kai, hace su olodo."[1] These lines are an exclamation, a meditation, in which the Orisha Yemaya is being invoked to touch the soul and bless the santera and her acolytes (and possibly enter into the santera, depending on tradition). Princess Nokia's decision to decenter her own work by prefacing it with the invocation is a decolonial act that the song asks the audience to mirror. As we watch/listen, we are invoking Yemaya ourselves and hear Princess Nokia as a messenger empowered by Yemaya. Thus, Nokia engages in speculative worldbuilding that imagines a future where Santería—a cosmology denigrated both within and without Latinx communities—provides a path to a decolonial future.

The power and importance of the invocation is made clear visually and musically; just after the invocation, the camera pans out to show to the santera facing the acolytes (and viewers) with her arms open wide, the beat dropping just as we see the acolytes facing the her with arms outstretched to the heavens. Here the song proper begins with a deep voice, perhaps representing the santera or Yemaya herself, repeating, "I'm your supreme / I'm your supreme."

Nokia's use of Santería is in and of itself a radical act. Santería is based on West African religious traditions, like its sister religions Vodou and Candomblé. The worship of the Orishas on which Santería is based was brought to the Americas and the Caribbean as early as the sixteenth century during the early slave trade of the Yoruba peoples. As Santería was illegal in many parts of the Americas, practitioners were forced to syncretize their Orishas with the Roman Catholic Church to survive. Yemaya herself was and still is often syncretized as Mother Mary. Princess Nokia represents a new tradition of Santería practitioners. While being proud of Santería's survivance through syncretism, "Brujas" reclaims Santería's West African roots. Through the song, Princess Nokia asserts that the previous shapeshifting necessitated by colonization is no longer required and that the reclaiming of precolonized identities and ways of being is possible.

Yet Princess Nokia does not aim for rejecting the hybridization of Santería and Latina identities created by colonization, but rather a wholehearted, aggressive embrace of her identity. This is also precisely what the song is urging women of color to do—aggressively embrace their identities and flaunt them in the face of disapproval by the oppressor. The Lukumi/Yoruba of the invocation is mixed with Spanish, so the song and video for "Brujas" has multiple reference points to the mixed identity created by colonization, with the song itself mostly English mixed with Spanglish. Here Nokia is showing that she has been colonized, but retains her power by celebrating her hybridity. One way Nokia celebrates her hybrid identity is through the song's continued play on words with witches and bitches. In the first chorus she asserts: "We is them ghetto witches / Speaking in tongue bitches." Through the play on witches and bitches, Nokia asserts her identity as an outsider/insider. As a "ghetto" bitch, she plays on standard hiphop tropes, while as a Lukumi/Yoruba speaking practitioner of Santería, she dismantles them. In addition, Princess Nokia incorporates US popular culture as seamlessly as she calls on her African and Indigenous ancestors. This provides a map to listeners, urging us to accept all facets of ourselves, even those connected to the trauma of colonization and the rape of Black and Indigenous women.

In her first verse, Nokia celebrates stereotypes often negatively associated with women of color in the US: "Long weaves, long nails / Corn rows, pig tails / Baby fathers still in jail," place her in an othered status, yet that othered status coexists with Westernized stereotypes of witches: "Good witches I fuck with / Hopped off my broomstick / Witchcraft, bitch craft." This image of a broom-riding witch is not consistent with cultural images of Santería's brujas, yet it is juxtaposed with references to Santería in the lyrics and visuals. Through this juxtaposition, Princess Nokia is affirming her diasporic status with pride, just as she does by juxtaposing visuals that strongly evoke traditional brujería with visuals that evoke an Afro-Latinx retelling of the 1996 classic teen witch film *The Craft*.

Princess Nokia evokes *The Craft* to reappropriate the traditions it commodifies and show that she belongs in the United States. The film itself begins as a seemingly feminist presentation of witchcraft for women's empowerment, but quickly vilifies it by playing on misogynistic tropes of women tied to heteronormativity (and the Global North's vilification of non-Judeo-Christian traditions), including an indictment of sexuality, anger, and power. In Princess Nokia's revision, sexuality, anger, and power are tools that can be wielded responsibly for radical self-care. We see the four acolytes defiantly leaning against a brick building and later on the stairs of that building in outfits that evoke the school uniforms of *The Craft*. The women of "Brujas," however, are all of color and their powers are not sexualized for the male gaze. Indeed, in the brick schoolhouse scenes, Princess Nokia displays gestures typically associated with male hip-hop to highlight her queerness and nonconformity to binary gender roles—by aggressively grabbing at her genitals, wiping her nose, and sitting with her legs spread wide. The brujas of Princess Nokia's vision are proudly aggressive and powerful. They serve as examples to the viewers of full self-acceptance and radical repurposing of not only stereotypes, but dominant culture, to enable women of color to thrive.

In these scenes, the women appear powerful and defiant; they have decolonized themselves, and they refuse to let the world judge or confine them to conformity. As they lean against the wall, Princess Nokia instructs women of color everywhere of the importance of rejecting internal colonization and negative energy, repeating, "Don't you fuck with my energy" eight times while she and the other acolytes raise their middle fingers.

Princess Nokia also shows listeners/viewers the path to achieve their own decolonization. First, the process is not solitary, as Nokia suggests through the presence of the santera and her fellow brujas. She references "Casting spells with my cousins / I'm the head of this coven," suggesting the importance of community and collective rebellion. Further, she also demonstrates this community in the visuals during both the invocation scene and scenes in the forest. We see Princess Nokia and her coven in the forest practicing rituals and community. In one scene, we see her and her coven dancing with an extended community of women, including the now unveiled santera as well as other young women and girls of color not previously shown. In another scene, we see the young women playing games and braiding hair. In still another, we see the santera and acolytes dressed once again in ritual clothes; though the acolytes remain dressed in white, this time the santera is dressed in yellow to evoke the orisha Oshún. The santera is seated in a chair in the middle of a forest path, flanked by the acolytes who walk down the paths as if in an aisle with sunflowers and then presents them as offerings to the orisha. This scene, interspersed with the others, shows the sacred nature of all community building, especially those revolving around self-care for women of color. Together, these women build their inner and collective power through ritual, dance, and play.

Despite the serious nature the ritual displays and defiance of stereotypes displayed in the song, the video is also intentionally playful. Nokia presents playing and playfulness as important elements of self-care. Indeed, it is not impossible to imagine white and non-Latinx audiences misreading this song as solely playful due to the high levels of play. For example, her playfulness with *witch* and *bitch* is significant in the context of both Santería and misogyny. Many practitioners of Santería do not wish to be associated with brujería and brujas, a label typically used to vilify Latin American women practicing Indigenous sciences and religions. Nokia reclaims the words *bruja*, *witch*, and *bitch* as a way of rejecting colonial values and decolonizing Santería. Similarly, by interspersing references of Santería with references of Western stereotypes of the witch, as she does through reference to *The Craft*, she boldly reclaims the legitimacy of brujería as a legitimate practice, rejecting colonial and neocolonial respectability politics.

The final verse of "Brujas" exemplifies Nokia's vision of decolonial, radical self-care:

> I'm a shapeshifting bitch, you don't know who you loving
> Better light you a candle
> I heard the nighttime was black
> And if you don't watch your step the greatest bitch will be back
> I cast a circle in white and I can vanquish your spite
> And if you hex me with hate then I'ma conjure the light
> Your evil ways put no fight
> I ain't no queen of the night
> I'm a bruja, I'm a bruja, and I'ma dress in all white

In these lines, Nokia once again emphasizes that anger and power are both not only acceptable, but tools of first survivance and then decolonization. Princess Nokia fiercely directs her detractors "to light you a candle," which is not only an indictment of Catholicism's treatment of Santería, but also the cowardice of the colonizer (as represented by her detractors). She, as a fully self-realized woman of color backed by her community, can "vanquish" the "evil" spite and hate of colonization, represented by hate and racism, by conjuring the light. Interestingly here, she also disrupts the binary of white and black/light and darkness with both the "dark" and "light" presented as positive forces; the dark is only to be feared by the colonizer, and the bruja is at home with both light and dark. As she disrupts these dichotomies, she recognizes their previous power and, in recognizing them, eschews them: she is not "the queen of the night," in the negative stereotypical sense, but brujería and darkness have power. This witch dresses in the sacred white of her Santería-practicing ancestors and the darkness of her skin is also presented as sacred.

Through these lyrics, Princess Nokia directs women of color to reject binaries and the thinking of the colonizers. She also calls on us not to code switch to appease white audiences. She demonstrates and celebrates the complexity of her identity as a member of the Afro-Indigenous-Latinx diaspora, referencing her hybridity in the second verse:

> I'm that Black a-Rican bruja straight out from the Yoruba
> And my people come from Africa diaspora, Cuba

And you mix that Arawak, that original people
I'm that Black Native American, I vanquish all evil
I'm that Black a-Rican bruja straight out from the Yoruba
And my ancestors Nigerian, my grandmas was brujas
And I come from an island and it's called Puerto Rico

In this verse Nokia recognizes the complexity of navigating her Latinx identity from a Global North perspective so intent on simple codification. She is Black and Indigenous—she is a Black a-Rican mix of Yoruba and Arawak. Her ancestry is Nigerian, Cuban, Arawak, and Puerto Rican—and those from her maternal lines were brujas. Santería serves as the unifying force—the thread that connects her to her ancestors. She does not reject a portion of her heritage as is so often the case not only in the anti-Black and anti-Indigenous racism of the Latinx diaspora in the United States, but also in Latin America and the Caribbean, thus presenting a futurist reimagining of Latinidades. For Princess Nokia, Santería is a way of celebrating her heritage: by claiming her bruja status, she is legitimizing and celebrating her mixed identity and the subjugated and oppressed histories and practices of her ancestors. Santería here is a tool for radical self-love and decolonization, one that enables young women of color to accept themselves and come into their power even when living in a society that does not value their lives. Through her Latinx Futurist imagining, Nokia shows us how to flourish in our uneven present and imagine a liberatory future.

Note

1. Thank you to Elizabeth Olaoye for helping me with the Yoruba. All translation mistakes are my own.

Bibliography

Princess Nokia. "Brujas—Princess Nokia." YouTube video, November 7, 2016. https://www.youtube.com/watch?v=iUcAPCxrSQs.

37 Lehua Parker, *One Truth, No Lie* (2016) / Indigenous Youth Activism through Mo'olelo and YA Literature

Caryn Lesuma

Throughout October and November of 2019, over two hundred people in my home region of Ko'olauloa on O'ahu, Hawai'i, were arrested by police in an attempt to block the installment of a second wind farm in the rural town of Kahuku (pop. 2,164). The project, brought to Hawai'i by the Fortune 500 AES Corporation and backed by both Honolulu City and County and the State of Hawai'i, installed eight 568-foot-tall industrial wind turbines less than one-third of a mile from schools, homes, farms, and the region's only hospital. While some supporters of the project have accused Kahuku residents of NIMBYism, the primary concerns cited by residents are less about aesthetics and more about the adverse health and environmental effects caused by immediate proximity to industrial infrasound and shadow flicker. In a rural community where the tallest buildings are three stories high at Kahuku High School, the fifty-three-story turbines loom dystopian and ominous, less an environmental triumph than symbols of corporate callousness and a reminder that when it comes to green initiatives, governments are frequently willing to sacrifice the well-being of humans and wildlife at the lower end of the socioeconomic spectrum "for the greater good."

The State of Hawai'i's energy policy initiatives include a laudable goal to eliminate the state's reliance on fossil fuels by becoming 100 percent reliant on renewable energy by 2045. This is essential on islands estimated by University of Hawai'i researchers to lose dozens of feet of shoreline to rising sea levels over the coming years.[1] Unfortunately, a lack of implementation guidelines surrounding the energy initiative means that in practice, there are very few protections in place for residents, wildlife, or land: in this case, a community comprising 0.3 percent of the island's population is being forced to shoulder 40 percent of the burden of wind energy.[2] Our predominantly Pacific Islander, working-class community is also home to a bird sanctuary and is a known habitat for the ʻōpeʻapeʻa (Hawaiian hoary bat), Hawai'i's only native land mammal and an endangered species. Despite this, AES has been granted legal permits allowing the turbines to kill certain numbers of these protected and endangered birds and bats each year, acts that would earn a private citizen hefty fines and jail time. Ironically, the state's lofty environmental goals—and equally ironic reliance on large, capitalist corporations to meet them—have resulted in additional environmental destruction. This is the definition of ecological injustice.

The situation here in Kahuku is, of course, multifaceted and complex, and I don't have the space here to address the nuances. Instead, my approach to thinking about this project will center on its relationship to Indigenous Futurisms, and in particular the implications of our community's activism for future generations of Koʻolauloa residents. As a scholar of youth culture and literature in the Pacific, I am struck by how this movement and larger ones at Mauna Kea against the Thirty Meter Telescope have engaged our Indigenous youth, who have powerfully expressed their visions for the future through song, chant, dance, and art. While "small" in numbers, resources, and visibility, the Kū Kiaʻi Kahuku movement—literally "stand to protect Kahuku," a name based on the Mauna Kea rallying cry, "Kū Kiaʻi Mauna," or stand to protect the mountain—is part of a larger pattern of global Indigenous resistance to corporate land grabs and unsustainable overdevelopment. As we relearn the history, language, and culture that has been suppressed for so long by colonial forces, Indigenous peoples are collectively choosing to act in order to protect our remaining resources and imagine how we might create more vibrant futures for our children. In many ways, I see the middle grade and YA literature being published for Indigenous Oceanic youth during this critical time as reflecting their positionality as contemporary Indigenous individuals while also modeling paths for resurgent community activism in the face of continued colonization.

A good example of one of these texts is Kanaka Maoli (Native Hawaiian) author Lehua Parker's 2016 YA novel *One Truth, No Lie*, the third and final book of the Niuhi Shark Saga. The series' protagonist, Zader Kaonakai

Westin, learns in books one and two of the series—*One Boy, No Water* and *One Shark, No Swim*—that the "water allergy" that has stigmatized him throughout his childhood is actually the manifestation of his ability to shapeshift into a feared niuhi, or human-eating shark. Part of this heritage also means that Zader is the grandson of Kanaloa, a major akua (deity) with dominion over the sea. It's important to note here that when Parker references beings like niuhi and Kanaloa, she is drawing on historical, spiritual, and Indigenous scientific knowledges that are fundamental elements of Kanaka Maoli belief systems. This ancestral knowledge is often conveyed through moʻolelo, a storytelling form that encompasses history, story, myth, legend, and tradition.[3] In *One Truth*, Zader learns to see his genealogical heritage as an opportunity rather than a liability, educating himself and developing his natural artistic gifts to launch a grassroots, guerilla art campaign that forces humans to confront the damage consumer capitalism is wreaking on the world's oceans. Zader's journey from timid, bullied child to empowered teen kiaʻi (protector) and activist mirrors what our small community has been doing to imagine a just future for our children and animal relatives: drawing on genealogical connections and Indigenous ways of knowing, being in good relation with people and the land/ocean, and speaking truth through art activism. Parker's innovative blend of moʻolelo and YA challenges youth to draw power from the wisdom of their Indigenous heritage in order to create the future that they envision. While my purpose is not to suggest that all Indigenous youth activism can or should be the same, looking at a few parallels between *One Truth, No Water* and Kahuku's fight against AES and city and state government demonstrates how literary imaginings for youth can complement real-life actions for just futures.

Embracing Identity

The first issue that needs to be addressed when it comes to Indigenous Hawaiian and Pacific Islander youth is that of identity and low self-esteem caused by centuries of colonization and stereotyping. In *One Truth*, Zader is unable to break free of self-loathing caused by the lifelong stigma of his "allergy" until he learns the truth of his ancestry and accepts his identity as a niuhi. He is initially resistant, believing that his identity as a human-male niuhi automatically makes him a human-eating "monster" like his infamous historical cousin, Nanaʻue, a human-male niuhi well-known in ancestral mo'olelo for his insatiable appetite for human flesh.[4] After taking the time to explore his newfound shapeshifting ability, however, he realizes that he can choose whether or not to be a human-eater—and that he actually has much better uses for his shark form. In reality, his identity as both Kānaka Maoli and niuhi gives him a new way of seeing and experiencing the ocean, which empowers him to share those perspectives with humans and change destructive behaviors like dynamite fishing, pollution, and other dangers.

With a large population of Native Hawaiian, Pacific Islander, and other ethnic minority youth, Kahuku High School is known as "The Pride of the North Shore" to residents, but is often stereotyped by the rest of the state as athlete-rich and academics-poor. In Hawai'i and other states with large populations of Native Hawaiian and Pacific Islanders, these youth are frequently stereotyped as violent troublemakers at worst and dumb jocks at best. Like Zader, they sometimes internalize these stigmas: I can't tell you how many times I've heard youth and even parents in the community—including my own relatives—say that their only shot at a higher education is through sports rather than academic scholarships, or that college is not even an option. While it is true that college is not for everyone, I am convinced that many who would flourish in a university setting often do not apply due to these pervasive stereotypes.

However, despite these stigmas, youth in our region have a strong sense of identity and community pride, partly borne out of defiance (a common slogan in the community is that we are the "enemy of the state"), but mostly developed from a strong community unity where everyone knows everyone and shares in triumphs and tragedies. The strength of that shared community identity prompted a group of over one hundred students to organize their own event independent from Kū Kia'i Kahuku, the main activist group. The youth gathered to wave signs and march to Kū Kia'i Kahuku's base camp at the entrance to the construction to present activist leaders with a symbolic lei woven with each of their names in its fibers. According to sixteen-year-old organizer Tealani Wasson, "Our main purpose was to visualize that the Kahuku students do have a purpose, have a voice and want it to be heard."[5] Without prompting from adult activists in the community, these youth used their strong collective identity to garner additional media attention to help support the cause.

Indigenous Adult Role Models

Another important element needed for youth empowerment reflected in the Niuhi Shark Saga is its consistent portrayal of responsible, reliable adult figures for its young protagonists. This is a significant break with mainstream American YA fiction, which generally requires the absence of responsible adults in order to facilitate protagonists' growth. Rather than leave Zader to figure out his own path, Parker surrounds him with strong, wise mentors throughout his journey. In books one and two, it's kupuna (elder) Uncle Kahana, who teaches Zader self-defense and introduces him to Hawaiian ways of knowing and understanding. In *One Truth*, it's Aunty Ake (short for Akeakamai, "a lover of wisdom; philosopher; scientist"), a mentor who teaches him to see truth as both a human and niuhi. He is also given personal instruction from a range of master artists across the globe, who teach him to develop his art from a variety of perspectives. This is a clear nod to Indigenous ways of learning, which emphasize reliance on the wisdom of elders learned through careful listening and observation.

The adults leading Kū Kia'i Kahuku likewise provided guidance and resources for youth throughout the process. While adult protectors prohibited children and youth from attending demonstrations where arrests were made, kia'i of all ages were consistently present during sign waving, visits to the state capitol and city hall, and at the base camp throughout the two months of physical actions. These actions required a great deal of coordination and sacrifice for a variety of reasons. First, rural Kahuku is located at the opposite end of the island from Honolulu, the state's decision-making center of political and economic power. As a result, kia'i needed to maintain a constant physical presence at the base camp (located at the entrance of the wind farm construction site in Kahuku town) while also sending groups to hearings, protest marches, and other events in Honolulu, over an hour's drive away. As a predominantly blue-collar community with a large percentage of young families, many community members had to make a choice between working to pay bills in a state with one of the nation's highest living costs and standing up to state and corporate interests that threatened their children's health and well-being. In addition to addressing these logistical concerns, Kū Kia'i Kahuku also chose to adopt the Native Hawaiian methodologies of Pu'uhonua O Pu'uhuluhulu at Mauna Kea,[6] including the organization of their own version of a university that brought in community members to teach activists—including large numbers of children and youth—about the meaning of Kapu Aloha, a Hawaiian embodiment of nonviolent action; mo'olelo, mele (songs), and oli (chants) about the local region of Ko'olauloa and other important sites in the islands; traditional practices like how to pound poi from kalo (taro root); and other Indigenous-based strategies of resistance and worldbuilding.

Community Organizing through Art Activism

The actions taken by Kū Kia'i Kahuku mirror Zader's path to enlightenment. Once he is comfortable with his true identity and learns all he can from his cultural and artistic mentors, he chooses to leverage his newfound understanding to "bridge the human and Niuhi world."[7] Zader's actions reflect Potawatomi scholar and activist Kyle Whyte's assertion that "[Indigenous] conservation and restoration projects . . . are about what relationships between humans and certain plants and animals we should focus on in response to the challenges we face."[8] As a result, Zader is able to advocate for changes that protect his nonhuman oceanic relatives because he is able to understand ecological destruction from both human and shark perspectives.

For Zader, bringing these relationships into focus means "showing" them through art. Throughout the second half of the book, he travels the world finding places where environmental injustices are harming the ocean habitats or wildlife. He then creates large art installations highlighting the injustices (murals, sculptures, etc.) and installs them overnight in places that are conspicuous and inconvenient for governments and corporations. In Kahuku, the focus has been on protecting the endangered 'ōpe'ape'a, which adult activists have done via lawsuits.[9] Children, however, have taken a page out of Zader's book and portrayed their activism in defense of the 'ōpe'ape'a through art, depicting their small, furry relatives being killed by the massive turbine blades. The images have been shared widely on social media and with the mayor's office, cutting through euphemistic legal terms like bat "takes" and revealing their true meaning: "kills."

The novel does have one shortcoming when it comes to modeling grassroots activism, however. Parker sidesteps issues of funding by creating an independently wealthy Uncle Kahana and later bestows Zader with a limitless credit card from his grandfather Kanaloa, which provides him with high-quality supplies, easy travel, and the ability to pay or bribe those who require incentive to cooperate. In reality, funding is scarce for small, hastily organized, and inexperienced groups like Kū Kia'i Kahuku, who needed to find sources of funding for bail and legal fees, portable toilets at base camp, food for activists, and other important needs. Without community donations and aid from the Hawaii Community Bail Fund, a crowdfunded project that supports activists and criminal justice reform throughout the state, most community members who were arrested would not have been able to afford to post bail.[10]

Prior to AES coming to town, the biggest activism in our community was our legendary support for the Kahuku High football team. But in a matter of weeks and months, people with no organizing or activist experience came together under an umbrella of Indigenous practices to create a new vision for what we imagine our community to be. Despite these incredible efforts, the fight is not over. Whether it happens soon or further down the road, we will continue to oppose the project and seek the turbines' removal with the knowledge that the future of our community is in good hands. The popularity and relevance of Parker's work and others like it throughout the broader Pacific—such as Lani Wendt Young's Telesā Series—underscore a pressing need for more Oceanic YA for Indigenous youth and allies. In a world marked by an increasing need for creative opposition to corporate overreach and environmental injustice, texts like these can help to reinforce the decisions that our youth are choosing to make as they work to build our collective futures.

Notes

1. Tavares, Fletcher, and Anderson, "Risk of Shoreline Hardening."
2. Horgan, "Oahu Residents Hold Peaceful Protest."
3. Pukui and Elbert, *Hawaiian Dictionary*, 254.
4. Nakuina, "Shark-Man."
5. Burgos, "Kahuku Students Join Protest."
6. See Bryan Kamaoli Kuwada's chapter, chapter 39, in this collection.
7. Parker, *One Truth, No Lie*, 251.

8. Whyte, "Our Ancestors' Dystopia Now," 207.

9. Pennybacker, "Wind Turbine Threats to Rare Bats Debated."

10. Hawaii Community Bail Fund, "About."

Bibliography

Burgos, Annalisa. "Kahuku Students Join Protest against Controversial Wind Farm Project." KITV Island News, October 27, 2019. https://www.wind-watch.org/news/2019/10/28/kahuku-students-join-protest-against-controversial-wind-farm-project/.

Hawaii Community Bail Fund. "About." Hawaii Community Bail Fund. Accessed February 4, 2022. https://hawaiicommunitybailfund.org/about/.

Horgan, T. J. "Oahu Residents Hold Peaceful Protest against Wind Turbine Project." *KITV Island News*, October 13, 2019. https://www.wind-watch.org/news/2019/10/14/oahu-residents-hold-peaceful-protest-against-wind-turbine-project/.

Nakuina, Emma. "The Shark-Man, Nanaue." In *Hawaiian Folk Tales*, edited by Thomas G. Thrum, 255–268. Honolulu: A. C. McClurg, 1907.

Parker, Lehua. *One Boy, No Water*. 2nd ed. Heber City, UT: Makena Press, 2016.

Parker, Lehua. *One Shark, No Swim*. 2nd ed. Heber City, UT: Makena Press, 2016.

Parker, Lehua. *One Truth, No Lie*. Heber City, UT: Makena Press, 2016.

Pennybacker, Mindy. "Wind Turbine Threats to Rare Bats Debated." *Honolulu Star-Advertiser*, October 19, 2019. https://www.staradvertiser.com/2019/10/19/hawaii-news/wind-turbine-threats-to-rare-bats-are-debated/.

Pukui, Mary Kawena, and Samuel H. Elbert. *Hawaiian Dictionary*. Honolulu: University of Hawai'i Press, 1986.

Tavares, Kammie-Dominique, Charles H. Fletcher, and Tiffany R. Anderson. "Risk of Shoreline Hardening and Associated Beach Loss Peaks before Mid-Century: O'ahu, Hawai'i." *Scientific Reports* 10, no. 13633 (August 2020). https://doi.org/10.1038/s41598-020-70577-y.

Whyte, Kyle Powys. "Our Ancestors' Dystopia Now: Indigenous Conservation and the Anthropocene." In *The Routledge Companion to the Environmental Humanities*, edited by Ursula K. Heise, Jon Christensen, and Michelle Niemann, 206–215. New York: Routledge, 2017.

38 Kim Stanley Robinson, *New York 2140* (2017) / Logistic Utopia

Fabio Fernandes

1. Kim Stanley Robinson (KSR): He who has published nineteen novels and numerous short stories, with work translated into twenty-four languages; who won numerous awards, including the Hugo for Best Novel, Nebula for Best Novel, and World Fantasy Award; who remains impossible to label, even from inside the genre, as he has been called many names since his debut in the late 1970s: hard SF writer, climate-obsessed sci-fi genius, even anticyberpunk author. (As he declared in a 2018 interview for *WIRED*: "Cyberpunk was an aberration. . . . They were somewhat antifeminist, with their hard noir gals. It was defeatist. Or nonpolitical. Or collaborationist—like noir. So I hated them, and they hated me."[1])

2. But perhaps KSR is best known as a *humanist*. The other SF writer to be embraced so broadly by cultural critics and scholars alike was Ursula K. Le Guin, whom KSR felt was his "mother" in SF writing. Particularly through her Hainish Cycle, Le Guin focused on people and ecosystems. With an anthropologist's eye, she wrote about socioeconomic and political relations. Though not an anthropologist, Robinson the PhD in English literature takes a sociopolitical approach. Similar to Le Guin, but with greater emphases on the economic dimension. His fiction is all about material problem-solving in near-future scenarios.

3. This is nothing new in SF, where Hugo Gernsback debuted *Ralph 124C 41+*, and, before that, the old Edisonades featured ace scientists who solved everything with new inventions. But the super science in those narratives seems more science fantasy than science fiction because the solutions are usually given by "handwavium." In KSR's novels, though, scientists (still very much heroes) work alongside other specialists within an organic

knowledge-producing structure in which they generate a holistic approach to the story's problems.

4. To wit: in *New York 2140* (2017), a protagonist says: "Have you ever noticed that our building is a kind of actor network that can do things? We got the cloud star, the lawyer, the building expert, the building itself, the police detective, the money man."[2] Such association of elements in a group without a center, a la Bruno Latour's actor-network theory, underpins the dynamics of KSR's fictional problem-solving scenarios. I call this a *logistic utopia*.

5. A logistic utopia is one whose horizon can be rather easily seen by those who had started building it, in contrast with earlier utopias—for instance, compared to the Russian Revolution, its horizon flung far in the future, that asked people to make sacrifices for the common good without necessarily living to see them bear fruit.[3] A democratic socialist rather than a Marxist,[4] KSR believes in an actor-network composed of democratically elected representatives, scientists, and pretty much everybody who can help with infrastructure, to address climate change by means of a "stepwise reform."[5]

6. Stepwise reformism reflects KSR's values: "The social democracies of north Europe and the name 'social democrat' also resonate (with me) . . . although these political parties, when in power in Europe, have had to make alliances and compromises with capitalism that make them far from satisfactory. But from the viewpoint of the United States, they look like at least a step along the path to more justice."[6]

7. Earlier, KSR had described this reform in the Science in the Capital trilogy (now rechristened as *Green Earth* in one volume), set in the present (early 2000s), but it's in *New York 2140* that we can see the full force of his imagination in action.

8. Breakthrough novel: *New York 2140* is what I regard as KSR's watershed moment—the author stops worrying about changing Earth for the better. He seems to grasp that this is not possible, that we have reached a point of no return caused by human interference in the global ecosystem.

9. The story: New York City in the twenty-second century has almost half of its surface covered by water due to the polar ice caps melting. A fifty-foot rise in the sea level turns Manhattan and other parts of the city into what its inhabitants call—not without irony—Super-Venice.

10. Like that watery Italian city, NYC is now the locus of *subsidence*—the gradual lowering of its ground, which creates the seasonal *Acqua alta*, occasionally covering its surface at high tide.

11. And just like Venice, New York City has learned to deal with it. The city is fully functional; its inhabitants endeavor to keep it this way, step by step, one day at a time.

12. Hence the term *logistic utopia*.

13. The novel opens with Vlade Marovich, super of the MetLife building, where most of the action takes place. He depicts the work needed to guarantee that NYC stays afloat as constant—both literally and metaphorically.

14. Literally: the building must be constantly treated with new materials to avoid crumbling from sea erosion.

15. Metaphorically: these things consume money. (We still need money and markets in this future.)

16. Andrew Russell and Lee Vinsel champion a similar perspective: "Maintenance and repair, the building of infrastructures, the mundane labour that goes into sustaining functioning and efficient infrastructures, simply has more impact on people's daily lives than the vast majority of technological innovations."[7]

17. After two pulses drowned New York City, capital retreated inland (namely, to Denver, CO). But the ones who couldn't get out, the homeless and undocumented, did what they could to rebuild the city, both literally and metaphorically.

18. The city now has *hotellos*, tents to accommodate guests, because physical habitation in NYC is now granted for life and only available through inheritance. For instance, protagonist Gen Octaviadottir, a Black female police detective (KSR's homage to Octavia E. Butler), inherits her apartment from her deceased mother.

19. The new NYC has been reconstructed socially as most of the city's inhabitants now live in communes. For example, the MetLife Tower hosts a huge co-op with gardens on its rooftop.

20. One frequent setting: MetLife's community cafeteria. During lunches and dinners, every sort of thing is discussed, from the disappearance of two community residents to economics and possible actions against encroaching gentrification. KSR had done this in the Mars trilogy, and also in *2312*: a huge part of the interactions between characters happen during communal meals.

21. Now, years after this reconstruction, the rich, helped by people who trade in futures (like Franklin Garr), want to come back and reclaim NYC.

22. So the concept of justice, against this new invasion of gentrifiers, is fairly specific: "There's something like two hundred major coastal cities, all just as drowned as New York. Like a billion people. And we're all wet, we're all in the precariat. . . . We all want justice and revenge," says one character.[8]

23. The book's inciting incident: the disappearance of Mutt and Jeff, two data analysts who go rogue after hacking a bank database to take revenge against the system by destroying it from the inside. (Something a bit similar to *Fight Club*, but with a more methodical strategy.)

24. What distinguishes *New York 2140* from your average dystopia in which the solo hacker takes down the evil corporation: *logistics*. Mutt and Jeff try to exact revenge against the system on their own, before the novel begins, but cannot. (They get kidnapped and held hostage in an underwater container, until rescued by accident.) They must end up joining forces with their salvage team rescuers to get justice.

25. KSR's novels emphasize the work of the collective whenever possible: his worlds are not the worlds of solo heroes but of the collectivity. A good logistic effort requires teamwork, after all.

26. KSR's science fiction may not be fiction in three hundred years, if we are to believe Scott Beauchamp, writing for *The Atlantic*. Beauchamp predicted this in 2013 when reviewing KSR's *2312*—when *New York 2140* was four years in the future. But judging by climate change, Beauchamp's prediction might have been true still earlier.[9]

27. KSR's stories have gradually altered since the Mars trilogy: he didn't stop advocating for the terraforming of Earth (something he's been doing since *Red Mars*), but he shifted gears to propose actions that would mitigate the effects of climate change.

28. "The revulsion against geoengineering has to be rethought," Robinson told *HuffPost* in 2018. "If a hundred million people die in one heat wave, and the government of India says we're going to imitate a volcanic explosion and throw dust into the air to block out the sun, are we going to tell them they can't?"[10]

29. (The India heat wave was later to be shown in the opening chapter of his latest novel, *The Ministry for the Future*. In my opinion, it's one of the bleakest scenes of not only science fiction, but also literature.)

30. *New York 2140*, according to Gerry Canavan, is "the first major science fictional artifact of the Trump era, anticipating even in its articulation of the conditions of victory the fragility of progress and the likelihood of reversal."[11] But it ends on a high note, with Mutt and Jeff rescued at the start of a new cycle; a big hurricane leaves a trail of destruction but also creates conditions for the communes to flourish, under the guidance of the MetLife co-op.

31. Community will still demand hard and never-ending work, exemplified by members of Idelba's (Vlade's ex-wife's) salvage crew, who will stabilize beaches to keep them above the tide line: "The crew seemed to regard this endless task as a good thing. It was like working on the Met; it would never

end. One of them raised a glass, and the others did likewise. 'One can easily imagine Sisyphus happy,' Abdul declared, and they drank to that."[12]

32. The conclusion? *New York 2140* is so crucial to the discussion of capital under the Anthropocene that it may very well be the great American novel of the twenty-first century (so far)—or of late US capitalism, if you will. Its action takes place in the future, but Kim Stanley Robinson is talking to his contemporaries. It's not a blueprint, but it suggests how we could make things better step by step in our communities.

33. It fulfills Lyotard's definition of postmodernism as the smaller narrative, opposite to the epic: no great, all-powerful protagonists, but people from literally all walks of life and more than a few countries, struggling to make ends meet while living their lives on a daily basis.

34. KSR's polyphonic style, alternating POVs with each chapter, and unclassifiable genre mix qualify *New York 2140* as not entirely science fiction. Nor is it entirely climate change literature. Nor is it solely a logistics manual. It manages to be all of these and more.

35. Paradoxical as it might be, this novel is probably the best novel ever written about New York City—or, on second thought, about any big city in the world.

Notes

1. Rogers, "Climate-Obsessed Sci-Fi Genius."

2. Robinson, *New York 2140*, Kindle loc. 7264.

3. Orlando Figes claims, in *Revolutionary Russia*, that this spirit of self-sacrifice of the Russian people helped them during World War II: "The Soviet people went to war with the [cult of sacrifice] psychology of the 1930s. Living in a state of constant revolutionary struggle, they became used to the idea of sacrifice" (312–314).

4. Famously a student of Marxist Fredric Jameson, KSR admitted in a February 28, 2019, interview with the *Antifada* podcast to being a dues-paying member of the Democratic Socialists of America.

5. Sethness, "Toward an Ecologically Based Post-Capitalism."

6. Sethness, "Toward an Ecologically Based Post-Capitalism."
7. Russell and Vinsel, "Hail the Maintainers."
8. Robinson, *New York 2140*, Kindle loc. 7282.
9. Beauchamp, "In 300 Years."
10. Kaufman, "King of Climate Fiction."
11. Canavan, "Utopia in the Time of Trump."
12. Robinson, *New York 2140*, Kindle loc. 11148.

Bibliography

Beauchamp, Scott. "In 300 Years, Kim Stanley Robinson's Science Fiction May Not Be Fiction." *The Atlantic*, April 1, 2013, https://www.theatlantic.com/entertainment/archive/2013/04/in-300-years-kim-stanley-robinsons-science-fiction-may-not-be-fiction/274392/.

Canavan, Gerry. "Utopia in the Time of Trump." *Los Angeles Review of Books*, March 11, 2017. https://lareviewofbooks.org/article/utopia-in-the-time-of-trump/.

Figes, Orlando. *Revolutionary Russia, 1891–1991*. New York: Metropolitan Books, 2014.

Kaufman, Alexander C. "The King of Climate Fiction Makes the Left's Case for Geoengineering." *Huffington Post*, 28 July 2018, https://www.huffpost.com/entry/climate-geoengineering-kim-stanley-robinson_n_5b4e54bde4b0de86f487b0b9.

Peck, Jamie, Sean KB, and AP Andy, hosts. "Antifada ft. Will Menaker: Fully Automated Luxury Gay Space Communism w/ Kim Stanley Robinson." *The Antifada* (podcast). February 28, 2019. https://fans.fm/p/57f.

Robinson, Kim Stanley. *New York 2140*. London: Orbit, 2017.

Rogers, Adam. "The Climate-Obsessed Sci-Fi Genius of Kim Stanley Robinson." *WIRED*, October 22, 2018. https://www.wired.com/story/kim-stanley-robinson-red-moon/.

Russell, Andrew, and Lee Vinsel. "Hail the Maintainers." *Aeon*, April 7, 2016. https://aeon.co/essays/innovation-is-overvalued-maintenance-often-matters-more.

Sethness, Javier. "Toward an Ecologically Based Post-Capitalism: Interview with Novelist Kim Stanley Robinson." *Truthout*, March 17, 2018. https://truthout.org/articles/toward-an-ecologically-based-post-capitalism-interview-with-novelist-kim-stanley-robinson/.

39 Nā Kia'i Mauna, Ka Pu'uhonua o Pu'uhuluhulu at the Mauna Kea Access Road (2019) / An SF Sovereignty Story

Bryan Kamaoli Kuwada

I have seen the future, and it is made out of tarps, tents, porta potties, and duct tape. It is not a cyberpunk metropolis or a shiny domed city standing upon the hill, though duct tape does have a particular sheen when the mountain sun strikes it just so. In the summer of 2019, a massive effort to block the construction of the Thirty Meter Telescope (TMT) upon the summit of Maunakea, Hawai'i Island, came to a head, and while the billion-dollar TMT has been touted as one of the most cutting-edge astronomical facilities on the planet, what offered the most striking vision of the future was much humbler, actually taking place in a parking lot across from the access road that leads up to the telescopes. Ka Pu'uhonua o Pu'uhuluhulu was, in essence, a protest camp cobbled together out of community donations and whatever supplies the kia'i, or protectors of the mountain, could fit in their cars. But it was also a new kind of science fiction text, one written on the land itself, showing us new possibilities and paradigms for living.

The struggle over Maunakea has been going on for at least fifty years, so an in-depth description will not fit here. Suffice it to say that these recent visible protests are the product of environmental conservation concerns, decades of mismanagement, deeply rooted cultural concerns, and issues over the governance of Indigenous land. Cultural practitioners, Hawaiians with familial connections to the mountain, and environmental groups like the Sierra Club and the Audubon Society have brought lawsuits or made other efforts to oppose the construction of the thirteen previous telescopes that predate the proposed TMT. Even the State of Hawai'i's own audits lambasted the way Maunakea has been managed, and environmental impact statements from NASA and others confirm that astronomy has caused significant, substantial, and adverse harm to the mountain.

So even though we have gone through over a generation of struggle on the mountain and demonstrated multiple environmental, cultural, and sovereignty concerns, both the multinational TMT corporation and the State of Hawai'i have tried to characterize the battle as simply one of science versus culture/religion. Hawaiians who opposed the telescope were cast as "the church," trying to keep Galileo from telling everyone that the earth revolved around the sun, and as "impediments to progress," trying to keep Hawai'i in the Stone Age. What we were really trying to do was live responsibly in this world and have an actual say in the future of our land and our culture.

It is into this battle of narratives that science fiction and our visions of the future come into play. While no one element is ubiquitous in all science fiction, certain abiding tropes help readers to recognize what belongs in the genre, whether they be spaceships, advanced technology, faster-than-light travel, wormholes, alien races, gleaming cities, galactic alliances, and so on. What you don't often see in SF, however, is Indigenous people. This is not to say that Indigenous authors are not producing science fiction and speculative works, just that Indigenous people (who are not cardboard cutouts of white fantasies or anxieties) do not populate the science fiction stories of our collective imagination. Even when people are portrayed as living with the land in a way that may seem Indigenous, it is only because their highly advanced technological society has collapsed and they are forced to live in diminished circumstances as a consequence. What almost never gets portrayed is the creation of a society where we care for the 'āina as our elder sibling, as what all of our technology and science should be advancing us toward. That perhaps living in a balanced and pono relationship with the land and people *is* the most advanced society that we could have.

Science fiction has long been the genre of dreams, and that is what has captivated me about it. But those of us who consume SF need to change our dreams, change our visions. It is not only novel to understand Ka Pu'uhonua o Pu'uhuluhulu as a science fiction text written into reality, but absolutely vital to do so. We cannot continue to dream within the confines of racist colonial heteropatriarchal systems. We cannot keep dreaming the same dreams that brought our planet and our peoples to this state: injured, oppressed, disconnected, deracinated. The Hawaiian word for science fiction tells me this. It demands that we ask for more from the genre.

Our word for science fiction is mōhihi'o. A hihi'o is a dream or a vision, and most Hawaiian-language speakers will assume that the mō is short for mo'olelo, our word for story, history, account, which would make mōhihi'o something akin to Walidah Imarisha's idea of visionary fiction. But mōhihi'o makes even further demands on us here. Mō isn't short for mo'olelo, or story, but is instead a contraction of the word mō'ike, to interpret dreams. According to Hawaiian-language teacher Pūlama Collier, there is a deeper dimension to mō'ike as well. Mō'ike means to be in the succession or genealogy of seeing or experiencing something. It is when you are somewhere on the 'āina and you see, feel, hear, or experience something in the way that your ancestors did. Almost like a cultural deja vu. You feel it in the native forest where all the plants, birds, and even insects are the same ones your ancestors saw and heard two hundred years ago. She described getting that feeling while she was flying in a helicopter over Waihe'e Valley on Maui—a place she was very familiar with, but being in the sky shifted her perspective. That new insight enabled her to align more closely with the traditional stories she already knew about that area and understand more deeply the things that our ancestors did when they were there.

Mōhihi'o still calls for science fiction to present visions for the future but also grounds us in the importance of echoing and experiencing what our ancestors taught us about relating to the 'āina, the land, and the kanaka, the person. The science-fictional narratives that we embrace now are leading us to bleak futures: the greater good can involve "science" being done at gunpoint; land is nothing more than real estate; we should be looking for another planet to live on; Indigenous values and cultures belong in the past. But when we understand Ka Pu'uhonua o Pu'uhuluhulu as mōhihi'o, as science fiction, we see how we can bring new stories into being that offer us shelter and offer us hope.

When the TMT tried to begin construction in 2015, it was greeted with lawsuits and human blockades that resulted in several dozen arrests and a moratorium on construction. The intervening years saw more lawsuits and a contested case hearing, but the TMT was given the go-ahead by the Hawai'i Supreme Court, based on something referred to as "the degradation principle"—essentially, the circular logic that the summit of the mountain had been so damaged already that new construction would not cause it further harm. A few days before construction trucks were scheduled to roll on the mauna, the Royal Order of Kamehameha, along with the kia'i, dedicated Pu'uhuluhulu as a pu'uhonua, a place of refuge. Those who were fleeing from violence were safe from harm within the confines of a pu'uhonua, which could be an entire district of an island, or a heiau (temple/consecrated area) complex, or even a single person, such as in the case of the ali'i wahine Ka'ahumanu. The kia'i felt that with the threat of a militarized police response and even the National Guard, such a sanctuary was necessary for their safety—that it was important for sanctuary to arise from our traditional practice, rather than from the Western system that has so often failed Kānaka Maoli and other BIPOC peoples.

Within a handful of days, Ka Pu'uhonua o Pu'uhuluhulu went from supporting a small group of people living in a parking lot eating beef jerky and canned Vienna sausage to housing and providing for over five thousand people the very first weekend of the blockade. Hundreds of kia'i maintained a constant presence at the Pu'uhonua, but many also drove or flew in from other parts of Hawai'i, even other states and countries, to stay for shorter amounts of time. The early weeks of the struggle were like watching a hyperlapse of a communal organism coming into fruit. If you had been gone for a few days, you would come back to find the entire Pu'uhonua rearranged. The common kitchen was in a completely different tent now, the portable toilets had been redistributed (though you still had to watch out for the one really unbalanced one), there were entirely new services available. And one of the most mōhihi'o things about it was that driving the way the Pu'uhonua grew and shifted were culturally grounded Hawaiians asking some of the speculative questions at the heart of science fiction: "What do our people need? Wouldn't it be cool if we had X?"

That driving force meant that the Pu'uhonua grew along the backbone of our cultural values—of what we were fighting for, of how we wanted to interact with the land, of how we wanted to treat the people around us. It meant that at the Pu'uhonua, everything provided was freely available to all. Everyone was fed way more than enough. So many people wanted to offer their support. Donations of all sorts came in from around the world: food, clothing, supplies, electronic equipment, services. The Mauna Medics, staffed by doctors, nurses, and trained assistants, offered health care. Pu'uhuluhulu University offered classes from cultural practitioners, college professors, elders, and community members on everything from Hawaiian language and history to sessions on the relevance of punk rock to the Hawaiian movement to nonviolent direct action training. Native plants were cared for and replanted. There were pu'uhonua within the pu'uhonua for women, for māhū and LGBTQI2S folx, places to take your children for daycare, places to go to learn art. The kūpuna, the elders, received delegations from other peoples and nations offering their support, reminding us that our struggles were linked with Palestine, Aotearoa, Sāmoa, BLM, a unified Korea, West Papua, Standing Rock, Okinawa, Guåhan, and so much more.

Undergirding everything was Hawaiian cultural belief and spiritual practice. Kapu Aloha, a modern framework based in traditional understanding, guided everyone's behavior on the mauna. Even practices of de-escalation were grounded in collective cultural responsibility and practice; when people were angry or distraught, groups of other kia'i would go near them and chant "E Aloha ē" or other mele together to reinvoke our collective responsibilities and calm them down. Ceremony, what we call protocol, was held three times a day: dawn, noon, and dusk. People gathered every day to offer both traditional and new chants and hula. Many of our cultural practices are often reserved only for people from certain lineages or who were taught under certain traditions, yet all of the protocol offered on the mauna were made noa, or free, for anyone to learn because we knew it was important to break down barriers, even within our own community.

And what did all this free childcare and education and hula make us to the State of Hawai'i's government? A threat. The state spent $15 million dollars on law enforcement and their efforts to clear the way for the TMT. The governor declared a state of emergency. Police were brought in from other islands, and the National Guard was mobilized, with several raids and sweeps being preempted by thousands of kia'i showing up when called and overwhelming law enforcement capacity. The governor even relied on the old trope of the no-good native, announcing at a press conference that the Pu'uhonua was actually a den of drunkenness and drugs.

It was truly surreal to have been in the midst of the camp, surrounded by people feeding each other, washing dishes, scrubbing toilets, playing music for elders, while listening to the governor describe it and us as debauched and destructive. But that is another thing that stands out about the encampment. The Pu'uhonua was not ever meant to be some utopic model for a future society; it was us trying to live a new story. The society we created there was a necessity born out of our struggle against cultural erasure and being severed from our land. It was a rejection of the colonialist and capitalist values that had been killing us and the planet for so long. We needed a place of safety because outside of the Puʻuhonua were guns and LRADs (long-range acoustic devices) and tear gas and riot gear. We needed to know culturally based methods of de-escalation because living in constant fear of raids and state-sanctioned violence affected our mental health. We made sure that learning was centered because everyone knew that the struggle was not just on the ground but in our minds as well. Everything had to be free because so many kiaʻi faced financial hardship or quit their jobs to live in and maintain the Puʻuhonua.

And because we were in struggle, it meant that the Puʻuhonua was not perfect. It was not the den of iniquity that the governor had described, but it was still a society made up of people trying to shed the legacies of hundreds of years of colonial depredation. The kiaʻi had solar power and tried to eliminate wasteful practices, but there was still too much Styrofoam and single-use plastic. There were agent provocateurs, people who came just to take selfies, people who thought it was a party. Some people still posed a threat to women and other vulnerable groups. Trying to create a safe place for everyone did not instantly cure our community of ingrained colonial ideals, heteropatriarchy, misogyny, racism, and queer- and transphobia. But the experience of living out our own science fiction put into stark relief the kinds of things we could not stand for in our communities. It made our community learn that we have to do better.

And this is the power of mōhihiʻo. It has given us Ka Puʻuhonua o Puʻuhuluhulu, a science fiction story cowritten by thousands of people. Each word was written through love for the land and each revision made through struggle. The worldwide pandemic was the only thing that could bring the kiaʻi off of the mountain, and even now some still remain. Maybe the Puʻuhonua will never come back as it was, but its story is out there now. We have seen what a society looks like when it is built upon Indigenous values and not chattel slavery and native genocide. Our children experienced a beautiful story of our sovereignty, and these stories beget more stories. Mōhihiʻo stories like kānaka standing for Black lives and Black joy, kiaʻi growing like groves of trees and protecting other ʻāina from unrestrained development, our people honoring our salt/blood connections with our Micronesian cousins. These are the stories that keep our oppressors up at night. So let us always reread and rewrite this mōhihi‘o story of Ka Pu‘uhonua o Pu‘uhuluhulu, and be dangerous. Let us be a threat to the ho-hum dreams of the status quo. Let us build new futures based on connection, based on caring for the land, caring for each other. Get out your duct tape, and let's go.

Contributors

Ben Abraham (he/him) is a digital games and sustainability researcher putting the finishing touches on a book titled *Digital Games after Climate Change.* He has publications in journals including *Games and Culture, Transformations,* and *The Fibreculture Journal* and is currently embarking on a postacademic career following the collapse of the Australian higher-education sector.

Emmet Asher-Perrin (they/them) is a writer, culture critic, and news and entertainment editor for Tor.com. Their work can also be found in *Queers Dig Time Lords* and *Lost Transmissions: The Secret History of Science Fiction and Fantasy* (under the name Emily Asher-Perrin). They live in Brooklyn, NY, with their counterpart and a dog named after a starship captain.

Brent Ryan Bellamy (he/him) teaches classes on comics, science fiction, other genre fictions, energy humanities, and worldbuilding at Trent University. You can read his work in the *Open Library of the Humanities, Paradoxa, Mediations, Resilience, Science Fiction Studies,* and *Western American Literature.* He coedited *An Ecotopian Lexicon* (2019) and *Materialism and the Critique of Energy* (2018). His book about the persistence of literary and social forms, *Remainders of the American Century: Post-Apocalyptic Novels in the Age of US Decline,* is available from Wesleyan University Press as of June 2021.

Gerry Canavan (he/him) is an associate professor of twentieth- and twenty-first-century literature in the Department of English at Marquette University, and the author of *Octavia E. Butler* (University of Illinois Press, 2016). He is the coeditor of *Green Planets: Ecology and Science Fiction, The Cambridge Companion to American Science Fiction,* and *The Cambridge History of Science Fiction,* and also serves as an editor at two academic journals focused on science fiction studies: *Extrapolation* and *Science Fiction Film and Television.*

Andrew Ferguson (he/him) is a college postdoctoral fellow at the University of Virginia, working on genre fiction, contemporary media, and pop culture, with a particular interest in what happens when stories and storytelling break down. His writing has appeared in *Textual Cultures, Science Fiction Studies,* and the *LA Review of Books,* among others. His most recent publication, in keeping with his long-term fascination with "bad" art, was on the *Star Wars Holiday Special*; upcoming articles include pieces on pulp modernism, homebrew videogames, zombies, Flann O'Brien, and Pac-Man.

Fabio Fernandes (he/him) lives in São Paulo, Brazil. He has published books in Portuguese (including a monograph on William Gibson's fiction, *A Construção do Imaginário Cyber*, and a novel, *Back in the USSR*) and in English (the collection *Love: An Archaeology* and the steampunk novella *Under Pressure*). Also a translator, he is responsible for the translation to Brazilian Portuguese of several SF novels, including *Neuromancer, Snow Crash*, and *A Clockwork Orange*. His short stories have been published in Brazil, Portugal, Italy, Romania, the UK, New Zealand, and the United States. Fernandes coedited (with Djibril al-Ayad) the postcolonialist anthology *We See a Different Frontier* and (with Francesco Verso) the anthology *Solarpunk: come ho imparato ad amare il futuro*. He is a graduate of Clarion West, class of 2013.

Dexter Gabriel (he/him) earned his PhD in history from Stony Brook University, New York. His research interests include the history of bondage, resistance, and freedom in the Black Atlantic, as well as interdisciplinary approaches to slavery within popular culture and media. He is currently a professor of history at the University of Connecticut and in his spare time writes speculative fiction under the penname P. Djéli Clark.

M. Elizabeth (Libby) Ginway (she/her) is an associate professor in the Department of Spanish and Portuguese Studies at the University of Florida. She is the author of *Brazilian Science Fiction: Cultural Myths and Nationhood in the Land of the Future* (2004), which was nominated for the MLA Katherine Singer Kovacs Prize by Bucknell University Press. She coedited a volume of essays, *Latin American Science Fiction: Theory and Practice* (Palgrave, 2012), with J. Andrew Brown. She has published articles in *Alambique, Brasil/Brazil, Extrapolation, Foundation, Hispania, Luso-Brazilian Review, Modern Language Studies, Revista Iberoamericana, Science Fiction Studies*, and *Paradoxa*. In addition to teaching nineteenth- and twentieth-century Brazilian literature, she has extended her SF interests to Spanish America, and her comparative study, *Cyborgs, Sexuality and the Undead: The Body in Mexican and Brazilian Speculative Fiction*, was published by Vanderbilt University Press in November 2020.

Sean Guynes (he/him) is a writer, critic, and editor who lives on Anishinaabe land in what is now Michigan. He is coeditor of the *Palgrave SFF: A New Canon* book series, two journal special issues, and several books. His shorter writing has appeared in public and academic venues including *Los Angeles Review of Books, Strange Horizons*, Tor.com, *American Quarterly*, and *World Literature Today*. He is on Twitter at @saguynes.

Ouissal Harize (she/her) is a doctoral researcher at Durham University with a primary research specialty in terror representations in postcolonial cultural productions. Her PhD thesis mainly focuses on exploring political violence as a colonial legacy and new directions of textually and visually documenting trauma and recovery. Her research interests include subaltern colonialism, symbolism of veiling in North African and Middle Eastern revolutions, representation of the Amazigh culture in fiction, and Arab science fiction studies. After earning a BA and MA from Badji Mokhtar University-Annaba in Algeria, she has been focusing on developing a model of decolonizing the syllabi in postcolonial universities. She works as a journalist, translator, and teacher of Arabic as a foreign language.

David M. Higgins (nonbinary/genderfluid/all pronouns acceptable) teaches in the English Department at Inver Hills College in Minnesota, and they are the speculative fiction editor for the *Los Angeles Review of Books*. She is the author of *Reverse Colonization: Science Fiction, Imperial Fantasy, and Alt-Victimhood* (2021), and her article "Toward a Cosmopolitan Science Fiction" won the SFRA Pioneer Award for excellence in scholarship. David's research has been published in journals such as *American Literature, Science Fiction Studies, Paradoxa,* and *Extrapolation,* and his work has appeared in edited volumes such as *The Cambridge History of Science Fiction* and *The Cambridge Companion to American Science Fiction*. David has been a featured speaker on NPR's radio show *On Point,* and they serve as the second vice president for the International Association for the Fantastic in the Arts (IAFA).

Veronica Hollinger (she/her) is emerita professor of cultural studies at Trent University in Ontario. She is a long-time coeditor of *Science Fiction Studies* and has coedited special issues on queer theory, Chinese science fiction, and the climate crisis. She has published widely on feminist and queer science fiction, cyberpunk, the climate crisis, postmodernism, and posthumanism. She is coeditor of *The Wesleyan Anthology of Science Fiction*.

Allanah Hunt (she/her) earned a PhD in creative writing at Anglia Ruskin University, England, for researching the production and analysis of fan fiction set in the Marvel Cinematic Universe. In addition to presenting academic papers at NAISA 2016, NIRAKN 2017, SHARP 2018, and SFRA 2019, she was awarded the black&write! project's Indigenous Writing fellowship in 2012 and 2013, a Boundless mentorship and a Next Chapter 2020 project, the Queensland Premier's Young Publishers and Writers Award, the 2021 Queensland Literary Award, the 2019 Nakata Brophy Fiction Prize, and the Griffith Review Fellowship, with her novella also placing in the Griffith Review Novella Project VII. She currently works as an editor intern through the black&write! project at the State Library of Queensland.

Nicola Hunte (she/her) is a lecturer in the Literatures in English discipline at the Cave Hill campus of the University of the West Indies. With her interest in the creative arts, she serves as the temporary editor of *POUi*, Cave Hill's journal of creative writing, as well as on the Frank Collymore Literary Endowment committee for the promotion of literary arts in Barbados. She has published in the area of literary criticism on Caribbean and African American texts in *Shibboleths*, an online journal of comparative theory, and the *Journal of West Indian Literature* (JWIL). Her critical work has also touched on popular culture, specific to Barbadian expression on- and offline. Her research focus includes the critical texts of Guyanese writer/theorist Wilson Harris and speculative fiction, particularly from the Caribbean and the African cultural diaspora.

Nathaniel Isaacson (he/him) is an associate professor of modern Chinese literature in the Department of Foreign Languages and Literature at North Carolina State University. His research interests include the history of Chinese science and science fiction, Chinese cinema, cultural studies, and literary translation. Nathaniel has published articles in the *Oxford Handbook of Modern Chinese Literatures* and in journals including *Osiris* and *Science Fiction Studies*. He has also published translations of nonfiction, poetry, and fiction in the translation journals *Renditions, Pathlight, Science Fiction Studies*, and *Chinese Literature Today*. His book *Celestial Empire: The Emergence of Chinese Science Fiction* (2017) examines the emergence of SF in late Qing China. A number of recent translations of SF author Han Song were included in the volume *Exploring Dark Fiction #5: A Primer to Han Song* (2020).

Ayana Jamieson (she/her) is an educator and founder of the Octavia E. Butler Legacy Network (@oeblegacy), a global community inspired and committed to uplifting and highlighting Butler's life, her work, and new works inspired by Butler's legacy. The Legacy Network grew out of her doctoral research on Butler's life. Her dissertation is entitled "'Certainty of the Flesh': A Biomythographical Reading of Octavia E. Butler's Fictions." She teaches ethnic studies courses at California State Polytechnic University, Pomona.

Darshana Jayemanne (he/him) is a lecturer in art, media, and computer games at Abertay University and the author of *Performativity in Art, Literature and Videogames* (Palgrave, 2017). This book's title names many of his main research interests, and it develops a media studies approach to performance in digital space and time. He was a co-investigator on the AHRC-funded Reality Remix project. He has served as a jurist for the Independent Games Festival's Award for Narrative Excellence, was convenor of the Game Engines Beyond Games symposium with Babycastles Gallery in New York City, and is the organizer of Keywords in Play, an interview series highlighting diverse games research. His academic work has appeared in *Games & Culture, The Journal of Broadcasting and Electronic Media, ToDIGRA*, and *Fibreculture Journal*.

Gwyneth Jones (she/her) is a feminist writer and critic of science fiction and fantasy who has also written for teenagers using the name Ann Halam. Awards include the Philip K. Dick Award, the Arthur C. Clarke Award, the Dracula Society's Children of the Night Award, the World Fantasy Award, and the Pilgrim Award for SF criticism. She lives in Brighton, UK, with her husband and her two cats, Milo and Tilly. Hobbies include curating assorted pond life in season, watching old movies, playing Zelda, and staring out of the window.

Brendan Keogh (he/him) is a video game industry and culture researcher at the Digital Media Research Centre, Queensland University of Technology. He is the author of *The Unity Game Engine and the Circuits of Cultural Software* (Palgrave, 2019; coauthored with Benjamin Nicoll), *A Play of Bodies: How We Perceive Videogames* (MIT Press, 2018), and *Killing is Harmless* (Stolen Projects, 2012).

Sami Ahmad Khan (he/him) is a writer, academic, and documentary producer. He writes, researches, edits, and teaches Indian science fiction. Sami is the recipient of a Fulbright grant to the University of Iowa and holds a PhD in science fiction from Jawaharlal Nehru University (JNU), New Delhi. His future war thriller *Red Jihad* won two awards, and his second novel—*Aliens in Delhi*—garnered rave reviews. Sami's creative writings and critical essays have appeared in leading journals, anthologies, and magazines; his overview of Indian SF has been translated into Czech; and his fiction has been the subject of formal academic research. His latest book is *Star Warriors of the Modern Raj: Materiality, Mythology and Technology of Indian Science Fiction* (University of Wales Press, 2021). Sami has taught at IIT Delhi, JNU, and GGSIP University and is presently a Marie Skłodowska-Curie Actions fellow at the University of Oslo, Norway.

Cameron Kunzelman (he/him) holds a PhD in moving image studies from Georgia State University. His scholarship focuses on the formal and aesthetic relationships between science fiction and video games. His public criticism has appeared in outlets such as *Kotaku, Polygon, Paste,* and *Vice*. He has a podcast on the academic field of game studies (cohosted with Michael Lutz) called *Game Studies Study Buddies*, which you might enjoy listening to.

Bryan Kamaoli Kuwada (he/him/ʻo ia) is a tiny part of a beautiful beloved community that fights every day for breath, for ea, for connection, for sovereignty. He is sometimes called tree, bear, Morris, hoa, Uncle Jacket, and more. He is also sometimes an academic, editor, translator, blogger (https://hehiale.wordpress.com/), poet (*The Offing, American Quarterly, Yellow Medicine Review*), writer of dorky sci-fi and speculative fiction stories set in Hawaiʻi (*Black Marks on the White Page, Pacific Monsters, Hawaiʻi Review, The Dark*), photographer, and/or videographer. What he mostly does is cook too much food and surf with his mother and a crew of fierce activist poet wahine who tease (and teach) him mercilessly.

Isiah Lavender III (he/him) is Sterling Goodman Professor of English at the University of Georgia, where he researches and teaches courses in African American literature and science fiction. In addition to his books *Race in American Science Fiction* (Indiana University Press, 2011), *Black and Brown Planets: The Politics of Race in Science Fiction* (University Press of Mississippi, 2014), *Dis-Orienting Planets: Racial Representations of Asia in Science Fiction* (University Press of Mississippi, 2017), *Afrofuturism Rising: The Literary Prehistory of a Movement* (Ohio State University Press, 2019), and *Literary Afrofuturism in the Twenty-First Century* (coedited with Lisa Yaszek; Ohio State University Press, 2020), his publications on science fiction include essays and reviews in journals such as *Extrapolation, Journal of the Fantastic in the Arts*, and *Science Fiction Studies*, and collections such as the *Cambridge History of Science Fiction* and the *Routledge Companion to Science Fiction*. He recently coedited with Yaszek *Beyond Afrofuturism*, the special double issue of *Extrapolation*. His current projects include *The Routledge Handbook of CoFuturisms* (coedited with Bodhisattva Chattopadhyay, Grace Dillon, and Taryne Jade Taylor), the interview collection *Conversations with Nalo Hopkinson*, and the monograph *Critical Race Theory and Science Fiction*. Finally, he edits for *Extrapolation*—the oldest science fiction journal—as one of its six editors.

Caryn Lesuma (she/her) is an assistant professor of English at Brigham Young University-Hawaii, where she also serves as the composition coordinator. Her research interests focus on young adult literature, literatures of the Pacific, and place-based pedagogy and rhetoric. She has published on contemporary adaptations of Pacific folklore and place-based composition pedagogy.

Karen Lord (she/her) is an award-winning author and independent research consultant in Barbados. Her academic qualifications range from a BSc (University of Toronto) in history of science and technology with a major in physics to a PhD (Bangor University, UK) in the sociological and statistical analysis of secular religiosity. In partnership with the Sir Arthur Lewis Institute of Social and Economic Studies (University of the West Indies), she has coauthored reports on development for the UNDP and on youth employment for the Caribbean Development Bank. Her debut novel, *Redemption in Indigo*, won the 2008 Frank Collymore Literary Award, the 2010 Carl Brandon Parallax Award, the 2011 William L. Crawford Award, the 2011 Mythopoeic Fantasy Award for Adult Literature, and the 2012 Kitschies Golden Tentacle (Best Debut), and it was nominated for the 2011 World Fantasy Award for Best Novel. Its sequel, the crime-fantasy novel *Unraveling*, was published in 2019. Her other books include the science fiction duology *The Best of All Possible Worlds* and *The Galaxy Game*. She also edited the anthologies *New Worlds, Old Ways: Speculative Tales from the Caribbean* and *Reclaim, Restore, Return: Futurist Tales from the Caribbean*.

Sarah Marrs (she/her) is a Chicago-based film critic who has written about film and pop culture for over ten years. Before that, Sarah studied writing and art at the University of Southern California. Today, she is the deputy editor of LaineyGossip and has had bylines on Pajiba, SYFY Fangrrls, and Decider. Sarah assists with the programming of the Chicago Critics Film Festival and is a member of the Chicago Film Critics Association, Online Film Critics Society, and Critics Choice Association.

Farah Mendlesohn (please refer to by name not pronoun) won a Hugo with Edward James in 2005 for *The Cambridge Companion to Fantasy Literature*. Mendlesohn is also the author of *Diana Wynne Jones: The Fantastic Tradition and Children's Literature* and *Rhetorics of Fantasy*; coauthor with Edward James of *A Short History of Fantasy* and *The Inter-galactic Playground: A Critical Study of Children's and Teens' Science Fiction*; and coauthor with Michael M. Levy of *Children's Fantasy Literature: An Introduction*, which won the World Fantasy Award and the Mythopoeic Award in 2017. In 2019, Mendlesohn published *The Pleasant Profession of Robert A. Heinlein*, and in

2020 published *Creating Memory: Historical Fiction and the English Civil Wars*. Mendlesohn is currently working on a monograph about the radical children's writer Geoffrey Trease and a short book about Joanna Russ's *The Female Man*. Mendlesohn is now the only three-time winner of the BSFA award for nonfiction and is neck and neck with John Clute for Hugo nominations (although sadly, not wins) for Best Related Work.

Cathryn Merla-Watson (she/her) holds a PhD in American studies with specializations in women's and gender studies and geography from the University of Minnesota, Twin Cities. She is currently an associate professor in Mexican American studies and codirector of gender and women's studies at the University of Texas-Río Grande Valley. Her research interests broadly include Latinx studies, Latinx speculative aesthetics, queer theory, performance studies, Chicana and Latina feminisms, and social justice research methodologies. She has published articles in *Aztlán* and *MELUS* and has published chapters in *The Un/Making of Latina/o Citizenship; Culture, Politics, and Aesthetics* (Palgrave, 2014); *Research Justice: Methodologies for Social Change* (Policy Press, 2015); and *Latina Outsiders: Remaking Latina Identity* (Routledge, 2019). She published with B. V. Olguín *Altermundos: Latin@ Speculative Literature, Film, and Popular Culture* (UCLA Chicano Studies Research Center Press, 2017), the first anthology to coalesce scholarship theorizing and codifying this new and emerging field of study. This anthology won the Before Columbus Foundation's American Book Award (2018). Her current book manuscript, *Latinx Eschatologies: Performing Apocalyptic Affect*, examines how recent queer hemispheric Latinx performances redeploy the (post)apocalyptic to dramatize the intersectional lived experience of necropower and enact affective politics.

Hugh Charles O'Connell (he/him) is an assistant professor of English at the University of Massachusetts Boston. His current research focuses on the utopian valences of Africanfuturism and examines the relationship between speculative fiction and speculative finance. He is the coeditor with David M. Higgins of *Speculative Finance/ Speculative Fiction*, a special issue of *CR: The New Centennial Review* 19, no. 1. His essays on contemporary and postcolonial science fiction have appeared in *Extrapolation, Utopian Studies, The Cambridge History of Science Fiction, Postcolonial Literary Inquiry, Modern Fiction Studies, Paradoxa, Science Fiction Film & Television, The Routledge Companion to Cyberpunk Culture*, and the *Los Angeles Review of Books*.

B. Pladek (he/they) is associate professor of romantic literature at Marquette University in Milwaukee and the author of *The Poetics of Palliation: Romantic Literary Therapy, 1790–1850* (Liverpool University Press, 2019).

John Rieder (he/him) is an emeritus professor of English at the University of Hawai'i at Mānoa. He is the author of *Colonialism and the Emergence of Science Fiction* (Wesleyan University Press, 2008) and *Science Fiction and the Mass Cultural Genre System* (Wesleyan University Press, 2017). In 2019, he was awarded the Science Fiction Research Association's Award for Lifetime Achievement.

Lysa Rivera (she/her) is an associate professor of English at Western Washington University, where she teaches Chicanx and African American literatures. Her research interests include Chicanxfuturism, Afrofuturism, and the potent fusions that are made possible when speculative fiction meets oppositional ideologies. She is currently at work on a book project on Chicanx cyberpunk after the Chicano Movement.

Kim Stanley Robinson (he/him) is a *New York Times* best-selling author and winner of the Hugo, Nebula, and Locus awards. He is the author of more than twenty books, including the best-selling Mars trilogy and the critically acclaimed *Forty Signs of Rain*, *The Years of Rice and Salt*, and *2312*. In 2008, he was named a "Hero of the Environment" by *Time* magazine, and he works with the Sierra Nevada Research Institute. He coedited *Green Planets: Ecology and Science Fiction* with Gerry Canavan (Wesleyan University Press, 2014). He lives in Davis, California.

Steven Shaviro (he/him) is DeRoy Professor of English at Wayne State University. His books include *Connected, or What It Means to Live in the Network Society* (2003), *Discognition* (University of Minnesota Press, 2016), and *Extreme Fabulations: Science Fictions of Life* (Goldsmiths Press, 2021).

Rebekah Sheldon (she/her) is an associate professor of English at Indiana University and the author of *The Child to Come: Life After the Human Catastrophe*, which received an Honorable Mention from the Science Fiction and Technoculture Studies Book Prize for 2016. She was the coeditor of "The Child Now" special issue of *GLQ* and has published articles in *Science Fiction Studies*, *Science Fiction Film and Television*, *Symploke*, *Angelaki*, *Rhizomes*, *LARB*, and *e-flux*, among other venues in speculative fiction and speculative philosophy.

Alison Sperling (she/her) is currently an IPODI International Postdoctoral Research Fellow at Technische Universität Berlin in the Center for Interdisciplinary Women's and Gender Studies and an affiliate research fellow at the ICI Institute for Cultural Inquiry Berlin. She researches in the fields of literary studies, feminist and queer theory, anthropocene studies, contemporary art, and the science-fictional.

Alfredo Suppia (he/him) is associate professor at the State University of Campinas (UNICAMP) in São Paulo, Brazil, where he teaches Brazilian and world cinema and film analysis, script writing, and film adaptation in the Department of Multi-Media Studies. He is author of over forty articles on film, including for the Oxford Bibliography of Latin American Studies, and two books on science fiction and Brazilian cinema. He has organized five speaker series on film and science fiction at UNICAMP and has edited several anthologies of essays on science fiction and film, including *Cartografias da ficção científica mundial* (*Cartographies of World Science Fiction*, 2015) and *Red Alert: Marxist Approaches to Science Fiction Cinema* (2016). His current book project, *Brazilian Science Fiction Cinema*, is the first in-depth critical history of Brazilian science fiction cinema to be published in English.

Bogi Takács (e/em/eir/emself or they pronouns) is a Hungarian Jewish agender trans person and an immigrant to the United States. E is a winner of the Lambda award for editing *Transcendent 2: The Year's Best Transgender Speculative Fiction*, the Hugo award for Best Fan Writer, and a finalist for other awards. Eir debut poetry collection *Algorithmic Shapeshifting* and eir debut short story collection *The Trans Space Octopus Congregation* were both released in 2019. You can find Bogi talking about books at http://www.bogireadstheworld.com, and on various social media as bogiperson.

Taryne Jade Taylor (she/her) is an assistant professor of English at Florida Atlantic University. Her research focuses on the politics of representation in speculative fiction, particularly feminist and Latinx futurisms. She is coeditor of the forthcoming *Routledge Handbook to CoFuturisms* (with Grace Dillon, Isiah Lavender III, and Bodhisattva Chattopadhyay). She is an associate editor for the *Journal of the Fantastic in the Arts*, coeditor of the Routledge series Studies in Global Genre Fiction (with Bodhisattva Chattopadhyay), and a juror for the Sturgeon Award.

Sherryl Vint (she/her) is Professor of Media and Cultural Studies at the University of California, Riverside, where she directs the Speculative Fictions and Cultures of Science program. Her books include *Bodies of Tomorrow, Animal Alterity, Science Fiction: A Guide to the Perplexed, Science Fiction: The Essential Knowledge*, and *Biopolitical Futures in Twenty-First Century Speculative Fiction*. She is an editor of *Science Fiction Studies* and the book series Science and Popular Culture. She has edited several books, most recently *After the Human: Theory, Culture and Criticism in the 21st Century*.

Kirin Wachter-Grene (she/her) is an assistant professor of liberal arts at the School of the Art Institute of Chicago, with an emphasis on African American literature and gender and sexuality studies. Wachter-Grene is the guest editor of *At the Limits of Desire: Black Radical Pleasure*, a special issue of *The Black Scholar* published in honor of the journal's fiftieth anniversary (2020), and she sits on the journal's active editorial board. Her academic writing has been published in journals including *African American Review, The Black Scholar, Callaloo, Feminist Formations*, and *Legacy: A Journal of American Women Writers* and is included in various edited collections. Currently, she is working on her manuscript titled *Into the Scorpion Garden: Samuel R. Delany and Transgressive African American Literature*.

Alternative media scholar, ethnic journalist, and nascent producer of Indigenous Futurist films **Ida Yoshinaga** (she/her) thanks Gerry Canavan and Sean Guynes for the chance to shape this collection, an experience that has given her utopian hope in the midst of global crises. An assistant professor of science fiction film at the Georgia Institute of Technology, and a longtime settler ally of Native struggles and cis-het ally of LGBTQIA+ movements, she teaches SF film/TV studies and cultural screenwriting.

Index

Page numbers in italics refer to figures.